THE
TOP
10
OF EVERYTHING
1998

THE

TOP

10

OF EVERYTHING

1998

RUSSELL ASH

DORLING KINDERSLEY

London • New York • Sydney • Moscow

A DORLING KINDERSLEY BOOK

Project Editor Adèle Hayward
Project Art Editor Jayne Jones
Editor Julie Oughton
Designer Austin Barlow
Managing Editor Stephanie Jackson
Managing Art Editor Nigel Duffield
Production Controller Alison Jones

Designed and Typeset by Blackjacks Limited
Designer Jonathan Baker
Project Editor Helen Freeman
Senior Editor Jack Buchan
Editor Casey Horton

Published in Great Britain in 1997 by
Dorling Kindersley Limited,
9 Henrietta Street,
London WC2E 8PS

A CIP catalogue record of this book is available
from the British Library.

ISBN 0 7513 0443 3

Reproduction by HBM Print Ltd, Singapore.
Printed and bound in Italy by Eurolitho.

CONTENTS

LIFE ON EARTH

THE HUMAN WORLD

SPORTS

THE GOOD & THE BAD

DISASTERS

CULTURE & LEARNING

MUSIC

STAGE, SCREEN & BROADCASTING

INTRODUCTION

This is the 9th annual edition of *The Top 10 of Everything*. If you have never seen one of the previous editions, welcome; if it is already familiar, welcome back. To both groups of readers it is worth mentioning what is new. Every year I try to introduce new categories and lists, and this year I have "starred" some of the lists that have never appeared in a previous edition of *The Top 10 of Everything*. Core lists and old favourites are still included, but this year, as every other year, every list that is featured has been checked and updated and the book is full of new information. Lists of the bestselling books or the most-watched films of a year, for instance, are replaced in their entirety by those for the latest complete year, and are thus completely different. In all other categories, new individual entries have been inserted, or whole lists have been replaced. Even some of the historical lists are revised as new evidence comes to light. In 1997 Hong Kong, a long-standing entry in many Top 10 lists, was handed back to China, and so no longer features as a separate country (although it does, of course, continue to feature in lists that are based on events that occurred when it had the status of a country). Lists on certain subjects alter very dramatically – those of tallest buildings frequently change while I am compiling them, and you will see in the list "10 Longest Cruise Ships" (p. 56–57) that four of them were launched in 1996 or 1997. During the course of 1998, this list will change yet again as a number of large new vessels are completed.

WHAT'S "TOP"?

Top 10 lists are not "bests" or favourites of mine or anyone else's, but almost invariably measurable rankings. Some are "worsts", as in the case of murder and disaster victims, because these are quantifiable. The lists encompass superlatives in many categories – tallest, longest, fastest, most produced, richest, most expensive, most common, and so on. Some are "firsts" or "lasts": these qualify as a special sort of Top 10 which recognizes, for instance, that the first 10 Moonwalkers were leaders in that endeavour. Such lists make up for the fact that most other sources usually give the first entry only, with the result that history's also-rans are in danger of being forgotten. "Lasts", as in the case of award winners in certain fields, for example, represent the most recent 10 achievers. Very occasionally an unquantified list of 10 is included if it throws light on a subject that does not readily submit to the Top 10 treatment.

IN THE BEGINNING…

I am often asked how I got the idea for *The Top 10 of Everything*. The vogue for books of lists started in the US with the pioneering *Book of Lists*, which was published in 1977. It was followed by specialist books of lists on topics from films to food. A few years after this ball started rolling, while on a visit to the US, someone gave me a copy of *The Book of Texas Lists* (which includes such lists as "The 9 worst street names in Dallas", with entries such as Microwave Avenue and Star Trek Lane). Back in England, I thought, "If you could do a whole book of lists on Texas, you could certainly do one on

London", and so I compiled a book which would have been called *The Book of London Lists* – except that the publishers decided to call it *The Londoner's Almanac*. While I was working on that book, which was published in 1985, it occurred to me that most of these books contained subjective lists that represented someone's opinion, or someone's favourites. I asked myself, "What if I included *only* lists that were definitively the biggest, or the fastest, or whatever?" – and the notion of *The Top 10 of Everything* was born. I did not imagine when the first edition was published in 1989 that it would become established as an annual, or that it would receive the interest and attention that it has. I am delighted that it is now published internationally, as a by-product of which I have been interviewed about it on everything from local radio stations to the *Oprah Winfrey Show*.

WHY MAKE LISTS?

Whether we like it or not, we are all bombarded with lists; it's impossible to open a newspaper without seeing lists created by market researchers or pollsters: lists of the safest cars, bestsellers, Oscar winners, annual crime lists, lists of the top schools, and so on, and so on . . . Essentially, lists are a way of simplifying our awareness of everyday activities in a form that we can easily digest and remember. In an age when we are being assailed with information of all kinds (and people are already starting to talk about "information overload"), lists provide a shorthand way of presenting what might otherwise be an impenetrable mass of data and figures. Lists, especially the sort that you will find in this book, can reflect life – and so, like life itself, they can be serious, bizarre, trivial, important, fascinating, revealing, entertaining, or a combination of all of these attributes. At least, that is my intention.

A VOTE OF THANKS

I would like to thank the many people who have helped with the book since its inception, especially those who have generously contributed information and suggestions. I am always grateful for corrections and owe particular thanks to specialists who have offered constructive advice on lists, or who have even compiled certain lists for me. In contemplating my work on *The Top 10 of Everything*, the analogy of painting the Forth Bridge springs to mind: no sooner have I finished at one end than it's time to start at the beginning again (sometimes, it seems, before the paint is completely dry). If, as a result, I have not found the time to respond to you personally, please take this as a big "thank you".

SUGGESTIONS OR CORRECTIONS

If you have ideas or corrections for future editions, you can contact me on our World Wide Web site at http://www.dk.com (where you will find more Top 10 lists and information about other Dorling Kindersley books), e-mail me direct at ash@pavilion.co.uk, or write to me care of the publishers.

PS: Watch out for the next edition of *The Top 10 of Everything* – appropriately, it will be the 10th!

TOWN & COUNTRY

TOP 10

LEAST POPULATED COUNTRIES IN THE WORLD

	Country	Population
1	Vatican City	738
2	Niue	2,239
3	Tuvalu	9,700
4	Nauru	10,200
5	Wallis and Futuna	13,750
6	Cook Islands	18,300
7	San Marino	24,801
8	Gibraltar	28,800
9	Monaco	29,972
10	Liechtenstein	30,310

These are all independent countries – although some are linked to larger ones. There are numerous dependencies with small populations, among them the Falkland Islands (2,121), and Midway Island (450) and Wake Atoll (300), both of which are under US military administration. The Pitcairn Islands, which were settled in 1790 by mutineers from the ship *Bounty*, have a population of 54.

TOP 10

MOST POPULATED COUNTRIES IN THE WORLD

	Country	Population 1980	1990	1996
1	China	984,736,000	1,133,710,000	1,210,005,000
2	India	692,394,000	855,591,000	952,108,000
3	USA	227,726,000	249,913,000	265,563,000
4	Indonesia	154,936,000	187,728,000	206,612,000
5	Brazil	122,830,000	150,062,000	162,661,000
6	Russia	139,045,000	148,081,000	148,078,000
7	Pakistan	85,219,000	113,914,000	129,276,000
8	Japan	116,807,000	123,537,000	125,450,000
9	Bangladesh	88,077,000	110,118,000	123,063,000
10	Nigeria	65,699,000	86,488,000	103,912,000
	UK	*56,314,000*	*57,418,000*	*58,490,000*
	World	*4,457,593,000*	*5,281,673,000*	*5,771,939,000*

Source: US Bureau of the Census

The population of China is now more than 20 times that of the UK and represents more than 20 per cent of the total population of the world in 1996, proving the commonly stated statistic that "one person in five is Chinese". Although differential rates of population increase result in changes in the order, the members of this Top 10 – which accounts for almost 60 per cent of the world's population – remain largely the same from one year to the next and represent every country with a population of more than 100,000,000. The population of the closest runner-up, Mexico, was reckoned to be 95,772,000 in 1996.

INDIA'S TEEMING MILLIONS
India's high birth rate has resulted in its population more than tripling during the 20th century. The population is set to exceed one billion by the millennium, closing the gap with China's slower-growing population.

TOP 10

COUNTRIES WITH THE HIGHEST ESTIMATED POPULATION IN THE YEAR 2000

	Country	Population
1	China	1,253,438,000
2	India	1,012,909,000
3	USA	274,943,000
4	Indonesia	219,267,000
5	Brazil	169,545,000
6	Russia	147,938,000
7	Pakistan	141,145,000
8	Bangladesh	132,081,000
9	Japan	126,582,000
10	Nigeria	117,328,000
	World	*6,090,914,000*

According to estimates prepared by the US Bureau of the Census, we will approach the year 2000 with a total world population of over 6 billion. India is scheduled to join China as the second country to achieve a population in excess of one billion, while Mexico is expected to ascend to the 100-million-plus club with a population of 102,912,000. In contrast, the populations of certain countries, such as Russia, are actually set to decline as birth rates fall.

TOP 10

COUNTRIES IN WHICH MEN MOST OUTNUMBER WOMEN

	Country	Men per 100 women
1	Qatar	197.1
2	United Arab Emirates	176.6
3	Bahrain	134.4
4	Saudi Arabia	125.8
5	Oman	110.4
6	Brunei	109.6
7	Libya	108.7
8	Pakistan	107.2
9	India	106.9
10	Papua New Guinea	106.6

TOP 10

COUNTRIES IN WHICH WOMEN MOST OUTNUMBER MEN

	Country	Women per 100 men
1	Latvia	116.7
2	Ukraine	115.2
3	Russia	113.3
4	Belarus	112.9
5=	Estonia	112.5
5=	Lithuania	112.5
7	Georgia	109.6
8	Moldova	109.4
9	Hungary	108.8
10	Swaziland	108.7

WORLD COUNTRIES

10

COUNTRIES WITH MOST NEIGHBOURS

	Country/neighbours	No. of neighbours
1	China	15

Afghanistan, Bhutan, India, Kazakhstan, Kyrgyzstan, Laos, Macau, Mongolia, Myanmar (Burma), Nepal, North Korea, Pakistan, Russia, Tajikistan, Vietnam

2	Russia	14

Azerbaijan, Belarus, China, Estonia, Finland, Georgia, Kazakhstan, Latvia, Lithuania, Mongolia, North Korea, Norway, Poland, Ukraine

3	Brazil	10

Argentina, Bolivia, Colombia, French Guiana, Guyana, Paraguay, Peru, Surinam, Uruguay, Venezuela

4=	Germany	9

Austria, Belgium, Czech Republic, Denmark, France, Luxembourg, Netherlands, Poland, Switzerland

4=	Sudan	9

Central African Republic, Chad, Egypt, Eritrea, Ethiopia, Kenya, Libya, Uganda, Congo (Zaïre)

4=	Congo (Zaïre)	9

Angola, Burundi, Central African Republic, Congo, Rwanda, Sudan, Tanzania, Uganda, Zambia

7=	Austria	8

Czech Republic, Germany, Hungary, Italy, Liechtenstein, Slovakia, Slovenia, Switzerland

7=	France	8

Andorra, Belgium, Germany, Italy, Luxembourg, Monaco, Spain, Switzerland

7=	Saudi Arabia	8

Iraq, Jordan, Kuwait, Oman, People's Democratic Republic of Yemen, Qatar, United Arab Emirates, Yemen Arab Republic

7=	Tanzania	8

Burundi, Kenya, Malawi, Mozambique, Rwanda, Uganda, Congo (Zaïre), Zambia

7=	Turkey	8

Armenia, Azerbaijan, Bulgaria, Georgia, Greece, Iran, Iraq, Syria

LONGEST FRONTIERS IN THE WORLD

	Country	km	miles
1	China	22,143	13,759
2	Russia	20,139	12,514
3	Brazil	14,691	9,129
4	India	14,103	8,763
5	USA	12,248	7,611
6	Congo (Zaïre)	10,271	6,382
7	Argentina	9,665	6,006
8	Canada	8,893	5,526
9	Mongolia	8,114	5,042
10	Sudan	7,697	4,783

The 12,248 km/7,611 miles of US frontiers include those shared with Canada (6,416 km/3,987 miles of which comprise the longest continuous frontier in the world), the 2,477-km/1,539-mile boundary between Canada and Alaska, that with Mexico (3,326 km/2,067 miles), and the frontier between the US naval base at Guantánamo and Cuba (29 km/18 miles). The total length of the world's land boundaries is estimated to be approximately 442,000 km/274,646 miles.

CHINESE PUZZLE
Although China has only the 3rd largest land area in the world, it has the most neighbours (15) and the longest frontiers of any country.

COUNTRIES WITH THE LONGEST COASTLINES

	Country	km	miles		Country	km	miles
1	Canada	243,791	151,485	**6**	Japan	29,751	18,486
2	Indonesia	54,716	33,999	**7**	Australia	25,760	16,007
3	Greenland	44,087	27,394	**8**	Norway	21,925	13,624
4	Russia	37,653	23,396	**9**	USA	19,924	12,380
5	Philippines	36,289	22,559	**10**	New Zealand	15,134	9,404

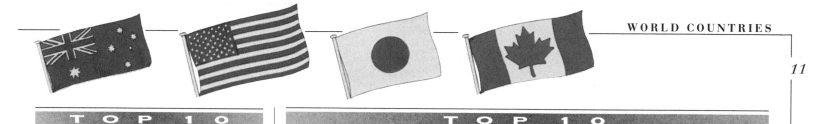

LARGEST LANDLOCKED COUNTRIES IN THE WORLD

	Country	Area sq km	sq miles
1	Kazakhstan	2,717,300	1,049,156
2	Mongolia	1,565,000	604,250
3	Chad	1,284,000	495,755
4	Niger	1,267,080	489,222
5	Mali	1,240,000	478,767
6	Ethiopia	1,128,221	435,609
7	Bolivia	1,098,581	424,165
8	Zambia	752,614	290,586
9	Afghanistan	647,497	250,000
10	Central African Republic	622,984	240,535

LARGEST COUNTRIES IN THE WORLD

	Country	Area sq km	sq miles
1	Russia	17,070,289	6,590,876
2	Canada	9,970,537	3,849,646
3	China	9,596,961	3,705,408
4	USA	9,372,614	3,618,787
5	Brazil	8,511,965	3,286,488
6	Australia	7,686,848	2,967,909
7	India	3,287,590	1,269,346
8	Argentina	2,766,889	1,068,302
9	Kazakhstan	2,717,300	1,049,156
10	Sudan	2,505,813	967,500
	UK	*244,101*	*94,247*
	World total	*136,597,770*	*52,740,700*

The list of the world's largest countries, the Top 10 of which comprise 53.8 per cent of the total Earth's surface, has undergone substantial revision of late: the break-up of the former Soviet Union has effectively introduced two new countries, with Russia taking pre-eminent position, while Kazakhstan, which enters in 9th position, ousts Algeria (2,381,741 sq km/919,595 sq miles) from the list.

LARGEST COUNTRIES IN EUROPE

	Country	Area sq km	sq miles
1	Russia (in Europe)	4,710,227	1,818,629
2	Ukraine	603,700	233,090
3	France	547,026	211,208
4	Spain	504,781	194,897
5	Sweden	449,964	173,732
6	Germany	356,999	137,838
7	Finland	337,007	130,119
8	Norway	324,220	125,182
9	Poland	312,676	120,725
10	Italy	301,226	116,304

MAP OF EUROPE

* Including offshore islands

The United Kingdom falls just outside the Top 10 at 244,101 sq km/94,247 sq ml. Excluding the Isle of Man and Channel Islands, its area comprises England (130,410 sq km/50,351 sq ml), Scotland (78,789 sq km/30,420 sq ml), Wales (20,758 sq km/8,015 sq ml), and Northern Ireland (14,144 sq km/5,461 sq ml). Geographically, rather than politically, the total area of the British Isles, including the whole island of Ireland (70,283 sq km/27,136 sq ml) is 314,384 sq km/121,383 sq ml.

MOST POPULOUS COUNTRIES NAMED AFTER REAL PEOPLE

	Country	Named after	Population
1	USA	Amerigo Vespucci (Italian; 1451–1512)	265,563,000
2	Philippines	Philip II (Spanish; 1527–98)	74,481,000
3	Colombia	Christopher Columbus (Italian; 1451–1506)	36,813,000
4	Saudi Arabia	Abdul Aziz ibn-Saud (Nejd; 1882–1953)	19,409,000
5	Bolivia	Simon Bolivar (Venezuelan; 1783–1830)	7,165,000
6	Marshall Islands	Capt. John Marshall (British; 1748–1818)	53,000
7	Northern Mariana	Maria Theresa (Austrian; 1717–80)	47,000
8	Cook Islands	Capt. James Cook (British; 1728–79)	17,000
9	Wallis and Futuna	Samuel Wallis (British; 1728–95)	14,000
10	Falkland Islands	Lucius Cary, 2nd Viscount Falkland (British; *c.* 1610–43)	2,000

It is questionable whether China, the world's most populous country, is named after the Emperor Chin. Rhodesia, which was named after the British statesman Cecil Rhodes, was re-named when Zambia was created from Northern Rhodesia in 1964 and Zimbabwe from Southern Rhodesia in 1980. Many countries were named after mythical characters, or were named after saints – often because they were discovered on the saint's day.

12

WORLD CITIES

TOP 10

MOST DENSELY POPULATED CITIES IN THE WORLD

	City/country	Population per sq km	sq mile
1	Hong Kong, China	98,053	253,957
2	Lagos, Nigeria	67,561	174,982
3	Dhaka, Bangladesh	63,900	165,500
4	Jakarta, Indonesia	56,650	146,724
5	Bombay, India	54,997	142,442
6	Ahmadabad, India	50,676	131,250
7	Ho Chi Minh City, Vietnam	50,617	131,097
8	Shenyang, China	44,125	114,282
9	Bangalore, India	43,583	112,880
10	Cairo, Egypt	41,413	107,260

* According to the US Bureau of the Census method of calculating population and population density; includes only cities with populations of over 2,000,000

TOP 10

LARGEST CITIES IN THE WORLD IN THE YEAR 2000

	City/country	Estimated population 2000*
1	Tokyo–Yokohama, Japan	29,971,000
2	Mexico City, Mexico	27,872,000
3	São Paulo, Brazil	25,354,000
4	Seoul, South Korea	21,976,000
5	Bombay, India	15,357,000
6	New York, USA	14,648,000
7	Osaka–Kobe–Kyoto, Japan	14,287,000
8	Tehran, Iran	14,251,000
9	Rio de Janeiro, Brazil	14,169,000
10	Calcutta, India	14,088,000

* Based on US Bureau of the Census's unique method of calculating city populations; this gives totals that differ from those calculated by other methods, such as those used by the United Nations

TOP 10

LARGEST NON-CAPITAL CITIES IN THE WORLD*

	City	Country	Population	Capital	Population
1	Shanghai	China	13,400,000	Beijing	10,940,000
2	Bombay	India	12,596,000	Delhi	8,419,000
3	Calcutta#	India	11,022,000	Delhi	8,419,000
4	São Paulo	Brazil	9,394,000	Brasília	1,864,000
5	Tianjin	China	9,090,000	Beijing	10,940,000
6	Karachi#	Pakistan	8,070,000	Islamabad	320,000
7	New York	USA	7,323,000	Washington, DC	598,000
8	Istanbul#	Turkey	6,293,000	Ankara	2,560,000
9	Rio de Janeiro#	Brazil	5,474,000	Brasília	1,864,000
10	St. Petersburg#	Russia	4,456,000	Moscow	8,967,000

* Based on a comparison of populations within administrative boundaries
 # Former capital city

MOST POPULATED CHINESE CITY
China is the most populous country on the Earth, with Shanghai, its foremost port and industrial centre, the world's largest non-capital city, with a total population of 13,400,000.

TOP 10

LARGEST CITIES IN EUROPE

	City/country	Population
1	Moscow*, Russia	10,769,000
2	London*, UK	8,897,000
3	Paris*, France	8,764,000
4	Istanbul#, Turkey	7,624,000
5	Essen, Germany	7,364,000
6	Milan, Italy	4,795,000
7	Madrid*, Spain	4,772,000
8	St. Petersburg, Russia	4,694,000
9	Barcelona, Spain	4,492,000
10	Manchester, UK	3,949,000

* Capital city
 # Located in the European part of Turkey

The problem of defining a city's boundaries means that population figures generally relate to "urban agglomerations", which often include suburbs sprawling over very large areas. The US Bureau of the Census' method of identifying city populations produces this list – although one based on cities minus their suburbs would present a very different picture. Using this method with other cities shows that Athens, Rome, and Berlin all have populations in excess of 3,000,000.

NOT BUILT IN A DAY
The building of the Colosseum, Rome, was begun in AD 72. Rome is one of Europe's oldest cities and was the capital of the Roman Empire. It was the first city to attain a population of one million.

THE 10

FIRST CITIES IN THE WORLD WITH POPULATIONS OF MORE THAN ONE MILLION

	City	Country
1	Rome	Italy
2	Angkor	Cambodia
3	Hangchow (Hangzhou)	China
4	London	UK
5	Paris	France
6	Beijing	China
7	Canton	China
8	Berlin	Germany
9	New York	USA
10	Vienna	Austria

Rome's population was reckoned to have exceeded 1,000,000 some time in the 2nd century BC, and Angkor and Hangchow both reached this figure by about AD 900 and 1200 respectively, but all three subsequently declined. Angkor was completely abandoned in the 15th century.

TOP 10

LARGEST CITIES IN THE US

	City/state	Population
1	New York, New York	7,311,966
2	Los Angeles, California	3,489,779
3	Chicago, Illinois	2,768,483
4	Houston, Texas	1,690,180
5	Philadelphia, Pennsylvania	1,552,572
6	San Diego, California	1,148,851
7	Dallas, Texas	1,022,497
8	Phoenix, Arizona	1,012,230
9	Detroit, Michigan	1,012,110
10	San Antonio, Texas	966,437

TOP 10

OLDEST CITIES IN THE UK

	City	Original charter granted
1	Ripon	886
2	London	1066
3	Edinburgh	1124
4	Chichester	1135
5=	Derby	1154
5=	Lincoln	1154
5=	Oxford	1154
8=	Nottingham	1155
8=	Winchester	1155
10	Exeter	1156

There are 48 cities in England, four in Scotland and Wales, and three in Northern Ireland. Although most of them were settled in earlier times – some as far back as the first century BC – their status as cities is dated from the years when their charters, issued by the Crown and establishing certain privileges, such as the power to enact local laws or collect taxes, were granted. Some dates are disputed: Norwich, for example, claims to have received its original charter in 996, but 1194 is the more accepted date. Contrary to popular belief, not all cities have cathedrals: Southampton, for example, does not, while, conversely, St David's has a cathedral but does not have a city charter.

TOP 10

MOST EXPENSIVE CITIES IN THE WORLD

	City/country	Index*
1	Tokyo, Japan	176.46
2	Osaka, Japan	164.68
3	Moscow, Russia	142.20
4	Zurich, Switzerland	138.84
5	Geneva, Switzerland	137.15
6	Oslo, Norway	135.33
7	Hong Kong, China	131.44
8	Beijing, China	131.43
9	Libreville, Gabon	131.27
10	Copenhagen, Denmark	130.14

* *Based on New York = 100*

The index on which this ranking is based is derived from research conducted by the Corporate Resources Group. Like the figures published by the United Nations in order to assess allowances for UN officials serving in the various cities, it takes into account the costs of a wide range of consumer goods and services. Runaway inflation and rapid price rises in cities that were once considered economical mean that Moscow and certain African cities now appear in close proximity to others that have traditionally been regarded as expensive.

COUNTIES OF BRITAIN

14

LARGEST BRITISH COUNTIES

	County	Area sq km	sq miles
1	Highland Region	24,100	9,305
2	Strathclyde Region	10,633	4,105
3	Grampian Region	8,757	3,381
4	North Yorkshire	8,312	3,209
5	Tayside Region	7,624	2,944
6	Cumbria	7,150	2,761
7	Devon	6,819	2,633
8	Dumfries and Galloway Region	6,457	2,493
9	Lincolnshire	6,083	2,349
10	Dyfed	5,854	2,260

Under the Local Government Act, new local authorities came into being on 1 April 1974. Some are similar in area to previous counties, but others are entirely new: Cumbria, for example, was created by amalgamating Cumberland and Westmorland and the Furness district of Lancashire, while Dyfed was formed from the former counties of Cardiganshire, Carmarthenshire, and Pembrokeshire.

SMALLEST BRITISH COUNTIES

	County	Area sq km	sq miles
1	Isle of Wight	394	152
2	South Glamorgan	433	167
3	Tyne and Wear	550	212
4	Cleveland	614	237
5	Gwynedd	746	288
6	Merseyside	823	318
7	West Glamorgan	871	336
8	West Midlands	896	346
9	Mid Glamorgan	1,019	393
10	Bedfordshire	1,232	476

Before the reorganization of British counties in 1974, the county of Rutland was the smallest at 394 sq km/152 sq miles – which is precisely the same area as the current smallest, the Isle of Wight. Loyalty to the old counties remains an emotive issue, but if recent proposals are adopted, there is every possibility that some of them will experience a comeback.

LEAST DENSELY POPULATED COUNTIES AND REGIONS IN THE UK

	County/region	Population per sq km
1	Highland, Scotland	7
2	Western Isles, Scotland	9
3	Argyll & Bute, Scotland	12
4	Shetland, Scotland	15
5	Orkney, Scotland	19
6	Borders, Scotland	21
7	Dumfries & Galloway, Scotland	22
8	Powys, Wales	23
9	Perthshire & Kinross, Scotland	24
10	Fermanagh, Northern Ireland	29

Of the present Western Isles, North and South Uist were once included with the closest mainland county of Inverness-shire, as was Harris, the southern extension of the island of Lewis, while Lewis itself was considered as part of Ross and Cromarty.

MOST DENSELY POPULATED COUNTIES AND REGIONS IN THE UK

	County/region	Population per sq km
1	Greater London, England	4,375
2	West Midlands, England	2,926
3	Merseyside, England	2,207
4	Tyne and Wear, England	2,112
5	Greater Manchester, England	1,996
6	West Yorkshire, England	1,029
7	South Yorkshire, England	836
8	Torfaen, Wales	719
9	North Lanarkshire, Scotland	686
10	Newport, Wales	680

Since the abolition of the Greater London Council in 1986, local government in the former area is under the control of 32 borough councils. Hence Greater London is in the unique position of being a county in name only, without the centralized power of the other metropolitan counties.

MOST HIGHLY POPULATED COUNTIES IN THE UK

	County	Population
1	Greater London	6,904,600
2	West Midlands	2,630,500
3	Greater Manchester	2,573,500
4	West Yorkshire	2,093,500
5	Hampshire	1,605,700
6	Essex	1,569,900
7	Kent	1,546,300
8	Merseyside	1,445,700
9	Lancashire	1,424,000
10	South Yorkshire	1,304,300

The metropolitan counties created in 1974 are now among the most populated in Britain. Even a century ago, Lancashire had the second largest population in the country, a total of 4,437,518. Under the revised county structure, it was divided into the metropolitan counties of Greater Manchester and Merseyside, with Lancashire comprising the remaining area.

TOP 10

COUNTIES OF ENGLAND AND WALES WITH THE LONGEST COASTLINES

	County	Total coastline	
		km	miles
1	Cornwall	1,104.89	686.27
2	Dyfed	1,043.04	647.85
3	Devon	857.34	532.51
4	Essex	839.44	521.39
5	Gwynedd	835.20	518.76
6	Norfolk	797.26	495.19
7	Cumbria	682.15	423.70
8	Kent	589.20	365.96
9	Humberside	485.32	301.44
10	Lancashire	476.50	295.96

TOP 10

BRITISH COUNTIES WITH THE LONGEST PERIMETERS

	County	Total perimeter	
		km	miles
1	Highland Region	2,417	1,052
2	Strathclyde Region	1,661	1,032
3	North Yorkshire	729	453
4	Dyfed	728	453
5	Dumfries and Galloway Region	709	441
6	Cornwall	672	417
7	Devon	665	413
8	Essex	592	368
9	Lincolnshire	572	355
10	Powys	569	354

Highland Region, Scotland, the largest British country or region, and the least populated, came into being with the 1974 amalgamation of Caithness, Sutherland, Ross and Cromarty (except the Isle of Lewis), Inverness-shire (except the Outer Hebrides), Nairnshire, and parts of Moray and North Argyll. During the same year Strathclyde absorbed Bute, Dunbarton, Lanarkshire, Ayrshire, Argyll, parts of Stirlingshire and Renfrewshire and the City of Glasgow.

TOP 10

COUNTIES OF ENGLAND AND WALES WITH THE SHORTEST COASTLINES

	County	Total coastline	
		km	miles
1	Powys	5.30	3.29
2	Durham	23.33	14.49
3	Mid Glamorgan	29.55	18.36
4	South Yorkshire	36.19	22.48
5	Nottinghamshire	59.48	36.94
6	South Glamorgan	101.13	62.81
7	Cambridgeshire	107.96	67.05
8	Isles of Scilly	109.89	68.25
9	Avon	126.34	78.48
10	Cheshire	126.56	78.61

It may be a surprise to see the landlocked counties of South Yorkshire, Nottinghamshire, and Cambridgeshire included here, but the Ordnance Survey, from whose database this list and the Longest Coastlines list were compiled, uses a method of measurement that includes tidal rivers by tracing coastlines up one riverbank to the NTL (Normal Tidal Limit), then down the opposite riverbank.

TOP 10

BRITISH COUNTIES WITH THE SHORTEST PERIMETERS

	County	Total perimeter	
		km	miles
1	South Glamorgan	115	71
2	Isle of Wight	122	76
3	Tyne & Wear	170	106
4	Cleveland	178	111
5	Mid Glamorgan	202	126
6	West Glamorgan	219	136
7	Bedfordshire	242	150
8	South Yorkshire	246	153
9	West Midlands	249	155
10	Greater Manchester	251	156

TOP 10

BRITISH COUNTIES WITH MOST PARISHES

	County	Parishes
1	North Yorkshire	762
2	Norfolk	539
3	Lincolnshire	513
4	Suffolk	471
5	Devon	422
6	Hereford and Worcester	347
7	Cheshire	328
8	Somerset	327
9	Oxfordshire	320
10	Essex	286

TOP 10

BRITISH COUNTIES WITH FEWEST PARISHES

	County	Parishes
1	Greater London	0
2	Tyne and Wear	10
3	Greater Manchester	13
4	West Midlands	14
5	Merseyside	22
6	Isle of Wight	26
7	Cleveland	32
8	South Glamorgan	54
9=	Surrey	78
9=	West Yorkshire	78

Civil parishes (not to be confused with ecclesiastical parishes) are the smallest units of local government in rural areas. There are few in urban or built-up areas, and many in predominantly rural areas. By law, parish councils must be established in parishes with more than 200 electors. There are more than 7,000 parish councils in England as well as 734 in Wales and more than 1,000 in Scotland (where they are correctly termed community councils).

PLACE NAMES

TOP 10

MOST COMMON PLACE NAMES IN THE US

	Name	Occurrences
1	Fairview	287
2	Midway	252
3	Riverside	180
4	Oak Grove	179
5	Five Points	155
6	Oakland	149
7	Greenwood	145
8=	Bethel	141
8=	Franklin	141
10	Pleasant Hill	140

TOP 10

MOST COMMON PLACE NAMES IN THE UK

	Name	Occurrences
1	Newton	150
2	Blackhill/Black Hill	141
3	Mountpleasant/Mount Pleasant	130
4	Castlehill/Castle Hill	127
5	Woodside/Wood Side	116
6	Newtown/New Town	111
7	Greenhill/Green Hill	108
8	Woodend/Wood End	106
9	Burnside	105
10	Beacon Hill	94

TOP 10

LONGEST PLACE NAMES IN THE US*

	Name	Letters
1	Chargoggagoggmanchauggagogg chaubunagungamaugg (*see* The Top 10 Longest Place Names in the World, No. 6)	45
2	Villa Real de la Santa Fe de San Francisco de Asis (*see* The Top 10 Longest Place Names in the World, No. 7=)	40
3	Nunathloogagamiutbingoi Dunes, Alaska	28
4	Winchester-on-the-Severn, Maryland	21
5	Scraper-Moechereville, Illinois	20
6	Linstead-on-the-Severn, Maryland	19
7=	Kentwood-in-the-Pines, California	18
7=	Lauderdale-by-the-Sea, Florida	18
7=	Vermilion-on-the-Lake, Ohio	18
10=	Chippewa-on-the-Lake, Ohio	17
10=	Fairhaven-on-the-Bay, Maryland	17
10=	Highland-on-the-Lake, New York	17
10=	Kleinfeltersville, Pennsylvania	17
10=	Mooselookmeguntic, Maine	17
10=	Palermo-by-the-Lakes, Ohio	17
10=	Saybrook-on-the-Lake, Ohio	17

TOP 10

COUNTRIES WITH THE LONGEST OFFICIAL NAMES

	Official name*	Common English name	Letters
1	Al Jamāhīrīyah al ʾArabīyah al Lībīyah ash Shaʿbīyah al Ishtirakīyah	Libya	56
2	Al Jumhūrīyah al Jazāʾirīyah ad Dīmuqrāṭīyah ash Shaʿbīyah	Algeria	49
3	United Kingdom of Great Britain and Northern Ireland	United Kingdom	45
4	Sri Lankā Prajathanthrika Samajavadi Janarajaya	Sri Lanka	43
5	Jumhūrīyat al-Qumur al-Ittihādīyah al-Islāmīyah	The Comores	41
6=	Al Jumhūrīyah al Islāmīyah al Mūrītānīyah	Mauritania	36
6=	The Federation of St. Christopher and Nevis	St. Kitts and Nevis	36
8	Jamhuuriyadda Dimuqraadiga Soomaaliya	Somalia	35
9=	al-Mamlakah al-Urdunnīyah al-Hāshimīyah	Jordan	34
9=	Repoblika Demokratikanʾi Madagasikara	Madagascar	34

* *Some official names have been transliterated from languages that do not use the Roman alphabet; their lengths may vary according to the method of transliteration used*

There is clearly no connection between the lengths of names and the longevity of the nation states that bear them. Since this list was first published in 1991, the following three countries have ceased to exist: Socijalisticka Federativna Republika Jugoslavija (Yugoslavia, 45 letters), Soyuz Sovetskikh Sotsialisticheskikh Respublik (USSR, 43), and Ceskoslovenská Socialistická Republika (Czechoslovakia, 36). Uruguay's official name of La República Oriental del Uruguay (29 letters) is sometimes given in full as the 38-letter La República de la Banda Oriental del Uruguay, which would place it in 6th position.

* *Including single-word, hyphenated, and multiple names (not counting hyphens as characters)*

A number of long American place names are of Native American origin, but some are not as long as they once were: in 1916 the US Board on Geographic Names saw fit to reduce the 26-letter New Hampshire stream known as Quohquinapassakessamanagno to "Beaver Creek". There are a number of street names that would qualify for entry, among them a Dr. Martin Luther King Jr. Boulevard in the Bronx, and a Dr. Martin Luther King Jr. Drive in Chicago.

TOP 10

MOST COMMON PLACE NAMES OF BIBLICAL ORIGIN IN THE US

	Name/meaning	Occurrences
1	Bethel (house of God)	141
2	Salem (peace)	134
3	Eden (pleasure)	101
4	Shiloh (peace)	98
5	Paradise (pleasure ground)	94
6	Antioch (named for Antiochus, king of Syria)	83
7	Sharon (plain)	72
8	Jordan (descender)	65
9=	Bethany/Bethania (house of affliction)	59
9=	Zion (mount, sunny)	59

An earlier version of this list based on a sampling of more than 60,000 US place names showed Salem to be the most frequent among more than 100 place names of biblical origin in the US. The name derives from that of the kingdom ruled over by king Melchizedek (Genesis XIV.18), which is often identified with Jerusalem. Salem, Massachusetts, founded in 1628 and the first town in the US to acquire a biblical name, became famous for the witch trials that were conducted there in 1691. However, this revised version, which takes account of all populated places (cities, towns, and villages) in the US and includes compound names, such as Salemville and Salem Heights, indicates that it falls into second place behind Bethel.

TOP 10

LONGEST PLACE NAMES IN THE WORLD*

Name	Letters
1 Krung thep mahanakhon bovorn ratanakosin mahintharayutthaya mahadilok pop noparatratchathani burirom udomratchanivetma hasathan amornpiman avatarnsa thit sakkathattiyavisnukarmprasit	167

When the poetic name of Bangkok, capital of Thailand, is used, it is usually abbreviated to "Krung Thep" (City of Angels).

| **2** Taumatawhakatangihangakoauau-otamateaturipukakapikimaunga-horonukupokaiwhenuakitanatahu | 85 |

This is the longer version (the other has a mere 83 letters) of the Maori name of a hill in New Zealand. It translates as "The place where Tamatea, the man with the big knees, who slid, climbed, and swallowed mountains, known as land-eater, played on the flute to his loved one".

| **3** Gorsafawddacha'idraigodanhed-dogleddollônpenrhynareur-draethceredigion | 67 |

A name contrived by the Fairbourne Steam Railway, Gwynedd, North Wales, UK, for publicity purposes and in order to out-do its rival, No. 4. It means "The Mawddach station and its dragon teeth at the Northern Penrhyn Road on the golden beach of Cardigan Bay".

| **4** Llanfairpwllgwyngyllgogerychwyrn-drobwllllantysiliogogogoch | 58 |

This is the place in Gwynedd, UK, famed especially for the length of its railway tickets. It means "St. Mary's Church in the hollow of the white hazel near to the rapid whirlpool of Llantysilio of the Red Cave". Its official name comprises only the first 20 letters.

Name	Letters
5 El Pueblo de Nuestra Señora la Reina de los Angeles de la Porciuncula	57

The site of a Franciscan mission and the full Spanish name of Los Angeles, USA, it means "the town of Our Lady the Queen of the Angels of the Little Portion".

| **6** Chargoggagoggmanchauggagogg-chaubunagungamaugg | 45 |

This is a lake near Webster, Massachusetts, USA. Its Native American name loosely means "You fish on your side, I'll fish on mine, and no one fishes in the middle". An invented extension of its real name (Chagungungamaug Pond, or "boundary fishing place"), this name was devised in the 1920s by Larry Daly, editor of the Webster Times.

| **7=** Lower North Branch Little Southwest Miramichi | 40 |

Canada's longest place name belongs to a short river in New Brunswick.

| **7=** Villa Real de la Santa Fe de San Francisco de Asis | 40 |

The full Spanish name of Santa Fe, New Mexico, USA, translates as "Royal city of the holy faith of St. Francis of Assisi".

| **9** Te Whakatakanga-o-te-ngarehu-o-te-ahi-a-Tamatea | 38 |

The Maori name of Hammer Springs, New Zealand, like the 2nd name in this list, refers to a legend of Tamatea, explaining how the springs were warmed by "the falling of the cinders of the fire of Tamatea".

| **10** Meallan Liath Coire Mhic Dhubhghaill | 32 |

The longest multiple name in Scotland, this is the name of a place near Aultanrynie, Highland, alternatively spelled Meallan Liath Coire Mhic Dhughaill.

* Including single-word, hyphenated, and multiple names

THE LONG SIDE OF THE TRACKS
For the benefit of its many visitors, the original 58-letter version of the name of this Welsh village is spelled phonetically on its station signboard. It is of dubious origin, however, the modern invention of local poet John Evans, and today ranks only as the world's second longest railway station name, having been overtaken by a similarly contrived Welsh place name.

NATIONAL PARKS

TOP 10

COUNTRIES WITH THE LARGEST PROTECTED AREAS

	Country	Per cent of total area	Designated area sq km	sq miles
1	Brazil	16.8	1,430,167	552,191
2	USA	10.6	993,547	383,611
3	Greenland	45.2	982,500	379,345
4	Australia	10.9	837,843	323,493
5	Colombia	71.9	818,346	316,158
6	Canada	5.6	554,369	214,092
7	Venezuela	60.7	553,496	213,706
8	Tanzania	38.9	365,115	140,972
9	Indonesia	17.2	330,059	127,437
10	China	3.2	308,970	119,294

The International Union for the Conservation of Nature has defined a national park as a relatively large area that is not altered by human exploitation and occupation. Many countries have such areas, the Yellowstone National Park in the US being the first, established in 1872. However, since there are also tracts of land that are worthy of protection, but which already have human habitation, the broader definition has evolved of "protected area"; this encompasses national parks, nature reserves, natural monuments, and other sites. There are at least 25,000 such designated areas around the world.

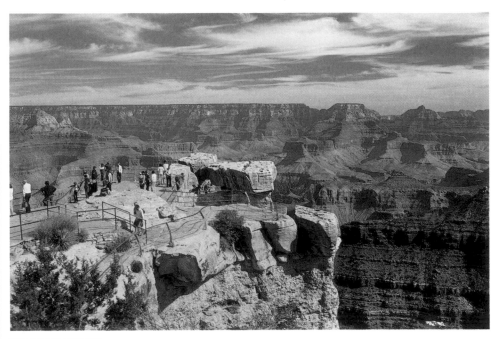

THE GRAND CANYON
The Grand Canyon National Park, which comprises 286 km/178 miles of the Colorado River valley, Arizona, is regarded as one of the great natural wonders of the world, and attracts over 4.5 million visitors annually.

TOP 10

MOST VISITED NATIONAL PARKS IN THE US

	Park/location	Visitors (1996)
1	Great Smoky Mountains National Park, North Carolina/Tennessee	9,265,667
2	Grand Canyon National Park, Arizona	4,537,703
3	Yosemite National Park, California	4,046,207
4	Olympic National Park, Washington	3,348,723
5	Yellowstone National Park, Wyoming	3,012,171
6	Rocky Mountain National Park, California	2,923,755
7	Grand Teton National Park, Wyoming	2,733,439
8	Acadia National Park, Maine	2,704,831
9	Zion National Park, Utah	2,498,001
10	Mammoth Cave, Kentucky	1,896,829

TOP 10

LONGEST HERITAGE COASTS IN THE UK

	Heritage Coast/defined	Length km	miles
1	Pembrokeshire, Jul 1974	232	145
2	North Northumberland, Feb 1973	96	60
3	Lleyn, Mar 1974	90	56
4	South Devon, Dec 1986	75	47
5=	Isles of Scilly, Dec 1974	64	40
5=	North Norfolk, Apr 1975	64	40
7	Gower, Jun 1973	59	37
8=	Suffolk, Sep 1979	57	35
8=	North Yorkshire and Cleveland, May 1981	57	35
10	Penwith, Apr 1986	54	34

The total length of Heritage Coasts in England and Wales is 1,539 km/956 miles. There are several further stretches of coast of more than 50 km/31 miles including Point-Widemouth and the Roseland (both defined April 1986), both of which measure 52 km/32 miles, and Purbeck (June 1981) at 50 km/31 miles.

T O P 1 0
LARGEST AREAS OF OUTSTANDING NATURAL BEAUTY IN ENGLAND AND WALES

	Area	Established	Area sq km	sq miles
1	Cotswolds	August 1966/December 1990	2,038	787
2	North Pennines	June 1988	1,983	766
3	North Wessex Downs	December 1972	1,730	668
4	High Weald	October 1983	1,460	564
5	Dorset	July 1959	1,129	436
6=	Sussex Downs	April 1966	983	380
6=	West Wiltshire Downs	October 1983	983	380
8	Cornwall/Camel Estuary	November 1959/October 1983	958	370
9	Kent Downs	July 1968	878	339
10	Chilterns	December 1965/March 1990	833	322

T O P 1 0
LARGEST NATIONAL PARKS IN ENGLAND AND WALES

	National Park	Established	Area sq km	sq miles
1	Lake District	May 1951	2,292	885
2	Snowdonia	October 1951	2,142	827
3	Yorkshire Dales	October 1954	1,769	683
4	Peak District	April 1951	1,438	555
5	North York Moors	November 1952	1,436	554
6	Brecon Beacons	April 1957	1,351	522
7	Northumberland	April 1956	1,049	405
8	Dartmoor	October 1951	954	368
9	Exmoor	October 1954	693	268
10	Pembrokeshire Coast	February 1952	584	225

Following the National Parks and Access to the Countryside Act of 1949, the National Parks were established in the 1950s to conserve and protect some of the most beautiful landscapes of England and Wales from unsuitable development, at the same time allowing the public free access to them. The total area is 14,011 sq km/ 5,410 sq miles (about nine per cent of the total area of the two countries), of which 9,934 sq km/3,836 sq miles is in England and 4,077 sq km/ 1,574 sq miles in Wales. In addition to the 10 National Parks, the Norfolk and Suffolk Broads (303 sq km/117 sq miles) became a National Park in all but name in April 1989. There are also plans for the New Forest and parts of Scotland to be designated National Parks or areas of special significance.

T O P 1 0
LONGEST NATIONAL TRAILS IN ENGLAND AND WALES

	National Trail/opened	Length km	miles
1	South West Coast Path, May 1973/Sep 1974/ May 1978	962	598
2	Pennine Way, Apr 1965	412	256
3	Thames Path, Jul 1996	344	214
4	Pembrokeshire Coast Path, May 1970	292	181
5	Offa's Dyke Path, Jul 1971	285	177
6	North Downs Way, Sep 1978	246	153
7	Cleveland Way, May 1969	176	109
8	South Downs Way, Jul 1972	171	106
9	Peddars Way and Norfolk Coast Path, Jul 1986	150	93
10	Ridgeway, Sep 1973	137	85

The Pennine Way, the first National Trail, was suggested in a newspaper article in 1935, but it was another 30 years before it was officially opened. There are now 11 Trails in total, with an overall length of 3,308 km/2,055 miles, of which the Top 10 comprise 3,175 km/1,972 miles (the Wolds Way, opened in October 1982 lies just outside this list at 133 km/83 miles). The Trails are managed by the Countryside Commission, which is responsible for repairing the erosion caused by the droves of walkers who use these popular routes.

TALL BUILDINGS

TALLEST HABITABLE BUILDINGS IN THE WORLD

	Building/location	Storeys	Height m	ft
1	Petronas Towers, Kuala Lumpur, Malaysia	96	452	1,482
2	Sears Tower, Chicago, USA *with spires*	110	443 *520*	1,454 *1,707*
3	World Trade Center*, New York, USA	110	417	1,368
4	Jin Mao Building, Shanghai, China *with spire*	93	382 *420*	1,255 *1,378*
5	Empire State Building, New York, USA *with spire*	102	381 *449*	1,250 *1,472*
6	T & C Tower, Kaohsiung, Taiwan	85	348	1,142
7	Amoco Building, Chicago, USA	80	346	1,136
8	John Hancock Center, Chicago, USA *with spire*	100	344 *450*	1,127 *1,476*
9	Shun Hing Square, Shenzhen, China *with spires*	80	330 *384*	1,082 *1,263*
10	Sky Central Plaza, Guangzhou, China *with spires*	80	323 *391*	1,060 *1,283*

* Twin towers; the second tower, completed in 1973, has the same number of storeys but is slightly smaller at 415 m/1,362 ft – although its spire takes it up to 521 m/1,710 ft

Heights are of buildings less their television and radio antennae and uninhabited extensions. The Sears Tower maintains its claim as the tallest building by virtue of having the most floors, the highest occupied floor, and the longest elevator ride.

TALLEST HABITABLE BUILDINGS IN THE SOUTHERN HEMISPHERE

	Building/location	Storeys	Height m	ft
1	Rialto Tower, Melbourne, Australia	60	242	794
2	MLC Centre, Sydney, Australia	60	228	748
3	Governor Phillip Tower, Sydney, Australia	54	227	745
4	Central Park Tower, Perth, Australia	52	226	742
5	Bourke Place*, Melbourne, Australia	48	224	735
6=	Carlton Centre, Johannesburg, South Africa	50	220	722
6=	120 Collins Street, Melbourne, Australia	52	220	722
8	Chifley Tower, Sydney, Australia	50	215	705
9	R & I Bank, Perth, Australia	52	214	702
10	Melbourne Central, Melbourne, Australia	55	211	692

* The BHP logo on the top of the building is Australia's highest sign

TALLEST RESIDENTIAL TOWERS IN THE WORLD

	Building/location	Storeys	Height m	ft
1	Lake Point Tower, Chicago, USA	70	197	645
2	Central Park Place, New York City, USA	56	191	628
3	Olympic Tower, New York City, USA	51	189	620
4	Huron Apartments, Chicago, USA	58	183	600
5	May Road Apartments, Hong Kong, China	58	180	590
6	Marina City Apartments, Chicago, USA	61	179	588
7	30 Broad Street, New York City, USA	48	171	562
8	Galleria, New York City, USA	57	168	552
9	Ritz Tower, New York City, USA	41	165	540
10	Amartapura Condominiums, Tangerang, Indonesia	54	163	535

These towers are all purely residential, rather than office buildings with a proportion given over to residential use. Above its 50 levels of office suites, the 343-m/1,127-ft John Hancock Center, Chicago, built in 1968, has 48 levels of apartments (floors 44 through to 92, at 155 m/509 ft to 315 m/1,033 ft above street level), which are thus the "highest" apartments in the world. The Metropolitan Tower, New York City, built in 1988, is 218 m/716 ft high with 66 storeys, of which the top 48 floors are residential. The 58-storey 198-m/650-ft Museum Tower, also in New York, similarly has mixed occupancy, with its top 40 levels residential.

TALLEST HOTELS IN THE WORLD

	Building/location	Storeys	Height m	ft
1	Baiyoke II Tower, Bangkok, Thailand	89	319	1,046
2	Yu Kyong, Pyong Yang, North Korea	105	300	985
3	Raffles Western Hotel, Singapore	73	226	742
4	Westin Peachtree Hotel, Atlanta, USA	71	220	723
5	Westin Hotel, Detroit, USA	71	219	720
6	Shangri-la, Hong Kong	60	215	705
7	Four Seasons Hotel, New York City, USA	52	208	682
8	Trump International Hotel, New York City, USA	45	207	679
9	Trump Tower, New York City, USA	68	202	664
10	Conrad International, Hong Kong	60	200	656

THE TOWERING CENTURY

Increasingly tall buildings have been one of the most visible signs of progress during the 20th century. The world's first skyscrapers were built over 100 years ago in Chicago, USA, but the city soon lost its crown to New York City. The Empire State Building was to maintain its role as the world's tallest building for more than 40 years, but since the 1980s other US cities, and increasingly those in the Far East, have joined the race. Even the Petronas Tower, Malaysia, the current world record holder, is scheduled to be overtaken by the end of the decade by the Chongqing Tower, China, a 114-storey building soaring to 457 m/1,500 ft.

BANK OF CHINA
Hong Kong's once tallest building prompted a surge of skyscraper construction that has been followed in other Asian cities.

WOOLWORTH BUILDING
Built in 1913, it pioneered New York's passion for skyscrapers.

TOP 10

WORLD CITIES WITH MOST SKYSCRAPERS*

	City	Country	Skyscrapers
1	New York City	USA	131
2	Chicago	USA	47
3	Hong Kong	China	30
4	Houston	USA	27
5	Los Angeles	USA	21
6	Kuala Lumpur	Malaysia	20
7=	Dallas	USA	17
7=	Melbourne	Australia	17
9=	San Francisco	USA	15
9=	Shanghai	China	15
9=	Singapore	Singapore	15

* Habitable buildings of over 152 m/500 ft

The word "skyscraper" was first used in the 18th century to mean a high-flying flag on a ship, and later to describe a tall horse or person. It was not used to describe buildings until the 1880s, when the first tall office blocks of 10 storeys or more were built in Chicago and New York, with the Eiffel Tower following at the end of the decade. The first modern, steel-framed skyscraper was the Woolworth Building, New York, built in 1913.

SEARS TOWER
After 22 years at the top, Chicago's Sears Tower has officially lost its status as "world's tallest".

SKYSCRAPER CITY
The Chicago skyline bears witness to the beginning of America's skyscraper age more than 100 years ago.

BRIDGES

TOP 10

LONGEST SUSPENSION BRIDGES IN THE WORLD

	Bridge/location	Year completed	Length of main span m	ft
1	Great Belt, Denmark	1997	1,624	5,328
2	Humber Estuary, UK	1980	1,410	4,626
3	Tsing Ma, Hong Kong, China	1997	1,377	4,518
4	Verrazano Narrows, New York, USA	1964	1,298	4,260
5	Golden Gate, San Francisco, USA	1937	1,280	4,200
6	Höga Kusten, Veda, Sweden	1997	1,210	3,970
7	Mackinac Straits, Michigan, USA	1957	1,158	3,800
8	Minami Bisano-seto, Kojima-Sakaide, Japan	1988	1,100	3,609
9	Fatih Sultan Mehmet (Bosphorus II), Istanbul, Turkey	1988	1,090	3,576
10	Bosphorus I, Istanbul, Turkey	1973	1,074	3,524

If constructed according to plan, the Messina Strait Bridge between Sicily and Calabria, Italy, will have the longest central span at 3,320 m/10,892 ft. However, at 3,910 m/12,828 ft, Japan's Akashi-Kaikyo Bridge, scheduled for completion in 1998, will be the longest overall.

TOP 10

TALLEST BRIDGE TOWERS IN THE WORLD

	Bridge/ location/year completed	Height m	ft
1	East Bridge, Great Belt Fixed Link, Sprogø, Denmark, 1997	254	833
2	Golden Gate, San Francisco, USA, 1937	227	754
3	Ponte de Normandie, Le Havre, France, 1994	214	702
4	Verrazano Narrows, New York City, USA, 1964	210	690
5	Tsing Ma, Hong Kong, China, 1997	206	675
6	Tagus, Lisbon, Portugal, 1965	190	625
7	George Washington, New York City, USA, 1931	183	600
8	Mackinac Straits, Michigan, USA, 1957	168	552
9	Humber Estuary, Hessle-Barton, UK, 1979	162	531
10	Firth of Forth Road, Queensferry, UK, 1964	156	512

TOP 10

HIGHEST-EARNING TOLL BRIDGES AND TUNNELS IN THE UK

	Crossing	Annual income (£)
1	Queen Elizabeth II (Dartford) Bridge	49,700,000
2	Severn Bridge	44,000,000
3	Mersey Tunnel	26,600,000
4	Humber Bridge	12,700,000
5	Forth Bridge	8,600,000
6	Tyne Tunnel	6,700,000
7	Tamar Bridge	4,700,000
8	Erskine Bridge	4,000,000
9	Tay Bridge	3,000,000
10	Itchen Bridge	2,400,000

Britain's two highest-earning crossings are also its longest cable-stayed bridges: the Second Severn Bridge, completed in 1996, has a span of 456 m/1,496 ft, and the Queen Elizabeth II Bridge at Dartford, completed in 1991, measures 450 m/1,476 ft.

THE 10

FIRST THAMES CROSSINGS IN LONDON

	Crossing	Years in operation
1	London Bridge	1st century AD–1014
2	Kingston Bridge	Medieval
3	Putney Bridge	1729–1886
4	Westminster Bridge	1750–1857
5	Kew Bridge	1759–89
6	Blackfriars Bridge	1769–1860
7	Battersea Bridge	1772–1890
8	Vauxhall Bridge	1816–98
9	Waterloo Bridge	1817–1934
10	Southwark Bridge	1819–1913

None of these first 10 crossings still exists, all having been replaced with new bridges on the same sites and with the same names (there have been at least five London Bridges). The 10 oldest crossings that are still operational – though some have changed their function and several have been widened or otherwise modified – are:

	Crossing	Opened
1	Richmond Bridge	1777
2	Kingston Bridge	1828
3	Thames Tunnel*	1843
4	Westminster Bridge	1862
5	Battersea Railway Bridge	1863
6	Hungerford Bridge	1864
7	Alexandra Bridge	1866
8	Kew Railway Bridge	1869
9	Blackfriars Bridge	1869
10	Tower Subway#	1870

* Built as a foot tunnel; rebuilt for London Underground's Metropolitan Line
# Built for pedestrian traffic; now used for water mains

LE PONT DE NORMANDIE
At 856 m/2,808 ft, the new bridge crossing the Seine near Le Havre, France, will be the world's longest cable stayed bridge until the 1999 completion of the 890-m/2,920-ft Tatara Bridge, Japan.

T O P 1 0

LONGEST CABLE-STAYED BRIDGES IN THE WORLD

	Bridge	Location	Year completed	Length of main span m	ft
1	Pont de Normandie	Le Havre, France	1994	856	2.808
2	Qunghzhou Minjiang	Fozhou, China	1996	605	1,985
3	Yangpu	Shanghai, China	1993	602	1,975
4=	Meiko-Chuo	Nagoya, Japan	1997	590	1,936
4=	Xupu	Shanghai, China	1997	590	1,936
6	Skarnsundet	Trondheim Fjord, Norway	1991	530	1,739
7	Ikuchi	Onomichi-Imabari, Japan	1994	490	1,608
8	Higashi-Kobe	Kobe, Japan	1992	485	1,591
9	Ying Kau	Hong Kong, China	1997	475	1,558
10	Seohae Grand	Asanman, South Korea	1997	470	1,542

T O P 1 0

LONGEST CANTILEVER BRIDGES IN THE WORLD

	Bridge/location	Year completed	Longest span m	ft
1	Pont de Québec, Canada	1917	549	1,800
2	Firth of Forth, Scotland	1890	521	1,710
3	Minato, Osaka, Japan	1974	510	1,673
4	Commodore John Barry, New Jersey/Pennsylvania, USA	1974	494	1,622
5=	Greater New Orleans 1, Louisiana, USA	1958	480	1,575
5=	Greater New Orleans 2, Louisiana, USA	1988	480	1,575
7	Howrah, Calcutta, India	1943	457	1,500
8	Gramercy, Gramercy, Louisiana, USA	1995	445	1,460
9	Transbay, San Francisco, USA	1936	427	1,400
10	Baton Rouge, Louisiana, USA	1969	376	1,235

T O P 1 0

LONGEST BRIDGES IN THE UK

	Bridge	Year completed	Length of main span m	ft
1	Humber Estuary	1980	1,410	4,626
2	Forth Road	1964	1,006	3,300
3	Severn Bridge	1966	988	3,240
4	Firth of Forth	1890	521	1,710
5	Second Severn Crossing	1994	456	1,496
6	Dartford	1992	450	1,476
7	Tamar, Saltash	1961	335	1,100
8	Runcorn–Widnes	1961	330	1,082
9	Clifton Suspension	1864	214	702
10	Menai Straits	1834	176	579

The bridge over the Humber Estuary is not only the longest single-span suspension bridge in the UK, but was the longest bridge in the world until the completion in 1997 of the East Bridge section of Denmark's Great Belt Fixed Link. Each of the Humber's twin concrete anchorages weighs 400,000 tons, and the suspension cables were spun from 41,000 miles of wire. It took eight years to build, at a cost of more than £90,000,000, and was officially opened by Queen Elizabeth II on 17 July 1981.

TUNNELS

LONGEST UNDERWATER TUNNELS IN THE WORLD

	Tunnel/location	Type	Year completed	Length km	miles
1	Seikan, Japan	Rail	1988	53.90	33.49
2	Channel Tunnel, France/England	Rail	1994	49.94	31.03
3	Dai-Shimizu, Japan	Rail	1982	22.17	13.78
4	Shin-Kanmon, Japan	Rail	1975	18.68	11.61
5	Great Belt Fixed Link (Eastern Tunnel), Denmark	Rail	1997	8.00	4.97
6	Severn, UK	Rail	1886	7.01	4.36
7	Haneda, Japan	Rail	1971	5.98	3.72
8	BART, San Francisco, USA	Rail	1970	5.83	3.62
9	Kammon, Japan	Rail	1942	3.60	2.24
10	Kammon, Japan	Road	1958	3.46	2.15

The need to connect the Japanese islands of Honshu, Kyushu, and Hokkaido has resulted in a wave of underwater-tunnel building in recent years, with the Seikan the most ambitious project of all. Connecting Honshu and Hokkaido, 23.3 km/14.4 miles of the tunnel are 100 m/328 ft below the sea bed, bored through strata that presented such enormous engineering problems that it took 24 years to complete. The Channel Tunnel's overall length is shorter than the Seikan Tunnel, but the undersea portion, at 38.0 km/23.6 miles, is longer.

LONGEST RAIL TUNNELS IN THE WORLD

	Tunnel/location	Year completed	Length km	miles
1	Seikan, Japan	1988	53.90	33.49
2	Channel Tunnel, France/England	1994	49.94	31.03
3	Moscow Metro (Medvedkovo/Belyaevo section), Russia	1979	30.70	19.07
4	London Underground (East Finchley/Morden Northern Line), UK	1939	27.84	17.30
5	Dai-Shimizu, Japan	1982	22.17	13.78
6	Simplon II, Italy/Switzerland	1922	19.82	12.31
7	Simplon I, Italy/Switzerland	1906	19.80	12.30
8	Shin-Kanmon, Japan	1975	18.68	11.61
9	Apennine, Italy	1934	18.52	11.50
10	Rokko, Japan	1972	16.25	10.10

LONGEST CANAL TUNNELS IN THE WORLD

	Tunnel	Canal/location	Length km	miles
1	Rôve	Canal de Marseille au Rhône, France	7.12	4.42
2	Bony	Canal de St. Quentin, France	5.67	3.52
3	Standedge	Huddersfield Narrow, UK	4.95	3.08
4	Mauvages	Canal de la Marne et Rhin, France	4.88	3.03
5	Balesmes	Canal Marne à Saône, France	4.82	3.00
6	Ruyaulcourt	Canal du Nord, France	4.35	2.70
7	Strood*	Thames and Medway, UK	3.57	2.22
8	Sapperton	Thames and Severn, UK	3.49	2.17
9	Lappal	Birmingham, UK	3.47	2.16
10	Pouilly-en-Auxois	Canal de Bourgogne, France	3.35	2.08

* *Later converted to a rail tunnel*

After a delay in construction during World War I, the Rôve tunnel on the Canal de Marseilles au Rhône was completed in 1927. Although it has been out of service since 16 June 1963, it remains the longest and the largest canal tunnel in the world, once capable of accommodating ocean-going ships. It is 18 m/59 ft wide and 15.4 m/50.5 ft high, with a bore area of 320 sq m/3,444 sq ft, or about six times the size of a double-track rail tunnel.

LONGEST RAIL TUNNELS IN EUROPE*

	Tunnel/location	Year completed	Length km	miles
1	Channel Tunnel, France/England	1994	49.94	31.03
2	Simplon II, Italy/Switzerland	1922	19.82	12.31
3	Simplon I, Italy/Switzerland	1906	19.80	12.30
4	Apennine, Italy	1934	18.52	11.50
5	Furka Base, Switzerland	1982	15.38	9.55
6	St. Gotthard, Switzerland	1882	15.00	9.32
7	Lötschberg, Switzerland	1913	14.61	9.08
8	Paola, Italy	1988	14.49	9.01
9	Mont-Cenis, France/Italy	1871	13.66	8.49
10	Inn Valley, Austria	1994	12.70	7.89

* *Excluding underground railways*

T O P 1 0

LONGEST ROAD TUNNELS IN THE WORLD

	Tunnel/location	Year completed	Length km	miles
1	St. Gotthard, Switzerland	1980	16.32	10.14
2	Arlberg, Austria	1978	13.98	8.69
3=	Fréjus, France/Italy	1980	12.90	8.02
3=	Pinglin Highway, Taiwan	*	12.90	8.02
5	Mt. Blanc, France/Italy	1965	11.60	7.21
6	Gudvangen, Norway	1992	11.40	7.08
7	Leirfjord, Norway	*	11.11	6.90
8	Kan–Etsu, Japan	1991	11.01	6.84
9	Kan–Etsu, Japan	1985	10.93	6.79
10	Gran Sasso, Italy	1984	10.17	6.32

Under construction

T O P 1 0

LONGEST ROAD AND RAIL TUNNELS IN THE US*

	Tunnel/location	Type	Year completed	Length km	miles
1	Cascade, Washington	Rail	1929	12.54	7.79
2	Flathead, Montana	Rail	1970	12.48	7.78
3	Moffat, Colorado	Rail	1928	10.00	6.21
4	Hoosac, Massachusetts	Rail	1875	7.56	4.70
5	BART Trans-Bay Tubes, San Francisco, California	Rail	1974	5.79	3.60
6	Brooklyn–Battery, New York	Road	1950	2.78	1.73
7	E. Johnson Memorial, Colorado	Road	1979	2.74	1.70
8	Eisenhower Memorial, Colorado#	Road	1973	2.72	1.69
9	Holland Tunnel, New York	Road	1927	2.61	1.62
10	Lincoln Tunnel I, New York	Road	1937	2.51	1.56

Excluding subways
 # The highest-elevation highway tunnel in the world

At 14.70 km/9.13 miles, Mount McDonald rail tunnel, on the Canadian Pacific line from Calgary, Alberta, to Vancouver, British Columbia is the longest transport tunnel in North America. In 1979 the US Air Force was reported to have built an experimental 6.00-km/3.73-mile missile transporting tunnel somewhere beneath the Arizona desert. Although longer than any US highway tunnel, its detailed specifications remain a military secret. The New York City West Delaware water tunnel, completed in 1944 and measuring 168.98 km/105.00 miles, is the longest tunnel in the world.

T O P 1 0

LONGEST TUNNELS IN THE UK*

	Tunnel/location	Type	Length km	miles
1	Severn, Avon/Gwent	Rail	7.02	4.36
2	Totley, South Yorkshire	Rail	5.70	3.54
3	Standedge, Manchester/West Yorkshire	Canal	5.10	3.17
4=	Standedge, Manchester/West Yorkshire	Rail	·4.89	3.04
4=	Woodhead New, South Yorkshire	Rail	4.89	3.04
6	Sodbury, Avon	Rail	4.07	2.53
7	Strood, Kent	Rail#	3.57	2.22
8	Disley, Cheshire	Rail	3.54	2.20
9	Ffestiniog, Gwynedd	Rail	3.52	2.19
10	Sapperton, Gloucestershire	Canal	3.49	2.17

Excluding underground railways # Formerly canal

THE CHANNEL TUNNEL
First proposed almost 200 years ago, the Channel Tunnel was finally opened in 1994. It is Europe's longest and the world's second longest undersea and rail tunnel.

OTHER STRUCTURES

TOP 10

OLDEST CHURCHES IN THE US

	Church/location	Built
1	Cervento de Porta Coeli, San German, Puerto Rico*	1609
2	San Estevan del Rey Mission, Valencia County, New Mexico	1629
3	St. Luke's Church, Isle of Wight County, Virginia	1632
4	First Church of Christ and the Ancient Burying Ground, Hartford County, Connecticut	1640
5	St. Ignatius Catholic Church, St. Mary's County, Maryland	1641
6	Merchant's Hope Church, Prince George County, Virginia	1657
7	Flatlands Dutch Reformed Church, King's County, New York	1660
8=	Claflin-Richards House, Essex County, Massachusetts	1661
8=	Church San Blas de Illesces of Coamo, Ponce, Puerto Rico*	1661
8=	St. Mary's Whitechapel, Lancaster County, Virginia	1661

* *Not US territory when built, but now a US National Historic Site*

TOP 10

OLDEST CATHEDRALS IN THE UK

	Cathedral	Founded
1	Canterbury	1071
2	Lincoln	1073
3	Rochester	1077
4=	Hereford	1079
4=	Winchester	1079
6	York	1080
7	Worcester	1084
8	London (now St. Paul's)	1087
9	Durham	1093
10	Exeter	1114

TOP 10

LARGEST DAMS IN THE WORLD

(Ranked according to the volume of material used in construction)

	Dam	Location	Completed	Volume (m³)
1	Syncrude Tailings	Alberta, Canada	1992	540,000,000
2	Pati	Paraná, Argentina	1990	230,180,000
3	New Cornelia Tailings	Ten Mile Wash, Arizona, USA	1973	209,500,000
4	Tarbela	Indus, Pakistan	1976	105,922,000
5	Fort Peck	Missouri, Montana, USA	1937	96,050,000
6	Lower Usuma	Usuma, Nigeria	1990	93,000,000
7	Atatürk	Euphrates, Turkey	1990	84,500,000
8	Yacyreta-Apipe	Paraná, Paraguay/Argentina	1991	81,000,000
9	Guri (Raul Leoni)	Caroni, Venezuela	1986	77,971,000
10	Rogun	Vakhsh, Tajikistan	1987	75,500,000

Despite the recent cancellation of several dams on environmental grounds, such as two in the Cantabrian Mountains, Spain, numerous major projects are in development for completion by the end of the century, when this Top 10 will contain some notable new entries. Among several in Argentina is the Chapeton dam under construction on the Paraná, and scheduled for completion this year; it will have a volume of 296,200,000 m³ and will thus become the 2nd largest dam in the world. The Pati, also on the Paraná, will have a volume of 238,180,000 m³ and the Kambaratinsk on the Nayrn, Kyrgyzstan, a volume of 112,000,000 m³. The Cipasang dam under construction on the Cimanuk, Indonesia, will have a volume of 90,000,000 m³.

TOP 10

LARGEST SPORTS STADIUMS IN THE WORLD

	Stadium	Location	Capacity
1	Strahov Stadium	Prague, Czech Republic	240,000
2	Maracaña Municipa Stadium	Rio de Janeiro, Brazil	205,000
3	Rungnado Stadium	Pyongyang, North Korea	150,000
4	Estadio Maghalaes Pinto	Belo Horizonte, Brazil	125,000
5=	Estadio Morumbi	São Paulo, Brazil	120,000
5=	Estadio da Luz	Lisbon, Portugal	120,000
5=	Senayan Main Stadium	Jakarta, Indonesia	120,000
5=	Yuba Bharati Krirangan	nr. Calcutta, India	120,000
9	Estadio Castelão	Fortaleza, Brazil	119,000
10=	Estadio Arrudão	Recife, Brazil	115,000
10=	Estadio Azteca	Mexico City, Mexico	115,000
10=	Nou Camp	Barcelona, Spain	115,000

T O P 1 0

HIGHEST DAMS IN THE WORLD

	Dam	Location	Completed	Height m	ft
1	Rogun	Vakhsh, Tajikstan	U/C*	335	1,099
2	Nurek	Vakhsh, Tajikstan	1980	300	984
3	Grand Dixence	Dixence, Switzerland	1961	285	935
4	Inguri	Inguri, Georgia	1980	272	892
5	Chicoasén	Grijalva, Mexico	U/C	261	856
6	Tehri	Bhagirathi, India	U/C	261	856
7	Kishau	Tons, India	U/C	253	830
8	Ertan	Yangtse-kiang, China	U/C	245	804
9	Sayano-Shushensk	Yeniesei, Russia	U/C	245	804
10	Guavio	Guavio, Colombia	U/C	243	797

* Uncompleted at time of publication

T O P 1 0

LARGEST MAN-MADE LAKES IN THE WORLD*

	Dam/lake	Location	Completed	Volume (m³)
1	Owen Falls	Uganda	1954	204,800,000,000
2	Bratsk	Russia	1964	169,900,000,000
3	High Aswan	Egypt	1970	162,000,000,000
4	Kariba	Zimbabwe	1959	160,368,000,000
5	Akosombo	Ghana	1965	147,960,000,000
6	Daniel Johnson	Canada	1968	141,851,000,000
7	Guri (Raul Leoni)	Venezuela	1986	135,000,000,000
8	Krasnoyarsk	Russia	1967	73,300,000,000
9	W.A.C. Bennett	Canada	1967	70,309,000,000
10	Zeya	Russia	1978	68,400,000,000

* Includes only those formed as a result of dam construction

The enlargement of the existing natural lake that resulted from the construction of the Owen Falls created the man-made lake with the greatest surface area: at 69,484 sq km/26,828 sq miles, it is almost as large as the Republic of Ireland.

T O P 1 0

LARGEST BELLS IN THE WESTERN WORLD

	Bell/location	Year cast	Weight (tonnes)
1	*Tsar Kolokol*, Kremlin, Moscow, Russia	1735	201.90
2	*Voskresenskiy (Resurrection)*, Ivan the Great Bell Tower, Kremlin, Moscow, Russia	1746	65.50
3	*Petersglocke*, Cologne cathedral, Germany	1923	25.40
4	Lisbon cathedral, Portugal	post-1344	24.40
5	St. Stephen's cathedral, Vienna, Austria	1957	21.39
6	Bourdon, Strasbourg cathedral, France	1521	20.00
7	*Savoyarde*, Sacre-Coeur basilica, Paris, France	1891	18.85
8	Bourdon, Riverside Church, New York, USA	1931	18.54
9	Olmütz, Czech Republic	1931	18.19
10	*Campagna gorda*, Toledo cathedral, Spain	1753	17.27

The largest bell in the world is the 6.14 m/20 ft 2 in high 6.6 m/21 ft 8 in diameter *Tsar Kolokol*, cast in Moscow for the Kremlin. It cracked before it had been installed and has remained there, unrung, ever since. New York's Riverside Church bell (the largest ever cast in England) is the bourdon (that sounding the lowest note) of the 74-bell Laura Spelman Rockefeller Memorial Carillon. This bell is one of the world's largest carillons, with a 3.10 m/ 10 ft 2 in diameter, and a total weight of 103.64 tonnes. Outside the West, large bells exist but were designed to be struck with a beam, not rung with a clapper like Western bells. A 164-tonne bell in Osaka, Japan, was destroyed in 1942, but there is a 154-tonne bell in the Shi-Tenno-Ji Temple, Kyoto, and a 75-tonne bell in Chonan, Japan. The Mingun or Mingoon bell in Mandalay, Myanmar (formerly Burma), cast in 1780, weighs approximately 88 tonnes, and there is a 54-tonne bell in Beijing, China.

T O P 1 0

LONGEST SEASIDE PIERS IN THE UK

	Pier	Length m	ft
1	Southend, Essex	2,158.0	7,080
2	Southport, Merseyside	1,107.3	3,633
3	Walton-on-the-Naze, Essex	792.5	2,600
4	Llandudno, Gwynedd	699.5	2,295
5	Ramsay, Isle of Man	691.9	2,270
6	Ryde, Isle of Wight	685.8	2,250
7	Hythe, Hampshire	640.1	2,100
8	Brighton (Palace Pier), East Sussex	536.5	1,760
9	Bangor (Garth Pier), Gwynedd	472.4	1,550
10	Blackpool (North Pier), Lancashire	430.0	1,410

THE COMMERCIAL WORLD

TOP 10

DUTY-FREE AIRPORTS IN THE WORLD

	Airport	Annual sales ($)
1	London Heathrow Airport	524,100,000
2	Honolulu Airport	419,500,000
3	Hong Kong Airport	400,000,000
4	Singapore Changi Airport	358,800,000
5	Tokyo Narita Airport	340,000,000
6	Amsterdam Schiphol Airport	326,600,000
7	Manila N. Aquino Airport	302,600,000
8	Frankfurt Airport	289,400,000
9	Paris Charles De Gaulle Airport	283,000,000
10	London Gatwick Airport	193,800,000

Although London Heathrow Airport achieved the greatest sales, Honolulu Airport had the highest average sales per passenger ($109.83 compared with $15.79).

TOP 10

DUTY-FREE PRODUCTS

	Product	Annual sales ($)
1	Women's fragrances	2,250,000,000
2	Cigarettes	2,235,000,000
3	Women's cosmetics	1,767,000,000
4	Scotch whisky	1,663,000,000
5	Cognac	1,235,000,000
6	Men's fragrances and toiletries	1,109,000,000
7	Accessories	1,050,000,000
8	Confectionery	1,049,000,000
9	Leather goods (handbags, belts, etc.)	902,000,000
10	Watches	703,000,000

TOP 10

DUTY-FREE COUNTRIES IN THE WORLD

	Country	Annual sales ($)
1	UK	1,827,000,000
2	USA	1,447,000,000
3	South Korea	1,052,000,000
4	Germany	1,019,000,000
5	Finland	936,000,000
6	Hong Kong	889,000,000
7	Japan	798,000,000
8	France	718,000,000
9	Denmark	706,000,000
10	Netherlands	668,000,000

In 1995 the UK led the world in duty- and tax-free shopping, accounting for 8.9 per cent of the total sales. Europe as a whole took 50.4 per cent of global sales, Asia and Oceania took 30.5 per cent, the Americas took 18.0 per cent. The entire continent of Africa accounted for just one per cent.

TOP 10

EXPORT MARKETS FOR GOODS FROM THE UK

	Country	Total value of exports (£)
1	Germany	17,649,000,000
2	USA	16,807,000,000
3	France	13,638,000,000
4	Netherlands	9,745,000,000
5	Belgium and Luxembourg	7,699,000,000
6	Italy	6,945,000,000
7	Ireland	6,707,000,000
8	Spain	5,073,000,000
9	Sweden	3,347,000,000
10	Japan	2,990,000,000

The union of West and East Germany has created a combined market that in 1990 placed it at the head of the list of UK export markets that had long been led by the US.

TOP 10

GOODS IMPORTED TO THE UK

	Product	Total value of imports (£)
1	Electrical machinery	26,940,000,000
2	Road vehicles	16,275,000,000
3	Chemicals	14,614,000,000
4	Mechanical machinery	13,423,000,000
5	Food and live animals	12,379,000,000
6	Clothing and footwear	6,369,000,000
7	Scientific and photographic equipment	4,988,000,000
8	Petroleum and petroleum products	4,843,000,000
9	Textile manufactures	4,550,000,000
10	Paper and paperboard manufactures	4,287,000,000
	Total (including goods not in this Top 10)	149,848,000,000

PORT TO PORT
Although service industries have become increasingly significant in recent years, the import and export of goods remains the driving force of international trade.

TOP 10

RETAILERS IN THE US

	Retailer	Annual sales ($)		Retailer	Annual sales ($)
1	Wal-Mart Stores	93,627,000,000	6	J.C. Penney Co., Inc.	20,562,000,000
2	KMart Corp.	34,389,000,000	7	American Stores Co.	18,308,894,000
3	Sears Roebuck & Co.	28,020,000,000	8	Price/Costco	17,905,926,000
4	The Kroger Co.	23,937,795,000	9	Safeway Stores	16,397,500,000
5	Dayton Hudson	23,516,000,000	10	Home Depot	15,470,358,000

TOP 10

SUPERMARKET GROUPS* IN THE UK

	Group	Sales (£)#
1	Tesco	11,600,000,000
2	J. Sainsbury+	9,500,000,000
3	Safeway/Presto	6,100,000,000
4	Asda/Dales	6,000,000,000
5	Kwik Save	3,300,000,000
6	Somerfield/Gateway	3,200,000,000
7	William Morrison	2,100,000,000
8	Iceland	1,400,000,000
9	Waitrose (John Lewis Partnership)	1,300,000,000
10	Aldi	500,000,000

* Excluding Co-ops and "mixed goods" retailers, such as Marks & Spencer, that achieved £2,500,000,000-worth of food sales in 1995–96
\# Excluding VAT
\+ Excluding Savacentre (£500,000,000 in 1995–6)

Based on The Retail Rankings (1997) published by Corporate Intelligence on Retailing

THE BIRTH OF THE BARCODE

Now a familiar feature of almost every product we buy, the barcode, or "Universal Product Code", was patented just 25 years ago. Although various similar ideas had been proposed earlier, the design that uses alternating bars was patented on 11 December 1973 by the American James L. Vanderpool of the Monarch Marking Systems Company of Dayton, Ohio, USA (the US Patent No. is 3,778,597). The patent established the method that is now used internationally. The first barcoded product to pass through a checkpoint was a packet of Wrigley's chewing gum that was purchased at the Marsh Supermarket, Troy, Ohio, at 8.01 a.m. on Wednesday, 26 June 1974.

COMMUNICATION

FIRST PLACES TO ISSUE POSTAGE STAMPS

	Place	Date issued
1	Great Britain	May 1840
2	New York City, USA	Feb 1842
3	Zurich, Switzerland	Mar 1843
4	Brazil	Aug 1843
5	Geneva, Switzerland	Oct 1843
6	Basle, Switzerland	Jul 1845
7	USA	Jul 1847
8	Mauritius	Sep 1847
9	France	Jan 1849
10	Belgium	Jul 1849

The first adhesive postage stamps issued in the US were designed for local delivery and produced by the City Despatch Post, New York City. They were inaugurated on 15 February 1842 and later that year were incorporated into the US Post Office Department. In 1847 the rest of the US followed suit, and the Post Office Department issued its first national stamps.

COUNTRIES SENDING THE MOST LETTERS PER PERSON

	Country	Average*
1	USA	670
2=	Liechtenstein	490
2=	Sweden	490
4	Norway	470
5=	Netherlands	420
5=	France	420
7=	Denmark	340
7=	Austria	340
9=	Belgium	330
9=	Luxembourg	330

* *Number of letters posted per person per annum*

According to the Universal Postal Union's figures, the world average for letters posted per person is 72.

COUNTRIES WITH THE MOST POST OFFICES

	Country	Post offices		Country	Post offices
1	India	153,000	6	Japan	25,000
2	China	64,000	7	UK	20,000
3	USA	50,000	8	Germany	19,000
4	Russia	47,000	9	France	17,000
5	Turkey	35,000	10	Ukraine	16,000

COUNTRIES WITH THE MOST TELEPHONES

	Country	Telephones
1	USA	155,749,790
2	Japan	60,700,000
3	Germany	40,869,190
4	France	31,600,000
5	UK	28,530,000
6	China	27,230,000
7	Italy	24,542,079
8	Russia	24,097,265
9	Republic of Korea	17,646,614
10	Canada	17,000,000

COUNTRIES WITH THE MOST TELEPHONES PER 100 PEOPLE

	Country	Telephones per 100 people
1	Sweden	68.67
2	Switzerland	61.35
3	Canada	60.74
4	Denmark	60.41
5	USA	59.86
6	Luxembourg	57.29
7	Iceland	56.19
8	Norway	55.37
9	Finland	55.36
10	France	54.73
	UK	49.41

TOP 10

COUNTRIES THAT MAKE THE MOST INTERNATIONAL PHONE CALLS

	Country	Calls per person	Total calls per annum
1	USA	9.0	2,342,728,000
2	Germany	17.0	1,384,000,000
3	UK	9.1	528,000,000 *
4	Italy	8.7	503,990,000
5	Switzerland	60.0	416,053,000
6	Netherlands	26.5	405,400,000
7	China	0.3	387,350,000
8	Canada	11.9	332,750,000 *
9	Spain	7.5	295,450,000
10	Belgium	29.4	291,037,000

* Estimated

TOP 10

COUNTRIES WITH THE MOST MOBILE PHONE USERS

	Country	Mobile users
1	USA	24,134,421
2	Japan	4,331,000
3	UK	3,956,000
4	Germany	2,466,432
5	Australia	2,289,000
6	Italy	2,240,039
7	Canada	1,890,000
8	China	1,566,000
9	Sweden	1,387,000
10	South Korea	960,300

MODERN BUSINESS ON THE LINE
The growth of communications – especially the use of mobile phones – in the 1980s and 1990s has revolutionized global business life.

TOP 10

COUNTRIES WITH THE MOST FAX MACHINES

	Country	Fax machines installed
1	USA	2,925,000
2	Japan	2,000,000
3	Germany	850,000
4	UK	454,000
5	France	401,000
6	Italy	260,000
7	Canada	199,000
8	China	187,000
9	India	180,000
10	Australia	135,000

Facsimile transmission from one point to another was suggested in the early 19th century and developed in a primitive form soon after the invention of the telephone. As new technology enables transmission from computer to computer, the number of new installations each year, as indicated by this list, will inevitably decline.

TOP 10

TYPES OF INTERNET SITE

	Type	Domain name	Number
1	Commercial	.com	3,965,417
2	Educational	.edu	2,654,129
3	Networks	.net	1,548,575
4	Japan	.jp	734,406
5	Germany	.de	721,847
6	Military	.mil	655,128
7	Canada	.ca	603,325
8	United Kingdom	.uk	591,624
9	United States	.us	587,175
10	Australia	.au	514,760
	Total (including domains not in this Top 10)		16,146,360

Source: Network Wizards (http://www.nw.com/)

TOP 10

MOST LINKED-TO SITES ON THE WORLD WIDE WEB

	Site	Links
1	Welcome to Netscape	84,052
2	Yahoo	35,818
3	WebCounter Home Page	30,394
4	WebCrawler Searching	25,783
5	The Blue Ribbon Campaign for Online Free Speech	19,667
6	Welcome to Microsoft	17,460
7	Lycos, Inc. Home Page	14,769
8	Infoseek	13,993
9	Discover NCSA: The National Center for Supercomputing Applications	12,478
10	Welcome to Starting Point™	11,195

Source: WebCrawler (http://webcrawler.com/), June 1997

A survey identified those sites on the Internet that were most frequently signposted, enabling users to "surf" to them.

TOYS & GAMES

TOP 10

TOYS AND GAMES IN THE UK, 1996*

	Product	Manufacturer
1	PreComputer Power Pad	V Tech Electronics
2	Talking Whizz Kid Power Mouse	V Tech Electronics
3	Monopoly	Waddingtons
4	Jenga	MB/Parker
5	Barbie Jewel Hair Mermaid	Mattel
6	Picnic Van	Mattel
7	Magna Doodle	Tyco Toys
8	Talking Barney	Playskool (Hasbro)
9	Five Star Table	Monneret
10	Strolling Sisters Gift Set	Mattel

* Ranked by value of retail sales

Sales of toys and games monitored through the UK's major outlets (Woolworths, Argos, Index, W.H. Smith, John Menzies, Grattan, Littlewoods, GUS, Gamleys, ELC, Beatties, Toptack, Freemans, Asda, and Tesco), which between them are responsible for approximately 70 per cent of all toys sales in the UK, are ranked here by value. An alternative Top 10 based on numbers of units sold would include "pocket money" items such as tins of paint used for model-making and sand used for sand-pits.

TOP 10

MOST LANDED-ON SQUARES IN MONOPOLY®*

US game		UK game
Illinois Avenue	1	Trafalgar Square
Go	2	Go
B. & O. Railroad Station	3	Fenchurch Street
Free Parking	4	Free Parking
Tennessee Avenue	5	Marlborough Street
New York Avenue	6	Vine Street
Reading Railroad	7	King's Cross Station
St. James Place	8	Bow Street
Water Works	9	Water Works
Pennsylvania Railroad	10	Marylebone Station

Monopoly® is a registered trade mark of Parker Brothers, a division of Tonka Corporation, USA, under licence to Waddington Games Ltd. in the UK

* Based on a computer analysis of the probability of landing on each square

Monopoly was patented in February 1936. It was devised in Philadelphia during the Great Depression by Charles Darrow, an unemployed heating engineer. Darrow's streets were derived from those of the New Jersey resort, Atlantic City. There were already several real estate board games around, such as The Landlord's Game, patented in 1904, which like Monopoly had a "Go to Jail" square, and Finance, which featured "Chance" and "Community Chest" cards. However, none of the earlier prototypes was commercially successful, and Darrow's version, with its subtle balance of skill and luck, was the first property game that was fun to play. His sales in 1934 rocketed to 20,000, and he entered into a licensing arrangement with Parker Brothers. Darrow rapidly became a millionaire.

TOP 10

MOST EXPENSIVE TOYS SOLD AT AUCTION BY CHRISTIE'S EAST, NEW YORK

	Toy/sale	Price ($)*
1	"The Charles", a fire hose-reel made by American manufacturer George Brown & Co, c. 1875, December 1991	231,000
2	Märklin fire station, December 1991	79,200
3	Horse-drawn, double-decker tram, December 1991	71,500
4	Mikado mechanical bank, December 1993	63,000
5	Märklin ferris wheel, June 1994	55,200

	Toy/sale	Price ($)*
6	Girl skipping rope mechanical bank, June 1994	48,300
7	Märklin battleship, June 1994	33,350
8	Märklin battleship, June 1994	32,200
9=	Bing keywind open phaeton tinplate automobile, December 1991	24,200
9=	Märklin fire pumper, December 1991	24,200

* Including 10 per cent buyer's premium

TOP 10

MOST POPULAR FANCY-DRESS COSTUME STYLES IN THE UK*

Women		Men
Georgian	1	Georgian
Pride and Prejudice	2	*Pride and Prejudice*
Hollywood	3	Uniforms
1920s Flapper	4	Edwardian
1930s	5	Victorian
1970s	6	1970s
Mardi Gras	7	*Braveheart*
Show Girls	8	1920s Gangster
Morticia (from *The Addams Family*)	9	Dracula
Saloon Girls	10	Musketeer

* Based on rentals from Angels & Bermans Fancy Dress Hire

HIGHEST-SCORING WORDS IN SCRABBLE

	Word/play	Score
1	Quartzy	(i) 164
		(ii) 162

(i) Play across a triple-word-score (red) square with the Z on a double-letter-score (light-blue) square.

(ii) Play across two double-word-score (pink) squares with Q and Y on pink squares.

2=	Bezique	(i) 161
4=		(ii) 158

(i) Play across a red square with either the Z or the Q on a light-blue square.

(ii) Play across two pink squares with the B and second E on two pink squares.

2=	Cazique	(i) 161
4=		(ii) 158

(i) Play across a red square with either the Z or the Q on a light-blue square.

(ii) Play across two pink squares with the C and E on two pink squares.

4=	Zinkify	158

Play across a red square with the Z on a light-blue square.

5=	Quetzal	155

Play across a red square with either the Q or the Z on a light-blue square.

5=	Jazzily	155

Using a blank as one of the Zs, play across a red square with the non-blank Z on a light-blue square.

5=	Quizzed	155

Using a blank as one of the Zs, play across a red square with the non-blank Z or the Q on a light-blue square.

8=	Zephyrs	152

Play across a red square with the Z on a light-blue square.

8=	Zincify	152

Play across a red square with the Z on a light-blue square.

8=	Zythums	152

Play across a red square with the Z on a light-blue square.

These Top 10 words all contain seven letters and therefore earn the premium of 50 for using all the letters in the rack.

BESTSELLING CD-ROM TITLES IN THE US, 1996

	Title	Manufacturer
1	Microsoft Windows 95 Upgrade	Microsoft
2	Myst	Broderbund
3	Warcraft II	CUC
4	Duke Nukem 3D	GT Interactive
5	Flight Simulator	Microsoft
6	Quicken Deluxe	Intuit
7	Corel Printhouse	Corel
8	Toy Story Animated Storybook	Disney
9	Netscape Navigator Personal Edition 3.0	Netscape
10	Civilization 2	MicroProse

Overall sales of PC software grew more than half a billion US dollars from 1995, although fewer new titles were released.

FROM PLAYROOM TO SALESROOM
Along with rare toys and teddy bears, fine examples of the doll-maker's craft often attain high prices at auction.

MOST EXPENSIVE DOLLS EVER SOLD AT AUCTION IN THE UK

	Doll/sale	Price (£)
1	Kämmer and Reinhardt bisque character doll, German, *c.* 1909, Sotheby's, London, 8 February 1994	188,500
2	Albert Marque bisque character doll, Sotheby's, London, 17 October 1996	71,900
3=	William and Mary wooden doll, English, *c.* 1690, Sotheby's, London, 24 March 1987	67,000
3=	17th-century wooden doll, Christie's, London, 18 May 1989	67,000
5	Albert Marque bisque character doll, Sotheby's, London, 17 October 1996	58,700
6	Mulatto pressed bisque swivel-head Madagascar doll, Sotheby's, London, 17 October 1996	56,500
7	Shellacked pressed bisque swivel-head doll, Sotheby's, London, 17 October 1996	45,500
8	Pressed bisque doll, Sotheby's, London, 17 October 1996	36,700
9	Kämmer and Reinhardt German doll, Christies, London, 3 June 1993	33,000
10	Victoria, a French doll of the 1880s, with a wardrobe of costumes, Christies, London, 2 June 1994	25,300

FUEL & POWER

TOP 10

ENERGY CONSUMERS IN THE WORLD

Energy consumption 1995*

	Country	Oil	Natural gas	Coal	Nuclear power	Hydro-electric power	Total
1	USA	806.8	559.5	494.4	182.9	25.8	2,069.4
2	China	157.5	15.8	640.3	3.3	16.2	833.1
3	Russia	146.1	317.9	119.4	25.6	15.2	624.2
4	Japan	267.3	55.0	85.9	74.3	7.7	490.2
5	Germany	135.1	67.0	92.5	39.8	1.8	336.2
6	France	89.0	29.6	13.0	97.3	6.5	235.4
7	India	72.5	17.0	128.3	2.0	7.5	227.3
8	Canada	80.0	66.8	24.7	25.0	28.7	225.2
9	UK	81.7	65.8	47.8	23.0	0.5	218.8
10	Italy	94.9	43.0	11.1	–	3.6	152.6
	World	*3,226.9*	*1,883.6*	*2,210.7*	*596.4*	*218.5*	*8,136.1*

* *Millions of tonnes of oil equivalent*

TOP 10

NATURAL GAS CONSUMERS IN THE WORLD

	Country	Consumption 1995 billion m³	billion ft³
1	USA	621.6	21,952
2	Russia	353.2	12,473
3	Ukraine	76.2	2,691
4	Germany	74.4	2,627
5	Canada	74.2	2,620
6	UK	73.1	2,582
7	Japan	61.2	2,161
8	Italy	47.8	1,688
9	Uzbekistan	42.4	1,497
10	Saudi Arabia	38.6	1,363
	World total	*2,093.0*	*73,914*

TOP 10

COUNTRIES WITH MOST NUCLEAR REACTORS

	Country	Reactors
1	USA	108
2	France	56
3	Japan	50
4	UK	35
5	Russia	29
6	Canada	21
7	Germany	19
8	Ukraine	15
9	Sweden	12
10	South Korea	11

Fewer than 30 countries around the world possess nuclear power. The proportion of total electricity production from nuclear sources averages approximately 30 per cent but varies considerably, accounting for almost 80 per cent in France and only about 20 per cent in the US. Russia's 12.5 per cent is the lowest in the Top 10.

TOP 10

ELECTRICITY PRODUCERS IN THE WORLD

	Country	Production kW/hr
1	USA	3,145,892,000,000
2	Russia	956,587,000,000
3	Japan	906,705,000,000
4	China	839,453,000,000
5	Canada	527,316,000,000
6	Germany	525,721,000,000
7	France	471,448,000,000
8	India	356,519,000,000
9	UK	323,029,000,000
10	Brazil	251,484,000,000

The Top 10 electricity consuming countries are virtually synonymous with these producers, since relatively little electricity is transmitted across national boundaries. Electricity production has burgeoned phenomenally in the post-war era: in 1948 US production was 336,600,000,000 kilowatt-hours, or almost one-tenth of its total today, while that of Japan was 33,600,000,000 kilowatt-hours, less than four per cent of its present amount.

TOP 10

COUNTRIES WITH THE GREATEST NATURAL GAS RESERVES

	Country	Known reserves (1995) trillion m³	trillion ft³ *
1	Russia	48.1	1,700.0
2	Iran	21.0	741.6
3	Qatar	7.1	250.0
4	United Arab Emirates	5.8	204.6
5	Saudi Arabia	5.3	185.9
6	USA	4.6	163.8
7	Venezuela	4.0	139.9
8	Algeria	3.6	128.0
9	Nigeria	3.4	120.0
10	Iraq	3.1	109.7

* *One trillion = 1 million million (10^{12})*

The world total reserves of natural gas are put at 139.7 trillion m³/4,933.6 trillion ft³ – these Top 10 countries thus hold 76 per cent of the world's supplies. At current rates of production, it is reckoned that natural gas supplies will last until 2060.

TOP 10

OIL PRODUCERS IN THE WORLD

	Producer	Production 1995 (tonnes)
1	Saudi Arabia	426,500,000
2	USA	382,500,000
3	Russia	306,800,000
4	Iran	182,800,000
5	Mexico	151,300,000
6	China	149,000,000
7	Venezuela	146,400,000
8	Norway	139,900,000
9	UK	130,300,000
10	United Arab Emirates	112,800,000

TOP 10

COUNTRIES WITH THE LARGEST CRUDE OIL RESERVES

	Country	Reserves (tonnes)		Country	Reserves (tonnes)
1	Saudi Arabia	35,700,000,000	6	Venezuela	9,300,000,000
2	Iraq	13,400,000,000	7	Mexico	7,100,000,000
3	Kuwait	13,300,000,000	8	Russia	6,700,000,000
4	United Arab Emirates	12,700,000,000	9	Libya	3,900,000,000
5	Iran	12,000,000,000	10	USA	3,700,000,000

Oil accounts for 40 per cent of the world energy market. At the end of 1995, the global known reserves of oil stood at 138,300,000,000 tonnes, dominated by a Top 10 that controls 117,800,000,000 tonnes, or 85 per cent of the world's oil. At the 1995 rate of production, the world supply will last for only another 43 years.

Despite its huge output, the US produces less than half the 806,800,000 tonnes a year of oil that it consumes, which is equivalent to 3 tonnes per person a year, consumed directly (through consumption of heating fuel, motor fuel, etc.) or indirectly (through consumption of electricity produced by oil-fired power stations, etc.).

TOP 10

LARGEST NUCLEAR POWER STATIONS IN THE WORLD

	Station	Country	Reactors in use	Output (megawatts)
1	Bruce	Canada	1–8	6,910
2	Gravelines	France	1–6	5,706
3	Paluel	France	1–4	5,528
4	Washington	USA	1–5	5,326
5	Fukushima Daichi	Japan	1–6	4,696
6	Fukushima Daini	Japan	1–4	4,400
7	Pickering	Canada	1–8	4,328
8	Chinon	France	A3; B1–B4	4,051
9=	Kursk	Russia	1–4	4,000
9=	St. Petersburg	Russia	1–4	4,000

TOP 10

COUNTRIES WITH LONGEST OIL PIPELINES

	Country	Total pipeline length km	miles
1	USA	276,000	171,498
2	Russia	63,000	39,146
3	Mexico	38,350	23,830
4	Canada	23,564	14,642
5	China	10,800	6,711
6	Iran	9,800	6,089
7	Germany	7,590	4,716
8	France	7,546	4,689
9	Argentina	6,990	4,343
10	Algeria	6,910	4,294

DIAMONDS & GOLD

TOP 10

MOST EXPENSIVE COINS EVER SOLD BY SPINK COIN AUCTIONS, LONDON

	Coin/sale date	Price (£)
1	George V 1920 Sydney Mint sovereign (1 March 1992)	104,000
2	Henry III gold penny (13 June 1985)	65,000
3	Brazilian Coronation peca, 1822 (18 June 1986)	58,000
4	George III pattern five guineas, 1773 (9 November 1989)	57,000
5	George III pattern five pounds, 1820 (9 November 1989)	47,500
6	Charles I triple unite, Oxford Mint, 1643 (31 May 1989)	44,000
7	Charles II gold pattern crown, 1662 (19 November 1990)	41,000
8	Edward VIII proof sovereign, 1937 (7 December 1984)	40,000
9	Anne Vigo five guineas, 1703 (9 November 1989)	39,000
10	Henry VIII sovereign (2 June 1983)	36,000

Founded in 1666, the year of the Great Fire of London, Spink & Son Ltd is the world's oldest-established firm of antique dealers and numismatists. In addition to the coins appearing in the list, on 3 July 1988 in Tokyo, Spink & Son, in association with the Taisei Stamp and Coin Co., achieved the world record price for a British coin when they sold a Victoria proof gothic crown – dating from 1847, and one of only two known – for the equivalent of £126,000.

TOP 10

LARGEST UNCUT DIAMONDS IN THE WORLD

	Diamond	Carats
1	Cullinan	3,106.00

Measuring approximately 10 x 6.5 x 5 cm/ 4 x 2¹/2 x 2 in, and weighing 621 gm/1 lb 6 oz, the Cullinan was unearthed in 1905. Bought by the Transvaal Government for £150,000, it was presented to King Edward VII. The King decided to have it cut, and the most important of the separate gems are now among the British Crown Jewels.

	Diamond	Carats
2	Braganza	1,680.00

All trace of this enormous stone has been lost.

3	Excelsior	995.20

Cut by the celebrated Amsterdam firm of Asscher in 1903, the Excelsior produced 21 superb stones, which were sold mainly through Tiffany's of New York.

4	Star of Sierra Leone	968.80

Found in Sierra Leone on St. Valentine's Day, 1972, the uncut diamond weighed 225 g/8 oz and measured 6.5 x 4 cm/2¹/2 x 1¹/2 in.

5	Zale Corporation "Golden Giant"	890.00

Its origin is so shrouded in mystery that it is not even known which country it came from.

	Diamond	Carats
6	Great Mogul	787.50

When found in 1650 in the Gani Mine, India, this diamond was presented to Shah Jehan, the builder of the Taj Mahal. After Nadir Shah conquered Delhi in 1739, it entered the Persian treasury and apparently vanished from history.

7	Woyie River	770.00

Found in 1945 beside the river in Sierra Leone, whose name it now bears, it was cut into 30 stones. The largest of these, known as Victory and weighing 31.35 carats, was auctioned at Christie's, New York, in 1984 for $880,000.

8	Presidente Vargas	726.60

Discovered in the Antonio River, Brazil, in 1938, it was named after the then President.

9	Jonker	726.00

In 1934 Jacobus Jonker found this massive diamond after it had been exposed by a heavy storm. Acquired by Harry Winston, it was exhibited in the American Museum of Natural History and attracted enormous crowds.

10	Reitz	650.80

Like the Excelsior, the Reitz was found in the Jagersfontein Mine in South Africa in 1895.

TOP 10

DIAMOND-PRODUCING COUNTRIES

	Country	Production per annum (carats)
1	Australia	41,000,000
2	Zaïre	16,500,000
3	Botswana	14,700,000
4	Russia	11,500,000
5	South Africa	9,800,000
6	Brazil	2,000,000
7	Namibia	1,100,000
8=	Angola	1,000,000
8=	China	1,000,000
10	Ghana	700,000
	World total	*100,850,000*

TOP 10

LARGEST POLISHED GEM DIAMONDS IN THE WORLD

	Diamond/last known whereabouts or owner	Carats
1	"Unnamed Brown" (De Beers)	545.67
2	Great Star of Africa/Cullinan I (British Crown Jewels)	530.20
3	Incomparable/Zale (sold in New York, 1988)	407.48
4	Second Star of Africa/Cullinan II (British Crown Jewels)	317.40
5	Centenary (De Beers)	273.85
6	Jubilee (Paul-Louis Weiller)	245.35
7	De Beers (sold in Geneva, 1982)	234.50
8	Red Cross (sold in Geneva, 1973)	205.07
9	Black Star of Africa (unknown)	202.00
10	Anon (unknown)	200.87

WORKING IN A GOLD MINE
South African gold mines have long been the world's No. 1 source of gold, producing almost a quarter of the world's total annual output of almost 2,300 tonnes.

TOP 10
COUNTRIES HOLDING GOLD RESERVES

	Country	Reserves (tonnes)
1	USA	8,138
2	France	3,182
3	Germany	3,101
4	Italy	2,592
5	Switzerland	2,590
6	Netherlands	1,052
7	Japan	754
8	UK	717
9	Portugal	612
10	Spain	608

Gold reserves are the government holdings of gold in each country – and are often far greater than the gold owned by private individuals. In the days of the "Gold Standard", this provided a tangible measure of a country's wealth. Though less significant today, gold reserves remain a component in calculating a country's international reserves, alongside its holdings of foreign exchange and SDRs (Special Drawing Rights).

TOP 10
COUNTRIES MAKING GOLD JEWELLERY

	Country	Gold used p.a. (tonnes)
1	Italy	446.0
2	India	400.6
3	China	191.0
4	Saudi Arabia and Yemen	153.1
5	USA	148.3
6	Indonesia	133.0
7	Turkey	110.4
8	Taiwan	102.0
9	Hong Kong	82.0
10	Japan	78.0

TOP 10
GOLD-MANUFACTURING COUNTRIES

	Country	Gold used in fabrication p.a. (tonnes)
1	Italy	457.9
2	India	426.1
3	USA	250.3
4	China	203.8
5	Japan	187.2
6	Saudi Arabia and Yemen	156.1
7	Indonesia	133.0
8	Turkey	125.6
9	Taiwan	110.0
10	Hong Kong	86.9

Gold fabrication accounted for a world total consumption of 3,257 tonnes in 1995. This comes from various sources including mined production, scrap, and the release of gold from official stockpiles. In addition to the manufacture of jewellery, 209 tonnes were used in electronics, 65.7 tonnes in dentistry, and 109.6 for other industrial and decorative purposes. Issues of official coins also comprise a large sector of the gold market (34.5 tonnes in 1995).

TOP 10
GOLD-PRODUCING COUNTRIES

	Country	Production 1995 (tonnes)
1	South Africa	522.4
2	USA	329.3
3	Australia	253.5
4	Canada	150.3
5	Russia	142.1
6	China	136.4
7	Indonesia	74.1
8	Brazil	67.4
9	Uzbekistan	63.6
10	Papua New Guinea	54.8

SAVE THE PLANET

TOP 10

PERSONAL ENVIRONMENTAL IMPROVEMENT ACTIVITIES

	Activity	Per cent undertaking*
1	Reading/watching TV programmes about environmental issues	85
2	Walking in the countryside	80
3	Taking bottles, glass, paper, or cans for recycling	70
4=	Giving money to environmental charities	51
4=	Using unleaded petrol	51
6	Selecting environmentally friendly products	36
7	Requesting information from an environmental organization	16
8	Subscribing to a magazine concerned with environmental issues	13
9	Joining an environmental organization	10
10	Visiting or writing a letter to a politician about an environmental issue	6

* *Of those taking part in* Business and the Environment, *a 1996 MORI survey of public attitudes and behaviour*

TOP 10

ENVIRONMENTAL CONCERNS

	Environmental problem	Per cent of people "very worried"
1	Litter in streets/countryside	43
2=	Air pollution	42
2=	Pollution of rivers, streams, and water	42
4	Exhaust fumes from cars/lorries	40
5	Pollution of seas; waste disposal at sea	39
6=	Too much traffic	36
6=	Asthma from pollution/increase in asthma rates	36
8	Loss of countryside/overbuilding	35
9	Pollution of beaches	34
10	Destruction of rainforests	33

THE 10

WORST CARBON DIOXIDE EMITTERS IN THE WORLD

	Country	CO_2 emissions per capita per annum (tonnes)
1	United Arab Emirates	42.28
2	USA	19.13
3	Singapore	17.99
4	Kazakhstan	17.48
5	Trinidad and Tobago	16.30
6	Australia	15.24
7	Canada	14.99
8	Russia	14.11
9	Norway	14.03
10	Saudi Arabia	13.85
	World average	*4.10*

THE 10

WORST SULPHUR DIOXIDE EMITTERS IN THE WORLD

	Country	Annual SO_2 emissions per capita kg	lb	oz
1	Canada	118.7	261	11
2	USA	81.2	179	0
3	Germany	70.7	155	14
4	UK	61.8	136	4
5	Spain	56.1	123	11
6	Ireland	52.9	116	10
7	Belgium	41.8	92	2
8	Finland	38.3	84	7
9	Denmark	35.0	77	3
10	Italy	34.4	75	13

Sulphur dioxide (SO_2), the principal cause of acid rain, is produced by fuel combustion in factories and power stations. During the 1980s, emissions by all countries declined: the UK's total production was estimated at 5,310,000 tonnes (equivalent to 96 kg per head) in 1975, and further reductions are planned so that the level in the year 2003 will be 60 per cent less than that in 1980. At present, some 70 per cent of the UK's SO_2 emissions are from power stations.

SAVE THE CAN
The recycling of aluminium and steel cans has become increasingly common: in the US alone, more than 170 million drinks cans and 13 million steel cans are recovered every day.

TOP 10

COMPONENTS OF HOUSEHOLD WASTE IN THE UK

	Waste	Average yearly per cent	weight (kg)
1	Putrescibles (kitchen and garden waste)	16.8	106
2	Newspapers	11.4	72
3	Other paper	9.5	60
4	Fines (ash, hoover dust)	6.8	43
5	Clear glass	5.4	34
6	Magazines	4.6	29
7	Disposable nappies	4.2	27
8	Plastic film	4.2	26
9	Miscellaneous combustibles (shoes, carpets, etc)	3.9	25
10	Card packaging	3.7	24

Source: AEA Technology, National Environmental Technology Centre

The average UK household generates 12.2 kg/26.9 lb of dustbin waste per week, or 634 kg/1,398 lb per annum – equivalent to the weight of 10 adults every year.

TOP 10

US STATES WITH THE HIGHEST RECYCLING RATE

	State	Waste recycled (%)
1	New Jersey	56
2	Wisconsin	50
3	Minnesota	41
4	Florida	40
5	Maine	35–40
6=	Ohio	35
6=	Vermont	35
8	Massachusetts	34
9	Virginia	33
10=	New York	32
10=	Oregon	32

Source: National Solid Waste Management Association

Through increasing public awareness and in response to state laws banning various types of packaging or levying additional taxes on the use of certain products, the recycling of solid waste has gathered considerable momentum in the US during the 1990s. All the states in the Top 10 report increased rates – Wisconsin, for example, had a rate of just 24 per cent in 1992, and has thus more than doubled its recycling rate (although New Jersey's position at the head of the list may reflect its inclusion of recycled cars, which are omitted from the statistics of most states). Targets of 50 per cent or more by the turn of the century or soon afterwards have been declared by most states.

TOP 10

RUBBISH PRODUCERS IN THE WORLD

	Country	Domestic waste per capita per annum kg	lb
1	USA	730	1,609
2	Australia	690	1,521
3	Canada	660	1,455
4	Finland	620	1,367
5	Iceland	560	1,235
6	Norway	510	1,124
7	Netherlands	500	1,102
8	Luxembourg	490	1,080
9	France	470	1,036
10	Denmark	460	1,014

THE 10

WORST DEFORESTING COUNTRIES IN THE WORLD

	Country	Average annual forest loss 1981–90 (sq km)
1	Brazil	36,710
2	Indonesia	11,120
3	Zaïre	7,320
4	Mexico	6,780
5	Bolivia	6,250
6	Venezuela	5,990
7	Thailand	5,150
8	Sudan	4,820
9	Tanzania	4,380
10	Paraguay	4,030

THE 10

US STATES RELEASING THE MOST TOXIC CHEMICALS

	State	Chemicals released kg	lb
1	Texas	113,454,931	250,125,291
2	Tennessee	70,680,602	155,824,043
3	Louisiana	69,773,417	153,824,043
4	Mississippi	55,160,212	121,607,444
5	Ohio	53,171,055	117,222,103
6	Illinois	44,305,676	97,677,290
7	Alabama	43,281,999	95,420,468
8	Florida	42,597,992	93,912,491
9	North Carolina	40,419,761	89,110,314
10	Michigan	37,475,820	82,620,035

THE BIGGEST DUMP IN THE WORLD

In 1948 the Fresh Kills Landfill site on New York's Staten Island was opened. It has since become the world's largest rubbish dump, covering 890 hectares/2,200 acres to a height of 53 m/175 ft. New York households generate an average of 2.8 kg/6.2 lb of solid waste each per day, 62 per cent of which is landfilled, with the remainder recycled, converted into energy, or incinerated. Every day up to 12,700 tonnes/ 14,000 tons of this garbage arrives at Fresh Kills. There it is handled by over 500 employees. Environmental concerns have been expressed about the site's future and will continue beyond its closure, which is scheduled for the year 2002.

THE WORLD'S RICHEST

TOP 10

COUNTRIES WITH THE MOST DOLLAR BILLIONAIRES*

	Country	Billionaires
1	USA	145
2	Germany	48
3	Japan	34
4=	Hong Kong	12
4=	Thailand	12
6	France	11
7=	Indonesia	10
7=	Mexico	10
9=	Brazil	8
9=	Switzerland	8

* *Individuals and families with a net worth of $1,000,000,000 or more*
Based on data published in Forbes Magazine

TOP 10

HIGHEST-EARNING ENTERTAINERS IN THE WORLD

	Entertainer	Profession	1995–96 income ($)
1	Oprah Winfrey	TV host/producer	171,000,000
2	Steven Spielberg	Film producer/director	150,000,000
3	Beatles	Rock group	130,000,000
4	Michael Jackson	Singer	90,000,000
5	Rolling Stones	Rock group	77,000,000
6	Eagles	Rock group	75,000,000
7=	David Copperfield	Illusionist	74,000,000
7=	Arnold Schwarzenegger	Actor	74,000,000
9	Jim Carrey	Actor	63,000,000
10=	Michael Crichton	Novelist/screenwriter	59,000,000
10=	Jerry Seinfeld	TV performer	59,000,000

Used by permission of Forbes Magazine

TOP 10

HIGHEST-EARNING SINGERS IN THE WORLD

	Singer(s)	1995–96 income ($)
1	Beatles	130,000,000
2	Michael Jackson	90,000,000
3	Rolling Stones	77,000,000
4	Eagles	75,000,000
5	Garth Brooks	51,000,000
6	R.E.M.	44,000,000
7	Luciano Pavarotti	36,000,000
8	Kiss	35,000,000
9	Maria Carey	32,000,000
10	Metallica	28,000,000

Used by permission of Forbes Magazine

Even though the Beatles no longer exist as a group, they continue to earn huge revenue from their recordings and videos. The Rolling Stones typify the huge income generated by major rock tours: their *Voodoo Lounge* tour made $300,000,000, while Microsoft paid $4,000,000 to use their song *Start Me Up* to promote Windows 95.

TOP 10

HIGHEST-EARNING ACTORS IN THE WORLD

	Actor(s)	1995–96 income ($)
1	Arnold Schwarzenegger	74,000,000
2	Jim Carrey	63,000,000
3	Tom Hanks	50,000,000
4	Tom Cruise	46,000,000
5=	Harrison Ford	44,000,000
5=	Clint Eastwood	44,000,000
5=	Sylvester Stallone	44,000,000
8	Robin Williams	42,000,000
9=	Roseanne	40,000,000
9=	Michael Douglas	40,000,000

Used by permission of Forbes Magazine

Actors with the audience magnetism of Arnold Schwarzenegger, Jim Carrey, and Clint Eastwood today routinely command $20,000,000 or more per movie, while percentage earnings can add further sums: Tom Hanks is reckoned to have made $35,000,000 from *Apollo 13*, and Tom Cruise could ultimately make over $60,000,000 for his role in *Mission: Impossible*.

TOP 10

HIGHEST-EARNING DECEASED PEOPLE

	Name	Year died
1	Elvis Presley	1977
2	John Lennon	1980
3	James Dean	1955
4	Jimi Hendrix	1970
5	Albert Einstein	1955
6	Marilyn Monroe	1962
7	Jim Morrison	1971
8	Humphrey Bogart	1957
9	Orson Welles	1985
10	Babe Ruth	1948

Under copyright law, the estates of numerous authors, film stars, singers, and songwriters continue to receive posthumous royalty income. Added to this, the commercial exploitation of iconic images in advertisements and other media has become a major business, with Einstein, for example, used to promote everything from whisky to computer software. The estates of innumerable other deceased celebrities accrue substantial income, but the actual amounts are jealously protected by lawyers.

RICHEST PEOPLE IN THE US

In 1996 *Forbes Magazine*, which annually surveys the 400 wealthiest people in the USA, ranked 145 American individuals and families as dollar billionaires – that is, with assets in excess of $1,000,000,000, more than double the total for the previous year. The Forbes 400 includes both the inheritors of great family fortunes and self-made individuals. A placing in the list is extremely volatile, however, particularly during recent times, when many who made vast fortunes in a short period lost them with even greater rapidity. At the same time, events such as stock market falls and the decline in property values have led to a fall in the assets of many members of this elite club, while deaths, such as that in 1996 of David Packard, have removed former entrants from the list, which now stands as:

	Name	Assets ($)
1	Bill Gates	18,500,000,000

In 1975, at the age of 19, Gates left law college to co-found (with Paul G. Allen, who rates 3rd place in this list) the Microsoft Corporation of Seattle, now one of the world's leading computer software companies, and one that has experienced phenomenal growth; a $2,000 investment in 1986 was worth nearly $70,000 in 1993. Gates, a self-described "hard-core technoid" first ascended to number one position in 1992. Formerly a bachelor devoted only to his business and fast cars, on 1 January 1994 he married Microsoft executive Melinda French. The launch of Windows 95 the following year further enhanced his fortune, which has since seen him branching into Internet software, cable news, and picture libraries. His book, The Road Ahead, *was a No. 1 bestseller.*

	Name	Assets ($)
2	Warren Buffett	15,000,000,000

Buffet was born and still lives in Omaha, Nebraska. His professional career started as a pinball service engineer, after which he published a horse race tip sheet. His diverse business interests include the New England textile company Berkshire Hathaway that has in turn acquired major stakes in the Washington Post, Coca-Cola, Gillette, *and other companies. In 1992 Buffett was ranked 4th in the* Forbes 400, *in 1993 was elevated to first place, but in 1994 dropped back behind Bill Gates.*

	Name	Assets ($)
3	Paul Allen	7,500,000,000

Co-founder with Bill Gates of Microsoft, Allen has maintained his connections with the computer and multimedia industry. He also pursues such interests as his ownership of the Portland Trail Blazers basketball team, and his passion for musicians such as Jimi Hendrix, one of the subjects of Experience Music Project, a museum founded by Allen.

	Name	Assets ($)
4	John Kluge	7,200,000,000

Kluge is founder of the Metromedia Company of Charlottesville, Virginia. The family of German-born Kluge settled in Detroit in 1922, where he worked on the Ford assembly line. He started a radio station and, in 1959, with partners, acquired the Metropolitan Broadcasting Company. This developed into Metromedia, a corporation that owns TV and radio stations and cellular telephone franchises and other varied properties. He also once owned an 80,000-acre estate and castle in Scotland. Kluge, who was placed as America's richest man in 1989, has diversified his interests and is developing Orion Pictures as part of a media group.

	Name	Assets ($)
5	Larry Ellison	6,000,000,000

California-based Ellison worked with IBM before establishing his own computer software company, Oracle Corporation, which plans to launch interactive television to provide video-on-demand.

	Name	Assets ($)
6	Phil Knight	5,300,000,000

A former athlete at the University of Oregon, Knight foresaw the burgeoning athletic shoe industry and founded Nike.

	Name	Assets ($)
7=	Jim Walton	4,800,000,000

Samuel Moore Walton, the founder of Wal-Mart Stores, headed the list of America's richest people for several years. He died in 1992, but the company he founded, today the largest retail chain in the US with 2,200 stores, has annual sales of $95,500,000,000. His widow Helen and four children share the fortune he created.

	Name	Assets ($)
7=	John Walton	4,800,000,000
9=	Alice Walton	4,700,000,000
9=	Helen Walton	4,700,000,000
9=	S. Robson Walton	4,700,000,000

Five runners-up with assets of more than $4 billion are listed in the *Forbes 400*. They are brothers Donald and Samuel Newhouse ($4,500,000,000 each), Sisters Barbara Cox Anthony and Anne Cox Chambers ($4,500,000,000 each), and Ronald Perelman ($4,500,000,000).

GOLDEN GATES OF FORTUNE
Seattle-born Bill Gates's fortune has grown along with the global success of his Microsoft Corporation, making him the world's richest non-royal with a fortune nudging $19 billion.

YOUNGEST BILLIONAIRES IN THE US

	Name/source of wealth/ assets ($)	Age
1	Daniel Morton Ziff (Ziff Brothers Investments), 1,000,000,000	25
2	Robert David Ziff (Ziff Brothers Investments), 1,000,000,000	31
3	Michael Dell (Dell Computer Corp.), 1,100,000,000	32
4	Dirk Edward Ziff (Ziff Brothers Investments), 1,000,000,000	33
5	Theodore W. Waitt (Gateway 2000 Computers), 1,700,000,000	34
6	Abigail Johnson (Fidelity Investments), 2,500,000,000	35
7	Kenneth Tuchman (TeleTech), 1,000,000,000	36
8	Steven Anthony Ballmer (Microsoft Corp.), 3,700,000,000	41
9	Lee Marshall Bass (oil, investments), 2,200,000,000	41
10	Ted Schwartz (APAC Teleservices Inc.), 1,100,000,000	43

Based on data published in Forbes Magazine

THE WEALTH OF NATIONS

TOP 10

RICHEST COUNTRIES IN THE WORLD

	Country	GDP per capita ($)
1	Luxembourg	39,833
2	Switzerland	37,179
3	Japan	34,629
4	Bermuda	29,857
5	Denmark	28,104
6	Norway	26,477
7	USA	25,860
8	Germany	25,578
9	Austria	24,949
10	Iceland	24,605
	UK	*18,411*

GDP (Gross Domestic Product) is the total value of all the goods and services that are produced annually within a country. (Gross National Product, GNP, also includes income from overseas.) Dividing the GDP by the country's population produces the GDP per capita, which is often used as a measure of how "rich" a country is. Some 32 industrialized nations have GDPs in excess of $10,000, while about 15 developing countries, particularly those in Africa, have per capita GDPs of less than $200.

TOP 10

COUNTRIES WITH THE HIGHEST PER CAPITA EXPENDITURE

	Country	Expenditure per capita ($)
1	Japan	19,700
2	Switzerland	19,570
3	USA	16,500
4	Iceland	15,550
5	Luxembourg	13,880
6	Germany	13,680
7=	France	13,400
7=	Norway	13,400
9	Belgium	13,060
10	Bermuda	12,690

THE 10

POOREST COUNTRIES IN THE WORLD

	Country	GDP per capita ($)
1	Sudan	63
2	Somalia	74
3	Mozambique	80
4	Tanzania	85
5	Afghanistan	111
6	Ethiopia	130
7	Malawi	144
8	Burundi	146
9	Sierra Leone	152
10	Chad	186

THE 10

COUNTRIES WITH THE LOWEST PER CAPITA EXPENDITURE

	Country	Expenditure per capita ($)
1	Somalia	17
2	Tanzania	61
3	Mozambique	87
4	Ethiopia	95
5	Kenya	120
6=	Burundi	130
6=	Malawi	130
8	Nepal	135
9=	Laos	140
9=	Sierra Leone	140

It is difficult for people in Western consumer cultures to comprehend the poverty of the countries appearing in this list, where the total average annual expenditure of an individual would barely cover the cost of a few meals in the West. These poorer economies inevitably rely on a greater degree of self-sufficiency in food production. In such countries, spending on transport, recreation, and other staple items of the household budgets of developed countries is virtually zero.

TOP 10

RICHEST STATES IN THE US

	State	Average income per capita ($)
1	Connecticut	30,303
2	New Jersey	28,858
3	New York	26,782
4	Massachusetts	26,694
5	Maryland	25,927
6	New Hampshire	25,151
7	Nevada	25,013
8	Illinois	24,763
9	Hawaii	24,738
10	Alaska	24,182

The US Bureau of Economic Analysis produces data to show the average income received by each resident. In the 20th century, average national incomes in the US have risen steadily from $418 in 1900, to $22,788 in 1995. If the District of Columbia was regarded as a State, it would be in 1st place, with an average income of $32,274.

THE 10

POOREST STATES IN THE US

	State	Average income per capita ($)
1	Mississippi	16,531
2	Arkansas	17,429
3	West Virginia	17,915
4	New Mexico	18,055
5	Oklahoma	18,152
6	Utah	18,223
7	Montana	18,482
8	Kentucky	18,612
9	North Dakota	18,663
10	Alabama	18,781

Historically, the southern states of the US have tended to be the poorest, with the average annual income in Mississippi barely half that of the annual income in the prosperous District of Columbia. The national average income ($22,788 in 1995) was exceeded in just 22 of the 50 states.

TOP 10

COINS AND NOTES IN CIRCULATION IN THE US*

	Unit	Value in circulation ($)
1	$100 bill	252,311,216,200
2	$20 bill	82,060,900,480
3	$50 bill	47,052,728,150
4	$10 bill	13,512,717,430
5	$1 bill	8,219,481,212
6	$5 bill	7,322,233,410
7	Dime	2,821,930,000
8	Quarter	1,831,908,000
9	Nickel	1,647,068,000
10	$2 bill	1,075,448,118

* As of 1 January 1997

As well as the denominations in this Top 10, there are 289,502 $500 bills (value $144,751,000), 168,006 $1,000 bills ($168,006,000), 354 $5,000 bills ($1,770,000), and 345 $10,000 bills ($3,450,000), along with 13,123,260,000 cents ($13,123,260,000) in circulation. In 1996 a total of 19,473,352,000 coins were minted at the US Mint production facilities.

TOP 10

COINS AND NOTES IN CIRCULATION IN THE UK*

	Unit	Value in circulation (£)
1	£20 note	8,579,000,000
2	£10 note	5,688,000,000
3	£50 note	3,104,000,000
4	£5 note	1,067,000,000
5	£1 coin	1,095,000,000
6	20p coin	326,000,000
7	50p coin	221,000,000
8	5p coin	149,500,000
9	10p coin	141,600,000
10	2p coin	88,220,000

* As of 1 January 1997

Notes in circulation in January 1997 (which included a total of £1,154,000,000 "other notes", such as the high-value notes used internally by the Bank of England) totalled £20,795,602,843 – the equivalent of a pile of £5 notes 416 km/259 miles high. There are also 7,239,000,000 1p coins worth £72,390,000, and 56,000,000 £1.00 notes – which are legal tender only in Scotland.

TOP 10

US COMPANIES MAKING THE GREATEST PROFIT PER SECOND

	Company	Profit per second ($)
1	General Motors	218
2	General Electric	208
3	Exxon Corporation	205
4	Philip Morris	172
5	IBM	132
6	Ford Motor Co.	131
7	Intel	113
8	Citicorp	109
9	Merck	105
10	E. I. Du Pont de Nemours	104

TOP 10

COUNTRIES IN WHICH IT IS EASIEST TO BE A MILLIONAIRE

	Country/ currency unit	Value of 1,000,000 units £	$
1	Ukraine, Karbovanets	3.62	5.52
2	Turkey, Lira	7.37	11.44
3	Zaïre, Zaïre	12.82	19.90
4	Angola, Kwanza	20.13	31.25
5	Guinea-Bissau, Peso	35.47	55.07
6	Belarus, Rouble	37.24	57.82
7	Mozambique, Metical	57.43	89.16
8	Vietnam, Dông	58.06	90.14
9	Russia, Rouble	119.23	185.10
10	Afghanistan, Afghani	134.69	209.11

Runaway inflation in many countries has reduced the value of their currencies to such an extent that they make them virtually worthless. Thus with an exchange rate running at an average of 275,869.6 Ukrainian Karbovanets to the pound sterling (428,287.55 to the $), total assets of just £3.62/$5.62 will qualify a person as a millionaire in the Ukraine.

TOP 10

COUNTRIES WITH MOST CURRENCY IN CIRCULATION 100 YEARS AGO

	Country	Currency in circulation 100 years ago (£) gold	silver	paper	total
1	France	178,000,000	150,000,000	115,000,000	443,000,000
2	USA	141,000,000	87,000,000	208,000,000	436,000,000
3	Germany	122,000,000	45,000,000	71,000,000	238,000,000
4	India	10,000,000	170,000,000	12,000,000	192,000,000
5	Russia	39,000,000	14,000,000	123,000,000	176,000,000
6	UK	102,000,000	22,000,000	39,000,000	163,000,000
7	China	–	150,000,000	–	150,000,000
8	Austria	8,000,000	19,000,000	76,000,000	103,000,000
9	Italy	22,000,000	11,000,000	57,000,000	90,000,000
10	Spain	19,000,000	24,000,000	30,000,000	73,000,000

It is interesting to consider that there are now individuals in these countries who, on paper at least, own more than the entire country's money supply in the late 1890s. Today there is in excess of $1,000,000,000,000 in circulation in the US.

CANDY IS DANDY

SWEET-CONSUMING COUNTRIES IN THE WORLD

	Country	chocolate kg	chocolate lbs	other sweets kg	other sweets lbs	total kg	total lbs
1	Denmark	7	15	10	22	17	37
2	Ireland	8	18	6	13	14	31
3=	UK	8	18	5	11	13	29
3=	Switzerland	10	22	3	7	13	29
3=	Germany	7	16	6	13	13	29
6=	Austria	8	17	3	7	11	24
6=	Belgium/Luxembourg	6	13	5	11	11	24
6=	Netherlands	5	11	6	13	11	24
6=	Australia	5	11	6	13	11	24
10	USA	5	11	5	11	10	22

Consumption per capita (per annum)

ICE CREAM-CONSUMING COUNTRIES IN THE WORLD

	Country	Production per capita litres	Production per capita pints
1	USA	26.58	46.78
2	Finland	21.67	38.13
3	Denmark	19.75	34.76
4	Australia	18.55	32.64
5	Canada	16.60	29.22
6	Sweden	16.39	28.84
7	Norway	15.97	28.10
8	Belgium/Luxembourg	14.30	25.16
9	UK	12.48	21.96
10	New Zealand	12.43	21.87

Source : International Dairy Foods Association

Global statistics for ice cream consumption are hard to come by, but this list presents recent and reliable International Ice Cream Association estimates for per capita production of ice cream and related products (frozen yoghurt, sherbert, water ices, etc.). Since only small amounts of such products are exported, consumption figures can be presumed to be similar.

ICE CREAM BRANDS IN THE US

	Brand	Sales ($)*
1	Private labels	773,100,000
2	Good Humor-Breyers	375,600,000
3	Dreyer's Grand Ice Cream	371,200,000
4	Blue Bell Creameries	174,300,000
5	Häagen-Dazs	138,500,000
6	Ben & Jerry's	113,300,000
7	Turkey Hill Dairy	63,000,000
8	Conagra	55,900,000
9	Marigold Foods	45,200,000
10	Friendly	44,900,000

* Year to 8 September 1996
Source: International Dairy Foods Association

The memorably titled Häagen-Dazs ice cream was the brainchild of Reuben Mattus, who in 1961 created a range of high quality ice creams, choosing a meaningless but Danish-sounding name to emphasize the rich, creamy nature of his product.

BEN & JERRY'S ICE CREAM/FROZEN YOGHURT FLAVOURS

1	Chocolate Chip Cookie Dough
2	Cherry Garcia
3	Chocolate Fudge Brownie
4	New York Super Fudge Chunk
5	Cherry Garcia Frozen Yoghurt
6	Chunky Monkey
7	Chocolate Fudge Brownie Frozen Yoghurt
8	Peanut Butter Cup
9	Vanilla with Heath Toffee Crunch
10	Phish Food

Grateful Dead founder the late Jerry Garcia is believed to be the only rock musician ever to have two bestselling frozen desserts named in his honour.

THE HOLE STORY

Polo Mints, "the mint with the hole", were launched in the UK in 1948, and are today Britain's bestselling mint. They are the British version of the US product, Life Savers, which used a similar slogan and became familiar in the UK when GIs were seen consuming them during World War II. Life Savers were first made in the early years of this century by Clarence A. Crane of Cleveland, Ohio, who named them after their resemblance to a lifebelt. He sold his business in 1913 for $2,900 to Edward John Noble. After changing the packaging and by ingenious marketing, Noble relaunched the product, which then became the world's bestselling sweet.

TOP 10

COCOA-CONSUMING COUNTRIES IN THE WORLD

	Country	Total cocoa consumption (tonnes)
1	USA	544,100
2	Germany	244,700
3	UK	184,000
4	France	156,500
5	Russian Federation	143,900
6	Japan	112,700
7	Brazil	100,700
8	Italy	85,400
9	Belgium/Luxembourg	62,100
10	Spain	60,200

Cocoa is the principal ingredient of chocolate, and its consumption is therefore closely linked to the production of chocolate in each consuming country. Like coffee, the consumption of chocolate tends to occur mainly in the Western world and in relatively affluent countries. Since some of these Top 10 consuming nations also have large populations, the figures for cocoa consumption per capita present a somewhat different picture, being dominated by those countries with a long-established tradition of manufacturing high-quality chocolate products:

	Country	Consumption per capita		
		kg	lb	oz
1	Belgium/Luxembourg	5.900	13	0
2	Iceland	4.444	9	13
3	Switzerland	3.491	7	11
4	UK	3.145	6	15
5	Denmark	3.122	6	14
6	Austria	3.071	6	12
7	Germany	2.997	6	10
8	Norway	2.771	6	2
9	Malta	2.711	6	0
10	France	2.692	5	15

TOP 10

CANDY BRANDS IN THE US

	Brand	Market share (%)
1	Reese's Peanut Butter Cup	5.0
2	Snickers Original	4.8
3	M&M's Plain	3.5
4	M&M's Peanut	3.2
5	Hershey's Kit Kat	2.4
6=	Hershey Kisses Milk	2.3
6=	Nestlé Butterfinger	2.3
8	Hershey's Milk Chocolate and Nougats Regular	2.1
9	Life Savers Original "Fruit Juicers"	2.0
10	Milky Way Original	2.0

TOP 10

GUM BRANDS IN THE US

	Brand	Sales ($)*
1	Wrigley's Doublemint	62,600,000
2	Winter Fresh	53,400,000
3	Freedent	50,800,000
4	Wrigley's Big Red	44,000,000
5	Wrigley's Spearmint	39,100,000
6	Wrigley's Juicy Fruit	37,500,000
7	Bubblicious	29,000,000
8	Bubble Yum	25,400,000
9	Dentyne Cinn A Burst	23,100,000
10	Dentyne	18,200,000

* *Through grocery stores only – total sales of some brands through drug stores, mass merchandisers, and other outlets (vending machines, gas stations, etc.) may more than double these figures*

Source: Information Resources, Inc.

TOP 10

HARRODS' BESTSELLING CHOCOLATES

1	Harrods Own Traditional English Chocolates	6	Harrods Belgian Fresh Cream Chocolates
2	Harrods Own Swiss Chocolates	7	Leysieffer
3	Harrods Own Belgian Chocolates	8	Godiva
4	Harrods Own Handmade Truffles	9	Nuehaus
5	Harrods Truffle Collection	10	Leonidas

FOOD FOR THOUGHT

T O P 1 0

CALORIE-CONSUMING COUNTRIES IN THE WORLD

	Country	Average daily consumption per capita
1	Ireland	3,847
2	Greece	3,815
3	Cyprus	3,779
4	USA	3,732
5	Spain	3,708
6	Belgium/Luxembourg	3,681
7	New Zealand	3,669
8	Denmark	3,664
9	Portugal	3,634
10	France	3,633
	UK	*3,317*
	World average	*2,718*

The Calorie requirement of the average man is 2,700 and of the average woman, 2,500. Inactive people need fewer Calories, while those engaged in heavy labour might need to increase, perhaps even to double, these figures. Calories that are not consumed as energy are stored as fat – which is why Calorie-counting is one of the key aspects of most diets.

T O P 1 0

SUGAR-CONSUMING COUNTRIES IN THE WORLD

	Country	Consumption per capita per annum kg	lb	oz
1	Swaziland	203.5	448	10
2	Singapore	82.5	181	14
3	Fiji	78.8	173	12
4	Malta	62.9	138	11
5	Belize	61.6	135	13
6	Israel	59.9	132	1
7	Tobago	59.7	131	10
8	Iceland	59.5	131	3
9	Denmark	57.2	126	2
10	Costa Rica	56.4	124	5

A Mars a day…

THE SWEET TASTE OF SUCCESS
The Mars bar, Milky Way bar, and other chocolate products such as Galaxy reflect the name of the Mars company's founder.

T H E 1 0

FIRST MARS PRODUCTS

	Product	Introduced
1=	Milky Way bar	1923
1=	Snickers bar (non-chocolate)	1923
3	Snickers bar (chocolate)	1930
4	3 Musketeers bar	1932
5	Maltesers	1937
6	Kitekat (catfood; now Whiskas)	1939
7	Mars almond bar	1940
8	M&M's plain chocolate candies	1941
9	Uncle Ben's Converted brand rice	1942
10=	M&M's peanut chocolate candies	1954
10=	Pal (dogfood)	1954

American candy manufacturer Franklin C. Mars established his first business in Tacoma, Washington, USA, in 1911 and formed the Mar-O-Bar company in Minneapolis (later moving it to Chicago) in 1922 with the first of its internationally known products, the Milky Way bar. The founder's son Forrest E. Mars set up in the UK in 1932, merging the firm with its American counterpart in 1964.

T O P 1 0

HOTTEST CHILLIES

	Typical example	Scoville Units
1	Datil, Habanero, Scotch Bonnet	100,000–350,000
2	Chiltepin, Santaka, Thai	50,000–100,000
3	Aji, Cayenne, Piquin, Tabasco	30,000–50,000
4	de Arbol	15,000–30,000
5	Serrano, Yellow Wax	5,000–15,000
6	Chipolte, Jalapeno, Mirasol	2,500–5,000
7	Cascabel, Sandia, Rocotillo	1,500–2,500
8	Ancho, Espanola, Pasilla, Poblano	1,000–1,500
9	Anaheim, New Mexico	500–1,000
10	Cherry, Peperoncini	100–500

Hot peppers contain substances called capsaicinoids, which determine how "hot" they are. In 1912 pharmacist Wilbur Scoville pioneered a test, based on which chillies are ranked by Scoville Units according to which one part of capsaicin (the principal capsaicinoid) per million equals 15,000 Scoville Units.

T H E 1 0

FIRST HEINZ PRODUCTS

	Product	Introduced
1	Horseradish	1869
2=	Sour gherkins	1870
2=	Sour mixed pickles	1870
2=	Chow chow pickle	1870
2=	Sour onions	1870
2=	Prepared mustard	1870
2=	Sauerkraut in crocks	1870
8=	Heinz & Noble catsup	1873
8=	Vinegar	1873
10=	Green pepper sauce	1879
10=	Red pepper sauce	1879
10=	Worcestershire sauce	1879

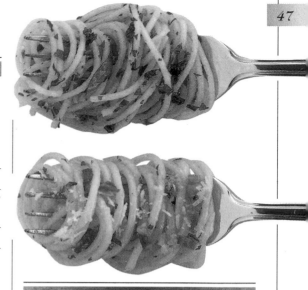

TOP 10

LARGEST CHEESES EVER MADE

1 26,085 kg/57,508 lb

Making gigantic cheeses is not a modern eccentricity: in his Natural History, *the Roman historian Pliny the Elder (AD 23–79) describes a 454-kg/1,000-lb cheese that was made in the Tuscan town of Luni. The current world record holder is this monster Cheddar made in 1995 in Quebec, Canada, by Loblaws Supermarkets and Agropur Dairies.*

2 18,171 kg/40,060 lb

This former world record-holder was manufactured on 13–14 March 1988 by Simon's Specialty Cheese of Little Chute, Wisconsin, USA. It was then taken on tour in a refrigerated "cheesemobile".

3 15,690 kg/34,591 lb

Made on 20–22 January 1964 for the World's Fair, New York, by the Wisconsin Cheese Foundation, it was 4.35 m/14½ ft long, 1.95 m/6½ ft wide, and 1.8 m/6 ft high. It toured and was displayed until 1968, when it was cut up to be sold.

4 6,096 kg/13,440 lb

Using the milk from 6,000 cows, production started on 12 July 1937. The cheese was exhibited at the New York State Fair.

5 5,359 kg/11,815 lb

This Cheddar was made in January 1957 in Flint, Michigan, from the milk pooled by a group of 367 farmers from their 6,600 cows.

6 3,629 kg/8,000 lb

This large Canadian Cheddar was made especially for the 1883 Toronto Fair.

7 669 kg/1,474 lb

A cheese 3.90 m/13 ft in circumference was made by James Elgar of Peterborough, UK, in 1849.

8 653 kg/1,400 lb

This Cheddar was given to President Jackson. After maturing for two years in the White House, it was given to the people of Washington, DC, on George Washington's birthday.

9= 544 kg/1,200 lb

A huge Cheshire presented to President Thomas Jefferson by a preacher, John Leland, in 1801, it was appropriately made by the town of Cheshire, Massachusetts.

9= 544 kg/1,200 lb

Made on 3 March 1989 in the village of West Pennard, Somerset, UK, by John Green, to recreate the 19th-century "Great Pennard Cheese" which was a 499-kg/1,100-lb, 2.7-m/ 9-ft circumference Cheddar named after the Somerset village in which it was made. It was presented to Queen Victoria as a wedding gift in 1840 and exhibited at the Egyptian Hall in Piccadilly, London. Its modern counterpart was shown at the May 1989 Festival of British Food and Farming. It took 5,455 litres/1,200 gallons of milk and measured 75 cm/3 ft in diameter and 2.7 m/9 ft in circumference.

TOP 10

PASTA PRODUCTS

	Pasta	Percentage market share
1	Spaghetti	26.0
2	Twists	18.0
3	Assorted shapes	13.5
4	Lasagne	9.2
5	Shells	9.0
6	Tagliatelle	8.0
7	Noodles	7.1
8	Macaroni	6.3
9	Tortellini	2.5
10	Cannelloni	0.4

THE 10

FIRST COCA-COLA PRODUCTS

	Product	Introduced
1	Coca-Cola	1886
2	Fanta	1960
3	Sprite	1961
4	TAB	1963
5	Fresca	1966
6	Mr. PiBB	1972
7	Hi-C Soft Drinks	1977
8	Mello Yello	1979
9	Ramblin' Root Beer	1979
10	Diet Coke	1982

TOP 10

CONSUMERS OF KELLOGG'S CORN FLAKES*

1	Ireland	**6**	Norway
2	UK	**7**	Canada
3	Australia	**8**	USA
4	Denmark	**9**	Mexico
5	Sweden	**10**	Venezuela

* Based on per capita consumption

In 1894 Dr. John Harvey and Will Keith Kellogg were running their "Sanatorium". Attempting to devise healthy foods for their patients, they experimented with wheat dough that they boiled and passed through rollers. By accident, they discovered that if the dough was left overnight it came out as flakes, and that when these were baked they turned into a tasty cereal.

TOP 10

COUNTRIES WITH THE MOST McDONALDS RESTAURANTS

	Country	Restaurants (1996)
1	USA	12,094
2	Japan	2,004
3	Canada	992
4	Germany	743
5	UK	650
6	Australia	608
7	France	541
8	Brazil	337
9	Taiwan	163
10	Netherlands	151

ALCOHOLIC BEVERAGES

48

ALCOHOL-DRINKING COUNTRIES IN THE WORLD

	Country	Annual consumption per capita (pure alcohol) litres	pints
1	Luxembourg	11.6	20.4
2	France	11.5	20.2
3	Portugal	11.0	19.3
4=	Hungary	10.2	18.0
4=	Spain	10.2	18.0
6	Czech Republic	10.1	17.8
7	Denmark	10.0	17.6
8	Germany	9.9	17.4
9	Austria	9.8	17.3
10	Switzerland	9.4	16.5
	UK	*7.3*	*12.9*
	USA	*6.8*	*12.0*

After heading this list for many years – and with an annual consumption that peaked at 17.4 litres/30.6 pints per head – France has been overtaken by Luxembourg, which is now acknowledged as the leading consumer of alcohol in the world.

FROM RUSSIA WITH LOVE

The first occasion on which the name of Smirnoff vodka appeared in print in English was on 26 April 1948, when the Official Gazette of the US Patent Office referred to the trademark. The Smirnovs were a family of Moscow distillers who established their company in the early 19th century. They were purveyors of vodka until the Russian Revolution of 1917, when Vladimir Smirnov was imprisoned and condemned to death. He escaped and fled to France, changing the spelling of his name to 'Smirnoff'. The family's vodka formula was later taken to the USA by a friend Rudolph Kunnett, and acquired by Heublein.

SPIRIT-DRINKING COUNTRIES IN THE WORLD

	Country	Annual consumption per capita (pure alcohol) litres	pints		Country	Annual consumption per capita (pure alcohol) litres	pints
1	Russia	4.60	8.09	6	Slovak Republic	2.80	4.93
2	Romania	3.96	6.97	7	Hungary	2.77	4.87
3=	China	3.80	6.69	8	Bulgaria	2.75	4.84
3=	Poland	3.80	6.69	9	Greece	2.70	4.75
5	Cyprus	3.60	6.34	10	France	2.52	4.43

WINE-DRINKING COUNTRIES IN THE WORLD

	Country	Annual consumption per capita litres	75 cl bottles
1	France	63.5	84.7
2	Italy	60.4	80.5
3	Portugal	58.4	78.9
4	Luxembourg	58.2	77.6
5	Argentina	43.8	58.4
6	Switzerland	43.6	58.1
7	Spain	36.3	48.4
8	Hungary	34.7	46.3
9	Greece	34.5	46.0
10	Austria	32.0	42.7
	UK	*12.8*	*17.1*
	USA	*6.8*	*9.1*

BEER-DRINKING COUNTRIES IN THE WORLD

	Country	Annual consumption per capita litres	pints
1	Czech Republic	160.0	281.6
2	Ireland	141.3	248.7
3	Germany	137.7	242.3
4	Denmark	120.1	211.4
5	Austria	115.6	203.4
6	Belgium	104.0	183.0
7	UK	102.7	180.7
8	Hungary	102.4	180.2
9	Luxembourg	99.4	174.9
10	New Zealand	98.8	174.0
	USA	*85.8*	*151.0*

TOP 10
LARGEST BREWERIES IN THE WORLD

	Brewery	Location	Annual sales litres	pints
1	Anheuser-Busch, Inc.	USA	10,421,000,000	18,338,000,000
2	Heineken NV	Netherlands	5,350,000,000	9,415,000,000
3	Miller Brewing Co.	USA	5,091,000,000	8,959,000,000
4	Kirin Brewery Co. Ltd.	Japan	3,240,000,000	5,702,000,000
5	Foster's Brewing Group	Australia	3,050,000,000	5,367,000,000
6	Companhia Cervejaria Brahma	Brazil	2,530,000,000	4,452,000,000
7	Groupe BSN	France	2,500,000,000	4,399,000,000
8	Coors Brewing Co.	USA	2,397,000,000	4,218,000,000
9	South Africa Breweries Ltd.	South Africa	2,270,000,000	3,995,000,000
10	Companhia Antartica Paulista	Brazil	2,000,000,000	3,520,600,000

TOP 10
MOST COMMON PUB NAMES IN THE UK

1	The Red Lion	6	The Bull
2	The Crown	7	The Coach and Horses
3	The Royal Oak	8	The George
4	The White Hart	9	The Plough
5	The King's Head	10	The Swan

TOP 10
MOST EXPENSIVE BOTTLES OF WINE EVER SOLD AT AUCTION

	Wine/sale	Price (£)
1	Château Lafite 1787, Christie's, London, 5 December 1985	105,000
2	Château d'Yquem 1784, Christie's, London, 4 December 1986	39,600
3	Château Mouton Rothschild 1945 (jeroboam – equivalent to 4 bottles), Christie's, Geneva, 14 May 1995 (S.Fr 68,200)	36,277
4	Château Lafite Rothschild 1832 (double magnum), International Wine Auctions, London, 9 April 1988	24,000
5	Château Pétrus 1945 (jeroboam), Sotheby's, New York, 16 September 1995 ($37,375)	23,360
6	Château Mouton Rothschild 1986 (Nebuchadnezzar – equivalent to 20 bottles), Sotheby's, New York, 22 April 1995 ($36,800)	22,870
7	Château Lafite 1806, Sotheby's, Geneva, 13 November 1988 (S.Fr 57,200)	21,700
8	Cheval-blanc 1947 (Imperial – equivalent to eight bottles), Christie's, London, 1 December 1994	21,450
9=	Château Mouton Rothschild 1985 (Nebuchadnezzar), Sotheby's, Los Angeles, 12 October 1996 ($33,350)	21,209
9=	Château Mouton Rothschild 1989 (Nebuchadnezzar), Sotheby's, Los Angeles, 12 October 1996 ($33,350)	21,209

TOP 10
IMPORTERS OF SCOTCH* IN THE WORLD

	Country	Annual imports litres	pints
1	USA	89,350,000	157,233,931
2	France	64,840,000	114,102,385
3	Spain	56,250,000	98,986,106
4	Japan	28,990,000	51,015,239
5	South Korea	23,510,000	41,371,793
6	Greece	22,310,000	39,260,089
7	Germany	21,870,000	38,485,798
8	South Africa	20,190,000	35,529,413
9	Australia	18,730,000	32,960,174
10	Italy	17,260,000	30,373,337

Including Northern Irish whiskey

More than 100 years ago, the expensive processes of distilling malt whisky and maturing it for several years were joined by the scientific blending of different grain and malt Scotch whiskies to achieve a consistent and less costly product.

SOFT DRINKS

TOP 10

SOFT-DRINK CONSUMERS IN THE WORLD

	Country	Annual consumption per capita litres	pints
1	Switzerland	105.0	184.8
2	Barbados	81.4	143.2
3	Bahamas	75.0	132.0
4	USA	74.7	131.5
5	Australia	73.9	130.0
6	Germany	72.0	126.7
7	Canada	69.3	122.0
8=	Belgium	65.0	114.4
8=	Japan	65.0	114.4
10	Singapore	61.4	108.1
	UK	39.0	68.6

As one might expect, affluent Western countries feature prominently in this list. Despite the spread of the so-called "Coca-Cola culture", former Eastern Bloc and developing countries rank very low – some African nations recording consumption of less than one litre/1.76 pints per annum.

TOP 10

SOFT DRINKS IN THE US

	Brand	Sales (gallons)*
1	Coca-Cola Classic	2,621,000,000
2	Pepsi	2,066,000,000
3	Diet Coke	1,268,000,000
4	Dr. Pepper	768,000,000
5	Diet Pepsi	760,000,000
6	Mountain Dew	683,000,000
7	Sprite	581,000,000
8	7-Up	381,000,000
9	Caffeine Free Diet Coke	265,000,000
10	Caffeine Free Diet Pepsi	153,000,000

Wholesale sales

Source: Beverage Marketing Corporation

Such is the international nature of the soft drinks market that a comparative British list would show Coca-Cola, Pepsi, and 7-Up in identical positions. Alongside them in a UK list, however, would be long-established domestic brands that include Lucozade and Schweppes products.

TOP 10

CONSUMERS OF COCA-COLA

	Country	Servings consumed per person (1995)
1	USA	343
2	Mexico	322
3	Germany	201
4=	Argentina	179
4=	Spain	179
6	South Africa	147
7	Japan	136
8	Brazil	122
9	UK	114
10	Philippines	105

The first Coca-Cola was served in Jacob's Pharmacy in Atlanta, Georgia, USA, on 8 May 1886. The first advertisement appeared in the *Atlanta Journal*, describing Coca-Cola as "Delicious! Refreshing! Exhilarating! Invigorating!" The new drink proved an immediate success – especially after a local Prohibition Act of July 1886 banned alcohol. "Coke" was first served in bottles in 1894.

TOP 10

MILK-DRINKING COUNTRIES IN THE WORLD

	Country*	Annual consumption per capita litres	pints
1	Iceland	174.2	306.6
2	Finland	165.1	290.6
3	Norway	142.9	251.5
4	Sweden	122.5	215.6
5	Spain	111.6	196.4
6	UK	111.5	196.2
7	Denmark	111.3	195.9
8	Switzerland	98.3	173.0
9	New Zealand	97.9	172.3
10	Australia	95.6	168.3
	USA	89.9	158.2

Those reporting to the International Dairy Federation only

TOP 10

CONSUMERS OF PERRIER WATER IN THE WORLD

1	France
2	USA
3	Belgium
4	Canada
5	UK
6	Greece
7	Germany
8	Hong Kong
9	Switzerland
10	Japan

In 1903 St. John Harmsworth, a wealthy Englishman on a tour of France, visited Vergèze, a spa town near Nîmes. Its spring, Les Bouillens (which was believed to have been discovered by the Carthaginian soldier Hannibal *c.* 218 BC), was notable for the occurrence of carbon dioxide, which is released from the surrounding rock, permeating through the water and making it "naturally sparkling". Harmsworth recognized the potential for selling the spa water and proceeded to buy the spring. He named it after Dr. Louis Perrier, a local doctor, and bottling it in green bottles said to have been modelled on the Indian clubs with which he exercised. The company was sold back to the French in 1948, and in 1992 the firm was bought by the Swiss company Nestlé. Perrier water has maintained a reputation as a popular drink in sophisticated circles. Perrier is now drunk in 145 countries around the world, and its name has become synonymous with mineral water.

T O P 1 0

COFFEE-DRINKING COUNTRIES IN THE WORLD

	Country	Annual consumption per capita			
		kg	lb	oz	cups*
1	Norway	9.04	19	15	1,356
2	Denmark	8.70	19	3	1,305
3	Finland	8.62	19	0	1,293
4	Austria	8.47	18	11	1,271
5	Belgium/Luxembourg	8.34	18	6	1,251
6	Sweden	8.17	18	0	1,226
7	Switzerland	7.97	17	9	1,196
8	Germany	7.38	16	4	1,107
9	Netherlands	6.67	14	11	1,001
10	France	5.48	12	1	822
	USA	*4.02*	*8*	*13*	*603*
	UK	*2.27*	*5*	*0*	*341*

AN AWFUL LOT OF COFFEE
Within the Top 10 alone, national tastes create a pattern of coffee consumption that varies from averages of almost four cups a day down to just two cups a day.

* Based on 150 cups per kg/2 lb 3 oz

T O P 1 0

CADBURY SCHWEPPES' WORLD BRANDS

1	Dr. Pepper
2	7-Up
3	Schweppes "Mixers"
4	Canada Dry Ginger Ale
5	Crush Orange
6	A&W (US – root beer and cream soda)
7	Sunkist
8	Penafiel (Mexico – mineral waters)
9	Squirt (US – fruit carbonates)
10	Cottee's (Australia)

German-born Jean Jacob Schweppe (1740–1821) moved to Geneva where he worked as a jeweller. An amateur scientist, he became interested in the manufacture of artificial mineral waters. He moved to London in 1792 and began producing his own brand of soda water, forming Schweppe & Co. (later Schweppes Ltd.). By the 1870s the company was also making ginger ale and "Indian Tonic Water" by adding quinine to sweetened soda water (after the style of the British in India who drank it as an antidote to malaria, thus beginning the fashion for gin and tonic). Schweppes merged with Cadbury Brothers Ltd. in 1969, forming Cadbury Schweppes. Schweppes' advertising has always been memorable, from its "Schweppervescence" campaign launched in 1946, to their long-running series with actor William Franklyn, using just the "Sch" sound of the name.

T O P 1 0

TEA-DRINKING COUNTRIES IN THE WORLD

	Country	Annual consumption per capita			
		kg	lb	oz	cups*
1	Irish Republic	3.16	7	0	1,390
2	UK	2.53	5	9	1,113
3	Kuwait	2.52	5	9	1,109
4	Turkey	2.02	4	7	889
5	Qatar	1.76	3	14	774
6	Bahrain	1.67	3	11	735
7	Syria	1.55	3	8	682
8	Hong Kong	1.48	3	4	651
9	Iran	1.32	2	15	581
10	Sri Lanka	1.29	2	13	568
	USA	*0.34*	*0*	*12*	*150*

* Based on 440 cups per kg/2 lb 3 oz

Notwithstanding the UK's traditional passion for tea, during recent years its consumption has consistently lagged behind that of Ireland. In the same period, Qatar's tea consumption has dropped from its former world record of 3.97 kg/8 lb 12 oz (1,747 cups) per head.

T O P 1 0

COFFEE BRANDS IN THE US*

	Brand	Sales ($)
1	Folgers	504,200,000
2	Maxwell House	394,900,000
3	Private label	135,800,000
4	Maxwell House Master Blend	89,500,000
5	Hills Bros	80,700,000
6	Chock Full O Nuts	57,500,000
7	Maxwell House Lite	50,300,000
8	Yuban	45,700,000
9	Folgers Coffee Singles	46,600,000
10	MJB	38,000,000

* Plain ground
Source: Information Research Inc.

The total sales of plain ground coffee for the year 1996 were $1,800,000,000, down 14.9 per cent from the previous year.

TRANSPORT & TOURISM

THE 10

FIRST MANNED BALLOON FLIGHTS

Date of flight

1 21 November 1783

François Laurent, Marquis d'Arlandes, and Jean-François Pilâtre de Rozier took off in a hot-air balloon designed by the Montgolfiers.

2 1 December 1783

The first-ever flight in a hydrogen balloon.

3 19 January 1784

This flight included the first aerial stowaway.

4 25 February 1784

The first-ever flight outside France.

5 2 March 1784

Flown by Jean-Pierre François Blanchard.

6 14 April 1784

The first ascent in the British Isles.

7 25 April 1784

Guyton de Morveau, a French chemist, and L'Abbé Bertrand flew at Dijon.

8 8 May 1784

Bremond and Maret flew at Marseilles.

9 12 May 1784

Brun and Comte Xavier de Maistre – both just 20 years old – ascended at Chambéry.

10 15 May 1784

This balloon crash-landed near Strasbourg.

THE 10

FIRST PEOPLE TO FLY IN HEAVIER-THAN-AIR AIRCRAFT

Pilot/nationality

1 Orville Wright (1871–1948), USA

On 17 December 1903 at Kitty Hawk, North Carolina, Wright made the first-ever manned flight in his Wright Flyer I. It lasted 12 seconds and covered a distance of 37 m/120 ft.

2 Wilbur Wright (1867–1912), USA

On the same day, Orville's brother made his first flight in the Wright Flyer I (59 seconds).

3 Alberto Santos-Dumont (1873–1932), Brazil

At Bagatelle, Bois de Boulogne, Paris, Santos-Dumont made a 60-m/193-ft hop on 23 October 1906 in his clumsy No. 14-bis.

4 Charles Voisin (1882–1912), France

Voisin made a short, six-second hop of 60m/197 ft at Bagatelle on 30 March 1907. The aircraft was built by himself and his brother.

Pilot/nationality

5 Henri Farman (1874–1958), UK (later a French citizen)

Farman first flew on 7 October 1907 and by 26 October had achieved 771 m/2,530 ft.

6 Léon Delagrange (1873–1910), France

On 5 November 1907 at Issy-les-Moulineaux, Delagrange flew his Voisin-Delagrange I for 40 seconds at 500 m/1,640 ft.

7 Robert Esnault-Pelterie (1881–1957), France

On 16 November 1907 at Buc, he first flew his REP 1 for 55 sec at 600 m/1,969 ft.

8 Charles W. Furnas (1880–1941), USA

On 14 May 1908 at Kitty Hawk, Wilbur Wright took Furnas, his mechanic, up in the Wright Flyer III for 29 sec at 600 m/1,968 ft.

9 Louis Blériot (1872–1936), France

After some earlier short hops, on 29 June 1908 at Issy, Blériot flew his Blériot VIII. On 25 July 1909 he became the first to fly across the English Channel.

10 Glenn Hammond Curtiss (1878–1930), USA

On 4 July 1908 at Hammondsport, New York, Curtiss flew an AEA June Bug for 1 min 42.5 sec at 1,551 m/5,090 ft, the first "official" flight in the US that was watched by a crowd.

FLIGHT TO FAME
Wilbur Wright flies the Wright brother's 1901 glider; the brother's experiments led the way to the first powered aircraft.

THE 10

FIRST TRANSATLANTIC FLIGHTS

Date*/crossing/aircraft

1 16–27 May 1919,
Trepassy Harbor,
Newfoundland to Lisbon, Portugal,
US Navy/Curtiss flying boat NC-4

2 14–15 June 1919,
St. John's, Newfoundland
to Galway, Ireland,
Twin Rolls-Royce-engined
converted Vickers Vimy bomber

3 2–6 July 1919,
East Fortune, Scotland to
Roosevelt Field, New York,
British R-34 airship

4 30 March–5 June 1922,
Lisbon, Portugal to Recife, Brazil,
Fairey IIID seaplane *Santa Cruz*

5 2–31 August 1924,
Orkneys, Scotland to
Labrador, Canada,
Two Douglas seaplanes, *Chicago*
and *New Orleans*

6 12–15 October 1924,
Friedrichshafen, Germany to
Lakehurst, New Jersey,
Los Angeles, a renamed German-built
ZR 3 airship

7 22 January–10 February 1926,
Huelva, Spain to Recife, Brazil,
Plus Ultra, a Dornier Wal
twin-engined flying boat

8 8–24 February 1927,
Cagliari, Sardinia to Recife, Brazil,
Santa Maria, a Savoia-Marchetti
S.55 flying boat

9 16–17 March 1927,
Lisbon, Portugal to Natal, Brazil,
Dornier Wal flying boat

10 28 April–14 May 1927,
Genoa, Italy to Natal, Brazil,
Savoia-Marchetti flying boat

* *All dates refer to the actual Atlantic legs of the journeys; some started earlier and ended beyond their first transatlantic landfalls*

FIRST FIGHTER
The German Messerschmitt 262 first flew in 1942 and became the first jet fighter in military use.

THE 10

FIRST ROCKET AND JET AIRCRAFT

	Aircraft	Country	First flight
1	Heinkel He 176*	Germany	20 June 1939
2	Heinkel He 178	Germany	27 August 1939
3	DFS 194*	Germany	#August 1940
4	Caproni-Campini N-1#	Italy	28 August 1940
5	Heinkel He 280V-1	Germany	2 April 1941
6	Gloster E.28/39	UK	15 May 1941
7	Messerschmitt Me 163 Komet*	Germany	13 August 1941
8	Messerschmitt Me 262V-3	Germany	18 July 1942
9	Bell XP-59A Airacomet	USA	1 October 1942
10	Gloster Meteor F Mk 1	UK	5 March 1943

* *Rocket-powered*
\# *Precise date unknown*

Prototypes of the rocket-powered Heinkel 176 and the turbojet Heinkel 178 first flew prior to the outbreak of World War II. The first operational jets were developed in the early years of the war, with the Messerschmitt Me 262 the first jet fighter in service. The German Arado Ar 234V-1Blitz ("Lightning"), which first flew on 15 June 1943, was the world's first jet bomber.

DEATH OF A PIONEER

Orville Wright died on 30 January 1948 at the age of 76. With his elder brother Wilbur, who had died in 1912, Orville had achieved fame when, on 17 December 1903 at Kitty Hawk, Carolina, he become the first person in the world to fly a powered aircraft. The Wright brothers went on to achieve total mastery of the air: no one else succeeded in getting airborne until 1906, by which time the Wrights were already regularly flying long distances under full control. The Smithsonian Institution in Washington, DC, long refused to accept the Wrights' claims as the first people to fly, and as a result of this their first aircraft, *Flyer I*, was "exiled" and exhibited in the Science Museum, London. It was finally returned to the US in the year of Orville's death.

AIR TRAVEL

TOP 10

BUSIEST AIRPORTS IN THE US

	Airport/location	Total enplaned passengers (1995)
1	Chicago O'Hare International, Illinois	31,433,002
2	Atlanta (Hartsfield), Georgia	28,090,978
3	Dallas/Fort Worth International, Texas	26,962,940
4	Los Angeles International, California	26,133,795
5	San Francisco International, California	17,187,766
6	Miami International, Florida	16,065,673
7	Denver (Stapleton), Colorado	14,858,763
8	John F. Kennedy International, New York	14,601,827
9	Detroit Metropolitan, Michigan	14,082,598
10	Phoenix Sky Harbor International, Arizona	13,738,433

Source: Federal Aviation Administration

THE WORLD'S LARGEST AIRPORT OPENS

In 1948, the year that aviation pioneer Orville Wright died, the airline industry that he and his brother Wilbur had made possible took an important step forward with the opening on 31 July of Idlewild Airport, New York. Developed on a site reclaimed from the marshland of Jamaica Bay, the international airport – then the largest in the world – derived its name from a golf course that had been swallowed up by its construction. In the same year the Atlantic was crossed by jets for the first time, heralding the era of the modern airliner. On Christmas Eve 1963 Idlewild was renamed John F. Kennedy Airport to honour the assassinated US president.

TOP 10

INTERNATIONAL FLIGHT ROUTES WITH MOST AIR TRAFFIC

	City A	City B	Passengers per route A to B	B to A	Total passengers
1	Hong Kong	Taipei	2,055,000	2,045,000	4,100,000
2	London	Paris	1,711,000	1,842,000	3,553,000
3	London	New York	1,322,000	1,311,000	2,633,000
4	Dublin	London	1,268,000	1,269,000	2,537,000
5	Kuala Lumpur	Singapore	1,196,000	1,119,000	2,315,000
6	Honolulu	Tokyo	1,157,000	1,137,000	2,294,000
7	Amsterdam	London	1,107,000	1,101,000	2,208,000
8	Seoul	Tokyo	1,089,000	1,081,000	2,170,000
9	Bangkok	Hong Kong	993,000	910,000	1,903,000
10	Hong Kong	Tokyo	940,000	937,000	1,877,000

TOP 10

BUSIEST AIRPORTS IN THE WORLD

	Airport	Location	Passengers per annum
1	Chicago O'Hare	Chicago, USA	66,468,000
2	Hartsfield Atlanta Int.	Atlanta, USA	53,630,000
3	Dallas/Fort Worth Int.	Dallas/Fort Worth, USA	52,601,000
4	London Heathrow	London, UK	51,368,000
5	Los Angeles Int.	Los Angeles, USA	51,050,000
6	Frankfurt	Frankfurt, Germany	34,376,000
7	San Francisco Int.	San Francisco, USA	33,965,000
8	Miami Int.	Miami, USA	30,203,000
9	John F. Kennedy Int.	New York, USA	28,807,000
10	Charles De Gaulle	Paris, France	28,363,000

TOP 10

BUSIEST AIRPORTS IN EUROPE

	Airport	Location	Passengers per annum
1	London Heathrow	London, UK	51,368,000
2	Frankfurt	Frankfurt, Germany	34,376,000
3	Charles de Gaulle	Paris, France	28,363,000
4	Orly	Paris, France	26,497,000
5	Schiphol	Amsterdam, Netherlands	23,069,000
6	London Gatwick	London, UK	21,045,000
7	Fiumicino	Rome, Italy	19,911,000
8	Madrid	Madrid, Spain	18,223,000
9	Palma	Mallorca, Spain	14,051,000
10	Zürich	Zürich, Switzerland	14,044,000

GIANTS OF THE SKIES
The increasing carrying capacity and distances flown by airliners such as Boeing 747 Jumbo jets have resulted in a huge growth in international air traffic.

T O P 1 0

AIRLINE-USING COUNTRIES IN THE WORLD

	Country	Passenger km p.a.*	Passenger miles p.a.*
1	USA	853,389,000,000	530,271,000,000
2	UK	152,453,000,000	94,730,000,000
3	Japan	129,981,000,000	80,766,000,000
4	Australia	67,145,000,000	41,722,000,000
5	France	66,932,000,000	41,590,000,000
6	China	64,204,000,000	39,895,000,000
7	Germany	62,158,000,000	38,623,000,000
8	Russia	61,035,000,000	37,925,000,000
9	Canada	49,288,000,000	30,626,000,000
10	Netherlands	48,474,000,000	30,120,000,000

* *Total distance travelled by scheduled aircraft of national airlines multiplied by number of passengers carried*

T O P 1 0

BUSIEST INTERNATIONAL AIRPORTS IN THE WORLD

	Airport	Location	International passengers per annum
1	London Heathrow	London, UK	44,262,000
2	Frankfurt	Frankfurt, Germany	27,546,000
3	Charles de Gaulle	Paris, France	25,690,000
4	Hong Kong Int.	Hong Kong, China	25,248,000
5	Schiphol	Amsterdam, Netherlands	22,943,000
6	New Tokyo International (Narita)	Tokyo, Japan	20,681,000
7	Singapore International	Singapore	20,203,000
8	London Gatwick	Gatwick, UK	19,417,000
9	John F. Kennedy Int.	New York, USA	15,898,000
10	Bangkok	Bangkok, Thailand	13,747,000

Other than New York's JFK, only five airports in the US handle more than 5,000,000 international passengers a year, notably Miami (13,071,000), Los Angeles (12,679,000), Chicago O'Hare (6,174,000), Honolulu (5,504,000), and San Francisco (5,238,000).

COCKPIT OF A BOEING 727-200

WATER TRANSPORT

SHIPPING COUNTRIES IN THE WORLD

	Country	Ships*
1	Panama	3,488
2	Russia	1,579
3	Liberia	1,534
4	Cyprus	1,436
5	China	1,387
6	Greece	981
7	Malta	925
8	Bahamas	910
9	Japan	812
10	Norway	678
	USA	543
	UK	152
	World total, including those not in this Top 10	25,092

* *The list includes only ships of more than 1,000 GRT – Gross Registered Tonnage*

The Top 10 countries in this list account for 55 per cent of the world's merchant ships of more than 1,000 gross tonnes.

BUSIEST PORTS IN THE WORLD

	Port	Location	Goods handled p.a. (tonnes)
1	Rotterdam	Netherlands	350,000,000
2	Singapore	Singapore	290,000,000
3	Chiba	Japan	173,700,000
4	Kobe	Japan	171,000,000
5	Hong Kong	Hong Kong	147,200,000
6	Houston	USA	142,000,000
7	Shanghai	China	139,600,000
8	Nagoya	Japan	137,300,000
9	Yokohama	Japan	128,300,000
10	Antwerp	Belgium	109,500,000

This Top 10 accounts for all but one of the world's ports handling more than 100,000,000 tonnes of goods a year: the other, Kawasaki, Japan (105,100,000 tonnes per annum), along with Chiba, serves the urban area of Tokyo.

THE IMPORTANCE OF THE ORIENTAL PORT
With the rise of the economies of the Far East, ports such as Singapore have steadily eclipsed many of those in Europe and the US, and now occupy half the world's Top 10 busiest ports.

LARGEST OIL TANKERS IN THE WORLD

	Tanker	Year built	Country of origin	Gross tonnage*	Deadweight tonnage#
1	*Jahre Viking*	1979	Japan	260,851	564,763
2	*Hellas Fos*	1979	France	261,862	555,051
3	*Kapetan Giannis*	1977	Japan	247,160	516,895
4	*Kapetan Michalis*	1977	Japan	247,160	516,423
5	*King Alexander*	1978	Sweden	237,768	491,120
6	*Nissei Maru*	1975	Japan	238,517	484,276
7	*Stena King*	1978	Taiwan	218,593	457,927
8	*Stena Queen*	1977	Taiwan	218,593	457,841
9	*Kapetan Panagiotis*	1977	Japan	218,447	457,062
10	*Kapetan Giorgis*	1976	Japan	218,447	456,368

* *The total weight of the vessel, including its cargo, crew, passengers, and supplies*

The 485.45 m/1,504 ft long *Jahre Viking* (formerly called *Happy Giant* and *Seawise Giant*) is the longest vessel ever built – it is as long as more than 20 tennis courts end-to-end and is 68.8 m/226 ft wide. It was extensively damaged during the Iran–Iraq War but was salvaged, refitted, and relaunched in 1991. The largest tanker afloat in the 1950s was the 104,521-ton Japanese-built *Universe Apollo*, launched in 1958. However, economic demands and technological improvements have enabled the size of oil tankers to increase. The dangerous, and potentially environmentally hazardous, operation of entering the relatively shallow water of ports to load and unload was overcome by advances in deep-water facilities, as a result of which the size of tankers grew to such an extent that the largest vessel of the 1960s was the *Universe Iran*, at 326,933 tonnes. A deadweight tonnage of 400,000 tonnes was first exceeded in 1972 with the launch of the *Globtik Tokyo* (483,662 tonnes), heralding the age of the "supertanker" with oil tankers of 500,000 tonnes or more.

LONGEST SHIP CANALS IN THE WORLD

	Canal/location/opened	Length km	miles
1	St. Lawrence Seaway, Canada/US, 1959	304	189
2	Main-Danube, Germany, 1992	171	106
3	Suez, Egypt, 1869	162	101
4=	Albert, Belgium, 1939	129	80
4=	Moscow-Volga, Russia, 1937	129	80
6	Kiel, Germany, 1895	99	62
7	Trollhätte, Sweden, 1916	87	54
8	Alphonse XIII, Spain, 1926	85	53
9	Panama, Panama, 1914	82	51
10	Houston, USA, 1914	81	50

The longest ship canal in the world is the St. Lawrence Seaway (Canada/USA). It opened in 1959 and is 304 km/189 miles in length. The Main-Danube Canal, Germany, completed in 1992, is the second longest at 171 km/106 miles. The Suez Canal, Egypt, opened in 1869, measures 162 km/101 miles – almost double the length of the Panama Canal (1914; 82 km/51 miles).

DID YOU KNOW

"THE BIGGEST SHIP IN THE WORLD"

The 211-m/692-ft steamship _Great Eastern_, designed by Isambard Kingdom Brunel, was five times bigger than any vessel ever built, a record held for nearly 50 years. Built in Millwall, London, and almost as long as the Thames was wide, it was decided to launch it sideways. Thousands turned out for the event, but the ship would not budge. She was finally launched in 1858 and in 1866 laid the first commercially successful transatlantic telegraph cable. However, the ship was dogged by misfortune, and 30 years after her launch, the _Great Eastern_ was broken up for scrap.

CATEGORIES OF BOAT NAMES IN THE US

	Category	No. in survey
1	Picturesque	144
2	Sea-going	75
3=	Children	67
3=	Geographical	67
5	Birds	63
6	Man and wife	62
7	Foreign	61
8	Whimsical	50
9	Alcoholic	45
10=	Fictitious/mythological	40
10=	Zoological	40

In a survey off the east coast of Florida, John McNamara noted the names of 1,000 vessels of all kinds and produced this analysis, which was published as "Reflections on Nautical Onomastics" in the journal _Names_. Among these and other categories, such as numbers, surnames, and "unexplained", he personally considered that the dullest name borne by a boat was _Investment Broker_.

COUNTRIES WITH THE LONGEST INLAND WATERWAY NETWORKS*

	Country	km	miles
1	China	138,600	86,122
2	Russia	101,000	62,758
3	Brazil	50,000	31,069
4	USA#	41,009	25,482
5	Indonesia	21,579	13,409
6	Vietnam	17,702	11,000
7	India	16,180	10,054
8	Congo (Zaïre)	15,000	9,321
9	France	14,932	9,278
10	Colombia	14,300	8,886

* _Canals and navigable rivers_
\# _Excluding Great Lakes_

LONGEST CRUISE SHIPS IN THE WORLD

	Ship/year built/country of origin	Length m	ft	in
1	_Norway_ (former _France_), 1961, France	315.53	1,035	2
2	_United States_, 1952, USA	301.76	990	0
3	_Queen Elizabeth 2_, 1969, UK	293.53	963	0
4=	_Grandeur of the Seas_, 1996, Finland	279.10	915	8
4=	_Enchantment of the Seas_, 1997, Finland	279.10	915	8
6	_Rhapsody of the Seas_, 1997, France	279.00	915	4
7	_Carnival Destiny_, 1996, Italy	272.35	893	6
8	_Sovereign of the Seas_, 1987, France	268.33	880	4
9=	_Monarch of the Seas_, 1991, France	268.32	880	4
9=	_Majesty of the Seas_, 1992, France	268.32	880	4

Source: Lloyds Register

THE MAJESTIC OCEAN LINER _QE2_
The QE2 was built as a replacement for the liner Queen Elizabeth. _It offers luxury accommodation for up to 1,700 passengers and made its maiden voyage in 1969._

ON THE ROAD

TOP 10

FASTEST PRODUCTION CARS IN THE WORLD

	Model	Maximum speed km/h	mph
1	Lamborghini Diablo	325	202
2	Ferrari Testarossa	290	180
3=	Ferrari 348ts	277	172
3=	Ferrari 348tb	277	172
5	Porsche 928 GT	274	170
6	Porsche 911 Turbo	270	168
7	Porsche 928S Series 4	266	165
8	Porsche 911 Carrera 2	259	161
9=	Lotus Esprit Turbo SE	257	160
9=	TVR 450SEAC	257	160

TOP 10

MOST COMMON CAUSES OF CAR BREAKDOWN

1	Battery	7	Distributor cap
2	Tyres	8	Clutch cable
3	Keys (lockouts/immobilizers)	9	Spark plugs
4	Fuel	10	Power unit
5	Starter motor		
6	Alternator		

Based on calls to the Automobile Association

WHEELS OF FORTUNE

Although the manufacture of motor cars was in its infancy in 1898, it was a milestone year for a number of innovations: the pneumatic tyre valve with a replaceable core was invented by George H.F. Schrader of New York, and in the same year the Goodyear Tyre & Rubber Company was started in Akron, Ohio, by brothers Frank and Charles Seiberling. They chose to name the tyre after Charles Goodyear (1800–60), the American inventor of the process for vulcanizing rubber, which made tyre manufacture technically and commercially possible. Today Goodyear is the leading tyre manufacturer in the US, making almost one in three of all tyres.

THE 10

FIRST COUNTRIES TO MAKE SEAT BELTS COMPULSORY

	Country	Introduced		Country	Introduced
1	Czechoslovakia	Jan 1969	7	Puerto Rico	Jan 1974
2	Ivory Coast	Jan 1970	8	Spain	Oct 1974
3	Japan	Dec 1971	9	Sweden	Jan 1975
4	Australia	Jan 1972	10=	Netherlands	Jun 1975
5=	Brazil	Jun 1972	10=	Belgium	Jun 1975
5=	New Zealand	Jun 1972	10=	Luxembourg	Jun 1975

Seat belts, long in use in aircraft, were not designed for use in private cars until the 1950s. Ford was the first manufacturer in Europe to fit anchorage-points, and belts were first fitted as standard equipment in Swedish Volvos from 1959. They were optional extras in most cars until the 1970s when they were fitted to all models, but their wearing was not compulsory in many countries until laws were enacted during the 1970s and 1980s.

TOP 10

VEHICLE-PRODUCING COUNTRIES IN THE WORLD

	Country	Cars	Commercial vehicles	Total registered vehicles
1	USA	6,350,367	5,634,724	11,985,091
2	Japan	7,610,533	2,585,003	10,195,536
3	Germany	4,360,235	307,129	4,667,364
4	France	3,050,929	423,776	3,474,705
5	South Korea	1,985,578	540,822	2,526,400
6	Canada	1,339,474	1,077,702	2,417,176
7	Spain	1,958,789	374,898	2,333,787
8	UK	1,532,084	233,001	1,765,085
9	Italy	1,422,359	244,911	1,667,270
10	Brazil	1,296,586	337,555	1,634,141

TOP 10

VEHICLE-OWNING COUNTRIES IN THE WORLD

	Country	Cars	Commercial vehicles	Total registered vehicles
1	USA	147,171,000	48,298,000	195,469,000
2	Japan	42,678,430	22,333,042	65,011,472
3	Germany	39,917,577	2,960,334	42,877,911
4	Italy	29,800,000	2,777,500	32,577,500
5	France	24,900,000	5,140,000	30,040,000
6	UK	23,831,906	3,604,972	27,436,878
7	Russia	13,549,000	9,856,000	23,405,000
8	Canada	13,700,000	3,739,600	17,439,600
9	Spain	13,739,794	2,952,838	16,692,632
10	Brazil	12,024,000	3,316,000	15,340,000

ROAD TO RUIN?

The first passenger cars took to the road a little over 100 years ago. There are now reckoned to be some 500 million cars and 150 million commercial vehicles in the world. The inexorable advance of motoring has contributed many benefits to the modern world. However, road safety and problems of pollution, road building, and the consumption of raw materials are engaging manufacturers who seek to improve safety, fuel economy, environmental friendliness, and the potential to recycle components as vehicles reach the end of their useful lives.

"TIN LIZZIE"
At one time, more than half the cars in the world were Model T Fords.

PRODUCTION LINE
The growth of mass production enabled the growth of the car culture that has dominated the 20th century.

TOP 10

BESTSELLING CARS OF ALL TIME

	Model	Year first produced	Estimated no. made
1	Volkswagen Beetle	1937*	21,220,000
2	Toyota Corolla	1963	20,000,000
3	Ford Model T	1908	16,536,075
4	Volkswagen Golf	1974	14,800,000
5	Lada Riva	1970	13,500,000
6	Ford Escort/Orion	1967	12,000,000
7	Nissan Sunny/Pulsar	1966	10,200,000
8	Mazda 323	1977	9,500,000
9	Renault 4	1961	8,100,000
10	Honda Civic	1972	8,000,000

* *Still produced in Mexico and Brazil*

Estimates of manufacturers' output of their bestselling models vary from the vague to the unusually precise 16,536,075 of the Model T Ford, with 15,007,033 produced in the US.

BEETLEMANIA
Designed by Ferdinand Porsche in 1937, production of the first Volkswagen Beetles began in 1945. Within 10 years more than one million had been sold.

FORD ESCORT
First produced in 1967, the Ford Escort and the Orion were among the most popular cars of the post-war period.

GOLF COURSE
The Golf, Volkswagen's successor to the Beetle, is the bestselling European car.

ON THE RIGHT TRACK

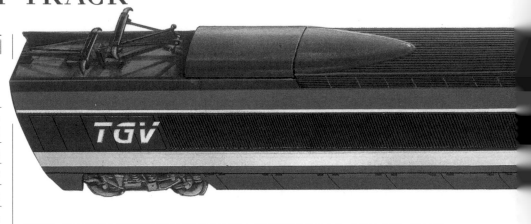

FIRST COUNTRIES WITH RAILWAYS

	Country	First railway established
1	UK	27 September 1825
2	France	7 November 1829
3	USA	24 May 1830
4	Ireland	17 December 1834
5	Belgium	5 May 1835
6	Germany	7 December 1835
7	Canada	21 July 1836
8	Russia	30 October 1837
9	Austria	6 January 1838
10	Netherlands	24 September 1839

Although there were earlier horse-drawn railways, the Stockton and Darlington Railway in the north of England inaugurated the world's first steam service. In their early years some of the countries listed here offered only limited services over short distances, but their opening dates mark the generally accepted beginning of each country's steam railway system.

GOING UNDERGROUND
London's Metropolitan Railway, the world's first underground service, opened on 10 January 1863. The wide-gauge track (2.134 m/7 ft) seen here at Bellmouth, Praed Street, was used in its early years.

LONGEST UNDERGROUND RAILWAY NETWORKS IN THE WORLD

	Location	Opened	Stations	Total track length km	miles
1	London, UK	1863	270	401	251
2	New York, USA	1904	469	398	249
3	Paris, France*	1900	432	323	202
4	Tokyo, Japan#	1927	250	289	181
5	Moscow, Russia	1935	150	244	153
6	Mexico City, Mexico	1969	154	178	112
7	Chicago, USA	1943	145	173	108
8	Copenhagen, Denmark+	1934	79	170	106
9	Berlin, Germany	1902	135	167	104
10	Seoul, Korea	1974	130	165	103

* *Metro + RER*
\# *Through-running extensions raise total to 683 km/391 miles, with 502 stations*
\+ *Only partly undergound*

OLDEST UNDERGROUND RAILWAY NETWORKS IN THE WORLD

	Location	Opened
1	London, UK	1863
2	Budapest, Hungary	1896
3	Glasgow, UK	1896
4	Boston, USA	1897
5	Paris, France	1900
6	Wuppertal, Germany	1901
7	Berlin, Germany	1902
8	New York, USA	1904
9	Philadelphia, USA	1907
10	Hamburg, Germany	1912

TRAIN À GRANDE VITESSE
The French TGV (Train à Grande Vitesse, or high-speed train) began service between Paris and Lyons in 1981. Its world record scheduled speed is set to be exceeded by even faster "bullet trains" now entering service in Japan.

T O P 1 0

COUNTRIES WITH THE FASTEST RAIL JOURNEYS*

	Country/journey/train	Distance km	miles	Speed km/h	mph
1	France, Paris–Lille (TGV 587)	204.2	126.9	250.0	155.3
2	Japan, Hiroshima–Kokuru (31 *Nozomi*)	192.0	119.3	230.4	143.2
3	Spain, Madrid–Ciudad Real (AVE 9744)	170.7	106.1	217.9	135.4
4	Germany, Fulda–Kassel (ICE *Frankfurter Römer*)	90.0	55.9	200.0	124.3
5	UK, Stevenage–Doncaster (InterCity 225)	206.6	128.4	177.1	110.0
6	Sweden, Hallsberg–Skövde (X2000 429)	113.8	70.7	175.1	108.8
7	Italy, Rome–Florence (*Cristoforo Colombo*)	261.9	162.7	162.0	100.7
8	USA, Baltimore–Wilmington (*Metroliner*)	110.1	68.4	153.6	95.4
9	Canada, Toronto–Dorval (*Metropolis*)	519.5	322.8	144.3	89.7
10	Russia, St. Petersburg–Moscow (ER 200)	649.9	403.8	130.4	81.0

* *Fastest journey for each country; all those in this Top 10 have other similarly or equally fast services*

The fastest international journeys are those on the Eurostar London–Paris route, via Eurotunnel (494.5 km/307.2 miles at 171.5 km/h/106.5 mph), and the TGVs between Paris and Brussels (332.2 km/206.4 miles at 148.8 km/h/92.4 mph). During 1997–98, two revolutionary high-speed trains, the E2 and E3, are scheduled to enter service in Japan, raising the speed to about 275 km/h/171 mph.

T O P 1 0

SURVIVING STEAM LOCOMOTIVES IN THE US

	Class	No. surviving
1	2-8-0	206
2	0-4-0	202
3	0-6-0	143
4	2-8-2	131
5	4-6-0	108
6	2-6-0	83
7	2-6-2	78
8	4-6-2	76
9	Shay	74
10	4-4-0	58

The number of surviving steam locomotives bears a close relation to the numbers of each class built – in the case of the 2-8-0s, some 21,000. Of these survivors, only a relatively small number is operational – again led by the 2-8-0s with 35 functioning examples, down to just 12 in the case of the 4-4-0s. There are instances of classes built in the thousands, such as the 2,200 2-10-2s, where fewer than 10 have survived and none are operational. The Shay was a geared, rather than wheeled, locomotive, introduced in 1880 and designed for steep gradients.

T O P 1 0

LONGEST RAIL PLATFORMS IN THE WORLD

	Station	Platform length m	ft
1	Washington–Monroe– Jackson, Chicago, Illinois, USA	1,067	3,500
2	Kharagpur, India	833	2,733
3	Perth, Australia	762	2,500
4	Sonepur, India	736	2,415
5	Bournemouth, UK	720	2,362
6	Bulawayo, Zimbabwe	702	2,302
7	New Lucknow, India	686	2,250
8	Bezwada, India	640	2,100
9	Jhansi, India	617	2,025
10	Colchester, UK	604	1,981

The presence of India in five out of the 10 entries in this list emphasizes the importance of the railways in the daily life of that country. India's railway network is the fourth longest in the world.

T O P 1 0

LONGEST RAIL NETWORKS IN THE WORLD

	Location	Total rail length km	miles
1	USA	240,000	149,129
2	Russia	154,000	95,691
3	Canada	70,176	43,605
4	India	62,462	38,812
5	China	58,399	36,287
6	Germany	43,966	27,319
7	Australia	38,563	23,962
8	Argentina	37,910	23,556
9	France	33,891	21,059
10	Brazil	27,418	17,037

Although remaining at the head of this list, US rail mileage has declined considerably since its 1916 peak of 408,773 km/ 254,000 miles, as the majority of people now travel by road. The total of all world networks is today reckoned to be some 1,201,337 km/746,476 miles.

TOURISM

TOP 10

AMUSEMENT AND THEME PARKS IN THE WORLD

	Park/location	Estimated visitors (1996)
1	Tokyo Disneyland, Tokyo, Japan	16,980,000
2	Disneyland, Anaheim, California, USA	15,000,000
3	Magic Kingdom at Walt Disney World, Lake Buena Vista, Florida, USA	13,803,000
4	Disneyland Paris, Marne-la-Vallée, France	11,700,000
5	EPCOT at Walt Disney World, Lake Buena Vista, Florida, USA	11,235,000
6	Disney-MGM Studios Theme Park at Walt Disney World, Lake Buena Vista, Florida, USA	9,975,000
7	Universal Studios Florida, Orlando, Florida, USA	8,400,000
8	Everland, Kyonggi-Do, South Korea	8,000,000
9	Blackpool Pleasure Beach, Blackpool, UK	7,500,000
10	Yokohama Hakkeijima Sea Paradise, Japan	6,926,000

Source: Amusement Business

ITALIAN ATTRACTION
Famous historic buildings such as the Leaning Tower of Pisa contribute to Italy's appeal, making it one of the world's most popular tourist destinations.

AMUSEMENT AND THEME PARKS IN EUROPE

	Park/location	Estimated visitors (1996)
1	Disneyland Paris, Marne-la-Vallée, France	11,700,000
2	Blackpool Pleasure Beach, Blackpool, UK	7,500,000
3	Tivoli Gardens, Copenhagen, Denmark	3,100,000
4	De Efteling, Kaatsheuvel, Netherlands	3,000,000
5=	Alton Towers, Staffordshire, UK	2,700,000
5=	Port Aventura, Salou, Spain	2,700,000
7	Europa Park, Rust, Germany	2,500,000
8=	Gardaland, Casteinuovo Del Garda, Italy	2,400,000
8=	Liseberg, Gothenburg, Sweden	2,400,000
10	Bakken, Klampenborg, Denmark	2,100,000

Source: Amusement Business

Despite appearing at the top of this list, Disneyland Paris continues to lose money at an alarming rate (in the six months to March 1997 its loss increased from F.Fr169,000,000/£21,400,000/$33,400,000 to F.Fr210,000,000/£26,600,000/ $41,500,000). Meanwhile, competition is mounting both from existing theme parks, among which those in the UK are especially well represented, and from newly-opened complexes, such as Spain's Port Aventura and Warner Brothers' Movie World in Bottrop-Krichhellen, Germany, which opened in 1996.

COUNTRIES EARNING MOST FROM TOURISM

	Country	World total %	Total ($) receipts (1996)
1	USA	15.1	64,373,000,000
2	Spain	6.7	28,428,000,000
3	France	6.6	28,241,000,000
4	Italy	6.4	27,349,000,000
5	UK	4.6	19,738,000,000
6	Germany	3.7	15,815,000,000
7	Austria	3.5	15,095,000,000
8	Hong Kong	2.5	10,836,000,000
9	China	2.4	10,200,000,000
10	Singapore	2.2	9,410,000,000

Source: World Tourism Organization

COUNTRIES OF ORIGIN OF TOURISTS TO THE US

	Country	Visitors per annum
1	Japan	3,506,000
2	UK	2,461,000
3	Germany	1,450,000
4	Mexico	1,324,000
5	France	686,000
6	Brazil	507,000
7	Italy	457,000
8	Korea	361,000
9=	China	353,000
9=	Venezuela	353,000

The enumeration methods of the US Immigration and Naturalization Service differ from those of the World Tourism Organization, presenting the paradoxical conclusion that, in the latest year for which figures are available, the USA received either 17,155,000 or 44,791,000 tourists.

TOP 10

TOURIST-SPENDING COUNTRIES IN THE WORLD

	Tourist country of origin	World total %	Total expenditure ($) (1996)
1	Germany	14.2	50,675,000,000
2	USA	12.9	45,855,000,000
3	Japan	10.3	36,792,000,000
4	UK	6.9	24,737,000,000
5	France	4.6	16,328,000,000
6	Italy	3.5	12,419,000,000
7	Austria	3.3	11,687,000,000
8	Russia	3.3	11,599,000,000
9	Netherlands	3.2	11,445,000,000
10	Canada	2.9	10,220,000,000

Source: World Tourism Organization

TOP 10

TOURIST COUNTRIES IN THE WORLD

	Country	World total %	Total visitors (1996)
1	France	10.3	61,500,000
2	USA	7.5	44,791,000
3	Spain	6.9	41,295,000
4	Italy	5.5	32,853,000
5	UK	4.4	26,025,000
6	China	3.8	22,765,000
7	Mexico	3.7	21,732,000
8	Hungary	3.5	20,670,000
9	Poland	3.3	19,420,000
10	Canada	2.9	17,345,000

Source: World Tourism Organization

TOP 10

MOST COMMON TYPES OF LOST PROPERTY ON LONDON TRANSPORT

	Type	Number of items found								
		1987–88	1988–89	1989–90	1990–91	1991–92	1992–93	1993–94	1994–95	1995–96
1	Books, cheque books and credit cards	19,329	19,148	20,006	20,270	20,436	20,187	18,818	20,038	19,695
2	"Value items" (handbags, purses, wallets, etc.)	19,868	18,628	18,397	18,634	17,342	18,270	17,364	17,708	18,088
3	Clothing	15,211	14,954	15,088	14,624	13,704	14,328	14,626	15,045	16,354
4	Cases and bags	9,317	9,155	9,272	9,034	8,513	8,056	8,432	9,029	10,034
5	Umbrellas	23,250	17,129	13,889	10,828	10,917	13,634	13,357	13,212	8,120
6	Keys	9,265	8,793	8,595	8,348	7,559	7,694	6,960	7,023	7,380
7	Spectacles	5,754	5,756	5,985	5,944	5,362	5,683	5,486	5,912	7,127
8	Cameras, electronic articles, and jewellery	5,304	5,493	5,352	5,732	5,298	5,394	5,426	6,129	6,117
9	Gloves (pairs)	4,402	3,770	3,428	3,446	3,268	3,188	3,380	2,886	3,661
10	Gloves (odd)	701	576	577	606	520	540	653	571	945
	Total items in Top 10:	*112,401*	*103,402*	*100,589*	*97,466*	*92,919*	*96,974*	*94,502*	*97,553*	*97,521*

As we have noted in previous editions of *The Top 10 of Everything*, there is an inexplicable consistency in the numbers of most categories of articles handed in to London Transport's Lost Property Office from year to year. Why, we may speculate, do an average of rather more than 100 individuals leave their spectacles on London's buses and tube trains every week? Why did the number losing their umbrellas halve and then begin to increase again? Books remain in the No. 1 position (oddly, cheque books and credit cards are now included in the same category), but changes in fashion have meant that hats no longer even warrant a separate category.

THE UNIVERSE & THE EARTH

T O P   1 0

BRIGHTEST STARS

	Star	Constellation	Distance*	Apparent magnitude
1	Sun	Solar System	149,598,020 km	−26.8
2	Sirius	Canis Major	8.64	−1.46
3	Canopus	Carina	1,200	−0.73
4	Alpha Centauri	Centaurus	4.35	−0.27
5	Arcturus	Boötes	34	−0.04
6	Vega	Lyra	26	+0.03
7	Capella	Auriga	45	+0.08
8	Rigel	Orion	900	+0.12
9	Procyon	Canis Minor	11.4	+0.38
10	Achernar	Eridanus	85	+0.46

* *From the Earth in light years, unless otherwise stated*

Based on apparent visual magnitude as viewed from the Earth – the lower the number, the brighter the star – Sirius, which has a diameter of 1,450,000 km/900,988 miles, is actually over 24 times brighter than the Sun, but its distance from the Earth relegates it into 2nd place. If the Sun is excluded, the 10th brightest star is Beta Centauri in the constellation of Centaurus. At its brightest, the star Betelgeuse in the constellation of Orion is brighter than some of these, but as it is variable its average brightness disqualifies it from this Top 10. The absolute magnitude of Cygnus OB2 No. 12, discovered in 1992, may make it the brightest star in the galaxy, but it is 5,900 light years away.

T O P   1 0

GALAXIES NEAREST TO THE EARTH

	Galaxy	Distance (light years)
1	Large Cloud of Magellan	169,000
2	Small Cloud of Magellan	190,000
3	Ursa Minor dwarf	250,000
4	Draco dwarf	260,000
5	Sculptor dwarf	280,000
6	Fornax dwarf	420,000
7=	Leo I dwarf	750,000
7=	Leo II dwarf	750,000
9	Barnard's Galaxy	1,700,000
10	Andromeda Spiral	2,200,000

These, and a number of other galaxies, are members of the so-called "Local Group" With such vast distances as these, "local" is clearly a relative term.

TOP 10

MOST FREQUENTLY SEEN COMETS

	Comet	Orbit period (years)
1	Encke	3.302
2	Grigg–Skjellerup	4.908
3	Honda–Mrkós–Pajdusáková	5.210
4	Tempel 2	5.259
5	Neujmin 2	5.437
6	Brorsen	5.463
7	Tuttle–Giacobini–Kresák	5.489
8	Tempel–L. Swift	5.681
9	Tempel 1	5.982
10	Pons–Winnecke	6.125

The comets in this Top 10, and several others, return with regularity, while others have such long periods of absence that they may not be seen again for many thousands – or even millions – of years. The most frequent visitor is Encke's Comet, which was named after the German astronomer Johann Franz Encke (1791–1865), who in 1818 calculated the period of its elliptical orbit. It had first been observed shortly before his birth, but without its orbit being calculated, and has been seen on almost all its subsequent returns. Encke's Comet is becoming extremely faint, and after its most recent return in 1994 it may very well be considered "lost".

TOP 10

MOST COMMON ELEMENTS IN THE UNIVERSE

	Element	Parts per 1,000,000
1	Hydrogen	739,000
2	Helium	240,000
3	Oxygen	10,700
4	Carbon	4,600
5	Neon	1,340
6	Iron	1,090
7	Nitrogen	970
8	Silicon	650
9	Magnesium	580
10	Sulphur	440

TOP 10

STARS NEAREST TO THE EARTH

(Excluding the Sun)

	Star	Light years*	Distance from the Earth km	miles
1	Proxima Centauri	4.22	39,923,310,000,000	24,792,500,000,000
2	Alpha Centauri	4.35	41,153,175,000,000	25,556,250,000,000
3	Barnard's Star	5.98	56,573,790,000,000	35,132,500,000,000
4	Wolf 359	7.75	73,318,875,000,000	45,531,250,000,000
5	Lalande 21185	8.22	77,765,310,000,000	48,292,500,000,000
6	Luyten 726-8	8.43	79,752,015,000,000	49,526,250,000,000
7	Sirius	8.64	81,833,325,000,000	50,818,750,000,000
8	Ross 154	9.45	89,401,725,000,000	55,518,750,000,000
9	Ross 248	10.40	98,389,200,000,000	61,100,000,000,000
10	Epsilon Eridani	10.80	102,173,400,000,000	63,450,000,000,000

* *One light year = 9,460,528,404,000 km/ 5,878,812,000 miles*

A spaceship travelling at a speed of 40,237 km/h/ 25,000 mph – which is faster than any speed yet achieved in space by a manufactured object – would take more than 113,200 years to reach Earth's closest star, Proxima Centauri.

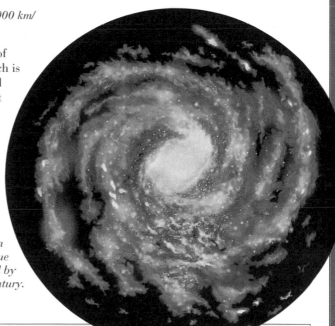

THE MILKY WAY
Often referred to as just "the Galaxy", the Milky Way is a giant spiral made up of several billion stars, including our sun. Its true nature has only been discovered by astronomers in the 20th century.

NEW ELEMENTS DISCOVERED

The British chemist Sir William Ramsay (1852–1916) knew that when nitrogen that was extracted from air, it appeared to be heavier than nitrogen prepared chemically. From this Ramsay concluded that there must be other gases present. He duly confirmed the presence of argon and helium, and in 1898, working with Morris W. Travers, discovered three more previously unknown gases: krypton, xenon, and neon. In 1904 Ramsay was awarded the Nobel Prize for Chemistry for his discoveries. As well as other uses for these gases, the wavelength of krypton is now used as the basis for the international standard measurement of one metre.

YEARS AGO · YEARS AGO · 100 · YEARS AGO · YEARS AGO

THE SOLAR SYSTEM

LIFE ON MARS?
Recent studies of a Martian meteorite have again raised the idea that life may once have existed on the seventh largest planet.

TOP 10

LARGEST BODIES IN THE SOLAR SYSTEM

	Body	Maximum diameter km	miles
1	The Sun	1,392,140	865,036
2	Jupiter	142,984	88,846
3	Saturn	120,536	74,898
4	Uranus	51,118	31,763
5	Neptune	49,532	30,778
6	The Earth	12,756	7,926
7	Venus	12,103	7,520
8	Mars	6,794	4,222
9	Ganymede	5,269	3,274
10	Titan	5,150	3,200

Most of the planets are visible with the naked eye. The exceptions are Uranus, discovered on 13 March 1781 by the British astronomer Sir William Herschel; Neptune, found by the German astronomer Johann Galle on 23 September 1846; and, outside this Top 10, Pluto, located using photographic techniques by American astronomer Clyde Tombaugh. Its discovery was announced on 13 March 1930; its diameter is uncertain, but is thought to be approximately 2,302 km/1,430 miles. Mercury, also outside this Top 10, has a diameter of 4,880 km/3,032 miles. Ganymede is the largest of Jupiter's satellites, and Titan the largest of Saturn's.

TOP 10

BODIES IN THE SOLAR SYSTEM WITH THE GREATEST ESCAPE VELOCITY*

	Body	Escape velocity (km/s)
1	The Sun	617.50
2	Jupiter	60.22
3	Saturn	32.26
4	Neptune	23.90
5	Uranus	22.50
6	The Earth	11.18
7	Venus	10.36
8	Mars	5.03
9	Mercury	4.25
10	Pluto	1.18

* *Excluding satellites*

TOP 10

BODIES IN THE SOLAR SYSTEM WITH THE GREATEST SURFACE GRAVITY*

	Body	Surface gravity	Weight#
1	The Sun	27.90	1,813.50
2	Jupiter	2.64	171.60
3	Neptune	1.20	78.00
4	Uranus	1.17	76.05
5	Saturn	1.16	75.40
6	The Earth	1.00	65.00
7	Venus	0.90	58.50
8	Mars	0.38	24.70
9	Mercury	0.38	24.70
10	Pluto	0.06	3.90

* *Excluding satellites*
\# *Of a 65 kg adult on the body's surface*

TOP 10

MOST COMMON SOURCES OF ASTEROID NAMES

	Sources	Asteroids
1	Astronomers	1,172
2	Places	833
3	Scientists other than astronomers	551
4	Mythological characters	439
5	Astronomers' family members and friends	406

	Sources	Asteroids
6	Historical persons	360
7	Writers	275
8	Composers and musicians	130
9	Literary characters	112
10	Organizations	93

SATURN'S NINTH MOON IS DISCOVERED

The first of Saturn's moons, Titan, was discovered in 1655, followed by seven more between 1671 and 1848. In 1898 the American astronomer William Pickering (1858–1938) found the most remarkable of them: Phoebe, Saturn's outermost moon, which lies some 12,952,000 km/8,048,000 miles distant from Saturn, taking 550 days to complete one orbit. Phoebe is 220 km/137 miles in diameter, and orbits in the opposite direction from all the other satellites. This suggests that it may in fact be an asteroid captured by Saturn's gravitational pull. Since Pickering's discovery, further moons have been observed, bringing Saturn's total to 18 satellites.

YEARS AGO 100 YEARS AGO

TOP 10

LARGEST PLANETARY MOONS IN THE SOLAR SYSTEM

	Moon	Planet	Diameter km	miles
1	Ganymede	Jupiter	5,269	3,274

Discovered by Galileo in 1609–10 and believed to be the largest moon in the Solar System, Ganymede – one of Jupiter's 16 satellites – is thought to have a surface of ice about 97 km/60 miles thick.

	Moon	Planet	Diameter km	miles
2	Titan	Saturn	5,150	3,200

Titan, the largest of Saturn's 18 confirmed moons, is actually larger than Mercury and Pluto. It was discovered by the Dutch astronomer Christian Huygens in 1655.

3	Callisto	Jupiter	4,820	2,995

Possessing a similar composition to Ganymede, Callisto is heavily pitted with craters, perhaps more than any other body in the Solar System.

4	Io	Jupiter	3,632	2,257

Most of what we know about Io was reported by the 1979 Voyager probe, which revealed a crust of solid sulphur, with massive eruptions hurling sulphurous material into space.

5	The Moon	The Earth	3,475	2,159

Our own satellite is a quarter of the size of the Earth, the 5th largest in the Solar System, and the only moon explored by humans.

6	Europa	Jupiter	3,126	1,942

Although Europa's ice-covered surface is apparently smooth and crater-free, it is covered with mysterious black lines, some of them 64 km/40 miles wide, resembling canals.

7	Triton	Neptune	2,750	1,708

This moon was discovered on 10 October 1846 by amateur astronomer William Lassell. Triton is the only known satellite in the Solar System that revolves around its planet in the opposite direction to the planet's rotation.

8	Titania	Uranus	1,580	982

The largest of Uranus's 15 moons, Titania was discovered by William Herschel in 1787, and has a snowball-like surface of ice.

9	Rhea	Saturn	1,530	951

Saturn's second largest moon was discovered by 17th-century, Italian-born French astronomer Giovanni Cassini.

10	Oberon	Uranus	1,516	942

Oberon, also discovered by Herschel, was given the name of the fairy-king husband of Queen Titania, both characters in Shakespeare's A Midsummer Night's Dream.

TOP 10

LARGEST PLANETARY MOONS IN THE SOLAR SYSTEM DISCOVERED IN THE 20TH CENTURY

	Moon	Planet	Year discovered	Discoverer	Diameter km	ml
1	Charon	Pluto	1978	James Christy	1,240	771
2	Miranda	Uranus	1948	Gerard Kuiper	472	293
3	Proteus	Neptune	1989	*Voyager 2*	403	250
4	Nereid	Neptune	1949	Gerard Kuiper	340	211
5	Larissa	Neptune	1989	*Voyager 2*	192	119
6	Janus	Saturn	1966	Audouin Dollfus	190	118
7	Himalia	Jupiter	1904	Charles Perrine	184	114
8	Puck	Uranus	1985	*Voyager 2*	170	106
9	Galatea	Neptune	1989	*Voyager 2*	158	98
10	Despina	Neptune	1989	*Voyager 2*	148	92

TOP 10

COLDEST BODIES IN THE SOLAR SYSTEM*

	Body	Lowest temperature (°C)
1	Pluto	–230
2	Uranus	–223
3	Neptune	–220
4	Mercury	–200
5	Saturn	–160
6	Jupiter	–145
7	Mars	–140
8	The Earth	–89
9	Venus	+464
10	The Sun	+5,500

* *Excluding satellites and asteroids*

Absolute zero, which has almost been attained on the Earth under laboratory conditions, is –273.15°C, only 38.15°C below the surface temperature of Triton, a moon of Neptune. At the other extreme, it has been calculated theoretically that the core of Jupiter attains 30,000°C, while the core of the Sun reaches 15,400,000°C.

TOP 10

LARGEST ASTEROIDS IN THE SOLAR SYSTEM

	Asteroid	Year discovered	Diameter km	miles
1	Ceres	1801	936	582
2	Pallas	1802	607	377
3	Vesta	1807	519	322
4	Hygeia	1849	450	279
5	Euphrosyne	1854	370	229
6	Interamnia	1910	349	217
7	Davida	1903	322	200
8	Cybele	1861	308	192
9	Europa	1858	288	179
10	Patienta	1899	275	171

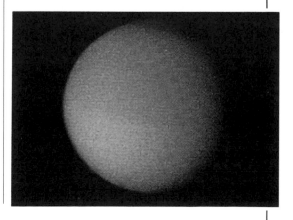

GIANT MOON
Titan, the first of Saturn's satellites to be discovered, is bigger than the planet Mercury.

SPACE FIRSTS

FIRST PEOPLE IN SPACE

	Name	Orbits	Duration hr:min	Spacecraft/ country	Date
1	Yuri Alekseyivich Gagarin	1	1:48	*Vostok I* (USSR)	12 Apr 1961
2	Gherman Stepanovich Titov	17	25:18	*Vostok II* (USSR)	6–7 Aug 1961
3	John Herschel Glenn	3	4:56	*Friendship 7* (USA)	20 Feb 1962
4	Malcolm Scott Carpenter	3	4:56	*Aurora 7* (USA)	24 May 1962
5	Andrian Grigoryevich Nikolayev	64	94:22	*Vostok III* (USSR)	11–15 Aug 1962
6	Pavel Romanovich Popovich	48	70:57	*Vostok IV* (USSR)	12–15 Aug 1962
7	Walter Marty Schirra	6	9:13	*Sigma 7* (USA)	3 Oct 1962
8	Leroy Gordon Cooper	22	34:19	*Faith 7* (USA)	15–16 May 1963
9	Valeri Fyodorovich Bykovsky	81	119:60	*Vostok* (USSR)	14–19 Jun 1963
10	Valentina Vladimirovna Tereshkova	48	70:50	*Vostok VI* (USSR)	16–19 Jun 1963

No. 2 was the youngest-ever astronaut, aged 25 years 329 days, and No. 10 was the first woman in space. Among early pioneering flights, neither Alan Shepard (5 May 1961: *Freedom 7*) nor Gus Grissom (21 July 1961: *Liberty Bell 7*) actually entered space, achieving altitudes of only 185 km/115 miles and 190 km/118 miles respectively.

FIRST MOONWALKERS

	Name/ spacecraft	Mission dates
1	Neil A. Armstrong (*Apollo 11*)	16–24 Jul 1969
2	Edwin E. ("Buzz") Aldrin (*Apollo 11*)	16–24 Jul 1969
3	Charles Conrad, Jr. (*Apollo 12*)	14–24 Nov 1969
4	Alan L. Bean (*Apollo 12*)	14–24 Nov 1969
5	Alan B. Shepard (*Apollo 14*)	31 Jan–9 Feb 1971
6	Edgar D. Mitchell (*Apollo 14*)	31 Jan–9 Feb 1971
7	David R. Scott (*Apollo 15*)	26 Jul–7 Aug 1971
8	James B. Irwin (*Apollo 15*)	26 Jul–7 Aug 1971
9	John W. Young (*Apollo 16*)	16–27 Apr 1972
10	Charles M. Duke (*Apollo 16*)	16–27 Apr 1972

SHANNON W. LUCID
The USA's 6th woman in space, and the most experienced, Lucid holds the record for time in space by an American woman. In 1996 she travelled 121 million km/75.2 million miles in 188 days in orbit, during which she transferred to the Russian Mir space station.

FIRST WOMEN IN SPACE

	Name/country/mission	Date
1	Valentina Vladimirovna Tereshkova, USSR, *Vostok 6*	16–19 Jun 1963

Tereshkova (b. 6 Mar 1937) was the first and, at 26, the youngest woman in space.

2	Svetlana Savitskaya, USSR, *Soyuz T7*	19 Aug 1982

On 25 Jul 1984 Savitskaya (b. 4 Aug 1948) also walked in space (from Soyuz T12*).*

3	Sally K. Ride, USA, *STS-7*	18–24 Jun 1983

Ride (b. 26 May 1951) was the first American woman in space.

4	Judith A. Resnik, USA, *STS-41-D*	30 Aug–5 Sep 1984

Resnik (b. 5 Apr 1949) was later killed in the STS-51-L *Shuttle disaster.*

5	Kathryn D. Sullivan, USA, *STS-41-G*	5–13 Oct 1984

Sullivan (b. 3 Oct 1951) was the first American woman to walk in space.

6	Anna L. Fisher, USA, *STS-51-A*	8–16 Nov 1984

Fisher (b. 24 Aug 1949) was the first American mother in space.

7	Margaret Rhea Seddon, USA, *STS-51-D*	12–19 Apr 1985

Seddon (b. 8 Nov 1947) flew again in STS-40 *(5–14 Jun 1991) and* STS-58 *(18 Oct–1 Nov 1993).*

8	Shannon W. Lucid, USA, *STS-51-G*	17–24 Jun 1985

Lucid (b. 14 Jan 1943) also flew in STS-34 *(18–23 Oct 1989),* STS-43 *(2–11 Aug 1991), STS-58 (18 Oct–1 Nov 1993). From* STS-76 *she transferred to the Russian* Mir *space station, then returned to Earth with* STS-79 *(22 Mar–26 Sep 1996).*

9	Bonnie J. Dunbar, USA, *STS-61-A*	30 Oct–6 Nov 1985

Dunbar (b. 3 Mar 1949) also flew in STS-32 *(9–20 Jan 1990),* STS-50 *(25 Jun–9 Jul 1992), and* STS-71 *(27 Jun–7 Jul 1995).*

10	Mary L. Cleave, USA, *STS-61-B*	26 Nov–3 Dec 1985

Cleave (b. 5 Feb 1947) also flew in STS-30 *(4–8 May 1989).*

THE 10

FIRST ARTIFICIAL SATELLITES

	Satellite	Country	Launch date
1	*Sputnik 1*	USSR	4 Oct 1957
2	*Sputnik 2*	USSR	3 Nov 1957
3	*Explorer 1*	USA	1 Feb 1958
4	*Vanguard 1*	USA	17 Mar 1958
5	*Explorer 3*	USA	26 Mar 1958
6	*Sputnik 3*	USSR	15 May 1958
7	*Explorer 4*	USA	26 Jul 1958
8	*SCORE*	USA	18 Dec 1958
9	*Vanguard 2*	USA	17 Feb 1959
10	*Discoverer 1*	USA	28 Feb 1959

Artificial satellites for use as radio relay stations were first proposed by the British science fiction writer Arthur C. Clarke in the October 1945 issue of *Wireless World*.

THE 10

FIRST BODIES TO HAVE BEEN VISITED BY SPACECRAFT

	Body	Spacecraft/country	Year
1	Moon	*Pioneer 4* (USA)	1959
2	Venus	*Mariner 2* (USA)	1962
3	Mars	*Mariner 4* (USA)	1965
4	Sun	*Pioneer 7* (USA)	1966
5	Jupiter	*Pioneer 10* (USA)	1973
6	Mercury	*Mariner 10* (USA)	1974
7	Saturn	*Pioneer 11* (USA)	1979
8	Comet Giacobini-Zinner	*International Sun-Earth Explorer 3* (International Cometary Explorer, USA/Europe)	1985
9	Uranus	*Voyager 2* (USA)	1986
10	Halley's Comet	*Giotto* (Europe)	1986

MARINER 9
More than six months after launch, Mariner 9 became the first probe to orbit another planet, sending back new data about Mars.

THE 10

FIRST COUNTRIES TO HAVE ASTRONAUTS OR COSMONAUTS IN SPACE

	Country	Name	Date*
1	USSR	Yuri Alekseyivich Gagarin	12 Apr 1961
2	USA	John Herschell Glenn	20 Feb 1962
3	Czechoslovakia	Vladimir Remek	2 Mar 1978
4	Poland	Miroslaw Hermaszewski	27 Jun 1978
5	East Germany	Sigmund Jahn	26 Aug 1978
6	Bulgaria	Georgi I. Ivanov	10 Apr 1979
7	Hungary	Bertalan Farkas	26 May 1980
8	Vietnam	Pham Tuan	23 Jul 1980
9	Cuba	Arnaldo T. Mendez	18 Sep 1980
10	Mongolia	Jugderdemidiyn Gurragcha	22 Mar 1981

* Of first space entry of a national of that country

Since the Soviet Union and the United States began and have dominated the exploration of space, all missions by non-Soviet and non-US citizens have been as guests of one of these countries. Especially since the era of the Space Shuttle and Mir space station, the list of nations with spaceflight experience has lengthened considerably and now includes Afghanistan, Austria, Belgium, Canada, France, Germany, India, Italy, Japan, Mexico, Netherlands, Romania, Saudi Arabia, Switzerland, Syria, and the UK.

THE 10

FIRST PLANETARY PROBES

	Probe/country	Planet	Arrival*
1	Venera 4 (USSR)	Venus	18 Oct 1967
2	Venera 5 (USSR)	Venus	16 May 1969
3	Venera 6 (USSR)	Venus	17 May 1969
4	Venera 7 (USSR)	Venus	15 Dec 1970
5	Mariner 9 (USA)	Mars	13 Nov 1971
6	Mars 2 (USSR)	Mars	27 Nov 1971
7	Mars 3 (USSR)	Mars	2 Dec 1971
8	Venera 8 (USSR)	Venus	22 Jul 1972
9	Venera 9 (USSR)	Venus	22 Oct 1975
10	Venera 10 (USSR)	Venus	25 Oct 1975

* Successfully entered orbit or landed

This list excludes "fly-bys" – those probes that passed by but did not land on the surface of another planet. The US's Pioneer 10, for example, which was launched on 2 March 1972, flew past Jupiter on 4 December 1973 but did not land. Venera 4 was the first unmanned probe to land on a planet, and Venera 9 the first to transmit pictures from a planet's surface. Mariner 9 was the first probe to orbit another planet; earlier and later Mariners had not been designed to land. These probes either are now in orbit around the Sun or have travelled beyond the Solar System.

ASTRONAUTS & COSMONAUTS

T O P 1 0

MOST EXPERIENCED NON-US AND NON-RUSSIAN ASTRONAUTS AND COSMONAUTS

	Name/country	No. of missions	Duration of missions			
			day	hr	min	sec
1	Thomas Reiter, Germany	1	179	02	41	37
2	Talgat A. Musabeyev, Kazakhstan	1	125	22	53	36
3	Ulf D. Merbold, Germany	3	49	21	38	04
4	Claude Nicollier, Switzerland	3	34	12	53	58
5	Jean-Loup Chrétien, France	2	32	15	59	00
6	Jean-Pierre Haignere, France	1	20	16	09	02
7	Marc J. Garneau, Canada	2	18	06	04	05
8=	Jean-Jacques Favier, France	1	16	21	47	47
8=	Robert B. Thirsk, Canada	1	16	21	47	47
10	Claudie André-Deshays, France	1	15	18	23	37

T O P 1 0

COUNTRIES WITH MOST SPACEFLIGHT EXPERIENCE*

	Country	Astronauts	Duration of missions			
			day	hr	min	sec
1	USSR/Russia*	83	12,112	20	27	05
2	USA	221	5,133	14	29	01
3	Germany	8	278	18	56	53
4	Kazakhstan	2	133	21	06	06
5	France	7	117	19	27	55
6	Canada	5	61	06	33	35
7	Japan	4	39	12	18	06
8	Italy	3	39	10	35	47
9	Switzerland	1	34	12	53	58
10	Bulgaria	2	11	19	11	06

* Russia became a separate independent state on 25 December 1991

T O P 1 0

MOST EXPERIENCED US ASTRONAUTS*

	Name	Duration of missions			
		day	hr	min	sec
1	Shannon W. Lucid	223	02	52	26
2	Norman E. Thagard	140	13	26	59
3	John E. Blaha	139	12	24	44
4=	Gerald P. Carr	84	01	16	00
4=	Edward G. Gibson	84	01	16	00
4=	William R. Pogue	84	01	16	00
7	Owen K. Garriott	69	18	56	23
8	Alan L. Bean	69	15	45	25
9	Jack R. Lousma	67	11	13	46
10	F. Story Musgrave	53	09	58	27

* To 1 January 1997

UNTETHERED SPACE WALK
On an eight-day US space mission in 1984, astronauts made their first untethered space walks, using their hands as instruments to guide a nitrogen-propelled manoeuvring unit.

TOP 10

YOUNGEST US ASTRONAUTS

	Astronaut	First flight	Age*
1	Janice E. Voss	21 Jun 1993	27
2	Kenneth D. Bowersox	25 Jun 1984	28
3	Sally K. Ride	18 Jun 1983	32
4	Tamara E. Jernigan	5 Jun 1991	32
5	Eugene A. Cernan	3 Jun 1966	32
6	Koichi Wakata	11 Jan 1996	32
7	Steven A. Hawley	30 Aug 1984	32
8	Mary E. Weber	13 Jul 1995	32
9	Kathryn D. Sullivan	5 Oct 1984	33
10	Ronald E. McNair#	3 Feb 1984	33

* *Those of apparently identical age have been ranked according to their precise age in days at the time of their first flight*
# *Killed in Challenger disaster, January 1986*

TOP 10

OLDEST US ASTRONAUTS

	Astronaut	Last flight	Age*
1	F. Story Musgrave	7 Dec 1996	61
2	Vance D. Brand	11 Dec 1990	59
3	Karl G. Henize	6 Aug 1985	58
4	William E. Thornton	6 May 1985	56
5	Don L. Lind	6 May 1985	54
6	Henry W. Hartsfield	6 Nov 1988	54
7	John E. Blaha	7 Dec 1996	54
8	William G. Gregory	18 Mar 1995	54
9	Robert A. Parker	11 Dec 1990	53
10	Shannon W. Lucid	31 Mar 1996	53

* *Those of apparently identical age have been ranked according to their precise age in days at the time of their last flight*

SPACE SALVAGE OPERATION
Discovery *Space Shuttle* 51-A astronaut *Dale A. Gardner uses his MMU (Manned Manoeuvring Unit) to recover the malfunctioning* Weststar VI *communications satellite.*

TOP 10

MOST EXPERIENCED SPACEWOMEN*

	Name#	No. of missions	Duration of missions day	hr	min	sec
1	Shannon W. Lucid	5	223	02	52	26
2	Yelena V. Kondakova	1	169	05	21	35
3	Tamara E. Jernigan	4	53	06	12	39
4	Bonnie J. Dunbar	4	41	12	37	50
5	Kathryn C. Thornton	4	40	15	15	18
6	Susan J. Helms	3	33	29	16	31
7	Marsha S. Ivins	3	32	19	32	22
8	Margaret Rhea Seddon	3	30	02	22	15
9	Ellen S. Baker	3	28	14	31	42
10	Linda M. Godwin	3	26	10	38	07

* *To 1 January 1997*
# *All US except No. 2 (Russian)*

Already a veteran of four missions, Shannon Lucid became America's most experienced astronaut and the world's most experienced female astronaut in 1996. She took off in US Space Shuttle *STS-76 Atlantis* on 22 March, and transferred to the Russian *Mir* Space Station, returning on board *STS-79 Atlantis* on 26 September, after travelling 121,000,000 km/75,200,000 miles.

TOP 10

LONGEST SPACE SHUTTLE FLIGHTS*

	Flight	Dates	Duration of flights hr	min	sec
1	STS-80 Columbia	19 Nov–7 Dec 1996	423	53	18
2	STS-78 Columbia	20 Jun–7 Jul 1996	405	48	30
3	STS-67 Endeavour	2–18 Mar 1995	399	9	46
3	STS-73 Columbia	20 Oct–5 Nov 1995	381	53	16
5	STS-75 Columbia	22 Feb–9 Mar 1996	377	41	25
6	STS-65 Columbia	8–23 Jul 1994	353	55	00
7	STS-58 Columbia	18 Oct–1 Nov 1993	336	12	32
8	STS-62 Columbia	9–18 Mar 1994	335	16	41
9	STS-50 Columbia	25 Jun–9 Jul 1992	331	30	04
10	STS-59 Endeavour	9–20 Apr 1994	269	49	30

* *To 1 January 1997*

The abbreviation STS (Space Transportation System) has been used throughout the Shuttle programme. The first nine flights were simply numbered *STS-1* (12–14 April 1981) to *STS-9*. Thereafter a more complex system was employed, until the digital system was reinstated after the ill-fated *Challenger* launch.

THE FACE OF THE EARTH

TOP 10

MOST COMMON ELEMENTS IN THE EARTH'S CRUST

	Element	Percentage*
1	Oxygen	45.6
2	Silicon	27.3
3	Aluminium	8.4
4	Iron	6.2
5	Calcium	4.7
6	Magnesium	2.8
7	Sodium	2.3
8	Potassium	1.8
9	Hydrogen	1.5
10	Titanium	0.6

* *Totals more than 100 per cent due to rounding*

This is based on the average percentages of the elements in igneous rock. At an atomic level, out of every million atoms, some 205,000 are silicon, 62,600 are aluminium, and 29,000 are hydrogen. However, in the Universe as a whole, hydrogen is by far the most common element, comprising some 927,000 out of every million atoms, followed by helium at 72,000 per million.

TOP 10

LIGHTEST ELEMENTS*

	Element	Year discovered	Density#
1	Lithium	1817	0.533
2	Potassium	1807	0.859
3	Sodium	1807	0.969
4	Calcium	1808	1.526
5	Rubidium	1861	1.534
6	Magnesium	1808	1.737
7	Phosphorus	1669	1.825
8	Beryllium	1798	1.846
9	Caesium	1860	1.896
10	Sulphur	Prehistoric	2.070

* *Solids only*
\# *Grams per cubic centimetre at 20°C*

TOP 10

ELEMENTS WITH THE HIGHEST MELTING POINTS

	Element	Melting point (°C)
1	Carbon	3,652
2	Tungsten	3,410
3	Rhenium	3,180
4	Osmium	3,045
5	Tantalum	2,996
6	Molybdenum	2,617
7	Niobium	2,468
8	Iridium	2,410
9	Ruthenium	2,310
10	Hafnium	2,227

Other elements that melt when heated to high temperatures include chromium (1,857°C), iron (1,535°C), and gold (1,064°C). For comparison, the surface of the Sun attains a temperature of 5,330°C.

TOP 10

HEAVIEST ELEMENTS

	Element	Year discovered	Density*
1	Osmium	1804	22.59
2	Iridium	1804	22.56
3	Platinum	1748	21.45
4	Rhenium	1925	21.01
5	Neptunium	1940	20.47
6	Plutonium	1940	20.26
7	Gold	Prehistoric	19.29
8	Tungsten	1783	19.26
9	Uranium	1789	19.05
10	Tantalium	1802	16.67

* *Grams per cubic centimetre at 20°C*

The two heaviest elements, the metals osmium and iridium, were discovered at the same time by the British chemist Smithson Tennant (1761–1815), who was also the first to prove that diamonds are made of carbon. A cubic foot (0.028317 m^3) of osmium weighs 640 kg/1,410 lb – equivalent to 10 people each weighing 64 kg/141 lbs.

TOP 10

ELEMENTS WITH THE LOWEST MELTING POINTS*

	Element	Melting point (°C)
1	Mercury	-38.9
2	Francium	27.0#
3	Caesium	28.4
4	Gallium	29.8
5	Rubidium	38.9
6	Phosphorus	44.1
7	Potassium	63.3
8	Sodium	97.8
9	Sulphur	112.8
10	Iodine	113.5

* *Solids only*
\# *Approximate*

Among other familiar elements that melt at relatively low temperatures are tin (232.0°C) and lead (327.5°C).

TOP 10

LARGEST METEORITES EVER FOUND

	Location	Estimated weight (tonnes)
1	Hoba West, Grootfontein, Namibia	54.4
2	*Ahnighito ("the Tent"),* Cape York, West Greenland	30.9
3	Bacuberito, Mexico	27.0
4	Mbosi, Tanganyika	26.0
5	Agpalik, Cape York, West Greenland	20.1
6	Armanti, Western Mongolia	20.0
7=	Willamette, Oregon, USA	14.0
7=	Chupaderos, Mexico	14.0
9	Campo del Cielo, Argentina	13.0
10	Mundrabila, Western Australia	12.0

Meteorites have been known since early times: fragments of meteorite have been found mounted in a necklace in an Egyptian pyramid and in ancient American Indian burial sites.

The shore of the Dead Sea is the lowest point on the world's surface. It takes its name from the scarcity of plants and animals in it that results from its high salt content.

TOP 10

DEEPEST DEPRESSIONS IN THE WORLD

	Depression/location	Maximum depth below sea level	
		m	ft
1	Dead Sea, Israel/Jordan	400	1,312
2	Turfan Depression, China	154	505
3	Qattâra Depression, Egypt	133	436
4	Poluostrov Mangyshlak, Kazakhstan	132	433
5	Danakil Depression, Ethiopia	117	383
6	Death Valley, USA	86	282
7	Salton Sink, USA	72	235
8	Zapadny Chink Ustyurta, Kazakhstan	70	230
9	Prikaspiyskaya Nizmennost', Kazakhstan/Russia	67	220
10	Ozera Sarykamysh, Turkmenistan/Uzbekistan	45	148

The shore of the Dead Sea, Israel/Jordan is the lowest exposed ground below sea level. However, its bed, at 728 m/2,388 ft below sea level, is only half as deep as that of Lake Baikal, Russia, which is 1,485 m/4,872 ft below sea level.

TOP 10

LARGEST DESERTS IN THE WORLD

	Desert	Location	Approx. area	
			sq km	sq miles
1	Sahara	North Africa	9,000,000	3,500,000
2	Australian	Australia	3,800,000	1,470,000
3	Arabian	Southwest Asia	1,300,000	502,000
4	Gobi	Central Asia	1,040,000	401,500
5	Kalahari	Southern Africa	520,000	201,000
6	Turkestan	Central Asia	450,000	174,000
7	Takla Makan	China	327,000	125,000
8=	Namib	Southwest Africa	310,000	120,000
8=	Sonoran	USA/Mexico	310,000	120,000
10=	Somali	Somalia	260,000	100,000
10=	Thar	India/Pakistan	260,000	100,000

THE NORTON COUNTY METEORITE

On 18 February 1948 people in New Mexico, Oklahoma, and Kansas, USA, reported seeing the spectacle of a fireball followed by a trail of smoke. It came to earth in Norton County, Kansas, and on investigation was discovered to be a meteorite weighing 1,070 kg/2,360 lb. Almost white, it is one of the largest stone meteorites ever discovered. Meteorites are composed principally of either iron or stone. More stone than iron meteorites fall to earth, but they usually break up on impact, and consequently all the largest known meteorites are iron. The Norton County Meteorite is now the prize exhibit in the Meteorite Museum of the University of New Mexico, Albuquerque.

This Top 10 presents the approximate areas and ranking of the world's great deserts. These are often broken down into smaller desert regions – the Australian Desert into the Gibson, Simpson, and Great Sandy Desert, for example. Of the total land surface of the Earth, as much as one-quarter may be considered "desert", or land where more water is lost through evaporation than is acquired through precipitation. However, deserts may range from the extremely arid and barren sandy desert, through arid, to semi-arid. Nearly every desert exhibits features that encompass all of these degrees of aridity without a precise line of demarcation between them.

RIVERS & WATERFALLS

TOP 10

LONGEST RIVERS IN THE WORLD

	River/location	Length km	miles
1	Nile, Tanzania/Uganda/ Sudan/Egypt	6,670	4,145
2	Amazon, Peru/Brazil	6,448	4,007
3	Yangtze–Kiang, China	6,300	3,915
4	Mississippi–Missouri– Red Rock, USA	5,971	3,710
5	Yenisey–Angara–Selenga, Mongolia/Russia	5,540	3,442
6	Huang Ho (Yellow River), China	5,464	3,395
7	Ob–Irtysh, Mongolia/ Kazakhstan/Russia	5,410	3,362
8	Zaïre (Congo), Angola/Congo (Zaïre)	4,700	2,920
9	Lena–Kirenga, Russia	4,400	2,734
10	Mekong, Tibet/China/ Myanmar (Burma)/Laos/ Cambodia/Vietnam	4,350	2,703

DID YOU KNOW

THE WORLD'S LONGEST RIVER?

The Nile's source was discovered in 1858 when British explorer John Hanning Speke reached Lake Victoria Nyanza. The river is today generally accepted to be the world's longest, with an overall length of 6,670 km/4,145 miles. It was not until almost 100 years later, in 1953, that the source of the Amazon was identified as a stream called Huarco flowing from the Misuie glacier in the Peruvian Andes. It joins the Amazon's main tributary at Ucayali, Peru, giving a total length of 6,448 km/4,007 miles. However, by following the Amazon from its source and up the Rio Pará it is possible to sail for some 6,750 km/4,195 miles, a greater distance than the length of the Nile. Since this route is not considered part of the Amazon basin, the Nile maintains its pre-eminence.

TOP 10

LONGEST RIVERS IN NORTH AMERICA

	River/location	Length km	miles
1	Mackenzie–Peace, Canada	4,241	2,635
2	Missouri–Red Rock, USA	4,088	2,540
3	Mississippi, USA	3,779	2,348
4	Missouri, USA	3,726	2,315
5	Yukon, Canada/USA	3,185	1,979
6	St. Lawrence, Canada	3,130	1,945
7	Rio Grande, USA	2,832	1,760
8	Nelson, Canada	2,575	1,600
9	Arkansas, USA	2,348	1,459
10	Colorado, USA	2,334	1,450

The principal reaches of the Mississippi, Missouri, and Red Rock rivers are often combined, thus becoming the 4th longest river in the world at 5,971 km/3,710 miles.

TOP 10

LONGEST RIVERS IN SOUTH AMERICA

	River/location	Length km	miles
1	Amazon, Peru/Brazil	6,448	4,007
2	Plata–Paraná, Brazil/ Paraguay/Argentina/ Uruguay	4,000	2,485
3	Madeira–Mamoré– Grande, Bolivia/Brazil	3,380	2,100
4	Purus, Peru/Brazil	3,207	1,993
5	São Francisco, Brazil	3,198	1,987
6	Orinoco, Colombia/Venezuela	2,736	1,700
7	Tocantins, Brazil	2,699	1,677
8	Paraguay, Paraguay/ Brazil/Argentina/Bolivia	2,549	1,584
9	Japurá–Caquetá Colombia/Brazil	2,414	1,500
10	Negro, Colombia/ Venezuela/Brazil	2,253	1,400

TOP 10

LONGEST RIVERS IN ASIA

	River/location	Length km	miles
1	Yangtze–Kiang, China	6,300	3,915
2	Yenisey–Angara–Selenga, Mongolia/Russia	5,540	3,442
3	Huang Ho, China	5,464	3,395
4	Ob–Irtysh, Mongolia/ Kazakhstan/Russia	5,410	3,362
5	Lena–Kirengal, Russia	4,400	2,734
6	Mekong, Tibet/China/ Myanmar/Laos/ Cambodia/Vietnam	4,350	2,703
7	Amur–Argun, China/Russia	4,345	2,700
8	Volga, Russia	3,530	2,193
9	Syr Darya–Naryn, Kyrgyzstan/Tajikistan/ Uzbekistan/Kazakhstan	3,019	1,876
10	Nizhnyaya Tunguska, Russia	2,989	1,857

TOP 10

LONGEST RIVERS IN AFRICA

	River/location	Length km	miles
1	Nile, Tanzania/Uganda/ Sudan/Egypt	6,670	4,145
2	Zaïre (Congo), Angola/Congo (Zaïre)	4,700	2,920
3	Niger, Guinea/Nigeria	4,100	2,550
4	Zambezi, Zambia/ Mozambique	2,650	1,650
5	Shebeli, Somalia	2,490	1,550
6	Ubangi, Congo (Zaïre)	2,460	1,530
7	Orange, Namibia/ South Africa	2,250	1,400
8	Kasai, Congo (Zaïre)	1,930	1,200
9	Senegal–Mauritania/ Bafing, Senegal	1,700	1,050
10	Blue Nile, Sudan	1,610	1,000

THE RIVER RHINE AT ST. GOAR
The Rhine, the longest river in Western Europe, is easily navigable. As a consequence it is the busiest waterway on the continent.

TOP 10

RIVERS PRODUCING THE MOST SEDIMENT

	River	Sediment discharged (tonnes per annum)
1	Yellow	1,900,000,000
2	Ganges	1,450,000,000
3	Brahmaputra	725,000,000
4	Yangtze	500,000,000
5	Indus	435,000,000
6	Amazon	360,000,000
7	Mississippi–Missouri	310,000,000
8	Irrawaddy	300,000,000
9	Mekong	170,000,000
10	Colorado	136,000,000

TOP 10

GREATEST WATERFALLS IN THE WORLD*

	Waterfall/location	Average flow (m³/sec)
1	Boyoma (Stanley), Congo (Zaïre)	17,000
2	Khône, Laos	11,610
3	Niagara (Horseshoe), Canada/USA	5,830
4	Grande, Uruguay	4,500
5	Paulo Afonso, Brazil	2,890
6	Urubupungá, Brazil	2,750
7	Iguaçu, Argentina/Brazil	1,700
8	Maribondo, Brazil	1,500
9	Churchill (Grand), Canada	1,390
10	Kabalega (Murchison), Uganda	1,200

* *Based on volume of water*

TOP 10

LONGEST RIVERS IN EUROPE

	River	Location	Length km	miles
1	Danube	Germany/Austria/Slovakia/Hungary/Serbia/Romania/Bulgaria	2,842	1,766
2	Rhine	Switzerland/Germany/Holland	1,368	850
3	Elbe	Czech Republic/Slovakia/Germany	1,167	725
4	Loire	France	1,014	630
5	Tagus	Portugal	1,009	627
6	Meuse	France/Belgium/Holland	950	590
7	Ebro	Spain	933	580
8	Rhône	Switzerland/France	813	505
9	Guadiana	Spain/Portugal	805	500
10	Seine	France	776	482

TOP 10

HIGHEST WATERFALLS IN THE WORLD

	Waterfall	River	Location	Total drop m	ft
1	Angel	Carrao	Venezuela	979	3,212*
2	Tugela	Tugela	South Africa	948	3,110
3	Utigård	Jostedal Glacier	Nesdale, Norway	800	2,625
4	Mongefossen	Monge	Mongebekk, Norway	774	2,540
5	Yosemite	Yosemite Creek	California, USA	739	2,425
6	Østre Mardøla Foss	Mardals	Eikisdal, Norway	657	2,154
7	Tyssestrengane	Tysso	Hardanger, Norway	646	2,120
8	Cuquenán	Arabopo	Venezuela	610	2,000
9	Sutherland	Arthur	South Island, New Zealand	580	1,904
10	Kjellfossen	Naero	Gudvangen, Norway	561	1,841

* *Longest single drop 807 m/2,648 ft*

OCEANS, SEAS & LAKES

TOP 10

LARGEST OCEANS AND SEAS IN THE WORLD

	Ocean/sea	Approx. area sq km	sq miles
1	Pacific Ocean	165,241,000	63,800,000
2	Atlantic Ocean	82,439,000	31,830,000
3	Indian Ocean	73,452,000	28,360,000
4	Arctic Ocean	13,986,000	5,400,000
5	Arabian Sea	3,864,000	1,492,000
6	South China Sea	3,447,000	1,331,000
7	Caribbean Sea	2,753,000	1,063,000
8	Mediterranean Sea	2,505,000	967,000
9	Bering Sea	2,269,000	876,000
10	Bay of Bengal	2,173,000	839,000

Geographers hold differing opinions as to whether certain bodies of water are regarded as seas in their own right or as parts of larger oceans – the Coral, Weddell, and Tasman Seas would be eligible for this list, but most authorities consider them part of the Pacific Ocean.

THE GREAT LAKES OF NORTH AMERICA
The vast expanse of the Great Lakes is particularly impressive when viewed from space. Lakes Superior and Huron are partly within Canada, making Lake Michigan the largest lake wholly situated within the US.

TOP 10

DEEPEST OCEANS AND SEAS IN THE WORLD

	Ocean/sea	Greatest depth m	ft	Average depth m	ft
1	Pacific Ocean	10,924	35,837	4,028	13,215
2	Indian Ocean	7,455	24,460	3,963	13,002
3	Atlantic Ocean	9,219	30,246	3,926	12,880
4	Caribbean Sea	6,946	22,788	2,647	8,685
5	South China Sea	5,016	16,456	1,652	5,419
6	Bering Sea	4,773	15,659	1,547	5,075
7	Gulf of Mexico	3,787	12,425	1,486	4,874
8	Mediterranean Sea	4,632	15,197	1,429	4,688
9	Japan Sea	3,742	12,276	1,350	4,429
10	Arctic Ocean	5,625	18,456	1,205	3,953

The deepest point in the deepest ocean is the Marianas Trench in the Pacific at a depth of 10,924 m/35,837 ft, according to a recent hydrographic survey, although a slightly lesser depth of 10,916 m/35,814 ft was recorded on 23 January 1960 by Jacques Piccard and Donald Walsh in their 17.7-m/58-ft long bathyscaphe *Trieste 2* during the deepest-ever ocean descent. Whichever measurement is correct, it is still close to 11 km/6.8 miles down, or almost 29 times the height of the Empire State Building.

MOST COMMON ELEMENTS IN SEAWATER

	Element	Tonnes per km³
1	Water*	991,000,000
2	Chlorine	19,600,000
3	Sodium	10,900,000
4	Magnesium	1,400,000
5	Sulphur	920,000
6	Calcium	420,000
7	Potassium	390,000
8	Bromine	67,000
9	Carbon	29,000
10	Strontium	8,300

* Composed of hydrogen and oxygen

A typical cubic kilometre of seawater is a treasury of often valuable elements, but sodium and chlorine (combined as sodium chloride, or common salt) are the only two that are extracted in substantial quantities. The cost of extracting such elements as gold (approximately 4 kilos of which are found in the average km³ of seawater) would be prohibitively expensive.

LARGEST FRESHWATER LAKES IN THE US*

	Lake/state	Approx. area sq km	sq miles
1	Michigan, Illinois/ Indiana/ Michigan/ Wisconsin	57,700	22,278
2	Iliamna, Alaska	2,590	1,000
3	Okeechobee, Florida	1,813	700
4	Becharof, Alaska	1,186	458
5	Red, Minnesota	1,168	451
6	Teshepuk, Alaska	816	315
7	Naknek, Alaska	627	242
8	Winnebago, Wisconsin	557	215
9	Mille Lacs, Minnesota	536	207
10	Flathead, Montana	510	197

* Excluding those partly in Canada

LARGEST LAKES IN THE WORLD

	Lake	Location	Approx. area sq km	sq miles
1	Caspian Sea	Azerbaijan/Iran/Kazakhstan/Russia/ Turkmenistan	378,400	146,101
2	Superior	Canada/USA	82,100	31,699
3	Victoria	Kenya/Tanzania/Uganda	62,940	24,301
4	Huron	Canada/USA	59,580	23,004
5	Michigan	USA	57,700	22,278
6	Aral Sea	Kazakhstan/Uzbekistan	40,000	15,444
7	Tanganyika	Burundi/Tanzania/Congo (Zaïre)/Zambia	31,987	12,350
8	Baikal	Russia	31,494	12,160
9	Great Bear	Canada	31,153	12,028
10	Great Slave	Canada	28,570	11,031

COUNTRIES WITH THE GREATEST AREA OF INLAND WATER

	Country	Percentage of total area	Water area sq km	sq miles
1	Canada	7.60	755,170	291,573
2	India	9.56	314,400	121,391
3	China	2.82	270,550	104,460
4	USA	2.20	206,010	79,541
5	Ethiopia	9.89	120,900	46,680
6	Colombia	8.80	100,210	38,691
7	Indonesia	4.88	93,000	35,908
8	Russia	0.47	79,400	30,657
9	Australia	0.90	68,920	26,610
10	Tanzania	6.25	59,050	22,799

Large areas of some countries are occupied by major rivers and lakes. Lake Victoria, for example, raises the water area of Uganda to 15.39 per cent of its total. In Europe, three Scandinavian countries have considerable areas of water: Sweden has 39,036 sq km/ 15,072 sq miles (8.68 per cent), Finland has 31,560 sq km/12,185 sq miles (9.36 per cent), and Norway has 16,360 sq km/6,317 sq miles (5.05 per cent).

TALLER THAN EVEREST?

Mountains are conventionally measured from sea level. Thus Everest, at 8,846 m/ 29,022 ft above sea level is the world's tallest mountain. However, the bases of some mountains lie far beneath the sea. The Hawaiian volcano Mauna Kea is 4,206 m/ 13,796 ft tall but has even greater height below sea level, some 6,000 m/19,683 ft, bringing its total height to 10,206 m/33,481 ft, or 1,360 m/4,461 ft taller than Everest. Its neighbour, Mauna Loa, at 4,171 m/13,681 ft tall with a further 5,500 m/18,043 ft below sea level, is also taller than Everest and is reckoned to be the world's most voluminous mountain at 42,000 km³/10,076 ml³. The tallest mountain wholly beneath the sea is in the Pacific Ocean's Tonga Trench, rising to 8,690 m/28,510 ft.

ON TOP OF THE WORLD

TOP 10

HIGHEST MOUNTAINS IN THE WORLD

(Height of principal peak; lower peaks of the same mountain are excluded)

	Mountain	Location	m	ft
1	Everest	Nepal/Tibet	8,846	29,022
2	K2	Kashmir/China	8,611	28,250
3	Kangchenjunga	Nepal/Sikkim	8,598	28,208
4	Lhotse	Nepal/Tibet	8,501	27,890
5	Makalu I	Nepal/Tibet	8,470	27,790
6	Dhaulagiri I	Nepal	8,172	26,810
7	Manaslu I	Nepal	8,156	26,760
8	Cho Oyu	Nepal	8,153	26,750
9	Nanga Parbat	Kashmir	8,126	26,660
10	Annapurna I	Nepal	8,078	26,504

Dhaulagiri was believed to be the world's tallest mountain until Kangchenjunga was surveyed and declared to be even higher. However, when the results of the so-called Great Trigonometrical Survey of India were studied, it became apparent that Everest (then called "Peak XV") was the tallest, its height being computed as 8,840 m/29,002 ft. Errors in measurement were corrected in 1955, giving the height as 8,848 m/29,029 ft. On 20 April 1993, using the latest measuring techniques, this was again revised to the current "official" figure. The mountain's name was suggested in 1865 as a tribute to Sir George Everest, the Surveyor General of India who had led the Great Trigonometrical Survey.

TOP 10

HIGHEST MOUNTAINS IN AFRICA

	Mountain/location	m	ft
1	Kibo (Kilimanjaro), Tanganyika/Tanzania	5,895	19,340
2	Batian (Kenya), Kenya	5,199	17,058
3	Ngaliema, Uganda/Congo (Zaïre)	5,109	16,763
4	Duwoni, Uganda	4,896	16,062
5	Baker, Uganda	4,843	15,889
6	Emin, Congo (Zaïre)	4,798	15,741
7	Gessi, Uganda	4,715	15,470
8	Sella, Uganda	4,627	15,179
9	Ras Dashen, Ethiopia	4,620	15,158
10	Wasuwameso, Congo (Zaïre)	4,581	15,030

TOP 10

HIGHEST ACTIVE VOLCANOES IN THE WORLD

	Volcano	Location	Latest activity	m	ft
1	Guallatiri	Chile	1987	6,060	19,882
2	Láascar	Chile	1991	5,990	19,652
3	Cotopaxi	Ecuador	1975	5,897	19,347
4	Tupungatito	Chile	1986	5,640	18,504
5	Popocatépetl	Mexico	1995	5,452	17,887
6	Ruiz	Colombia	1992	5,400	17,716
7	Sangay	Ecuador	1988	5,230	17,159
8	Guagua Pichincha	Ecuador	1988	4,784	15,696
9	Purace	Colombia	1977	4,755	15,601
10	Kliuchevskoi	Russia	1995	4,750	15,584

This list includes all volcanoes that have been active at some time during the 20th century. Although it does not qualify for the list above, the highest currently active volcano in Europe is Mt. Etna in Italy (3,311 m/10,855 ft), which was responsible for numerous deaths in earlier times. Although still active, Etna's last major eruption took place on 11 March 1669, killing at least 20,000.

TOP 10

HIGHEST DORMANT VOLCANOES IN THE WORLD

	Volcano	Location	Latest activity	m	ft
1	Llullaillaco	Chile	1877	6,723	22,057
2	El Misti	Peru	*c.* 1870	5,822	19,101
3	Orizaba	Mexico	1687	5,610	18,405
4	Rainier	USA	*c.* 1894	4,392	14,410
5	Shasta	USA	1786	4,317	14,162
6	Fuji	Japan	1708	3,776	12,388
7	Tolbachik	Russia	1876	3,682	12,080
8	Turrialba	Costa Rica	1866	3,246	10,650
9	Baitoushan	China/Korea	1702	2,774	9,003
10	Bandai	Japan	1888	1,819	5,968

This list comprises the world's tallest volcanoes that are known to have been active at some time before the 20th century, but which now appear to be dormant – although some, including Mt. Rainier, Mt. Shasta, and Mt. Fuji still emit steam. Mt. Rainier and Mt. Fuji are both classic examples of "composite cones" or "strato-volcanoes" – those that have been built up during sequential eruptions over many thousands of years.

TOP 10

HIGHEST MOUNTAINS IN NORTH AMERICA

	Mountain/location	m	ft
1	McKinley, USA	6,194	20,320
2	Logan, Canada	6,050	19,850
3	Citlaltépetl (Orizaba), Mexico	5,700	18,700
4	St. Elias, USA/Canada	5,489	18,008
5	Popocatépetl, Mexico	5,452	17,887
6	Foraker, USA	5,304	17,400
7	Ixtaccihuatl, Mexico	5,286	17,343
8	Lucania, Canada	5,226	17,147
9	King, Canada	5,173	16,971
10	Steele, Canada	5,073	16,644

TOP 10

HIGHEST MOUNTAINS IN OCEANIA

	Mountain/location	m	ft
1	Jaya, Indonesia	5,030	16,500
2	Daam, Indonesia	4,920	16,150
3	Pilimsit, Indonesia	4,800	15,750
4	Trikora, Indonesia	4,750	15,580
5	Mandala, Indonesia	4,700	15,420
6	Wilhelm, Papua New Guinea	4,690	15,400
7	Wisnumurti, Indonesia	4,590	15,080
8	Yamin, Papua New Guinea	4,530	14,860
9	Kubor, Papua New Guinea	4,360	14,300
10	Herbert, Papua New Guinea	4,270	14,000

TOP 10

HIGHEST MOUNTAINS IN SOUTH AMERICA

	Mountain/location	m	ft
1	Cerro Aconcagua, Argentina	6,960	22,834
2	Ojos del Salado, Argentina/Chile	6,885	22,588
3	Bonete, Argentina	6,873	22,550
4	Pissis, Argentina/Chile	6,780	22,244
5	Huascarán, Peru	6,768	22,205
6	Llullaillaco, Argentina/Chile	6,723	22,057
7	Libertador, Argentina	6,721	22,050
8	Mercadario, Argentina/Chile	6,670	21,884
9	Yerupajá, Peru	6,634	21,765
10	Tres Cruces, Argentina/Chile	6,620	21,720

TOP 10

HIGHEST MOUNTAINS IN EUROPE

	Mountain/location	m	ft
1	Mont Blanc, France/Italy	4,807	15,771
2	Monte Rosa, Italy/Switzerland	4,634	15,203
3	Dom, Switzerland	4,545	14,911
4	Liskamm, Italy/Switzerland	4,527	14,853
5	Weisshorn, Switzerland	4,505	14,780
6	Täschorn, Switzerland	4,491	14,734
7	Matterhorn, Italy/Switzerland	4,477	14,688
8	La Dent Blanche, Switzerland	4,357	14,293
9	Nadelhorn, Switzerland	4,327	14,196
10	Le Grand Combin, Switzerland	4,314	14,153

DID YOU KNOW

HIGH FLIERS

On 3 April 1933, 20 years before any climbers had reached the top of Mount Everest, British pilots Lord Clydesdale, in a Westland P.V3, and Flt. Lt. David McIntyre, in a Westland Wallace biplane, succeeded in flying over it. Using oxygen and wearing electrically-heated flying suits, they battled against high winds, almost crashed, and suffered from failed oxygen equipment, but both achieved their objective and landed safely.

TOP 10

COUNTRIES WITH THE HIGHEST ELEVATIONS IN THE WORLD*

	Country/mountain	m	ft
1	Nepal#, Everest	8,846	29,022
2	Pakistan, K2	8,611	28,250
3	India, Kangchenjunga	8,598	28,208
4	Bhutan, Khula Kangri	7,554	24,784
5	Tajikstan, Mt. Garmo (formerly Kommunizma)	7,495	24,590
6	Afghanistan, Noshaq	7,499	24,581
7	Kyrgystan, Pik Pobedy	7,439	24,406
8	Kazakhstan, Khan Tengri	6,995	22,949
9	Argentina, Cerro Aconcagua	6,960	22,834
10	Chile, Ojos del Salado	6,885	22,588

* *Based on the tallest peak in each country*
\# *Everest straddles Nepal and Tibet, which – now known as Xizang – is a province of China*

While an elevation of more than 305 m/ 1,000 ft is commonly regarded as a mountain, there is no international agreement. Using this criterion, almost every country in the world can claim to have at least one mountain.

WORLD WEATHER

THE 10

LAYERS OF CLOUDS

	Cloud layer	Altitude of layer	
		m	ft
1	Stratus	below 450	below 1,456
2=	Cumulus	450–2,000	1,476–6,562
2=	Stratocumulus	450–2,000	1,476–6,562
2=	Cumulonimbus	450–2,000	1,476–6,562
5	Nimbostratus	900–3,000	2,953–9,843
6=	Altostratus	2,000–7,000	6,562–22,966
6=	Altocumulus	2,000–7,000	6,562–22,966
8=	Cirrus	5,000–13,500	16,404–44,291
8=	Cirrostratus	5,000–13,500	16,404–44,291
8=	Cirrocumulus	5,000–13,500	16,404–44,291

TOP 10

WETTEST INHABITED PLACES IN THE WORLD

	Location	Average annual rainfall	
		mm	in
1	Buenaventura, Colombia	6,743	265.47
2	Monrovia, Liberia	5,131	202.01
3	Pago Pago, American Samoa	4,990	196.46
4	Moulmein, Myanmar (Burma)	4,852	191.02
5	Lae, Papua New Guinea	4,645	182.87
6	Baguio, Luzon Island, Philippines	4,573	180.04
7	Sylhet, Bangladesh	4,457	175.47
8	Conakry, Guinea	4,341	170.91
9=	Bogor, Java, Indonesia	4,225	166.34
9=	Padang, Sumatra Island, Indonesia	4,225	166.34

WET, WET, WET
All 10 of the world's wettest places receive more than 4 metres/12 feet of rain each year, with the rainiest of all experiencing over 6.7 metres/22 feet.

TOP 10

HOTTEST CITIES IN THE WORLD*

	City	Highest recorded temperature	
		°C	°F
1	Arouane, Mali	54.4	130
2=	Abadan, Iran	52.8	127
2=	Cloncurry, Australia	52.8	127
2=	Wadi Halfa, Sudan	52.8	127
5=	Aswan, Egypt	51.1	124
5=	Fort Flatters, Algeria	51.1	124
5=	Mosul, Iraq	51.1	124
8=	Cufra, Libya	50.0	122
8=	Gabes, Tunisia	50.0	122
8=	Multan, Pakistan	50.0	122

* Hottest city in each country only

Phoenix, Arizona (47.8°C/118°F), and Seville, Spain (47.2°C/117°F), are the hottest cities in the US and Europe.

TOP 10

HOTTEST INHABITED PLACES IN THE WORLD

	Location	Average temperature	
		°C	°F
1	Djibouti, Djibouti	30.0	86.0
2=	Timbuktu, Mali	29.3	84.7
2=	Tirunelveli, India	29.3	84.7
2=	Tuticorin, India	29.3	84.7
5=	Nellore, India	29.2	84.6
5=	Santa Marta, Colombia	29.2	84.6
7=	Aden, South Yemen	28.9	84.0

	Location	Average temperature	
		°C	°F
7=	Madurai, India	28.9	84.0
7=	Niamey, Niger	28.9	84.0
10=	Hudaydah, North Yemen	28.8	83.8
10=	Ouagadougou, Burkina Faso	28.8	83.8
10=	Thanjāvūr, India	28.8	83.8

TOP 10
WETTEST PLACES IN GREAT BRITAIN

	Location	Average annual rainfall	
		mm	in
1	Dalness, Glen Etive, Strathclyde	3,306	130.16
2	Seathwaite, nr Borrowdale, Cumbria	3,150	124.02
3	Glenfinnan, Loch Shiel, Highland	3,022	118.98
4	Inveraran, Loch Lomond, Central	2,701	106.34
5	Inveruglas, Loch Lomond, Central	2,662	104.80
6	Capel Curig, Gwynedd	2,555	100.59
7	Wythburn, Lake Thirlmere, Cumbria	2,535	99.80
8=	Tyndrum and Crianlarich, Central	2,500	98.43
8=	Chapel Stile, Cumbria	2,500	98.43
10	Lochgoilhead, Strathclyde	2,464	97.01

TOP 10
SNOWIEST CITIES IN THE US

	City	Mean annual snowfall	
		mm	ins
1	Blue Canyon, California	6,116	240.8
2	Marquette, Michigan	3,282	129.2
3	Sault Ste. Marie, Michigan	2,949	116.1
4	Syracuse, New York	2,896	114.0
5	Caribou, Maine	2,794	110.0
6	Mount Shasta, California	2,664	104.9
7	Lander, Wyoming	2,596	102.2
8	Flagstaff, Arizona	2,560	100.8
9	Sexton Summit, Oregon	2,484	97.8
10	Muskegon, Michigan	2,466	97.1

TOP 10
DRIEST INHABITED PLACES IN THE WORLD

	Location	Average annual rainfall	
		mm	in
1	Aswan, Egypt	0.5	0.02
2	Luxor, Egypt	0.7	0.03
3	Arica, Chile	1.1	0.04
4	Ica, Peru	2.3	0.09
5	Antofagasta, Chile	4.9	0.19
6	Minya el Qamn, Egypt	5.1	0.20
7	Asyût, Egypt	5.2	0.20
8	Callao, Peru	12.0	0.47
9	Trujillo, Peru	14.0	0.54
10	Fayyum, Egypt	19.0	0.75

TOP 10
COLDEST INHABITED PLACES IN THE WORLD

	Location	Average temperature	
		°C	°F
1	Norlísk, Russia	−10.9	12.4
2	Yakutsk, Russia	−10.1	13.8
3	Yellowknife, Canada	−5.4	22.3
4	Ulaanbator, Mongolia	−4.5	23.9
5	Fairbanks, Alaska, USA	−3.4	25.9
6	Surgut, Russia	−3.1	26.4
7	Chita, Russia	−2.7	27.1
8	Nizhnevartosvsk, Russia	−2.6	27.3
9	Hailar, Mongolia	−2.4	27.7
10	Bratsk, Russia	−2.2	28.0

TOP 10
HOTTEST YEARS IN GREAT BRITAIN SINCE 1659

	Year	Average temperature	
		°C	°F
1	1990	10.67	51.21
2	1949	10.64	51.15
3	1989	10.54	50.97
4	1959	10.52	50.94
5=	1834	10.51	50.92
5=	1921	10.51	50.92
7	1733	10.50	50.90
8	1779	10.41	50.74
9	1868	10.40	50.72
10	1736	10.33	50.59

TOP 10
HOTTEST CITIES IN THE US

	City	Average temperature			City	Average temperature	
		°C	°F			°C	°F
1	Key West, Florida	25.4	77.8	6	Brownsville, Texas	23.1	73.8
2	Miami, Florida	24.2	75.9	7=	Tampa, Florida	22.2	72.4
3	West Palm Beach, Florida	23.7	74.7	7=	Vero Beach, Florida	22.4	72.4
4	Fort Myers, Florida	23.3	74.4	9	Corpus Christi, Texas	22.3	71.6
5	Yuma, Arizona	23.3	74.2	10	Daytona Beach, Florida	21.3	70.4

LIFE ON EARTH

TOP 10

LARGEST DINOSAURS EVER DISCOVERED

1 *Seismosaurus*
Length: 30–36 m/98–119 ft
Estimated weight: 50–80 tonnes

A skeleton of this colossal plant-eater was excavated in 1985 near Albuquerque, New Mexico, USA, by US palaeontologist David Gillette, and given a name that means "earth-shaking lizard". It is being studied by the New Mexico Museum of Natural History, which may confirm its position as the largest dinosaur, with some claiming a length of up to 52 m/170 ft.

2 *Supersaurus*
Length: 24–30 m/80–100 ft
Estimated weight: 50 tonnes

The remains of Supersaurus *were found in Colorado, USA, in 1972. Some scientists have suggested a length of up to 42 m/138 ft.*

3 *Antarctosaurus*
Length: 18–30 m/60–98 ft
Estimated weight: 40–50 tonnes

Named Antarctosaurus *("southern lizard") by German palaeontologist Friedrich von Huene in 1929, this creature's thigh bone alone measures 2.3 m/ 7 ft 6 in.*

4 *Barosaurus*
Length: 23–27.5 m/75–90 ft
Weight uncertain

Barosaurus *(meaning "heavy lizard", so named by US palaeontologist Othniel C. Marsh in 1890) has been found in both North America and Africa, thus proving the existence of a land link between these continents in Jurassic times (205–140 million years ago).*

5 *Mamenchisaurus*
Length: 27 m/89 ft
Weight uncertain

An almost complete skeleton discovered in 1972 showed it had the longest neck of any known animal, comprising more than half its total body length. It was named by Chinese palaeontologist Yang Zhong-Jian (known in palaeontological circles as "C.C. Young") after the place in China where it was found.

6 *Diplodocus*
Length: 23–27 m/75–89 ft
Estimated weight: 12 tonnes

Diplodocus *was probably one of the most stupid dinosaurs, having the smallest brain in relation to its body size.*

7 *Ultrasauros*
Length: Over 25 m/82 ft
Estimated weight: 50 tonnes

Ultrasauros *was discovered by James A. Jensen in Colorado in 1979 but has not yet been fully studied. It was originally called "Ultrasaurus" ("ultra lizard"), which, it turned out, was a name also given to another, smaller dinosaur. To avoid confusion, its spelling was altered.*

8 *Brachiosaurus*
Length: 25 m/82 ft
Estimated weight: 50 tonnes

Some palaeontologists have put the weight of Brachiosaurus *as high as 190 tonnes, but this seems improbable.*

9 *Pelorosaurus*
Length: 24 m/80 ft
Weight uncertain

The first fragments of Pelorosaurus *("monstrous lizard") were found in Sussex and named by British doctor and geologist Gideon Algernon Mantell as early as 1850.*

10 *Apatosaurus*
Length: 20–21 m/66–70 ft
Estimated weight: 20–30 tonnes

Apatosaurus *(its name means "deceptive lizard") is better known by its former name of* Brontosaurus *("thunder reptile"). The bones of the first one ever found, in Colorado in 1879, caused great confusion for many years because its discoverer attached a head from a different species to the rest of the skeleton.*

DIPLODOCUS

FIRST DINOSAURS TO BE NAMED

Name/meaning/named by	Year
1 *Megalosaurus*, Great lizard, William Buckland	1824
2 *Iguanodon*, Iguana tooth, Gideon Mantell	1825
3 *Hylaeosaurus*, Woodland lizard, Gideon Mantell	1832
4 *Macrodontophion*, Large tooth snake, A. Zborzewski	1834
5= *Thecodontosaurus*, Socket-toothed lizard, Samuel Stutchbury and H. Riley	1836
5= *Palaeosaurus*, Ancient lizard, Samuel Stutchbury and H. Riley	1836
7 *Plateosaurus*, Flat lizard, Hermann von Meyer	1837
8= *Cladeiodon*, Branch tooth, Richard Owen	1841
8= *Cetiosaurus*, Whale lizard, Richard Owen	1841
10 *Pelorosaurus*, Monstrous lizard, Gideon Mantell	1850

The first 10 dinosaurs were all identified and named within a quarter of a century – although subsequent research has since cast doubt on the authenticity of certain specimens. The name *Megalosaurus*, the first to be given to a dinosaur, was proposed by William Buckland (1784–1856), an English geologist who was also Dean of Westminster and a noted eccentric. Acknowledging that the name had been suggested to him by another clergyman-geologist, the Rev. William Daniel Conybeare, Buckland first used it in an article, "Notice on the *Megalosaurus* or Great Fossil Lizard of Stonesfield," which was published in 1824. *Iguanodon*, the second dinosaur to be named, was identified by Gideon Algernon Mantell (1790–1852). Mantell found the first *Iguanodon* teeth in 1822 in a pile of stones being used for road repairs in the Tilgate Forest area of Sussex. After detailed study, he concluded that they resembled an enormous version of the teeth of the Central American iguana lizard, and hence suggested the name *Iguanodon*.

AS DEAD AS A DODO
The dodo, a flightless member of the dove family, was discovered in 1598, and specimens were taken to Europe where its ungainly appearance was greeted with astonishment. Within 100 years, entirely as a result of human activity in hunting them down, the Dodo had disappeared, its name becoming a synonym for "extinct", as in "dead as a dodo".

FINAL DATES THAT 10 ANIMALS WERE LAST SEEN ALIVE

Animal	Last seen alive
1 Aurochs	1627

This giant wild ox, once described by Julius Caesar, was last recorded in central Europe after the advance of agriculture forced it to retreat from its former territory, which once stretched to the west as far as Britain. It was extensively hunted, and the last few specimens died on the Jaktorow Forest in Poland.

2 *Aepyornis*	1649

Also known as the "Elephant bird", the 3 m/10 ft wingless bird was a native of Madagascar.

3 Dodo	1681

Discovered by European travellers in 1507, specimens of this curious bird were extensively collected – its lack of flight and tameness making it extremely vulnerable to being caught. Its name comes from the Portuguese word duodo, *meaning "stupid". The last dodo seen alive was on the island of Mauritius in 1681, where it was observed by English naturalist Benjamin Harry.*

4 Steller's sea cow	1768

This large marine mammal, named after its 1741 discoverer, German naturalist Georg Wilhelm Steller, and one of the creatures that gave rise to the legend of the mermaid, was rapidly hunted to extinction. The spectacled cormorant, which Steller also found, became extinct at about the same time.

5 Great auk	1844

The last example in Britain of a breeding Pinguinus impennis *– a flightless North Atlantic seabird – was seen nesting in the Orkneys in 1812; the last example ever seen in Britain was in 1821 when one was killed for food on St. Kilda. The last surviving pair in the world was killed on 4 June 1844 on Eldey island on behalf of an Icelandic collector called Carl Siemsen. A stuffed example, collected in 1821 by Count F.C. Raben, was sold at Sotheby's, London, in 1971 to the Natural History Museum of Iceland. A further example was sold by the University of Durham on 21 September 1977 for £4,200. There are possibly as many as 80 specimens in natural history collections around the world.*

6 Tarpan	1851

This European wild horse was last seen in the Ukraine. Przewalski's horse, another wild horse thought to be extinct, has been rediscovered in Mongolia. New, captive-bred stock has been re-introduced into its former range around the fringes of the Gobi Desert.

7 Quagga	1883

This zebra-like creature, found in South Africa and first recorded in 1685, was hunted by European settlers for food and leather to such an extent that by 1870 the last specimen in the wild had been killed. Examples sent to European collectors and zoos survived but failed to reproduce in captivity and steadily died out. The last example, a female in Amsterdam Zoo, died on 12 August 1883.

8 Pilori muskrat	1902

The species became extinct following the 8 May 1902 eruption of Mont Pelée, Martinique, which destroyed its habitat.

9 Passenger pigeon	1914

The passenger pigeon's last moment can be stated precisely. At 1.00 pm on 1 September 1914 at Cincinnati Zoo, a 29-year-old bird named Martha expired. There had once been vast flocks of passenger pigeons, with estimated totals running to a staggering five to nine billion in the 19th century. However as they were remorselessly killed for food and to protect farm crops in the US, and since the bird laid just one egg each season, its decline was almost inevitable. By 24 March 1900 (when the last passenger pigeon in the wild was shot), it was virtually extinct, with only a few specimens, such as Martha, in zoos.

10 Heath hen	1932

*The grouse-like prairie chicken known as the Heath hen (*Tympanuchus cupido cupido*) was extensively hunted in the New England states until only a few specimens survived, all on the island of Martha's Vineyard, Massachusetts. Despite conservation measures to protect them, many birds were killed in a forest fire in 1916, and a virus decimated the survivors, the last of them dying on 11 March 1932.*

ENDANGERED ANIMALS

THE 10

MOST ENDANGERED MAMMALS IN THE WORLD

	Mammal	Estimated number
1=	Tasmanian wolf	?
1=	Halcon fruit bat	?
1=	Ghana fat mouse	?
4	Javan rhinoceros	50
5	Iriomote cat	60
6	Black lion tamarin	130
7	Pygmy hog	150
8	Kouprey	100–200
9	Tamarau	200
10	Indus dolphin	400

THE 10

MOST ENDANGERED BIRDS IN THE UK

1	Red-backed shrike
2	Common crane
3	White-tailed eagle
4	Bittern
5	Marsh warbler
6	Corncrake
7	Roseate tern
8	Red-necked phalarope
9	Montagu's harrier
10	Tree sparrow

TOP 10

RAREST MARINE MAMMALS

	Mammal	Estimated no.
1	Caribbean monk seal	200
2	Mediterranean monk seal	400
3	Juan Fernandez fur seal	750
4	West Indian manatee	1,000
5	Guadeloupe fur seal	1,600
6	New Zealand fur seal	2,000
7=	Hooker's sea lion	4,000
7=	Right whale	4,000
9	Fraser's dolphin	7,800
10	Amazon manatee	8,000

The hunting of seals for their fur and of whales for oil and other products has resulted in a sharp decline in their populations. Populations of some species of seal formerly numbering millions have shrunk to a few thousand, and it has been estimated that the world population of humpback whales has dwindled from 100,000 to 10,000.

PYGMY HOG
It is hoped that the smallest known pig, the pygmy hog, a rare inhabitant of the Himalayan foothills, will be rescued through the creation of a forest reserve in India.

THE 10

COUNTRIES IMPORTING MOST RAW IVORY

	Country	Weight per annum kg	lb
1	Hong Kong	179,608	395,967
2	Japan	100,985	222,634
3	China	50,384	111,078
4	Belgium	38,730	85,385
5	Singapore	17,722	39,070
6	USA	4,803	10,589
7	France	4,486	9,890
8	UK	4,222	9,308
9	India	3,879	8,552
10	Taiwan	2,955	6,515

Most elephant ivory comes from Africa and goes to the Far East as raw material for a carving industry that then re-exports its products worldwide. Western countries such as Belgium have acted as conduits for this trade, as have several African countries, including Burundi and Djibouti, which have virtually no wild elephants of their own.

THE 10

COUNTRIES EXPORTING MOST IVORY

	Country	Weight per annum kg	lb
1	Hong Kong	299,692	135,938
2	Singapore	100,586	221,754
3	Japan	33,139	73,059
4	Belgium	24,034	52,986
5	Somalia	22,638	49,908
6	Tanzania	22,581	49,783
7	Congo	18,806	41,460
8	Gabon	13,542	29,855
9	Zaïre	11,009	24,271
10	Djibouti	10,901	24,033

SAVING NATURE

The US Endangered Species Act is regarded as one of the most important pieces of legislation ever enacted to protect animals and plants. The Act made it an offence to destroy species or their habitats, or to engage in such activities as importing or trading in certain animals, birds' eggs, and rare plants, and established recovery plans for many species. Endangered species that are at risk of extinction, and threatened species (at risk of becoming endangered) are included. Animals on the list encompass large, popular creatures, such as bears and deer, and rare but less familiar birds, reptiles, fish, and insects. At 31 January 1997, the total stood at 444 animals and 623 plants.

ELEPHANTS UNDER THREAT

The elephant has been associated with humans for thousands of years, and has been used for hunting, in warfare, for transport, and in the logging industry. There were once millions of African elephants, and as recently as the beginning of this century there were at least 100,000 Asian elephants. Destruction of natural habitats, extensive poaching for ivory and hide and, in Asia, for use in traditional medicine, has reduced the populations of both African and Asian elephants. In 1996 their total populations were reckoned to be 286,234 and between 37,860 and 48,740 respectively. Extensive programmes have been established to rescue them from their threatened status.

TUSK TRADE
Despite an international ban since 1991, the illegal poaching and smuggling of ivory continues to endanger the elephant populations of certain countries.

BABY ELEPHANT
Protected in game reserves, elephants can now breed without threat.

TOP 10

COUNTRIES WITH THE MOST ELEPHANTS

	Country	Elephants
1	Tanzania	73,459*
2	Zaïre	65,974 #
3	Botswana	62,998*
4	Gabon	61,794 +
5	Zimbabwe	56,297*
6	Congo	32,563 #
7	India	20,000 ★
8	Zambia	19,701*
9	Kenya	13,834*
10	South Africa	9,990*

* Definite
\# Probable
+ Possible
★ Minimum

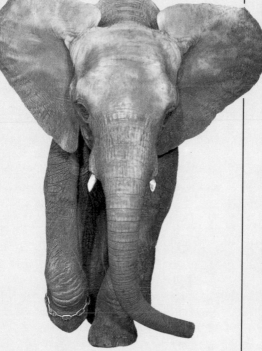

BIG GAME
Once numbered in their millions, hunting has decimated the huge herds of elephants that once roamed Africa and Asia.

LAND ANIMALS

SLOTHFUL SLOTH
One of nature's most somnolent creatures, even the name of the sloth has become a synonym for extreme laziness.

TOP 10

DEADLIEST SNAKES IN THE WORLD

	Snake	Native region
1	Saw-scales or carpet viper	Africa and Asia

This snake is considered the most dangerous for various reasons: it is relatively common, prone to biting, and injects a large amount of highly toxic venom. It probably kills as many as 8,000 people a year in Asia alone.

2=	Taipan	Australia and New Guinea

Taipans have very long fangs and are able to deliver a large quantity of venom. Mortality is practically 100 per cent unless antivenin is administered immediately.

2=	Black mamba	Southern and Central Africa

Death is nearly 100 per cent without antivenin.

4	Tiger snake	Australia

Mortality is very high without antivenin.

5	Common krait	South Asia

Even with antivenin mortality is up to 50 per cent.

6	Death adder	Australia

Without antivenin mortality is over 50 per cent, but prompt treatment saves most victims.

7	Yellow or Cape cobra	Southern Africa

This is the most dangerous type of cobra in the world, with a high mortality rate.

8	King cobra	India and Southeast Asia

At 4.9 m/16 ft long, the king cobra is the largest poisonous snake in the world. It also injects the most venom into its victims.

9=	Bushmaster	Central and South America
9=	Green mamba	Africa

Most people fear snakes, but only a few dozen of the 3,500-odd snake species that exist cause serious harm. Measuring the strength of the venom of snakes is technically possible, but this factor does not indicate how dangerous they may be. This Top 10 takes account of the degree of threat posed by those snakes that have a record of causing fatalities.

TOP 10

LAZIEST ANIMALS IN THE WORLD

	Animal	Average hours of sleep		Animal	Average hours of sleep
1	Koala	22	**6=**	Hamster	14
2	Sloth	20	**6=**	Squirrel	14
3=	Armadillo	19	**8=**	Cat	13
3=	Opossum	19	**8=**	Pig	13
5	Lemur	16	**10**	Spiny anteater	12

This list excludes periods of hibernation, which can last up to several months among creatures such as the ground squirrel. At the other end of the scale comes the frantic shrew, which has to hunt and eat constantly, or else perish: it literally has no time for sleep. The incredible swift contrives to sleep on the wing, "turning off" alternate halves of its brain for shifts of two hours or more. Flight control is entrusted to whichever hemisphere of the brain is on duty at the time.

TOP 10

LONGEST SNAKES IN THE WORLD

	Snake	Maximum length m	ft
1	Reticulated (Royal) python	10.7	35
2	Anaconda	8.5	28
3	Indian python	7.6	25
4	Diamond python	6.4	21
5	King cobra	5.8	19
6	Boa constrictor	4.9	16
7	Bushmaster	3.7	12
8	Giant brown snake	3.4	11
9	Diamondback rattlesnake	2.7	9
10	Indigo or gopher snake	2.4	8

Although the South American anaconda is sometimes claimed to be the longest snake, this has not been authenticated, and therefore the python remains at No. 1.

TOP 10

LONGEST LAND ANIMALS IN THE WORLD

	Animal	Maximum length m	ft
1	Reticulated (Royal) python	10.7	35
2	Tapeworm	10.0	33
3	African elephant	7.3	24
4	Crocodile	5.9	19
5	Giraffe	5.8	19
6	White rhinoceros	4.2	14
7	Hippopotamus	4.0	13
8	American bison	3.9	13
9	Arabian camel (dromedary)	3.5	12
10	Siberian tiger	3.3	11

TOP 10

HEAVIEST TERRESTRIAL MAMMALS IN THE WORLD*

Mammal	Length		Weight	
	m	ft	kg	lb
1 African elephant	7.3	24	7,000	14,432
2 Whiterhinoceros	4.2	14	3,600	7,937
3 Hippopotamus	4.0	13	2,500	5,512
4 Giraffe	5.8	19	1,600	2,527
5 American bison	3.9	13	1,000	2,205
6 Arabian camel (dromedary)	3.5	12	690	1,521
7 Polar bear	3.0	10	600	1,323
8 Moose	3.0	10	550	1,213
9 Siberian tiger	3.3	11	300	661
10 Gorilla	2.0	7	220	485

* *Excluding domesticated cattle and horses*

TOP 10

MOST COMMON MAMMALS IN THE UK

Mammal	Estimated number
1 Common rat	76,790,000
2 House mouse	75,192,000
3 Field vole	75,000,000
4 Common shrew	41,700,000
5 Wood mouse	38,000,000
6 Rabbit	37,500,000
7 Mole	31,000,000
8 Bank vole	23,000,000
9 Pygmy shrew	8,600,000
10 Grey squirrel	2,520,000

TOP 10

MOST PROLIFIC WILD MAMMALS IN THE WORLD

Animal	Average litter
1 Malagasy tenrec	25
2 Virginian opossum	22
3 Golden hamster	11
4 Ermine	10
5 Prairie vole	9
6 Coypu	8.5
7= European hedgehog	7
7= African hunting dog	7
9= Meadow vole	6.5
9= Wild boar	6.5

TOP 10

FASTEST MAMMALS IN THE WORLD

Mammal	Maximum recorded speed		Mammal	Maximum recorded speed	
	km/h	mph		km/h	mph
1 Cheetah	105	65	5= Thomson's gazelle	76	47
2 Pronghorn antelope	89	55	7 Brown hare	72	45
3= Mongolian gazelle	80	50	8 Horse	69	43
3= Springbok	80	50	9= Greyhound	68	42
5= Grant's gazelle	76	47	9= Red deer	68	42

TOP 10

MOST INTELLIGENT MAMMALS

1	Human
2	Chimpanzee
3	Gorilla
4	Orang-utan
5	Baboon
6	Gibbon
7	Monkey
8	Smaller toothed whale
9	Dolphin
10	Elephant

This list is based on research conducted by Edward O. Wilson, Professor of Zoology at Harvard University, USA, who defined intelligence as speed and extent of learning performance over a wide range of tasks, also taking account of the ratio of an animal's brain size to its body bulk. It may come as a surprise that the dog does not make it into this Top 10; a recent study of 133 dog breeds by the US psychologist Stanley Coren showed that there is a wide range of intelligence within the species.

DID YOU KNOW

WORLD CHAMPION SPRINTER

Although animals such as pronghorn antelopes can sustain high speeds for longer periods of time, the cheetah is the fastest animal over short distances. It can accelerate to 96 km/h/60 mph in three seconds from a standing start. Tests conducted in 1937 at Harringay Stadium, a greyhound racing track in London, UK, and further tests carried out in the US in 1960, were inconclusive since cheetahs in captivity are reluctant to run. However, analysis of films of cheetahs in the wild indicate that they can easily cover 7 m/23 ft with a single stride of 0.28 seconds duration – equivalent to 90 km/h/56 mph – and exceed that in short bursts of speed.

MARINE ANIMALS

T O P 1 0

HEAVIEST MARINE MAMMALS

	Mammal	Length m	ft	in	Weight (tonnes)
1	Blue whale	33.5	110	0	130.0
2	Fin whale	25.0	82	0	45.0
3	Right whale	17.5	57	5	40.0
4	Sperm whale	18.0	59	0	36.0
5	Gray whale	14.0	46	0	32.7
6	Humpback whale	15.0	49	2	26.5
7	Baird's whale	5.5	18	0	11.0
8	Southern elephant seal	6.5	21	4	3.6
9	Northern elephant seal	5.8	19	0	3.4
10	Pilot whale	6.4	21	0	2.9

Probably the largest animal that ever lived, the blue whale dwarfs even the other whales listed here, all but one of which far outweigh the biggest land animal, the elephant.

T O P 1 0

FISHING COUNTRIES

	Country	Annual catch (tonnes)
1	China	17,567,907
2	Peru	8,450,600
3	Japan	8,128,121
4	Chile	6,037,985
5	USA	5,939,339
6	Russia	4,461,375
7	India	4,232,060
8	Indonesia	3,637,700
9	Thailand	3,348,149
10	South Korea	2,648,977

T O P 1 0

LARGEST TURTLES AND TORTOISES

	Turtle/tortoise	Maximum weight kg	lb
1	Pacific leatherback turtle	865	1,908
2	Atlantic leatherback turtle	454	1,000
3=	Green sea turtle	408	900
3=	Aldabra giant tortoise	408	900
5	Loggerhead turtle	386	850
6	Galapagos giant or elephant tortoise	385	849
7	Alligator snapping turtle	183	403
8	Black sea turtle	126	278
9	Flatback turtle	84	185
10	Hawksbill turtle	68	150

Both the size and the longevity of turtles and tortoises remain hotly debated by zoologists. Although the weights on which this Top 10 are ranked are from corroborated sources, there are many claims of even larger specimens among the 265 living species of *Chelonia* (turtles and tortoises). The largest are marine turtles, while the Aldabra giant tortoises are the largest of the land-dwellers – and probably the longest-lived land creatures of all, at more than 150 years. The Alligator snapping turtle is the largest freshwater species. However, all living examples would be dwarfed in size by prehistoric monster turtles such as *Stupendemys geographicus*, that measured up to 3 m/10 ft in length and weighed over 2,040 kg/4,497 lb.

T O P 1 0

FASTEST FISH IN THE WORLD

	Fish	Maximum recorded speed km/h	mph
1	Sailfish	110	68
2	Marlin	80	50
3	Bluefin tuna	74	46
4	Yellowfin tuna	70	44
5	Blue shark	69	43
6	Wahoo	66	41
7=	Bonefish	64	40
7=	Swordfish	64	40
9	Tarpon	56	35
10	Tiger shark	53	33

Flying fish have a top speed in the water of only 37 km/h/23 mph, but airborne they can reach 56 km/h/35 mph. Many sharks qualify for this list: only two are listed here to prevent the list becoming overly shark-infested. But just in case you thought it was safe to go back in the water, the great white shark (of *Jaws* fame) can manage speeds of 48 km/h/30 mph with ease. For any smaller fish (up to the size of a pike or salmon) a handy formula for estimating an individual's top speed is just over 10 times its own length in centimetres per second: thus a trout 15 cm/5½ in long swims at 160 cm/58 in per second, or 5.8 km/h/3.6 mph.

BLUEFIN TUNA

MARLIN

SAILFISH

TOP 10

LARGEST SPECIES OF SALTWATER FISH CAUGHT IN THE WORLD

	Species	Angler/location/date	Weight kg	g	lb	oz
1	Great white shark	Alfred Dean, Ceduna, South Australia, 1959	1,208	39	2,664	0
2	Tiger shark	Walter Maxwell, Cherry Grove, Southern California, USA, 1964	807	41	1,780	0
3	Greenland shark	Terje Nordtvedt, Trondheimsfjord, Norway, 1987	775	0	1,708	9
4	Black marlin	A. C. Glassell, Jr., Cabo Blanco, Peru, 1953	707	62	1,560	0
5	Bluefin tuna	Ken Fraser, Aulds Cove, Nova Scotia, Canada, 1979	678	59	1,496	0
6	Pacific blue marlin	Jay W. de Beaubien, Kaaiwi Point, Kona, Honolulu, 1982	624	15	1,376	0
7	Atlantic blue marlin	Larry Martin, St. Thomas, Virgin Islands, 1977	581	52	1,282	0
8	Swordfish	L. Marron, Iquique, Chile, 1953	536	16	1,182	0
9	Mako shark	Patrick Guillanton, Black River, Mauritius, 1988	505	76	1,115	0
10	Hammerhead shark	Allen Ogle, Sarasota, Florida, USA, 1982	449	52	991	0

TOP 10

LARGEST SPECIES OF FRESHWATER FISH CAUGHT IN THE WORLD

	Species	Angler/location/date	Weight kg	g	lb	oz
1	White sturgeon	Joey Pallotta III, Benicia, California, USA, 1983	212	28	468	0
2	Alligator gar	Bill Valverde, Rio Grande, Texas, USA, 1951	126	55	279	0
3	Nile perch	Kurt M. Fenster, Tende Bay, Entebbe, Uganda, 1989	68	98	152	1
4	Chinook salmon	Les Anderson, Kenai River, Arkansas, USA, 1985	44	11	97	4
5=	Blue catfish	Edward B. Elliott, Missouri River, South Dakota, USA, 1959	44	00	97	0
5=	Tigerfish	Raymond Houtmans, Zaïre River, Kinshasa, Zaïre, 1988	44	00	97	0
7	Lake sturgeon	James M. DeOtis, Kettle River, Montana, USA, 1986	41	84	92	4
8	Flathead catfish	Mike Rogers, Lake Lewisville, Texas, USA, 1982	41	39	91	4
9	Atlantic salmon	Henrik Henrikson, Tana River, Norway, 1928	35	89	79	2
10	Carp	Leo van der Gugten, Lac de St Cassien, France, 1987	34	33	75	11

IN THE CAN
Sardines, along with other species of herring and pilchard, are components of a world fishing industry that in the 1990s first topped 100 million tonnes a year.

TOP 10

SPECIES OF FISH MOST CAUGHT WORLDWIDE

	Species	Tonnes caught per annum
1	Anchoveta	11,896,808
2	Alaska pollock	4,298,619
3	Chilean jack mackerel	4,254,629
4	Silver carp	2,333,669
5	Atlantic herring	1,886,105
6	Grass carp	1,821,606
7	South American pilchard	1,793,425
8	Common carp	1,627,198
9	Chubb mackerel	1,507,497
10	Skipjack tuna	1,462,637

The Food and Agriculture Organization of the United Nations estimates the volume of the world's fishing catch, which totals almost 110,000,000 tonnes a year, of which about 75,000,000 tonnes is reckoned to be destined for human consumption – equivalent to approximately 13 kg/29 lbs a year for every inhabitant. The foremost species, anchoveta, are small anchovies used principally as bait to catch tuna. In recent years, the amount of carp has increased markedly. Among broader groupings, some 3,000,000 tonnes of shrimps and prawns and a similar tonnage of squids, cuttlefish, and octopuses, are caught annually.

FLYING ANIMALS

TOP 10
SMALLEST BATS IN THE WORLD

Bat/habitat	Weight gm	oz	Length cm	in
1 Kitti's hognosed bat (*Craseonycteris thonglongyai*), Thailand	2.0	0.07	2.9	1.10
2 Proboscis bat (*Rhynchonycteris naso*), Central and South America	2.5	0.09	3.8	1.50
3= Banana bat (*Pipistrellus nanus*), Central Africa	3.0	0.11	3.8	1.50
3= Smoky bat (*Furiptera horrens*), Central and South America	3.0	0.11	3.8	1.50
5= Little yellow bat (*Rhogeessa mira*), Central America	3.5	0.12	4.0	1.57
5= Lesser bamboo bat (*Tylonycteris pachypus*), Southeast Asia	3.5	0.12	4.0	1.57
7 Disc-winged bat (*Thyroptera tricolor*), Central and South America	4.0	0.14	3.6	1.42
8 Lesser horseshoe bat (*Rhynolophus hipposideros*), Europe and Western Asia	5.0	0.18	3.7	1.46
9 California myotis (*Myotis californienses*), North America	5.0	0.18	4.3	1.69
10 Northern blossom bat (*Macroglossus minimus*), Southeast Asia to Australia	15.0	0.53	6.4	2.52

TOP 10
LARGEST FLIGHTED BIRDS

Bird	Weight kg	lb	oz
1 Great bustard	20.9	46	1
2 Trumpeter swan	16.8	37	1
3 Mute swan	16.3	35	15
4= Albatross	15.8	34	13
4= Whooper swan	15.8	34	13
6 Manchurian crane	14.9	32	14
7 Kori bustard	13.6	30	0
8 Grey pelican	13.0	28	11
9 Black vulture	12.5	27	8
10 Griffon vulture	12.0	26	7

TOP 10
LARGEST BIRDS OF PREY*

Bird	Length cm	in
1 Californian condor	124	49
2= Steller's sea eagle	114	45
2= Lammergeier	114	45
4 Bald eagle	109	43
5= Andean condor	107	42
5= European black vulture	107	42
5= Ruppell's griffon	107	42
8 Griffon vulture	104	41
9 Wedge-tailed eagle	102	40
10 Lappet-faced vulture	100	39

* Diurnal only – hence excluding owls

The entrants in this Top 10 all measure more than 1 m/39 in from beak to tail, but birds of prey generally have smaller body weights than those appearing in the list of 10 largest flighted birds. All of these raptors, or aerial hunters, have remarkable eyesight and can spot their victims from great distances. However, even if they kill animals heavier than themselves, they are generally unable to take wing with them: stories of eagles carrying off lambs and small children are usually fictitious.

GROUNDED
Some of the largest living birds – as well as some that are now extinct – are incapable of flight, and have become adapted to life on the ground.

OSTRICH
274.3 cm (108 in)

CASSOWARY
152.4 cm (60 in)

EMPEROR PENGUIN
114 cm (45 in)

TOP 10
LARGEST FLIGHTLESS BIRDS

Bird	Weight kg	lb	oz	Height cm	in
1 Ostrich	156.5	345	0	274.3	108
2 Emu	40.0	88	3	152.4	60
3 Cassowary	33.5	73	14	152.4	60
4 Rhea	25.0	55	2	137.1	54
5 Emperor penguin	29.4	64	13	114.0	45
6 Flightless cormorant	4.5	9	15	95.0	37¹/₃
7 Flightless steamer	5.5	12	2	84.0	33
8 Kakapo	2.5	5	8	66.0	26
9 Kagu	5.0	11	0	59.9	23³/₅
10 Kiwi	3.5	7	12	55.9	22

TOP 10
MOST COMMON BIRDS IN GREAT BRITAIN

	Species	Estimated number of breeding pairs
1	Wren	7,100,000
2	Chaffinch	5,400,000
3	Blackbird	4,400,000
4	Robin	4,200,000
5	House sparrow	3,600,000
6	Blue tit	3,300,000
7	Willow warbler	2,300,000
8	Wood pigeon	2,150,000
9	Hedge sparrow	2,000,000
10	Great tit	1,600,000

TOP 10
BIRDS WITH THE LARGEST WINGSPANS

	Bird	Maximum wingspan m	ft
1	Marabou stork	4.0	13
2	Albatross	3.7	12
3	Trumpeter swan	3.4	11
4=	Mute swan	3.1	10
4=	Whooper swan	3.1	10
4=	Grey pelican	3.1	10
4=	Californian condor	3.1	10
4=	Black vulture	3.1	10
9=	Great bustard	2.7	9
9=	Kori bustard	2.7	9

WINGED WONDER
The albatross is among the world's largest birds, with one of the most impressive wingspans. It is compared here with a seagull.

TOP 10
LARGEST BIRDS IN THE UK

	Bird	Beak to tail length cm	in
1=	Mute swan	145–160	57–63
1=	Whooper swan	145-160	57-63
3	Bewick's swan	116–128	46–50
4	Canada goose	up to 110	up to 43
5	Grey heron	90–100	35–39
6	Cormorant	84–98	33–39
7	Gannet	86–96	34–38
8	Golden eagle	76–91	30–36
9	White-tailed sea eagle	69–91	27–36
10	Capercaillie (male)	82–90	32–35

SWIFT BY NAME...
...and swift by nature, it holds the world record for avian speed.

TOP 10
FASTEST BIRDS IN THE WORLD

	Bird	Maximum recorded speed km/h	mph
1	Spine-tailed swift	171	106
2	Frigate bird	153	95
3	Spur-winged goose	142	88
4	Red-breasted merganser	129	80
5	White-rumped swift	124	77
6	Canvasback duck	116	72
7	Eider duck	113	70
8	Teal	109	68
9=	Mallard	105	65
9=	Pintail	105	65

Until pilots cracked 306 km/h/190 mph in 1919, birds were the fastest creatures on the Earth: diving peregrine falcons approach 298 km/h/185 mph.
However, most comparisons of the air speed of birds rule out diving or wind-assisted flight: most small birds on migration can manage a ground speed (speed relative to ground) of 97 km/h/60 mph to 113 km/h/70 mph. This list therefore picks out star performers among the medium- to large-sized birds that do not need help from wind or gravity to hit their top speed.

TOP 10
LONGEST AERIAL MIGRATIONS

	Bird	Maximum migration km	miles
1	Arctic tern	20,117	12,500
2	Parasitic jaeger	16,093	10,000
3=	Baird's sandpiper	15,450	9,600
3=	Pectoral sandpiper	15,450	9,600
5=	Gray-headed albatross	14,967	9,300
5=	Hudsonian godwit	14,967	9,300
5=	Lesser yellowlegs	14,967	9,300
5=	Light-mantled sooty albatross	14,967	9,300
5=	Northern giant petrel	14,967	9,300
5=	Pomarine jaeger	14,967	9,300
5=	Red phalarope	14,967	9,300
5=	Royal albatross	14,967	9,300
5=	Ruddy turnstone	14,967	9,300
5=	Southern polar skua	14,967	9,300
5=	Surfbird	14,967	9,300
5=	Wandering tattler	14,967	9,300
5=	Whimbrel	14,967	9,300
5=	White-rumped sandpiper	14,967	9,300

LIVESTOCK

T O P 1 0

TYPES OF LIVESTOCK IN THE WORLD

	Livestock	World total
1	Chickens	12,664,000,000
2	Cattle	1,306,476,000
3	Sheep	1,067,566,000
4	Pigs	900,480,000
5	Ducks	715,000,000
6	Goats	639,400,000
7	Turkeys	230,000,000
8	Buffaloes	151,514,000
9	Horses	60,894,000
10	Donkeys	43,762,000

The 17,779,092,000 animals accounted for by this Top 10 outnumber the world's human population by three to one. The world's chicken population is more than double the human population, while the world's cattle population outnumbers the population of China.

COUNTING SHEEP
Ranking third in the global livestock inventory, sheep actually outnumber the human populations of certain countries.

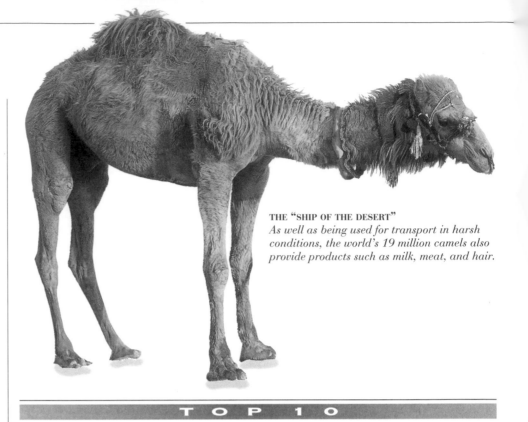

THE "SHIP OF THE DESERT"
As well as being used for transport in harsh conditions, the world's 19 million camels also provide products such as milk, meat, and hair.

T O P 1 0

COUNTRIES WITH MOST CAMELS

	Country	Camels		Country	Camels
1	Somalia	6,200,000	6	Ethiopia	1,000,000
2	Sudan	2,903,000	7	Kenya	810,000
3	India	1,520,000	8	Chad	600,000
4	Pakistan	1,119,000	9	Saudi Arabia	418,000
5	Mauritania	1,087,000	10	Mongolia	390,000
				World total	*19,241,000*

T O P 1 0

COUNTRIES WHERE SHEEP MOST OUTNUMBER PEOPLE

	Country	Sheep	Human population	Sheep per person
1	Falkland Islands	717,000	2,121	338.05
2	New Zealand	47,144,000	3,494,300	13.49
3	Uruguay	22,685,000	3,116,800	7.28
4	Australia	120,651,000	18,114,000	6.66
5	Mongolia	13,719,000	2,363,000	5.81
6	Mauritania	5,288,000	2,217,000	2.39
7	Kazakhstan	33,524,000	16,963,600	1.98
8	Iceland	470,000	266,786	1.76
9	Namibia	2,620,000	1,500,000	1.75
10	Somalia	13,500,000	9,077,000	1.49

The estimated total world sheep population is 1,067,566,000 – a global average of one sheep for every 5.62 people (or 0.2 people per sheep) – but as this Top 10 shows, there are a number of countries where the tables are turned, and sheep considerably outnumber humans.

TOP 10

WOOL-PRODUCING COUNTRIES

	Country	Annual production (tonnes)
1	Australia	700,000
2	New Zealand	280,000
3	China	260,000
4	Russia	94,100
5	Argentina	92,000
6	Kazakhstan	90,000
7	Uruguay	85,345
8	UK	66,714
9	South Africa	61,100
10	Pakistan	53,200
	World total	*2,590,255*

TOP 10

FARM ANIMALS MOST OFTEN TREATED BY VETS IN THE UK

1	Cattle
2	Sheep
3	Goats
4	Pigs
5	Horses
6	Donkeys
7	Deer
8	Poultry
9	Farmed fish
10=	Llamas
10=	Ostriches

The most common livestock naturally receives the greatest proportion of British vets' time (there are 126,000,000 chickens, 29,484,000 sheep, and more than 11,000,000 head of cattle alone in the UK to occupy their attention). It is therefore surprising to find two rare species that are farmed in comparatively minute numbers jostling for position at the bottom of the British Veterinary Association's Top 10.

TOP 10

COUNTRIES WITH MOST TURKEYS

	Country	Turkeys
1	USA	88,000,000
2	France	36,000,000
3	Italy	22,000,000
4	UK	10,000,000
5=	Brazil	6,000,000
5=	Canada	6,000,000
5=	Mexico	6,000,000
8=	Portugal	5,000,000
8=	Germany	5,000,000
10=	Argentina	4,000,000
10=	Israel	4,000,000
10=	Madagascar	4,000,000
	World total	*230,000,000*

TOP 10

BEEF-PRODUCING COUNTRIES

	Country	Annual production (tonnes)
1	USA	11,552,000
2	Brazil	4,620,000
3	China	3,474,000
4	Russia	2,799,000
5	Argentina	2,466,000
6	France	1,899,000
7	Australia	1,803,000
8	Germany	1,407,000
9	Mexico	1,329,000
10	India	1,292,000
	World total	*53,217,000*

China's beef production has increased almost 15-fold since the period 1979–81, during which it was estimated to be 229,000 tonnes per annum. The UK's recent concerns with BSE, or "mad cow disease", have resulted in a decline in beef production that has evicted it from its place in this Top 10.

TOP 10

COUNTRIES WITH MOST PIGS

	Country	Pigs
1	China	424,680,000
2	USA	59,992,000
3	Brazil	35,350,000
4	Germany	24,698,000
5	Russia	22,631,000
6	Poland	20,418,000
7	Spain	18,332,000
8	Mexico	18,000,000
9	Vietnam	16,500,000
10	France	14,593,000
	World total	*900,480,000*

The distribution of the world's pig population is determined by cultural, religious, and dietary factors – few pigs are found in African and Islamic countries, for example – with the result that there is a disproportionate concentration of pigs in countries that do not have such prohibitions – 73 per cent of the world total is found in these Top 10 countries. Denmark, with 11,190,000 pigs and a human population of 5,215,718, is the country in which the pig population most outnumbers the human population (there are others with marginally more pigs than people, such as Tuvalu, with 13,000 pigs and 12,000 humans). The UK has 7,879,000 pigs, or one pig for every eight people.

BRINGING HOME THE BACON
The omnivorous pig has long been domesticated and figures prominently in the mythology and literature of many nations.

CATS, DOGS & OTHER PETS

TOP 10

TYPES OF PET IN THE US

	Pet	Estimated number
1	Cats	66,150,000
2	Dogs	58,200,000
3	Parakeets	14,190,000
4	Small animal pets*	12,740,000
5	Freshwater fish	10,800,000#
6	Reptiles	7,540,000
7	Finches	7,350,000
8	Cockatiels	6,320,000
9	Canaries	2,580,000
10	Parrots	1,550,000

* Includes rabbits, ferrets, hamsters, guinea pigs, and gerbils
# Number of households owning, rather than individual specimens

Source: Pet Industry Joint Advisory Council

TOP 10

TYPES OF PET IN THE UK

	Pet	Percentage of households
1	Dog	26.9
2	Cat	21.5
3	Goldfish	9.1
4	Rabbit	4.5
5	Budgerigar	4.2
6	Tropical fish	2.9
7	Other caged bird(s)	2.8
8	Hamster	2.3
9	Guinea pig	1.5
10	Canary	1.2

TOP 10

PEDIGREE CAT BREEDS IN THE US

	Breed	No. registered*
1	Persian	42,578
2	Maine Coon	4,747
3	Siamese	2,865
4	Abyssinian	2,383
5	Exotic	1,981
6	Oriental	1,371
7	Scottish Fold	1,264
8	American Shorthair	1,032
9	Birman	933
10	Ocicat	868

Of the 36 different breeds of cat listed with the Cat Fancier's Association, these were the Top 10 registered in 1996 out of a total of 68,948. The biggest increase in popularity since the 1980s has been for the Exotic, the rank of which has leapt from 14th in 1982 to its current No. 5 position. The Maine Coon has also consolidated its popularity. Many legends surround this breed: for example, that it is so-called because it resulted from cross-breeding a cat and a racoon; and that it descends from the Angora cats that were owned by Marie Antoinette during the French Revolution.

* To year ending 31 December 1996

TOP 10

PEDIGREE CAT BREEDS IN THE UK

	Breed	No. registered		Breed	No. registered
1	Persian Long Hair	9,312	7	Maine Coon	1,235
2	Siamese	4,896	8	Bengal	787
3	British Short Hair	4,322	9	Ragdoll	771
4	Burmese	3,577	10	Exotic Short Hair	756
5	Birman	2,445			
6	Oriental Short Hair	1,346			

This list is based on a total of 33,579 cats registered with the Governing Council of the Cat Fancy in 1996.

TOP 10
CATS' NAMES IN THE UK*

1	Sooty	6	Tom
2	Tigger	7	Fluffy
3	Tiger	8	Lucy
4	Smokey	9	Sam
5	Ginger	10	Lucky

Based on an RSPCA survey

TOP 10
DOG BREEDS IN THE US

	Breed	No. registered by American Kennel Club, Inc. (1996)
1	Labrador Retriever	149,505
2	Rottweiler	89,867
3	German Shepherd	79,076
4	Golden Retriever	68,993
5	Beagle	56,946
6	Poodle	56,803
7	Dachshund	48,426
8	Cocker Spaniel	45,305
9	Yorkshire Terrier	40,216
10	Pomeranian	39,712

Source: The American Kennel Club

The total registered in 1996 was 1,332,557 – up from 1,277,039 in 1995. The Labrador Retriever tops the list for the sixth consecutive year.

TOP 10
STICK INSECTS' NAMES IN THE UK*

1	Sticky	6	Stick
2	Fred	7	Sam
3	Twiggy	8	Billy
4	Tom	9	Freddie
5	George	10	Charlie

Based on an RSPCA survey

TOP 10
DOG BREEDS IN THE UK

	Breed	No. registered by Kennel Club
1	Labrador Retriever	34,844
2	German Shepherd (Alsatian)	25,690
3	West Highland White Terrier	16,461
4	Golden Retriever	16,442
5	Cocker Spaniel	14,468
6	English Springer Spaniel	14,099
7	Cavalier King Charles Spaniel	13,941
8	Yorkshire Terrier	10,850
9	Boxer	9,827
10	Staffordshire Bull Terrier	8,251

As in the previous year, the 10 principal breeds of dogs registered by the Kennel Club in 1996 remained identical, but with some adjustments to the order. Independent surveys present a similar picture, though certain other popular breeds make a stronger showing than in this list.

TOP 10
BUDGERIGARS' NAMES IN THE UK*

1	Joey	6	Peter
2	Billy	7	Charlie
3	Bluey	8	Magic
4	Bobby	9	George
5	Snowy	10	Tweety

Based on an RSPCA survey

TOP 10
GOLDFISH NAMES IN THE UK*

1	Jaws	6	George
2	Goldie	7	Flipper
3	Fred	8	Ben
4	Tom	9	Jerry
5	Bubbles	10	Sam

Based on an RSPCA survey

TOP 10
DOGS' NAMES IN THE UK

Female		Male
Trixie	1	Sam
Polly	2	Spot
Jessie	3	Pip
Lucy	4	Duke
Bonnie	5	Piper
Cassie	6	Max
Daisy	7	Charlie
Heidi	8	Rocky
Susie	9	Zak
Holly	10	Tiny

As we have observed in previous editions of *The Top 10 of Everything*, a move away from traditional dogs' names occurred during the 1980s, with the demise of perennial (and specifically canine) names such as Shep, Brandy, Whisky, Rex, and Lassie, and an increasing tendency toward human first names. The latest research conducted by the British dog welfare organization, the National Canine Defence League, reveals the arrival of several new names. These include Polly, Jessie, and Cassie for female dogs and Sam, Spot, and Pip for males.

PLANT LIFE

COUNTRIES WITH THE LARGEST AREAS OF FOREST

	Country	Forest cover hectares	acres
1	Russia	765,912,000	1,892,607,000
2	Canada	494,000,000	1,220,699,000
3	Brazil	488,000,000	1,205,872,000
4	USA	295,990,000	731,406,000
5	Congo (Zaïre)	173,800,000	429,468,000
6	Australia	145,000,000	358,302,000
7	China	130,496,000	322,462,000
8	Indonesia	111,774,000	276,199,000
9	Peru	84,800,000	209,545,000
10	India	68,500,000	169,267,000
	World total	4,138,009,000	10,225,227,000

Despite the felling of trees for commercial use and land clearance for other human settlements and agriculture, particularly in the world's rainforests, the planet's total area of forests and woodlands has barely fluctuated in the past quarter-century. In 1972 the forested proportion stood at just over 32 per cent of the world's total land area, and today it is only fractionally under 32 per cent.

MOST ANCIENT BRITISH YEW TREES

	Location	Girth m	ft	Estimated age (years)
1	Fortingall, Tayside*	17.1	56	over 5,000
2=	Llangernyw, Clwyd#	12.2	40	5,000
2=	Discoed, Powys	11.0	36	5,000
4=	Defynnog, Powys	12.2	40	4,000
4=	Linton, Hereford	10.1	33	4,000
4=	Crowhurst, Surrey	9.8	32	4,000
4=	Tisbury, Wilts	9.1	30	4,000
8=	Bettwys Newydd, Gwent	10.1	33	3,000
8=	Farringdon, Hampshire	9.1	30	3,000
10	Ashbrittle, Somerset#+	12.2	40	?#

* Measured in 1769, but now split
\# Estimated measurement, but now split
+ Grows on an ancient tumulus, but impossible to estimate age

THE MIGHTY REDWOOD
Originally there were 40 species of redwood (sequoia), but now there are only three – two in the US and one in China.

TALLEST TREES IN THE US

(The tallest-known example of each of the 10 tallest species)

	Tree	Location	m	ft
1	Coast Douglas fir	Coos County, Oregon	100.3	329
2	Coast redwood	Humboldt Redwoods State Park, California	95.4	313
3	General Sherman giant sequoia	Sequoia National Park, California	83.8	275
4	Noble fir	Mount St. Helens National Monument, Washington	82.9	272
5	Grand fir	Olympic National Park, Washington	76.5	251
6	Western hemlock	Olympic National Park, Washington	73.5	241
7	Sugar pine	Dorrington, California	70.7	232
8	Ponderosa pine	Plumas National Forest, California	68.0	223
9	Port-Orford cedar	Siskiyou National Forest, Oregon	66.8	219
10	Pacific silver fir	Forks, Washington	66.1	217

A coast redwood known as the Dyerville Giant (from Dyerville, California), which stood 110.3 m/362 ft high, fell in a storm on 27 March 1991, and a slightly taller (110.6-m/363-ft) coast redwood, which formerly topped this list, fell during 1992. The General Sherman giant sequoia is reckoned to be the planet's most colossal living thing, weighing some 1,400 tons, which is equivalent to the weight of nine blue whales or 360 elephants.

T O P 1 0

OLDEST BOTANIC GARDENS IN NORTH AMERICA

	Garden	Founded
1	Pierce's Park,* Kennett Square, Pennsylvania	1800
2	United States Botanic Garden, Washington, DC	1820
3	Painter's Arboretum,# Media, Pennsylvania	1830
4	Missouri Botanical Garden, St. Louis, Missouri	1859
5	Arnold Arboretum, Jamaica Plain, Massachusetts	1872
6	Beal-Garfield Botanic Garden, East Lansing, Michigan	1873
7	Dominion Arboretum & Botanic Garden, Ottawa, Ontario, Canada	1886
8	University of California – Berkeley Botanic Garden, Berkeley, California	1890
9	New York Botanical Garden, Bronx, New York	1891
10	Botanic Garden of Smith College, Northampton, Massachusetts	1893

* *Now Longwood Gardens*
\# *Now Tyler's Arboretum*

T O P 1 0

MOST FORESTED COUNTRIES IN THE WORLD
(By per cent of forest cover)

	Country	Forest cover		Country	Forest cover
1	Surinam	92	6	Gabon	74
2	Papua New Guinea	91	7	Finland	69
3	Solomon Islands	85	8=	Bhutan	66
4	French Guiana	81	8=	Japan	66
5	Guyana	77	10	North Korea	65

RAIN FOREST IN SOUTH AMERICA

T O P 1 0

OLDEST BOTANIC GARDENS IN THE UK

	Garden	Founded
1	University Botanic Garden, Oxford	1621
2	Royal Botanic Garden, Edinburgh	1670
3	Chelsea Physic Garden, London	1673
4	Royal Botanic Gardens, Kew	1759
5	Cambridge University Botanic Garden	1762
6	Bath Botanical Gardens	1779
7	Glasgow Botanic Gardens	1817
8	Museum Gardens, York	1827
9	Belfast Botanic Garden	1828
10	Birmingham Botanical Gardens	1839

T O P 1 0

TALLEST TREES IN THE UK*
(The tallest-known example of each of the 10 tallest species)

	Tree	Location	m	ft
1	Douglas fir	The Hermitage, Dunkeld, Tayside	64.5	212
2	Grand fir	Strone House, Argyll, Strathclyde	63.0	207
3	Sitka spruce	Private estate, Strathearn, Tayside	61.5	202
4=	Giant sequoia	Castle Leod, Strathpeffer, Highland	53.0	174
4=	Low's fir	Diana's Grove, Blair Castle, Strathclyde	53.0	174
6=	Noble fir	Ardkinglas House, Argyll, Strathclyde	52.0	171
6=	Norway spruce	Moniac Glenn, Highland	52.0	171
8	Western hemlock	Benmore Younger Botanic Gardens, Argyll, Strathclyde	51.0	167
9	European silver fir	Armadale Castle, Skye, Highland	50.0	164
10	London plane	Bryanstone School, Blandford, Dorset	48.0	157

* *Based on data supplied by* The Tree Register of the British Isles

FOOD FROM THE LAND

TOP 10

WORLD VEGETABLE RECORDS*
(As held by Bernard Lavery)

	Vegetable/ record year	Weight kg	lb	oz
1	Pumpkin (1989 – held for 3 days)	322.06	710	0
2	Cabbage (1989)	56.24	124	0
3	Vegetable marrow (1990)	49.04	108	2
4	Courgette (1990)	29.25	64	8
5	Kohl-rabi (1990)	28.18	62	2
6	Celery (1990)	20.89	46	1
7	Radish (1990)	12.73	28	1
8	Cucumber (1991)	9.10	20	1
9	Brussels sprout (1992)	8.25	18	3
10	Carrot (1996)	5.20	11	7½

* *Current world record unless otherwise stated*

Bernard Lavery, who lives in Llanharry, Mid Glamorgan, UK, holds 19 world and 10 British records for his giant vegetables. Through books and a telephone helpline, he offers practical advice to enable others to achieve similar results.

TOP 10

BANANA-PRODUCING COUNTRIES IN THE WORLD

	Country	Annual production (tonnes)
1	India	9,500,000
2	Brazil	5,679,000
3	Ecuador	5,503,000
4	China	3,309,000
5	Philippines	3,200,000
6	Colombia	2,500,000
7	Indonesia	2,300,000
8	Mexico	2,141,000
9	Costa Rica	1,996,000
10	Thailand	1,700,000
	World total	*54,467,000*

TOP 10

VEGETABLE CROPS IN THE WORLD

	Crop	Annual production (tonnes)
1	Sugar cane	1,147,992,000
2	Rice	550,193,000
3	Wheat	541,120,000
4	Maize	514,506,000
5	Potatoes	280,679,000
6	Sugar beet	265,963,000
7	Cassava	163,776,000
8	Barley	142,746,000
9	Soybeans	125,930,000
10	Sweet potatoes	122,034,000

TOP 10

FRUIT CROPS IN THE WORLD

	Crop	Annual production (tonnes)
1	Oranges	57,796,000
2	Bananas	54,467,000
3	Grapes	53,255,000
4	Apples	49,682,000
5	Coconuts	45,068,000
6	Plantains	30,189,000
7	Mangoes	19,003,000
8	Melons	14,018,000
9	Tangerines, clementines, satsumas	13,543,000
10	Pears	11,597,000

TOP 10

COCONUT-PRODUCING COUNTRIES IN THE WORLD

	Country	Annual production (tonnes)		Country	Annual production (tonnes)
1	Indonesia	13,868,000	**6**	Mexico	1,201,000
2	Philippines	10,300,000	**7**	Malaysia	1,043,000
3	India	8,000,000	**8**	Vietnam	1,000,000
4	Sri Lanka	1,997,000	**9**	Brazil	950,000
5	Thailand	1,465,000	**10**	Papua New Guinea	700,000

RICE-PRODUCING COUNTRIES IN THE WORLD

	Country	Annual production (tonnes)
1	China	187,192,000
2	India	122,372,000
3	Indonesia	49,860,000
4	Bangladesh	24,659,000
5	Vietnam	24,000,000
6	Thailand	21,130,000
7	Myanmar (Burma)	20,109,000
8	Japan	12,625,000
9	Brazil	11,236,000
10	Philippines	11,002,000
	World total	*550,193,000*

World production of rice has risen dramatically during this century. It remains the staple diet for a huge proportion of the global population, especially in Asian countries. Relatively small quantities are grown elsewhere: the USA's output is 7,888,000 tonnes, and the total for the whole of Europe is just 2,115,000 tonnes, with Italy the leading producer at 1,284,000 tonnes.

COFFEE-PRODUCING COUNTRIES IN THE WORLD

	Country	Annual production (tonnes)
1	Brazil	930,000
2	Colombia	810,000
3	Mexico	408,000
4	Indonesia	346,000
5	Ethiopia	228,000
6	Uganda	220,000
7	Guatemala	210,000
8	Ecuador	197,000
9	Côte d'Ivoire	194,000
10	Vietnam	185,000
	World total	*5,603,000*

In recent years there has been a decline in coffee production from the former world peak of over 6,000,000 tonnes. While this list continues to prove the saying, "There's an awful lot of coffee in Brazil", Kenya, perhaps surprisingly, does not appear, since its annual total of 93,000 tonnes ranks the country in only 17th place.

TEA-PRODUCING COUNTRIES IN THE WORLD

	Country	Annual production (tonnes)
1	India	715,000
2	China	613,000
3	Kenya	245,000
4	Sri Lanka	242,000
5	Indonesia	140,000
6	Turkey	135,000
7	Japan	86,000
8	Georgia	74,000
9	Iran	56,000
10	Bangladesh	51,000
	World total	*2,627,000*

FLOWER POWER
Sunflowers come from North and Central America, but the plant has been successfully introduced into many other parts of the world. The oil derived from its seeds is used in cooking and for manufacturing food products such as margarine, while the residue is made into animal feed.

SUNFLOWER SEED-PRODUCING COUNTRIES IN THE WORLD

	Country	Annual production (tonnes)
1	Argentina	5,520,000
2	Russia	4,200,000
3	Ukraine	2,680,000
4	France	1,993,000
5	USA	1,817,000
6	India	1,470,000
7	China	1,269,000
8	Romania	933,000
9	Turkey	900,000
10	Hungary	777,000
	World total	*26,186,000*

THE HUMAN WORLD

T O P 1 0

MOST COMMON PHOBIAS

	Object of phobia	Medical term
1	Spiders	Arachnephobia or arachnophobia
2	People and social situations	Anthropophobia or sociophobia
3	Flying	Aerophobia or aviatophobia
4	Open spaces	Agoraphobia, cenophobia, or kenophobia
5	Confined spaces	Claustrophobia, cleisiophobia, cleithrophobia, or clithrophobia
6	Vomiting	Emetophobia or emitophobia
7	Heights	Acrophobia, altophobia, hypsophobia, or hypsiphobia
8	Cancer	Carcinomaphobia, carcinophobia, carcinomatophobia, cancerphobia, or cancerophobia
9	Thunderstorms	Brontophobia or keraunophobia; related phobias are those associated with lightning (astraphobia), cyclones (anemophobia), and hurricanes and tornadoes (lilapsophobia)
10	Death	Necrophobia or thanatophobia

A phobia is a morbid fear that is out of all proportion to the object of the fear. Many people would admit to being uncomfortable about these principal phobias, as well as others such as snakes (ophiophobia), injections (trypanophobia), or ghosts (phasmophobia), but most do not become obsessive about them or allow such fears to rule their lives. True phobias often arise from some incident in childhood when a person has been afraid of some object and has developed an irrational fear that has persisted into adulthood.

T O P 1 0

MOST COMMON ALLERGENS

(Substances that cause allergies)

Food allergen		Environmental allergen
Nuts	1	House dust mite (*Dermatophagoides pteronyssinus*)
Shellfish/seafood	2	Grass pollens
Milk	3	Tree pollens
Wheat	4	Cats
Eggs	5	Dogs
Fresh fruit (apples, oranges, strawberries, etc.)	6	Horses
Fresh vegetables (potatoes, cucumber, etc.)	7	Moulds (*Aspergillus fumigatus, Alternaria, Cladosporium*, etc.)
Cheese	8	Birch pollen
Yeast	9	Weed pollen
Soya protein	10	Wasp/bee venom

An allergy has been defined as "an unpleasant reaction to foreign matter, specific to that substance, which is altered from the normal response and peculiar to the individual concerned". Allergens, the substances that cause allergies, are usually foods but may also be environmental agents, such as pollen, which causes hay fever. Reactions can cause symptoms ranging from severe mental or physical disability to minor irritations such as a mild headache.

"Elimination dieting" to pinpoint and avoid food allergens, and identifying and avoiding environmental allergens, can often result in the complete cure of many allergies.

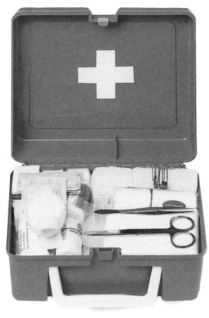

TOP 10

CAUSES OF STRESS-RELATED ILLNESSES

	Event	Value
1	Death of spouse	100
2	Divorce	73
3	Marital separation	65
4=	Detention in prison or other institution	63
4=	Death of close family member	63
6	Major personal injury or illness	53
7	Marriage	50
8	Losing one's job	47
9=	Marital reconciliation	45
9=	Retirement	45

Psychiatrists Dr. Thomas Holmes and Dr. Richard Rahe joined forces and devised what they called the "Social Readjustment Rating Scale" to place a value on the likelihood of illness occurring as a result of stress caused by various "life events". Even agreeable occasions have been evaluated for their stress value. The cumulative effect of several incidents increases the risk factor – if an individual's points total over 300 in a given year, they are reckoned to have a 79 per cent chance of developing major illness.

TOP 10

MOST COMMON REASONS FOR VISITS TO THE DOCTOR

	Complaint	Rate*
1	Acute upper respiratory infections	772
2	Acute bronchitis and bronchitis	719
3	Asthma	425
4	Disorders of conjunctiva (eye)	415
5	Hypertension (high blood pressure)	412
6=	Disorders of external ear	409
6=	Acute pharyngitis (sore throat)	409
8	Acute tonsillitis	407
9	Ill-defined intestinal infections	394
10	Various unspecified disorders of the back	372

* Per 10,000 visits per annum

TOP 10

MOST COMMON HOSPITAL CASUALTY COMPLAINTS

1	Cuts
2	Bruises
3	Dog bites
4	Sprained ankles
5	Eye injuries
6	Head injuries
7	Minor burns
8	Fractures
9	Upper respiratory tract infections
10	Gastroenteritis

TOP 10

COUNTRIES WITH MOST PATIENTS PER DOCTOR

	Country	Patients per doctor
1	Niger	54,472
2	Eritrea	49,200
3	Malawi	49,118
4	Mozambique	36,428
5	Ethiopia	30,195
6	Chad	27,765
7	Burkina Faso	27,158
8	Rwanda	24,697
9	Liberia	24,600
10	Ghana	22,452

Comparing countries' populations, their declared numbers of doctors, and hence the ratios of patients to doctors, is fraught with problems, especially since some countries include dentists with their doctors (Russia and the Ukraine among them), while China includes practitioners of traditional Chinese medicine as well as conventional doctors.

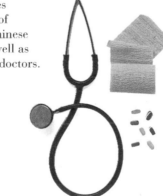

PAIN-KILLER PATENTED

Although it was discovered in 1853, acetyl salicylic acid was disregarded for 40 years until Felix Hoffman, a chemist working for the German company Bayer, rediscovered it and used it to treat his father's rheumatism. Bayer patented the process for producing it commercially in 1898, and it was first sold the following year. It was given the name "aspirin" ("a" for acetyl, "spir" from the Latin name of the flower meadowsweet, while "in" was a popular ending for the names of drugs). After Germany's defeat in World War I, the country's patents lapsed, and other companies began making aspirin, which became the world's bestselling over-the-counter drug.

MATTERS OF LIFE & DEATH

TOP 10

COUNTRIES WITH THE HIGHEST MALE LIFE EXPECTANCY

	Country	Life expectancy at birth (years)
1	San Marino	77.2
2	Iceland	76.8
3	Japan	76.1
4	Andorra	76.0
5	Hong Kong	75.4
6	Israel	75.1
7	Canada	74.9
8	Sweden	74.8
9=	Martinique	74.7
9=	Switzerland	74.7
	UK	*73.2*
	USA	*72.0*

The relatively high, and generally increasing, life expectancy for males in these Top 10 countries contrasts sharply with that in many developing countries, particularly most African countries, where it rarely exceeds 45 years. Sierra Leone is at the bottom of the league with an average life expectancy of 37.5 years.

TOP 10

COUNTRIES WITH THE HIGHEST FEMALE LIFE EXPECTANCY

	Country	Life expectancy at birth (years)
1	San Marino	85.3
2	Japan	82.2
3	Andorra	82.0
4	Switzerland	81.4
5	France	81.1
6=	Canada	81.0
6=	Hong Kong	81.0
6=	Martinique	81.0
9	Australia	80.8
10	Iceland	80.7
	USA	*78.9*
	UK	*78.6*

Female life expectancy in all these Top 10 countries – as well as a further seven – now exceeds 80 years. The comparative figure for such developing countries as Sierra Leone, where it is 40.6 years for women, makes for less encouraging reading. The world over, women generally live longer than men; in certain countries, such as Iraq, they live longer by as much as 11 years.

BORN IN 1875
At her 122nd birthday on 21 February 1997, Jeanne Louise Calment of Arles, France, became the world's oldest living person.

THE 10

COUNTRIES WITH THE MOST DEATHS FROM HEART DISEASE

	Country	Death rate per 100,000
1	Czech Republic	314.4
2	Scotland	258.3
3	New Zealand	248.6
4	Finland	243.2
5	Hungary	240.0
6	Bulgaria	230.1
7	Denmark	211.1
8	England & Wales	210.0
9	Sweden	209.3
10	Australia	200.5
	USA	*188.1*

TOP 10

COUNTRIES WITH THE LOWEST INFANT MORTALITY

	Country	Death rate per 1,000 live births
1	Iceland	3.2
2	Sweden	3.4
3	Singapore	4.3
4	Finland	4.4
5=	Japan	4.5
5=	Norway	4.5
7=	Hong Kong	4.8
7=	Taiwan	4.8
9	Liechtenstein	5.3
10	Denmark	5.6
	USA	*8.5*
	UK	*10.9*

THE 10

COUNTRIES WITH THE HIGHEST INFANT MORTALITY

	Country	Death rate per 1,000 live births
1	Sierra Leone	166.0
2	Afghanistan	161.0
3	Western Sahara	149.0
4	Mozambique	148.0
5	Guinea	147.0
6	Malawi	144.0
7	Guinea-Bissau	140.0
8	Central African Republic	137.2
9	The Gambia	132.0
10	Liberia	126.0

THE 10
MOST COMMON CAUSES OF DEATH IN THE US

	Cause	Deaths p.a.
1	Diseases of the heart	738,781
2	Cancer	537,781
3	Cerebrovascular diseases	158,061
4	Chronic obstructive pulmonary diseases and allied conditions	104,756
5	Accidents and adverse effects	89,703
6	Pneumonia and influenza	83,528
7	Diabetes	59,085
8	Human Immunodeficiency Virus (HIV)	42,506
9	Suicide	30,893
10	Chronic liver disease and cirrhosis	24,848

Source: National Center for Health Statistics.

Figures are for 1995 based on a total number of 2,312,203 estimated deaths in the US for that year. "Accidents and adverse effects" includes 41,786 deaths resulting from motor vehicle accidents. The category "Homicide and legal intervention" (which includes murders, executions, and deaths resulting from actions by members of the police force), formerly at No. 10, fell to 11th place with 21,577 deaths.

THE 10
MOST COMMON CAUSES OF DEATH IN THE UK

	Cause	Deaths p.a.
1	Diseases of the circulatory system	275,879
2	Cancer and other neoplasms	159,838
3	Diseases of the respiratory system	100,418
4	Diseases of the digestive system	22,091
5	Injury and poisoning	19,187
6	Diseases of the nervous system and sense organs	10,702
7	Mental disorders	10,691
8	Endocrine, nutritional, and metabolic diseases, and immunity disorders	8,663
9	Diseases of the genito-urinary system	8,264
10	Infectious and parasitic diseases	3,960

Total annual deaths from all causes (including some that do not appear in this Top 10): **641,712**

The 10 principal causes of death remain the same and in approximately the same order from year to year, with only slight fluctuations in total numbers. Of deaths that resulted from accidents and violence, motor vehicle accidents accounted for most – 4,744 in total, 434 fewer than in 1991 – and represent the continuation of a promising downward trend.

TOP 10
LONGEST-LIVED PROFESSIONS

	Profession	SMR*
1	Shop assistants	48
2=	Hairdressing supervisors	49
2=	Mechanical and aeronautical engineers	49
2=	Local government officers	49
5=	General administration, national government	52
5=	Site and other managers, clerks of works	52
5=	Teachers in higher education	54
8=	Managers, works foremen	58
8=	Professionals in science, engineering, and other technologies	58
10	Laboratory and engineering technicians	59

* Standard Mortality Ratio; figures for men in the UK only

Standard Mortality Ratios are a commonly used method of comparing the risk of death in one group with that in another. If an SMR of 100 is the average, then one of 50 is low.

THE 10
SHORTEST-LIVED PROFESSIONS

	Profession	SMR
1	Deckhands, engine-room hands, bargemen, lightermen, boatmen	304
2	Hairdressers and barbers	263
3	General labourers	243
4	Foremen on ships, lighters, and other vessels	236
5	Fishermen	234
6	Steel erectors, scaffolders, etc.	180
7	Foremen in product inspection and packaging	160
8	Chemical and petroleum processing-plant operators	154
9	Travel stewards and attendants, hospital and hotel porters	150
10	Foremen on production lines	149

HEALTH FOR ALL

The World Health Organization (WHO) came into being on 7 April 1948. An arm of the United Nations, itself founded three years earlier, the WHO now has 189 member states. Its primary objective is "the attainment by all peoples of the highest possible level of health". For the past 20 years the WHO has been operating a programme with the ambitious aim of "Health for All by the Year 2000". This it proposes to achieve through education and activities in such medical fields as the combating of high levels of infant mortality, smoking, and the spread of infectious diseases due to poor drinking water. The WHO spearheaded the campaign that successfully eradicated smallpox from the world in 1979. It has adopted a similar programme that aims to eliminate polio by the end of the century.

FOR BETTER OR FOR WORSE

TOP 10

PROFESSIONS OF COMPUTER-DATING MEMBERS

MEN

	Profession	Per cent of those registered
1	Engineers	6.1
2	Company directors	5.0
3	Computer programmers	4.7
4	Architects/designers	4.6
5	Accountants	4.4
6	Teachers	4.2
7	Doctors	4.0
8	Managers	3.7
9	Civil servants	2.5
10	Farmers	1.4

WOMEN

	Profession	Per cent of those registered
1	Teachers	7.8
2	Solicitors	5.1
3	Nurses	4.9
4	Accountants	4.5
5	Civil servants	3.9
6	Secretaries	3.8
7	Women at home	3.5
8	Doctors	3.1
9	Social workers	2.8
10	Students	1.3

TOP 10

WEDDING GIFTS IN THE UK

1	China
2	Glass
3	Kitchenware
4	Bed linen
5	Bath linen
6	Electrical
7	Silverware
8	Table accessories
9	Garden furniture
10	Lighting

Source: John Lewis Partnership

TOP 10

COUNTRIES WITH THE HIGHEST MARRIAGE RATE

	Country	Marriages per 1,000 p.a.*
1	Cuba	17.7
2	Bermuda	15.1
3	Philippines	14.0
4	Liechtenstein	13.1
5	Benin	12.8
6	Seychelles	12.7
7	Puerto Rico	12.6
8	Maldives	11.7
9=	Bangladesh	10.7
9=	Turkmenistan	10.7
	USA	8.9
	UK	5.9

* *During latest period for which figures available*

The apparent world record marriage rate of 31.2 per 1,000 often reported for the US territory of the Northern Mariana Islands – which has a total population of under 44,000 – and that of 18.0 for the US Virgin Islands are statistical "blips".

TOP 10

MONTHS FOR MARRIAGES IN THE US

	Month	Marriages
1	June	263,000
2	August	254,000
3	May	238,000
4=	July	224,000
4=	October	224,000
6	September	219,000
7	November	174,000
8	December	169,000
9	April	165,000
10	March	148,000

Source: National Center for Health Statistics

Figures are estimates for 1995 from a US total of some 2,336,000 weddings, a one per cent decline compared with the previous year (in 1995 the US marriage rate of 8.9 per 1,000 of the population hit its lowest level since 1963). February was at No. 11 with 146,000, and January the least popular with only 111,000.

TOP 10

MONTHS FOR MARRIAGES IN ENGLAND AND WALES

	Month	Marriages
1	July	41,855
2	August	40,151
3	September	39,547
4	June	33,125
5	May	32,769
6	October	25,248
7	April	22,327
8	March	15,411
9	December	14,210
10	November	13,459

SINGLES REQUESTED AT WEDDINGS

	Title/artist	Year
1	*Endless Love*, Diana Ross and Lionel Richie	1981
2	*Your Song*, Elton John	1971
3	*Everything I Do (I Do It for You)*, Bryan Adams	1991
4	*The Best*, Tina Turner	1989
5	*Crazy for You*, Madonna	1985
6	*(Where Do I Begin) Love Story*, Andy Williams	1971
7	*I Will Always Love You*, Whitney Houston	1992
8	*Love Me Tender*, Elvis Presley	1956
9	*I Just Can't Stop Loving You*, Michael Jackson	1987
10	*Unchained Melody*, Righteous Brothers	1965

FIRST WEDDING ANNIVERSARY GIFTS

1	Cotton
2	Paper
3	Leather
4	Fruit and flowers
5	Wood
6	Sugar (or iron)
7	Wool (or copper)
8	Bronze (or electrical appliances)
9	Pottery (or willow)
10	Tin (or aluminium)

In the UK and US most of the earlier anniversary themes listed above are generally disregarded in favour of the "milestone" anniversaries: the 25th (silver), 40th (ruby), 50th (gold), and 60th (diamond). Correctly, the 75th anniversary is the "diamond", but since Queen Victoria's so-called "Diamond Jubilee" was celebrated on the 60th anniversary of her succession to the throne, it has usually been commemorated as the 60th.

MOST COMMON CAUSES OF MARITAL DISCORD AND BREAKDOWN

1	Lack of communication
2	Continual arguments
3	Infidelity
4	Sexual problems
5	Financial problems
6	Work (usually one partner devoting excessive time to work)
7	Physical or verbal abuse
8	Children (whether to have them; attitudes towards their upbringing)
9	Step-parenting
10	Addiction (to drinking, gambling, spending, etc.)

Source: Relate National Marriage Guidance

COUNTRIES WITH THE LOWEST DIVORCE RATES

	Country	Divorce rate per 1,000 p.a.
1	Mozambique	0.01
2=	Western Samoa	0.2
2=	Sri Lanka	0.2
2=	North Korea	0.2
2=	Guatemala	0.2
2=	Antigua and Barbuda	0.2
7=	St. Lucia	0.3
7=	Pakistan	0.3
7=	Macedonia	0.3
7=	Bosnia and Herzegovina	0.3

The legal or religious sanctioning of or opposition to divorce around the world results in a remarkable range between those countries where divorce rates are high and those that appear in this list. Here, just one divorce is granted each year for every 3,333 inhabitants – or, in the case of Mozambique, one in 100,000.

DESTINATIONS FOR BRITISH COUPLES MARRYING ABROAD

1	St. Lucia
2	Kenya
3	Jamaica
4	Barbados
5	Antigua
6	The Seychelles
7	Mauritius
8	Florida, USA
9	Bali
10	Fiji

COUNTRIES WITH THE HIGHEST DIVORCE RATE

	Country	Divorce rate per 1,000 p.a.
1	Latvia	5.6
2	Russia	4.5
3	Belarus	4.3
4=	Cuba	4.2
4=	Ukraine	4.2
6	USA	4.1
7	Puerto Rico	4.0
8	Estonia	3.8
9	Lithuania	3.7
10	Moldova	3.3

WHAT'S IN A NAME?

TOP 10

GIRLS' AND BOYS' NAMES IN THE US

Girls		Boys
Brittany	1	Michael
Ashley	2	Christopher
Jessica	3	Matthew
Amanda	4	Joshua
Sarah	5	Andrew
Megan	6	James
Caitlin	7	John
Samantha	8	Nicholas
Stephanie	9	Justin
Katherine	10	David

American name fashions are highly volatile and vary considerably according to a child's ethnic background and the influences of popular culture. Jennifer, for example, once rose to the No. 2 position because the heroine of the book and 1970 film *Love Story* had this name, and Tiffany entered this Top 10 in 1980 in the wake of the TV series *Charlie's Angels*, and its character Tiffany Welles. This pattern has been mirrored in the 1990s with Brittany, a name that does not even make an appearance among the Top 100 British girls' names. In contrast, three of the Top 10 US boys' names (Matthew, Joshua, and James) also appear in the British Top 10.

TOP 10

GIRLS' AND BOYS' NAMES IN THE US 100 YEARS AGO

Girls		Boys
Mary	1	John
Ruth	2	William
Helen	3	Charles
Margaret	4	Robert
Elizabeth	5	Joseph
Dorothy	6	James
Catherine	7	George
Mildred	8	Samuel
Frances	9	Thomas
Alice/Marion	10	Arthur

TOP 10

GIRLS' AND BOYS' NAMES 50 YEARS AGO IN THE US

Girls		Boys
Mary	1	Robert
Patricia	2	James
Barbara	3	John
Judith	4	William
Carol/Carole	5	Richard
Sharon	6	Thomas
Nancy	7	David
Joan	8	Ronald
Sandra	9	Donald
Margaret	10	Michael

TOP 10

GIRLS' AND BOYS' NAMES IN ENGLAND AND WALES 1996

Girls		Boys
Sophie +3*	1	Jack 0
Jessica -1	2	Daniel 0
Chloe +6	3	Thomas 0
Emily +4	4	James 0
Lauren -3	5	Joshua 0
Rebecca -3	6	Matthew 0
Charlotte -2	7	Ryan 0
Hannah -2	8	Samuel +1
Amy -2	9	Joseph +2
Megan +4	10	Liam +2

* *The numbers alongside each name indicate the change in its popularity since the previous year – thus Sophie, which was in 4th place in 1995, moved up three places in 1996, and so on. (0 shows that the name has stayed in the same position from the previous year.)*

Fashions in boys' names are much less volatile than those of girls, as exemplified by the lack of movement in the first seven in this list. Outside this Top 10, Molly showed the greatest increase in popularity, rising 19 places to 28th. Leah entered the Top 50 for the first time in 1996, while Jennifer, Kayleigh, and Kirsty all dropped out.

TOP 10

GIRLS' AND BOYS' NAMES 50 YEARS AGO IN THE UK

Girls		Boys
Margaret	1	John
Patricia	2	David
Christine	3	Michael
Mary	4	Peter
Jean	5	Robert
Ann	6	Anthony
Susan	7	Brian
Janet	8	Alan
Maureen	9	William
Barbara	10	James

TOP 10

GIRLS' AND BOYS' NAMES IN AUSTRALIA

Girls		Boys
Jessica	1	Matthew
Sarah	2	James
Emily	3	Thomas
Rebecca	4	Joshua
Emma	5	Benjamin
Hannah	6	Daniel
Stephanie	7	Samuel
Amy	8	Nicholas
Caitlin	9	Alexander
Lauren	10	Michael

TOP 10

MOST COMMON SURNAMES IN THE TELEPHONE DIRECTORY IN LONDON, UK

1	Smith	6	Harris/Harrison
2	Brown/Browne	7	Taylor
3	Jones	8	Roberts/Robertson
4	Williams/Williamson	9	Patel
5	Clark/Clarke	10	James

MOST COMMON SURNAMES IN THE US

	Surname	Number
1	Smith	2,382,509
2	Johnson	1,807,263
3	Williams/Williamson	1,568,939
4	Brown	1,362,910
5	Jones	1,331,205
6	Miller	1,131,205
7	Davis	1,047,848
8	Martin/Martinez/Martinson	1,046,297
9	Anderson/Andersen	825,648
10	Wilson	787,825

Over 20 years ago the United States Social Security Administration published its survey of the most common surnames. It was based on the number of people for whom it had more than 10,000 files, which covered a total of 3,169 names. The SSA has not repeated the exercise, but it is probable that the ranking order has remained very similar.

MOST COMMON SURNAMES DERIVED FROM OCCUPATIONS IN THE US

1 Smith

2 Miller

3 Taylor

4 Clark (cleric)

5 Walker (cloth worker)

6 Wright (workman)

7 Baker

8 Carter (driver or maker of carts)

9 Stewart (steward)

10 Turner (woodworker)

It is reckoned that about one in six US surnames recalls the occupation of the holder's ancestors. Several US Presidents have borne such surnames, including Zachary Taylor and Jimmy Carter, both of which feature in this Top 10.

MOST COMMON SURNAMES IN THE UK

1 Smith		**6** Davies/Davis
2 Jones		**7** Evans
3 Williams		**8** Thomas
4 Brown		**9** Roberts
5 Taylor		**10** Johnson

MOST COMMON SURNAMES IN THE MANHATTAN TELEPHONE DIRECTORY

1 Smith/Smyth/Smythe

2 Lee/Lea/Leigh/Ley/Li

3 Brown/Browne

4 Cohen/Coan/Coen/Cohn/Cone/Kohn

5 Johnson/Johnston/Johnsen

6 Rodriguez

7 Miller

8 Williams

9 Jones

10 Davis/Davies

MOST COMMON PATRONYMS IN THE US

1 Johnson ("son of John")

2 Williams/Williamson ("son of William")

3 Jones ("son of John")

4 Davis ("son of Davie/David")

5 Martin/Martinez/Martinson ("son of Martin")

6 Anderson/Andersen ("son of Andrew")

7 Wilson ("son of Will")

8 Harris/Harrison ("son of Harry")

9 Thomas ("son of Thomas")

10 Thomson/Thompson ("son of Thomas")

MOST COMMON DESCRIPTIVE SURNAMES IN THE US

1 Brown (brown-haired)

2 White (light-skinned, or white-haired)

3 Young (youthful, or a younger brother)

4 Gray (grey-haired)

5 Long (tall)

6 Russell (red-haired)

7 Black/Blake (black-haired, or dark-skinned)

8 Little (small)

9 Reid (red-haired)

10 Curtis (courteous, or well-educated)

As many as one in ten of all US surnames may be derived from a physical description that was once applied to an ancestor. The list is headed by the Browns, whose role as labourers and pioneers was recognized by the 19th-century British author Thomas Hughes in his novel *Tom Brown's Schooldays* (1857), writing: "For centuries, in their quiet, dogged, homespun way, they have been subduing the earth in most English counties, and leaving their mark in American forests and Australian uplands."

TERMS OF ENDEARMENT USED IN THE US*

1 Honey

2 Baby

3 Sweetheart

4 Dear

5 Lover

6 Darling

7 Sugar

8= Angel

8= Pumpkin

10= Beautiful

10= Precious

* Based on survey of romance conducted by a US champagne company

ORGANIZATIONS & CHARITIES

ROBERT BADEN-POWELL
After serving in the army in India and Africa, Robert Baden-Powell, known as "BP", founded the worldwide scouting movement.

TOP 10
ENVIRONMENTAL ORGANIZATIONS IN THE US

	Organization	Approximate membership
1	National Wildlife Federation	5,600,000
2	Greenpeace	1,400,000
3	Sierra Club	553,246
4	National Audubon Society	516,220
5	The Wilderness Society	330,000
6=	Environmental Defense Fund	125,000
6=	Natural Resources Defense Council	125,000
8	National Parks and Conservation Association	100,000
9	Defenders of Wildlife	80,000
10	Friends of the Earth	50,000

TOP 10
ANIMAL CHARITIES IN THE UK

	Charity	Voluntary income (£)
1	Royal Society for the Prevention of Cruelty to Animals	30,009,000
2	Royal Society for the Protection of Birds	26,839,000
3	World Wide Fund for Nature	17,716,000
4	People's Dispensary for Sick Animals	16,887,000
5	Donkey Sanctuary	6,242,000
6	Blue Cross Animals' Hospital	6,006,000
7	Redwings Horse Sanctuary	5,051,000
8	National Canine Defence League	4,934,000
9	Cats Protection League	3,895,000
10	Animal Health Trust	3,871,000

TOP 10
COUNTRIES WITH THE HIGHEST SCOUT MEMBERSHIP

	Country	Membership*
1	Indonesia	10,059,131
2	USA	4,602,844
3	Philippines	2,685,767
4	India	1,657,780
5	Thailand	1,000,348
6	UK	637,905
7	Bangladesh	602,492
8	Pakistan	420,775
9	Republic of Korea	273,046
10	Canada	270,402

* As at 1 December 1996

Following an experimental camp held in 1907 on Brownsea Island, Dorset, England, Sir Robert Baden-Powell (1857–1941) launched the scouting movement. There are believed to be just 13 countries in the world where scouting either does not exist or is forbidden for political reasons; of the later, China is among the largest.

TOP 10
COUNTRIES WITH THE HIGHEST GIRL GUIDE AND GIRL SCOUT MEMBERSHIP

	Country	Membership
1	USA	3,318,006
2	Philippines	1,275,113
3	India	853,396
4	UK	698,361
5	Poland	238,469
6	Canada	232,668
7	Kenya	100,000
8	Indonesia	98,656
9	South Korea	90,932
10	Italy	89,797

The Girl Guide Movement was started in 1910 by Sir Robert Baden-Powell and his sister, Agnes (1858–1945). Today the World Association of Girl Guides and Girl Scouts has 129 national member organizations with a total membership of 9,000,000 around the world.

TOP 10
MEMBERSHIP ORGANIZATIONS IN THE US

	Organization	Approximate membership
1	American Automobile Association	35,291,651
2	American Association of Retired Persons	32,000,000
3	YMCA of America	14,447,270
4	National Congress of Parents and Teachers	6,500,000
5	National Right to Life Committee	6,000,000
6	Boy Scouts of America National Council	5,628,806
7	National Committee to Preserve Social Security and Medicare	5,500,000
8	Evangelical Lutheran Church in America	5,200,000
9	National Council of Senior Citizens	5,000,000
10	American Farm Bureau Federation	4,700,000

T O P 1 0

MEMBERSHIP ORGANIZATIONS IN THE UK

	Organization	Membership
1	Automobile Association	9,185,000
2	Trades Union Congress	8,089,000
3	Royal Automobile Club	5,500,000
4	National Trust	2,396,346
5	UNISON	1,355,000
6	Royal Society for the Protection of Birds	943,000
7	Transport & General Workers' Union	897,000
8	GMB	740,000
9	Amalgamated Engineering and Electrical Union	726,000
10	Royal British Legion	708,159

T O P 1 0

FUND-RAISING CHARITIES IN THE UK

	Charity	Voluntary income in 1996 (£)
1	Oxfam	92,308,000
2	National Trust	77,014,000
3	Imperial Cancer Research Fund	70,980,000
4	Cancer Research Campaign	60,211,000
5	British Heart Foundation	57,204,000
6	Royal National Lifeboat Institution	55,741,000
7	Barnardos	47,300,000
8	Help the Aged	43,178,000
9	British Red Cross Society	38,446,000
10	SCOPE	37,237,000

T O P 1 0

CHILDREN'S CHARITIES IN THE UK

	Charity	Voluntary income in 1996 (£)
1	Barnardo's	47,300,000
2	National Society for the Prevention of Cruelty to Children	35,091,000
3	Children's Society	15,641,000
4	NCH Action for Children	13,323,000
5	BBC Children in Need Appeal	13,322,000
6	Variety Club Children's Charity	8,980,000
7	Childline Charitable Trust	4,123,000
8	Children in Crisis	2,376,000
9	Norwood Child Care	2,286,000
10	Children First	2,004,000

* Excluding charities that aid both children and adults

T O P 1 0

OLDEST ESTABLISHED CLUBS* IN THE UK

	Club	Location	Established
1	White's Club	London	1693
2	Boodle's	London	1762
3	Brooks's	London	1764
4	Norfolk Club	Norwich	1770
5	Royal Thames Yacht Club	London	1775
6	New Club	Edinburgh	1787
7	Marylebone Cricket Club	London	1787
8	The Athenaeum	Liverpool	1797
9	Royal Anglesey Yacht Club	Beaumaris	1802
10	City Club	Chester	1807

* Other than golf clubs

T O P 1 0

ENVIRONMENTAL ORGANIZATIONS IN THE UK

	Organization	Membership		Organization	Membership
1	National Trust	2,396,346	6	World Wide Fund for Nature	236,174
2	Royal Society for the Protection of Birds	943,000	7	National Trust for Scotland	230,000
3	English Heritage	407,000	8=	Greenpeace	215,000
4	Civic Trust	315,000	8=	Woodland Trust	215,000
5	Royal Society for Nature Conservation	260,000	10	Friends of the Earth	200,000

ROYAL HIGHNESSES & PRESIDENTS

TOP 10
LONGEST-REIGNING MONARCHS IN THE WORLD

	Monarch	Country	Reign	Age at accession	Years reigned
1	Louis XIV	France	1643–1715	5	72
2	John II	Liechtenstein	1858–1929	18	71
3	Franz-Josef	Austria–Hungary	1848–1916	18	67
4	Victoria	UK	1837–1901	18	63
5	Hirohito	Japan	1926–89	25	62
6	George III	UK	1760–1820	22	59
7	Louis XV	France	1715–74	5	59
8	Pedro II	Brazil	1831–89	6	58
9	Wilhelmina	Netherlands	1890–1948	10	58
10	Henry III	England	1216–72	9	56

Extravagant claims have been made for long-reigning monarchs in the ancient world. One example is the alleged 94-year reign of Phiops II, a 6th Dynasty Egyptian pharaoh. Since his dates cannot be verified, he has not been included in this Top 10.

TOP 10
LONGEST-REIGNING BRITISH MONARCHS

	Monarch	Reign	Age at accession	Age at death	Years reigned
1	Victoria	1837–1901	18	81	63
2	George III	1760–1820	22	81	59
3	Henry III	1216–72	9	64	56
4	Edward III	1327–77	14	64	50
5	Elizabeth II	1952–	25	–	45
6	Elizabeth I	1558–1603	25	69	44
7	Henry VI	1422–61 (deposed, d. 1471)	8 months	49	38
8	Henry VIII	1509–47	17	55	37
9	Charles II	1660–85	19	54	36
10	Henry I	1100–35	31–32*	66–67*	35

* *Henry I's birth date is unknown, so his ages at accession and death are uncertain*

TOP 10
CURRENT MONARCHIES* WITH MOST RULERS

	Monarchy	Line commenced	No. rulers#
1	Japan	40 BC	125
2	England	802	64
3	Sweden	980	59
4	Denmark	940	55
5	Norway	858	42
6	Monaco	1458	20
7	Spain	1516	18
8=	Netherlands	1572	14
8=	Liechtenstein	1699	14
10	Thailand	1782	9

* *Including principalities*
# *Monarchs deposed and later restored counted once only*

Among the dwindling ranks of monarchies, these are the longest-established, at least according to the number of successive incumbents. There are many other countries that had innumerable monarchs, but which no longer have hereditary rulers, among them China, France, and Russia.

TOP 10
BUSIEST MEMBERS OF THE ROYAL FAMILY

	Member	Events attended 1996
1	Princess Royal	514
2	The Queen	509
3	Prince of Wales	417
4	Duke of Edinburgh	364
5	Duke of Kent	206
6	Duke of Gloucester	151
7	Duchess of Gloucester	128
8	Princess Alexandra	119
9	Prince Edward	115
10	Princess Margaret	114

In 1996 the members of the Royal Family appearing in this list attended a total of 2,637 events in the UK, while three other members (the Duke of York, the Duchess of Kent, and the Queen Mother) attended 199 events between them. In addition, those in this Top 10 carried out a total of 813 engagements while abroad on official tours, the Duke of Edinburgh carrying out the greatest number, 255.

TOP 10
HIGHEST-PAID MEMBERS OF THE ROYAL FAMILY

	Member	Annual payment (£)
1	The Queen	7,900,000
2	The Queen Mother	643,000
3	The Duke of Edinburgh	359,000
4	The Duke of York	249,000
5	The Duke of Kent	236,000
6	The Princess Royal	228,000
7	Princess Alexandra	225,000
8	Princess Margaret	219,000
9	The Duke of Gloucester	175,500
10	Prince Edward	96,000

The Civil List is not technically the Royal Family's "pay", but the allowance made by the Government for their staff and the costs incurred in the course of performing their public duties. The amount of the Civil List was fixed for 10 years from 1 January 1991 and provides a total annual allocation of £10,417,000. Of that sum, £1,515,000 is refunded to the Treasury. Princess Alice, Duchess of Gloucester, is the 11th recipient, with £87,000 per annum.

T H E   1 0

FIRST PRESIDENTS OF THE US

	President/dates	Period of office
1	George Washington (1732–99)	1789–97
2	John Adams (1735–1826)	1797–1801
3	Thomas Jefferson (1743–1826)	1801–09
4	James Madison (1751–1836)	1809–17
5	James Monroe (1758–1831)	1817–25
6	John Quincy Adams (1767–1848)	1825–29
7	Andrew Jackson (1767–1845)	1829–37
8	Martin Van Buren (1782–1862)	1837–41
9	William H. Harrison (1773–1841)	1841
10	John Tyler (1790–1862)	1841–45

T O P   1 0

LONGEST-SERVING US PRESIDENTS

	President	Period in office years	days
1	Franklin D. Roosevelt	12	39
2=	Grover Cleveland	8*	
2=	Dwight D. Eisenhower	8*	
2=	Ulysses S. Grant	8*	
2=	Andrew Jackson	8*	
2=	Thomas Jefferson	8*	
2=	James Madison	8*	
2=	James Monroe	8*	
2=	Ronald Reagan	8*	
2=	Woodrow Wilson	8*	

* Two four-year terms – now the maximum any US President may remain in office

PRESIDENT OF THE US, BILL CLINTON
As well as featuring in the list of tallest US presidents, Bill Clinton would appear in a list of the youngest and in a list of the most popular US presidents.

T H E   1 0

LAST US PRESIDENTS AND VICE PRESIDENTS TO DIE IN OFFICE

	Name/date of death	Office
1	John F. Kennedy* 22 November 1963	P
2	Franklin D. Roosevelt 12 April 1945	P
3	Warren G. Harding 2 August 1923	P
4	James S. Sherman 30 October 1912	VP
5	William McKinley* 14 September 1901	P
6	Garret A. Hobart 21 November 1899	VP
7	Thomas A. Hendricks 25 November 1885	VP
8	James A. Garfield* 19 September 1881	P
9	Henry Wilson, 10 November 1875	VP
10	Abraham Lincoln* 15 April 1865	P

* Assassinated

T O P   1 0

TALLEST US PRESIDENTS

	President	Height m	ft in
1	Abraham Lincoln	1.93	6 4
2	Lyndon B. Johnson	1.91	6 3
3=	Bill Clinton	1.89	6 2½
3=	Thomas Jefferson	1.89	6 2½
5=	Chester A. Arthur	1.88	6 2
5=	George Bush	1.88	6 2
5=	Franklin D. Roosevelt	1.88	6 2
5=	George Washington	1.88	6 2
9=	Andrew Jackson	1.85	6 1
9=	Ronald Reagan	1.85	6 1

T O P   1 0

US PRESIDENTS WITH THE MOST ELECTORAL VOTES

	President	Year	Votes
1	Ronald Reagan	1984	525
2	Franklin D. Roosevelt	1936	523
3	Richard Nixon	1972	520
4	Ronald Reagan	1980	489
5	Lyndon B. Johnson	1964	486
6	Franklin D. Roosevelt	1932	472
7	Dwight D. Eisenhower	1956	457
8	Franklin D. Roosevelt	1940	449
9	Herbert C. Hoover	1928	444
10	Dwight D. Eisenhower	1952	422

HUMAN ACHIEVEMENTS

THE 10

FIRST EXPLORERS TO LAND IN THE AMERICAS

	Explorer	Nationality	Discovery/exploration	Year
1	Christopher Columbus	Italian	West Indies	1492
2	John Cabot	Italian/English	Nova Scotia/Newfoundland	1497
3	Alonso de Hojeda	Spanish	Brazil	1499
4	Vicente Yañez Pinzón	Spanish	Amazon	1500
5	Pedro Alvarez Cabral	Portuguese	Brazil	1500
6	Gaspar Corte Real	Portuguese	Labrador	1500
7	Rodrigo de Bastidas	Spanish	Central America	1501
8	Vasco Nuñez de Balboa	Spanish	Panama	1513
9	Juan Ponce de León	Spanish	Florida	1513
10	Juan Díaz de Solís	Spanish	Río de la Plata	1515

THE 10

FIRST PEOPLE TO GO OVER NIAGARA FALLS AND SURVIVE

	Name	Method	Date
1	Annie Edison Taylor	Barrel	24 Oct 1901
2	Bobby Leach	Steel barrel	25 Jul 1911
3	Jean Lussier	Rubber ball fitted with oxygen cylinders	4 Jul 1928
4	William Fitzgerald (aka Nathan Boya)	Rubber ball	15 Jul 1961
5	Karel Soucek	Barrel	3 Jul 1984
6	Steven Trotter	Barrel	18 Aug 1985
7	Dave Mundy	Barrel	5 Oct 1985
8=	Peter deBernardi	Metal container	28 Sep 1989
8=	Jeffrey Petkovich	Metal container	28 Sep 1989
10	Dave Mundy	Diving bell	26 Sep 1993

Source: Niagara Falls Museum

THE 10

LAST *TIME* MAGAZINE "MEN OF THE YEAR"

	Recipient	Year
1	Dr. David Ho (1952–), AIDS researcher	1996
2	Newt Gingrich (1943–), US politician	1995
3	Pope John Paul II (1920–)	1994
4	Yasser Arafat (1929–), F.W. de Klerk (1936–), Nelson Mandela (1918–), Yitzhak Rabin (1922–95), "Peacemakers"	1993
5	Bill Clinton (1946–), US President	1992
6	George Bush (1924–), US President	1991
7	Ted Turner (1938–), US businessman	1990
8	Mikhail Gorbachev (1931–), Soviet leader	1989
9	"Endangered Earth"	1988
10	Mikhail Gorbachev, Soviet leader	1987

THE 10

FIRST PEOPLE TO REACH THE NORTH POLE

	Name/nationality	Date		Name/nationality	Date
1=	Robert Edwin Peary (US)	6 Apr 1909	7=	Pavel Afanaseyevich Geordiyenko (USSR)	23 Apr 1948
1=	Matthew Alexander Henson (US)	6 Apr 1909	7=	Mikhail Yemel'yenovich Ostrekin (USSR)	23 Apr 1948
1=	Ooqueah (Eskimo)	6 Apr 1909	7=	Pavel Kononovich Sen'ko (USSR)	23 Apr 1948
1=	Ootah (Eskimo)	6 Apr 1909	7=	Mikhail Mikhaylovich Somov (USSR)	23 Apr 1948
1=	Egingwah (Eskimo)	6 Apr 1909			
1=	Seegloo (Eskimo)	6 Apr 1909			

THE FIRST SOLO CIRCUMNAVIGATION OF THE EARTH

Although there have now been several hundred solo voyages around the world, the first ever such voyage was completed on 3 July 1898 when 54-year-old Captain Joshua Slocum arrived in Fairhaven, Massachusetts, after a voyage of more than three years. The Canadian-born professional sailor had set off from Boston on 24 April 1895 in *Spray*, an 11.2-mm/36-ft-9 in replica of an old oyster boat he had built himself at a cost of $553.32. Slocum was hailed as a hero and later wrote a book about his exploit. At the end of 1909, he embarked on another solo journey in *Spray*, this time to the Orinoco, but after setting sail Slocum was never seen again.

CONQUEST OF EVEREST

As early as the mid 19th century, it was realized that Mount Everest was the world's highest peak, but it was 100 years before anyone was able to climb it successfully. No attempts were made until the 1920s, and in 1922 the second expedition reached a height of 8,320 m/27,297 ft. Although a member of the 3rd expedition attained 8,580 m/ 28,150 ft, two members of the party vanished. The first successful ascent, that of Hillary and Tenzing, culminated on 29 May 1953. The first woman to climb Everest was Junko Tabei of Japan on 16 May 1975, and on 20 August 1980 Italian climber Reinhold Messner became the first to climb solo, and without the benefit of oxygen.

THE 10
FIRST MOUNTAINEERS TO CLIMB EVEREST

	Mountaineer	Nationality	Date
1	Edmund Hillary	New Zealander	29 May 1953
2	Tenzing Norgay	Nepalese	29 May 1953
3	Jürg Marmet	Swiss	23 May 1956
4	Ernst Schmied	Swiss	23 May 1956
5	Hans-Rudolf von Gunten	Swiss	24 May 1956
6	Adolf Reist	Swiss	24 May 1956
7	Wang Fu-chou	Chinese	25 May 1960
8	Chu Ying-hua	Chinese	25 May 1960
9	Konbu	Tibetan	25 May 1960
10=	Nawang Gombu	Indian	1 May 1963
10=	James Whittaker	US	1 May 1963

Nawang Gombu and James Whittaker are 10th equal because, neither wishing to deny the other the privilege of being first, they ascended the last feet to the top side by side.

THIRD EXPEDITION
The third Mount Everest expedition was led by Edward Norton. Two of the team lost their lives.

LOST ON EVEREST
British mountaineer George Leigh Mallory disappeared in June 1924 while attempting the final assault on the summit.

FIRST EXPEDITION
Led by Lt-Col. C.K. Howard-Bury, the 1921 British Everest Reconnaissance Expedition first assessed the scale of the challenge posed by the world's tallest mountain.

PEAK OF SUCCESS
Edmund Hillary and Sherpa Tenzing Norgay became the first to conquer Everest.

NOBEL PRIZE WINNERS

TOP 10

NOBEL PRIZE-WINNING COUNTRIES

	Country	Phy	Che	Ph/Med	Lit	Pce	Eco	Total
1	USA	63	41	74	10	17	25	230
2	UK	21	23	24	8	11	7	94
3	Germany	19	27	15	6	4	1	72
4	France	11	7	7	12	9	1	47
5	Sweden	4	4	7	7	5	2	29
6	Switzerland	2	5	6	2	3	–	18
7	USSR	7	1	2	3	2	1	16
8	Stateless institutions	–	–	–	–	15	–	15
9=	Italy	3	1	3	5	1	–	13
9=	Netherlands	6	3	2	–	1	1	13

Phy – Physics; Che – Chemistry; Ph/Med – Physiology or Medicine; Lit – Literature; Pce – Peace; Eco – Economic Sciences. Germany includes the united country before 1948, West Germany to 1990, and the united country since 1990.

DID YOU KNOW

THE ULTIMATE PRIZE

Having made a fortune through his invention of dynamite and many other patents, the Swedish scientist Alfred Nobel (1833–96) left his wealth in a fund to sponsor the prizes that bear his name. Winners in the six categories each receive a sum of money: in 1901 this amounted to 150,800 Swedish krona, but today it is worth 7,400,000 krona, or approximately $1,119,000/£716,000. Winners also receive a 66-mm/2½-in diameter, 18-carat gold medal weighing about 175 gm/6⅛ oz, which is engraved with the laureate's name. All the medals feature a portrait of Alfred Nobel, but their design and inscriptions vary according to the prize: those for the Physics, Chemistry, Physiology or Medicine, and Literature prizes have a quotation in Latin from Virgil's *Aeneid*, "Inventions enhance life which is beautified through art", while the Peace medal states "For the peace and brotherhood of men". The Economic Sciences prize is inscribed "The Bank of Sweden, in Memory of Alfred Nobel, 1968" – the year that the Prize was established.

THE 10

LAST WINNERS OF THE NOBEL PRIZE FOR LITERATURE

	Winner/country/dates	Prize year
1	Wislawa Szymborska (Poland, 1923–)	1996
2	Seamus Heaney (Ireland, 1939–)	1995
3	Kenzaburo Oe (Japan, 1935–)	1994
4	Toni Morrison (USA, 1931–)	1993
5	Derek Walcott (Saint Lucia, 1930–)	1992
6	Nadine Gordimer (South Africa, 1923–)	1991
7	Octavio Paz (Mexico, 1914–)	1990
8	Camilo José Cela (Spain, 1916–)	1989
9	Naguib Mahfouz (Egypt, 1911–)	1988
10	Joseph Brodsky (Russia/USA, 1940–96)	1987

THE 10

LAST WINNERS OF THE NOBEL PRIZE FOR ECONOMIC SCIENCES

	Winner/country/dates	Prize year
1=	James A. Mirrlees (UK, 1936–)	
1=	Professor William Vickrey (Canada, 1914–)	1996

The analysis of informational asymmetries.

3	Robert E. Lucas (USA, 1937–)	1995

The hypothesis of rational expectations as an aid to macroeconomic analysis and economic policy.

4=	John C. Harsanyi (Hungary/USA, 1920–)	
4=	Reinhard Selten (Germany, 1930–)	
4=	John F. Nash (USA, 1928–)	1994

The analysis of equilibria in the theory of non-cooperative games.

7=	Robert W. Fogel (USA, 1926–)	
7=	Douglass C. North (USA, 1920–)	1993

The application of economic theory and quantitative methods to explain economic and institutional change.

9	Gary S. Becker (USA, 1930–)	1992

Extending microeconomic analysis to a wide range of human behaviours and interactions.

10	Ronald H. Coase (UK/USA, 1910–)	1991

The discovery and clarification of the significance of transaction costs and property rights for the traditional structure and functioning of the economy.

The Nobel Prize for Economic Sciences is a recent addition to the Nobel prizes, first awarded in 1969. It is presented annually by the Royal Swedish Academy of Sciences and consists of a gold medal, a diploma, and a sum of money. The Nobel laureate for Economic Sciences, along with that of the other prizes, is announced annually in October, and the presentation is made to the winner on 10 December, the anniversary of Alfred Nobel's death.

T H E 1 0

LAST WINNERS OF THE NOBEL PEACE PRIZE

Winner/country/dates	Prize year	Winner/country/dates	Prize year
1= Carlos Filipe Ximenes Belo (East Timor, 1948–)	1996	**4=** Itzhak Rabin (Israel, 1922–1995)	1994
1= José Ramos-Horta (East Timor, 1949–)	1996	**7=** Nelson Rolihlahla Mandela (South Africa, 1918–)	1993
3 Joseph Rotblat (UK, 1908–)	1995	**7=** Frederik Willem de Klerk (South Africa, 1936–)	1993
4= Yasir Arafat (Palestine, 1929–)	1994	**9** Rigoberta Menchú (Guatemala, 1959–)	1992
4= Shimon Peres (Israel, 1923–)	1994	**10** Aung San Suu Kyi (Burma, 1945–)	1991

T H E 1 0

LAST WINNERS OF THE NOBEL PRIZE FOR CHEMISTRY

Winner/country/dates	Prize year
1= Sir Harold W. Kroto (UK, 1939–)	
1= Richard E. Smalley (USA, 1943–)	1996

The discovery of new forms of carbon known as fullerenes.

3= Paul Crutzen (Netherlands, 1933–)	
3= Mario Molina (Mexico, 1943–)	
3= Frank Sherwood Rowland (USA, 1927–)	1995

Work in atmospheric chemistry concerning the formation and decomposition of ozone.

6 George A. Olah (Hungary/USA, 1927–)	1994

The preparation of positively charged hydrocarbons, or 'carbocations'.

7= Michael Smith (UK/Canada, 1932–)	1993

The development of site-specific mutagenesis.

7= Kary Banks Mullis (USA, 1944–)	1993

The invention of the polymerase chain reaction.

9 Rudolph A. Marcus (USA, 1923–)	1992

Theories of electron transfer.

10 Richard Robert Ernst (Switzerland, 1933–)	1991

The development of high-resolution nuclear magnetic resonance (NMR) spectroscopy.

T H E 1 0

LAST WINNERS OF THE NOBEL PRIZE FOR PHYSIOLOGY OR MEDICINE

Winner/country/dates	Prize year
1– Peter C. Doherty (Australia, 1940–)	
1= Rolf M. Zinkernagel (Switzerland, 1944–)	1996

The discovery of how the immune system recognizes virus-infected cells.

3= Christiane Nüsslein-Volhard (Germany, 1942–)	
3= Eric F. Wieschaus (USA, 1947–)	
3= Edward B. Lewis (USA, 1918–)	1995

Discoveries about the involvement of genes in the spatial organization of organisms.

6= Alfred G. Gilman (USA, 1941–)	
6= Martin Rodbell (USA, 1925–)	1994

Discovery of G-proteins and their role in signal transduction within cells.

8= Richard J. Roberts (USA, 1943–)	
8= Phillip A. Sharp (USA, 1944–)	1993

The discovery of mosaic genes.

10= Edmond H. Fischer (USA, 1920–)	
10= Edwin G. Krebs (USA, 1918–)	1992

The discovery of mechanisms for the regulation of proteins in the human body.

T H E 1 0

LAST WINNERS OF THE NOBEL PRIZE FOR PHYSICS

Winner/country/dates	Prize year
1= David M. Lee (USA, 1931–)	
1= Douglas D. Osheroff (USA, 1945–)	
1= Robert C. Richardson (USA, 1937–)	1996

The discovery of superfluidity of helium-3.

4= Martin L. Perl (USA, 1927–)	1995

The discovery of the tau lepton.

4= Frederick Reines (USA, 1918–)	1995

The detection of the neutrino.

6= Bertram Neville Brockhouse (Canada, 1918–)	
6= Clifford G. Shull (USA, 1915–)	1994

Studies of neutron beams.

8= Russell A. Hulse (USA, 1950–)	
8= Joseph H. Taylor, Jr. (USA, 1941–)	1993

The discovery of a new type of pulsar.

10 Georges Charpak (France, 1924–)	1992

The invention of detectors for the detection of interactions of elementary particles.

SPORTS

TOP 10

PGA TOUR EARNERS IN 1996

	Player*	Winnings ($)		Player*	Winnings ($)
1	Tom Lehman	1,780,159	6	Fred Couples	1,248,694
2	Phil Mickelson	1,697,799	7	Davis Love III	1,211,139
3	Mark Brooks	1,429,396	8	Brad Faxon	1,055,050
4	Steve Stricker	1,383,739	9	Scott Hoch	1,039,564
5	Mark O'Meara	1,255,749	10	David Duval	977,079

Source: ESPNET Sports Zone
* *All US players*

TOP 10

PLAYERS TO WIN THE MOST MAJORS IN A CAREER

	Player	Country	British Open	US Open	Masters	PGA	Total
1	Jack Nicklaus	USA	3	4	6	5	18
2	Walter Hagen	USA	4	2	0	5	11
3=	Ben Hogan	USA	1	4	2	2	9
3=	Gary Player	South Africa	3	1	3	2	9
5	Tom Watson	USA	5	1	2	0	8
6=	Harry Vardon	UK	6	1	0	0	7
6=	Gene Sarazen	USA	1	2	1	3	7
6=	Bobby Jones	USA	3	4	0	0	7
6=	Sam Snead	USA	1	0	3	3	7
6=	Arnold Palmer	USA	2	1	4	0	7

TOP 10

BIGGEST WINNING MARGINS IN THE US MASTERS

	Player*	Year	Winning margin
1	Tiger Woods	1997	12
2	Jack Nicklaus	1965	9
3	Raymond Floyd	1976	8
4	Cary Middlecoff	1955	7
5	Arnold Palmer	1964	6
6=	Claude Harmon	1948	5
6=	Ben Hogan	1953	5
6=	Nick Faldo (UK)	1996	5
9=	Jimmy Demaret	1940	4
9=	Sam Snead	1952	4
9=	Severiano Ballesteros (Spain)	1980	4
9=	Severiano Ballesteros (Spain)	1983	4
9=	Bernhard Langer (Germany)	1993	4

* *All golfers from the United States unless otherwise stated*

TOP 10

WINNERS OF WOMEN'S MAJORS

	Player	Titles
1	Patty Berg	16
2=	Mickey Wright	13
2=	Louise Suggs	13
4	Babe Didrikson Zaharias	12
5	Betsy Rawls	8
6	JoAnne Gunderson Carner	7
7=	Kathy Whitworth	6
7=	Pat Bradley	6
7=	Julie Simpson Inkster	6
7=	Glenna Collett Vare	6

The present-day Majors are: the US Open, Mazda LPGA Championship, du Maurier Classic, and Nabisco Dinah Shore Classic. Also taken into account are wins in the former Majors: the Western Open, Titleholders Championship, and the amateur championships of both Britain and the US.

HAPPY GOLFER
Arnold Palmer was the world's highest-earning golfer for many years; his income in 1996 was over $15 million.

TOP 10

LOWEST WINNING SCORES IN THE US MASTERS

	Player*	Year	Score
1	Tiger Woods	1997	270
2=	Jack Nicklaus	1965	271
2=	Raymond Floyd	1976	271
4=	Ben Hogan	1953	274
5=	Ben Crenshaw	1995	274
6=	Severiano Ballesteros (Spain)	1980	275
6=	Fred Couples	1992	275
8=	Arnold Palmer	1964	276
8=	Jack Nicklaus	1975	276
8=	Tom Watson	1977	276
8=	Nick Faldo (UK)	1996	276

* All US players unless otherwise stated

The US Masters is the only Major played on the same course each year, at Augusta, Georgia. The course was built on the site of an old nursery, and the abundance of flowers and shrubs is a reminder of its former days, with each of the holes named after the plants growing adjacent to it.

TOP 10

LOWEST WINNING SCORES IN THE US OPEN

	Player	Country	Year	Venue	Score
1=	Jack Nicklaus	USA	1980	Baltusrol	272
1=	Lee Janzen	USA	1993	Baltusrol	272
3	David Graham	Australia	1981	Merion	273
4=	Jack Nicklaus	USA	1967	Baltusrol	275
4=	Lee Trevino	USA	1968	Oak Hill	275
6=	Ben Hogan	USA	1948	Riviera	276
6=	Fuzzy Zoeller	USA	1984	Winged Foot	276
8=	Jerry Pate	USA	1976	Atlanta	277
8=	Scott Simpson	USA	1987	Olympic Club	277
10=	Ken Venturi	USA	1964	Congressional	278
10=	Billy Casper	USA	1966	Olympic Club	278
10=	Hubert Green	USA	1977	Southern Hills	278
10=	Curtis Strange	USA	1988	Brookline	278
10=	Curtis Strange	USA	1989	Oak Hill	278
10=	Steve Jones	USA	1996	Oakland Hills	278

TOP 10

LOWEST FOUR-ROUND SCORES IN THE BRITISH OPEN

	Player	Country	Year	Venue	Score
1	Greg Norman	Australia	1993	Sandwich	267
2=	Tom Watson	USA	1977	Turnberry	268
2=	Nick Price	South Africa	1994	Turnberry	268
4=	Jack Nicklaus	USA	1977	Turnberry	269
4=	Nick Faldo	UK	1993	Sandwich	269
4=	Jesper Parnevik	Sweden	1994	Turnberry	269
7=	Nick Faldo	UK	1990	St. Andrews	270
7=	Bernhard Langer	Germany	1993	Sandwich	270
9=	Tom Watson	USA	1980	Muirfield	271
9=	Fuzzy Zoeller	USA	1994	Turnberry	271
9=	Tom Lehman	USA	1996	Lytham	271

The first time the Open Championship was played over four rounds of 18 holes was at Muirfield in 1892, when the amateur Harold H. Hilton won with scores of 78, 81, 72, and 74 for a total of 305.

WORLD TENNIS

TOP 10

WINNERS OF MEN'S GRAND SLAM SINGLES TITLES

	Player/country	A	F	W	US	Total
1	Roy Emerson (Australia)	6	2	2	2	12
2=	Björn Borg (Sweden)	0	6	5	0	11
2=	Rod Laver (Australia)	3	2	4	2	11
4=	Jimmy Connors (USA)	1	0	2	5	8
4=	Ivan Lendl (Czechoslovakia)	2	3	0	3	8
4=	Fred Perry (UK)	1	1	3	3	8
4=	Ken Rosewall (Australia)	4	2	0	2	8
4=	Pete Sampras (USA)	2	0	3	3	8
9=	René Lacoste (France)	0	3	2	2	7
9=	William Larned (USA)	0	0	0	7	7
9=	John McEnroe (USA)	0	0	3	4	7
9=	John Newcombe (Australia)	2	0	3	2	7
9=	William Renshaw (UK)	0	0	7	0	7
9=	Richard Sears (USA)	0	0	0	7	7
9=	Mats Wilander (Sweden)	3	3	0	1	7

A = *Australian Open*; F = *French Open*; W = *Wimbledon*; US = *US Open*

TOP 10

WINNERS OF WOMEN'S GRAND SLAM SINGLES TITLES

	Player/country	A	F	W	US	Total
1	Margaret Court (Australia)	11	5	3	5	24
2	Steffi Graf (Germany)	4	5	7	7	21
3	Helen Wills-Moody (USA)	0	4	8	7	19
4=	Chris Evert-Lloyd (USA)	2	7	3	6	18
4=	Martina Navratilova (Czechoslovakia/USA)	3	2	9	4	18
6	Billie Jean King (USA)	1	1	6	4	12
7=	Maureen Connolly (USA)	1	2	3	3	9
7=	Monica Seles (Yugoslavia/USA)	4	3	0	2	9
9=	Suzanne Lenglen (France)	0	2	6	0	8
9=	Molla Mallory (USA)	0	0	0	8	8

A = *Australian Open*; F = *French Open*; W = *Wimbledon*; US = *US Open*

TOP 10

MALE PLAYERS IN THE WORLD*

	Player	Country
1	Pete Sampras	USA
2	Thomas Muster	Austria
3	Michael Chang	USA
4	Yevgeny Kafelnikov	Russia
5	Goran Ivanisevic	Croatia
6	Richard Krajicek	Netherlands
7	Thomas Enqvist	Sweden
8	Carlos Moya	Spain
9	Marcelo Rios	Chile
10	Wayne Ferreira	South Africa

* *ATP rankings as at 17 March 1997*

WIMBLEDON RECORD-HOLDER
Martina Navratilova's nine singles wins between 1978 and 1990 make her Wimbledon's unrivalled singles champion.

TOP 10

FEMALE PLAYERS IN THE WORLD*

	Player	Country
1	Steffi Graf	Germany
2	Martina Hingis	Switzerland
3	Arantxa Sanchez Vicario	Spain
4	Jana Novotna	Czech Republic
5	Monica Seles	USA
6	Conchita Martinez	Spain
7	Lindsay Davenport	USA
8	Anke Huber	Germany
9	Irinia Spirlea	Romania
10	Iva Majoli	Croatia

* *WTA rankings as at 17 March 1997*

PLAYERS WITH THE MOST WIMBLEDON TITLES

	Player/country	Years	Singles	Doubles	Mixed	Total
1	Billie Jean King (USA)	1961–79	6	10	4	20
2	Elizabeth Ryan (USA)	1914–34	0	12	7	19
3	Martina Navratilova (Czechoslovakia/USA)	1976–95	9	7	2	18
4	Suzanne Lenglen (France)	1919–25	6	6	3	15
5	William Renshaw (UK)	1880–89	7	7	0	14
6=	Louise Brough (USA)	1946–55	4	5	4	13
6=	Lawrence Doherty (UK)	1897–1905	5	8	0	13
8=	Helen Wills-Moody (USA)	1927–38	8	3	1	12
8=	Reginald Doherty (UK)	1897–1905	4	8	0	12
10=	Margaret Court (Australia)	1953–75	3	2	5	10
10=	Doris Hart (USA)	1947–55	1	4	5	10

Billie Jean King's first and last Wimbledon titles were in the ladies' doubles. The first, in 1961, as Billie Jean Moffitt, was with Karen Hantze when they beat Jan Lehane and Margaret Smith 6–3, 6–4. When Billie Jean won her record-breaking 20th title in 1979, she partnered Martina Navratilova to victory over Betty Stove and Wendy Turnbull. Billie Jean could have increased her total in 1983 but was defeated in the mixed doubles.

PLAYERS WITH THE MOST FRENCH CHAMPIONSHIP SINGLES TITLES

	Player*	Years	Titles
1	Chris Evert-Lloyd (USA)	1974–86	7
2	Björn Borg (Sweden)	1974–81	6
3=	Margaret Court (Australia)	1962–73	5
3=	Steffi Graf (Germany)	1987–96	5
5=	Henri Cochet	1926–32	4
5=	Helen Wills-Moody (USA)	1928–32	4
7=	René Lacoste	1925–29	3
7=	Hilde Sperling (Germany)	1935–37	3
7=	Yvon Petra	1943–45	3
7=	Ivan Lendl (Czechoslovakia)	1984–7	3
7=	Mats Wilander (Sweden)	1982–88	3
7=	Monica Seles (Yugoslavia)	1990–92	3

* *Players are from France unless otherwise stated*

PLAYERS WITH THE MOST AUSTRALIAN CHAMPIONSHIP SINGLES TITLES

	Player*	Years	Titles
1	Margaret Court	1960–73	11
2=	Nancy Bolton	1937–51	6
2=	Roy Emerson	1961–67	6
4	Daphne Akhurst	1925–30	5
5=	Pat Wood	1914–23	4
5=	Jack Crawford	1931–35	4
5=	Ken Rosewall	1953–72	4
5=	Evonne Cawley	1974–77	4
5=	Steffi Graf (Germany)	1988–94	4
5=	Monica Seles (Yugoslavia)	1991–96	4

* *Players are from Australia unless otherwise stated*

PLAYERS WITH THE MOST US SINGLES TITLES

	Player*	Years	Titles
1	Molla Mallory	1915–26	8
2=	Richard Sears	1881–87	7
2=	William Larned	1901–11	7
2=	Bill Tilden	1920–29	7
2=	Helen Wills-Moody	1923–31	7
2=	Margaret Court (Australia)	1962–70	7
7	Chris Evert-Lloyd	1975–82	6
8=	Jimmy Connors	1974–83	5
8=	Steffi Graf (Germany)	1988–96	5
10=	Robert Wrenn	1893–97	4
10=	Elisabeth Moore	1896–1905	4
10=	Hazel Wightman	1909–19	4
10=	Helen Jacobs	1932–35	4
10=	Alice Marble	1936–40	4
10=	Pauline Betz	1942–46	4
10=	Maria Bueno (Brazil)	1959–66	4
10=	Billie Jean King	1967–74	4
10=	John McEnroe	1979–84	4
10=	Martina Navratilova	1983–87	4

* *Players are from the US unless otherwise stated*

TEST CRICKET

WICKET-TAKERS OF ALL TIME IN TEST CRICKET

	Player/country	Years	Tests	Wickets
1	Kapil Dev (India)	1978–94	131	434
2	Richard Hadlee (New Zealand)	1973–90	86	431
3	Ian Botham (England)	1977–92	102	383
4	Malcolm Marshall (West Indies)	1978–91	81	376
5	Imran Khan (Pakistan)	1971–92	88	362
6	Dennis Lillee (Australia)	1971–84	70	355
7	Courtney Walsh (West Indies)	1984–97	89	330
8	Bob Willis (England)	1971–84	90	325
9	Wasim Akram (Pakistan)	1985–96	72	311
10	Lance Gibbs (West Indies)	1958–76	79	309

RUN-MAKERS OF ALL TIME IN TEST CRICKET

	Player/country	Years	Tests	Runs
1	Allan Border (Australia)	1978–92	156	11,174
2	Sunil Gavaskar (India)	1971–87	125	10,122
3	Graham Gooch (England)	1975–95	118	8,900
4	Javed Miandad (Pakistan)	1976–94	124	8,832
5	Viv Richards (West Indies)	1974–91	121	8,540
6	David Gower (England)	1978–92	117	8,231
7	Geoff Boycott (England)	1964–82	108	8,114
8	Gary Sobers (West Indies)	1954–74	93	8,032
9	Colin Cowdrey (England)	1954–75	114	7,624
10	Gordon Greenidge (West Indies)	1974–91	108	7,558

HIGHEST INDIVIDUAL TEST INNINGS

	Player/year/match	Runs
1	Brian Lara, 1993–94, West Indies *vs.* England	375
2	Gary Sobers, 1957–58, West Indies *vs.* Pakistan	365*
3	Len Hutton, 1938, England *vs.* Australia	364
4	Hanif Mohammad, 1957–58, Pakistan *vs.* West Indies	337
5	Walter Hammond, 1932–33, England *vs.* New Zealand	336*
6	Don Bradman, 1930, Australia *vs.* England	334
7	Graham Gooch, 1990, England *vs.* India	333
8	Andrew Sandham, 1929–30, England *vs.* West Indies	325
9	Bobby Simpson, 1964, Australia *vs.* England	311
10	John Edrich, 1965, England *vs.* New Zealand	310*

* Not out

PARTNERSHIPS IN TEST CRICKET

	Player/match/year	Runs
1=	Andrew Jones/Martin Crowe, New Zealand *vs.* Sri Lanka, 1990–91	467
1=	Bill Ponsford/Don Bradman, Australia *vs.* England, 1934	467
3	Mudasser Nazar/Javed Miandad, Pakistan *vs.* India, 1982–83	451
4	Conrad Hunte/Gary Sobers, West Indies *vs.* Pakistan, 1957–58	446
5	Vinoo Mankad/Pankaj Roy, India *vs.* New Zealand, 1955–56	413
6	Peter May/Colin Cowdrey, England *vs.* West Indies, 1957	411
7	Sidney Barnes/Don Bradman, Australia *vs.* England, 1946–47	405
8	Gary Sobers/Frank Worrell, West Indies *vs.* England, 1959–60	399
9	Qasim Omar/Javed Miandad, Pakistan *vs.* Sri Lanka, 1985–86	397
10	Bill Ponsford/Don Bradman, Australia *vs.* England, 1934	388

Gundappa Viswanath, Yashpal Sharma, and Dilip Vengsarkar put on 415 runs for India's third wicket against England at Madras in 1981–82. Vengsarkar retired hurt when the partnership was on 99.

FIRST TEST CENTURIES SCORED BY ENGLISH BATSMEN

	Player/venue	Score	Date
1	W.G. Grace, The Oval	152	6–8 Sep 1880
2	George Ulyett, Melbourne	149	10–14 Mar 1882
3	Allan Steel, Sydney	135*	17–21 Feb 1883
4	Allan Steel, Lord's	148	21–23 Jul 1884
5	Walter Read, The Oval	117	11–13 Aug 1884
6	William Barnes, Adelaide	134	12–16 Dec 1884
7	John Briggs, Melbourne	121	1–5 Jan 1885
8	Arthur Shrewsbury, Melbourne	105*	21–25 Mar 1885
9	Arthur Shrewsbury, Lord's	164	19–21 Jul 1886
10	W.G. Grace, The Oval	170	12–14 Aug 1886

* Not out

All 10 centuries were scored against Australia. W.G. Grace's two centuries were the only ones he scored in Test Cricket. Grace's total of 170 runs at the Oval in 1886 was the highest in a Test Match in England for 35 years.

TOP 10

HIGHEST TEAM TOTALS IN TEST CRICKET

	Match (winners first)	Venue	Year	Score
1	England vs. Australia	The Oval	1938	903–7 dec
2	England vs. West Indies	Kingston	1929–30	849
3	West Indies vs. Pakistan	Kingston	1957–58	790–3 dec
4	Australia vs. West Indies	Kingston	1954–55	758–8 dec
5	Australia vs. England	Lord's	1930	729–6 dec
6	Pakistan vs. England	The Oval	1987	708
7	Australia vs. England	The Oval	1934	701
8	Pakistan vs. India	Lahore	1989–90	699–5 dec
9	Australia vs. England	The Oval	1930	695
10	West Indies vs. England	The Oval	1995	692–8 dec

Still holding the record for the highest test cricket total after nearly 60 years, England went into the 4th and final Test against the Australians at the Oval in 1938 needing a win to square the series. They achieved this by a massive margin of an innings and 579 runs, still their biggest winning margin in Test Cricket. Australian bowler "Chuck" Fleetwood-Smith returned figures of 87 overs, 11 maidens, 1 wicket for 298 runs, the greatest number of runs conceded by a bowler in Test Cricket. After being padded up for a day and a half while Len Hutton piled on the runs, England No. 5 Eddie Paynter was eventually dismissed for a duck.

England's record-breaking high scorecard:
L. Hutton, c Hassett b O'Reilly 364; W. J. Edrich, lbw O'Reilly 12; M. Leyland, run out 187; W. R. Hammond, lbw Fleetwood-Smith 59; E. Paynter, lbw O'Reilly 0; D. C. S. Compton, b Waite 1; J. Hardstaff Jr., not out 169; A. Wood, c & b Barnes 53; H. Verity, not out 8; Extras (b22, lb19, w1, nb8) 50. Total (7 wickets dec) 903. Did not bat: K. Farnes, W. E. Bowes.

TOP 10

BATSMEN WITH MOST TEST CENTURIES

	Batsman	Country	Centuries
1	Sunil Gavaskar	India	34
2	Don Bradman	Australia	29
3	Allan Border	Australia	27
4	Gary Sobers	West Indies	26
5=	Greg Chappell	Australia	24
5=	Viv Richards	West Indies	24
7	Javed Miandad	Pakistan	23
8=	Walter Hammond	England	22
8=	Geoff Boycott	England	22
8=	Colin Cowdrey	England	22

TOP 10

LOWEST COMPLETED INNINGS IN TEST CRICKET

	Match (losers first)	Venue	Year	Total
1	New Zealand vs. England	Auckland	1954–55	26
2=	South Africa vs. England	Port Elizabeth	1895–96	30
2=	South Africa vs. England	Birmingham	1924	30
4	South Africa vs. England	Cape Town	1898–99	35
5=	Australia vs. England	Birmingham	1902	36
5=	South Africa vs. Australia	Melbourne	1931–32	36
7=	Australia vs. England	Sydney	1887–88	42
7=	New Zealand vs. Australia	Wellington	1945–46	42
7=	India* vs. England	Lord's	1974	42
10	South Africa vs. England	Cape Town	1888–89	43

* India batted one player short

New Zealand's record-breaking low scorecard:
Second innings – B. Sutcliffe, b Wardle 11; J. G. Leggat, c Hutton, b Tyson 1; M. B. Poore, b Tyson 0; J. R. Reid, b Statham 1; N. McGregor, c May, b Appleyard 1; G. O. Rabone, lbw Statham 7; H. B. Cave, c Graveney, b Appleyard 5; A. R. MacGibbon, lbw Appleyard 0; I. A. Colquhoun, c Graveney, b Appleyard 0; A. M. Moir, not out 0; J. A. Hayes, b Statham 0; Extras 0. Total 26. Fall of wickets: 1–6, 2–8, 3–9, 4–14, 5–14, 6–22, 7–22, 8–22, 9–26. Bowling: Tyson 7–2–10–2; Statham 9–3–9–3; Appleyard 6–3–7–4; Wardle 5–5–0–1.

TOP 10

RUN-MAKERS IN A TEST SERIES

	Player	Series (tests)	Year	Runs
1	Don Bradman	Australia vs. England (5)	1930	974
2	Walter Hammond	England vs. Australia (5)	1928–29	905
3	Mark Taylor	Australia vs. England (6)	1989	839
4	Neil Harvey	Australia vs. South Africa (5)	1952–53	834
5	Viv Richards	West Indies vs. England (4)	1976	829
6	Clyde Walcott	West Indies vs. Australia (5)	1954–55	827
7	Gary Sobers	West Indies vs. Pakistan (5)	1957–58	824
8	Don Bradman	Australia vs. England (5)	1936–37	810
9	Don Bradman	Australia vs. South Africa (5)	1931–32	806
10	Brian Lara	West Indies vs. England (5)	1993–94	798

Don Bradman's remarkable tally against England in 1930 came only a year after Walter Hammond had become the first man to score 900 runs in a series. Bradman scored his runs in just seven innings at an average of 139.

SPORTS

AMERICAN FOOTBALL

122

TOP 10
BIGGEST WINNING MARGINS IN THE SUPER BOWL

	Winners	Runners-up	Year	Score	Margin
1	San Francisco 49ers	Denver Broncos	1990	55–10	45
2	Chicago Bears	New England Patriots	1986	46–10	36
3	Dallas Cowboys	Buffalo Bills	1993	52–17	35
4	Washington Redskins	Denver Broncos	1988	42–10	32
5	LA Raiders	Washington Redskins	1984	38–9	29
6	Green Bay Packers	Kansas City Chiefs	1967	35–10	25
7	San Francisco 49ers	San Diego Chargers	1995	49–26	23
8	San Francisco 49ers	Miami Dolphins	1985	38–16	22
9	Dallas Cowboys	Miami Dolphins	1972	24–3	21
10=	Green Bay Packers	Oakland	1968	33–14	19
10=	New York Giants	Denver Broncos	1987	39–20	19

TOP 10
PLAYERS WITH THE MOST PASSING YARDS IN AN NFL CAREER*

	Player	Passing yards
1	Dan Marino	51,636
2	Fran Tarkenton	47,003
3	John Elway	45,034
4	Warren Moon	43,787
5	Dan Fouts	43,040
6	Joe Montana	40,551
7	Johnny Unitas	40,239
8	Dave Krieg	37,946
9	Boomer Esiason	36,442
10	Jim Kelly	35,467

* To end of 1996–97 season

TOP 10
COLLEGES WITH THE MOST BOWL WINS

	College	Wins
1	Alabama	27
2	University of Southern California (USC)	25
3=	Penn State	21
3=	Tennessee	21
5	Oklahoma	20
6=	Georgia Tech	17
6=	Texas	17
6=	Nebraska	17
9=	Georgia	15
9=	Florida State	15

Source: National Football League

Bowl games are annual end-of-season college championship games, played at the end of December or the beginning of January. The "Big Four" bowl games are: Rose Bowl, Cotton Bowl, Sugar Bowl, and Orange Bowl. The Rose Bowl, one of college football's great occasions, dates to 1902, when the leading Eastern and Western teams met at Pasadena as part of the Tournament of Roses floral celebration, which was first held in 1890. By the turn of the century it had become a major attraction.

TOP 10
PLAYERS WITH THE MOST TOUCHDOWNS IN AN NFL CAREER*

	Player	Touchdowns
1	Jerry Rice	165
2	Marcus Allen	134
3	Walter Payton	126
4	Jim Brown	125
5	John Riggins	116
6	Emmitt Smith	115
7	Lenny Moore	113
8	Don Hutson	105
9	Steve Largent	101
10	Franco Harris	100

* To end of 1996–97 season
Source: National Football League

TOP 10
COACHES IN AN NFL CAREER

	Coach	Games won
1	Don Shula	347
2	George Halas	324
3	Tom Landry	270
4	Curly Lambeau	229
5	Chuck Noll	209
6	Chuck Knox	193
7	Paul Brown	170
8	Bud Grant	168
9	Steve Owen	153
10	Dan Reeves*	149

* Still active at end of 1996–97 season

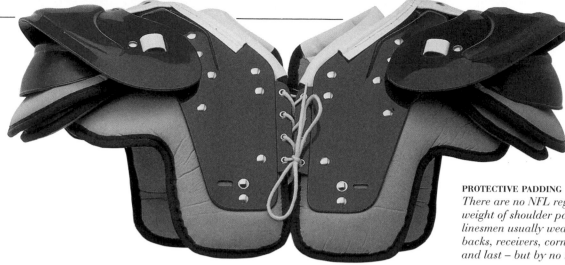

PROTECTIVE PADDING
There are no NFL regulations concerning the size and weight of shoulder pads, but offensive and defensive linesmen usually wear the biggest, followed by the backs, receivers, corners and safeties, quarterbacks, and last – but by no means least – kickers.

TOP 10
LARGEST NFL STADIUMS

	Stadium	Home team	Capacity
1	Pontiac Silverdrome	Detroit Lions	80,365
2	Rich Stadium	Buffalo Bills	80,024
3	Arrowhead Stadium	Kansas City Chiefs	79,101
4	Giants Stadium	New York Giants/Jets	77,716
5	Mile High Stadium	Denver Broncos	76,123
6	Pro Player Stadium	Miami Dolphins	74,916
7	Houlihan's Stadium	Tampa Bay Buccaneers	74,321
8	Sun Devil Stadium	Arizona Cardinals	73,273
9	Jacksonville Municipal Stadium	Jacksonville Jaguars	73,000
10	Ericsson Stadium	Carolina Panthers	72,520

Source: National Football League

TOP 10
FOOTBALL TEAMS*

	Team	Wins	Runners-up	Points
1	Dallas Cowboys	5	3	13
2	San Francisco 49ers	5	0	10
3	Pittsburgh Steelers	4	1	10
4	Washington Redskins	3	2	8
5	Oakland/Los Angeles Raiders	3	1	7
6	Miami Dolphins	2	3	7
7	Green Bay Packers	3	0	6
8	New York Giants	2	0	4
9=	Buffalo Bills	0	4	4
9=	Denver Broncos	0	4	4
9=	Minnesota Vikings	0	4	4

* Based on two points for a Super Bowl win, and one for runner-up

TOP 10
POINT SCORERS IN AN NFL SEASON

	Player	Team	Year	Points
1	Paul Hornung	Green Bay Packers	1960	176
2	Mark Moseley	Washington Redskins	1983	161
3	Gino Cappelletti	Boston Patriots	1964	155*
4	Emitt Smith	Dallas Cowboys	1995	150
5	Chip Lohmiller	Washington Redskins	1991	149
6	Gino Cappelletti	Boston Patriots	1961	147
7	Paul Hornung	Green Bay Packers	1961	146
8=	Jim Turner	New York Jets	1968	145
8=	John Kasay	Carolina Panthers	1996	145
10=	John Riggins	Washington Redskins	1983	144
10=	Kevin Butler#	Chicago Bears	1985	144

* Including a two-point conversion   # The only rookie in this Top 10

TOP 10
RUSHERS IN AN NFL CAREER

	Player	Total yards gained rushing
1	Walter Payton	16,726
2	Eric Dickerson	13,259
3	Tony Dorsett	12,739
4	Jim Brown	12,312
5	Franco Harris	12,120
6	Marcus Allen*	11,738
7	Barry Sanders*	11,725
8	John Riggins	11,352
9	O.J. Simpson	11,236
10	Thurman Thomas*	10,762

* Still active at end of 1996–97 season

BASKETBALL

PLAYERS WHO HAVE PLAYED MOST GAMES IN THE NBA AND THE ABA

	Player	Games played
1	Robert Parish*	1,611
2	Kareem Abdul-Jabbar	1,560
3	Moses Malone*	1,455
4	Artis Gilmore	1,329
5	Elvin Hayes	1,303
6	Caldwell Jones	1,299
7	John Havlicek	1,270
8	Buck Williams*	1,266
9	Paul Silas	1,254
10	Julius Erving	1,243

* *Still active at end of 1996–97 season*

The ABA (American Basketball Association) was established as a rival to the National Basketball Association (NBA) in 1968 and survived until 1976. Because many of the sport's top players "defected", their figures are still included in this list. During the 1995–96 season, Robert Parish moved to the top of this list by playing his 1,561st game on 6 April 1996 at the Gateway Arena in Cleveland, between the Charlotte Hornets and the Cleveland Cavaliers.

POINT SCORERS IN AN NBA CAREER*

	Player	Total points
1	Kareem Abdul-Jabbar	38,387
2	Wilt Chamberlain	31,419
3	Moses Malone	27,409
4	Elvin Hayes	27,313
5	Michael Jordan#	26,920
6	Oscar Robertson	26,710
7	Dominique Wilkins#	26,534
8	John Havlicek	26,395
9	Alex English	25,613
10	Karl Malone#	25,574

* *Regular season games only*
# *Still active at end of 1996–97 season*

If points from the ABA were also considered, then Abdul-Jabbar would still be number one, with the same total. He was born as Lew Alcindor but adopted a new name when he converted to the Islamic faith in 1969. The following year he turned professional, playing for Milwaukee. His career spanned 20 seasons before Abdul-Jabbar retired at the end of the 1989 season. Despite scoring an NBA record 38,387 points, he could not emulate the great Wilt Chamberlain by scoring 100 points in a game, which Chamberlain achieved for Philadelphia against New York at Hershey, Pennsylvania, on 2 March 1962. Chamberlain also scored 70 points in a game six times, a feat that Abdul-Jabbar never succeeded in rivaling.

HIGHEST-EARNING PLAYERS IN THE NBA, 1996–97

	Player/team	Earnings ($)*
1	Michael Jordan, Chicago Bulls	30,140,000
2	Horace Grant, Orlando Magic	14,857,000
3	Reggie Miller, Indiana Pacers	11,250,000
4	Shaquille O'Neal, Los Angeles Lakers	10,714,000
5	Gary Payton, Seattle Supersonics	10,212,000
6	David Robinson, San Antonio Spurs	9,952,000
7	Juwan Howard, Washington Bullets	9,750,000
8	Hakeem Olajuwon, Houston Rockets	9,655,000
9	Alonzo Mourning, Miami Heat	9,380,000
10	Dennis Rodman, Chicago Bulls	9,000,000

* *Salary only*

PLAYERS WITH THE MOST CAREER ASSISTS

	Player	Assists
1	John Stockton*	12,170
2	Magic Johnson	10,141
3	Oscar Robertson	9,887
4	Isiah Thomas	9,061
5	Maurice Cheeks	7,392
6	Lenny Wilkens	7,211
7	Bob Cousy	6,995
8	Guy Rodgers	6,917
9	Nate Archibald	6,476
10	John Lucas	6,454

* *Still active at end of 1996–97 season*

TOP 10

NBA COACHES

	Coach	Games won*		Coach	Games won*
1	Lenny Wilkens#	1,070	6	Pat Riley#	854
2	Red Auerbach	938	7	Don Nelson	851
3	Dick Motta#	936	8	Cotton Fitzsimmons	832
4	Bill Fitch#	924	9	Gene Shue	784
5	Jack Ramsay	864	10	John MacLeod	707

Regular season games only   # *Still active at end of 1996–97 season*

TOP 10

BIGGEST ARENAS IN THE NBA

	Arena	Location	Home team	Capacity
1	The Alamodome	San Antonio, Texas	San Antonio Spurs	25,666
2	Charlotte Coliseum	Charlotte, North Carolina	Charlotte Hornets	23,696
3	SkyDome	Toronto, Ontario	Toronto Raptors	22,911
4	United Center	Chicago, Illinois	Chicago Bulls	21,500
5	The Palace of Auburn Hills	Auburn Hills, Michigan	Detroit Pistons	21,454
6	The Rose Garden	Portland, Oregon	Portland Trailblazers	21,400
7	Gund Arena	Cleveland, Ohio	Cleveland Cavaliers	20,562
8	Byrne Meadowlands Arena	East Rutherford, New Jersey	New Jersey Nets	20,049
9	General Motors Place	Vancouver, British Columbia	Vancouver Grizzlies	19,193
10	Delta Center Arena	Salt Lake City, Utah	Utah Jazz	19,911

The smallest arena in the NBA is the 15,200 capacity Miami Arena, the home of the Miami Heat. The largest ever NBA stadium was the Louisiana Superdome, used by Utah Jazz between 1975 and 1979, which was capable of holding crowds of 47,284.

WARRIORS BATTLE ON
Kevin Wallis is one of the more recent members of the successful Golden State Warriors. The team, formerly the Philadelphia Warriors (1946–62) and San Francisco Warriors (1962–71), won the first ever NBA title in 1947.

TOP 10

TEAMS WITH THE MOST NBA TITLES

	Team*	Titles
1	Boston Celtics	16
2	Minnesota/Los Angeles Lakers	11
3	Chicago Bulls	5
4=	Philadelphia/Golden State Warriors	3
4=	Syracuse Nationals/ Philadelphia 76ers	3
6=	Detroit Pistons	2
6=	Houston Rockets	2
6=	New York Knicks	2
9=	Baltimore Bullets	1
9=	Houston Rockets	1
9=	Milwaukee Bucks	1
9=	Rochester Royals#	1
9=	St. Louis Hawks+	1
9=	Seattle Supersonics	1
9=	Portland Trail Blazers	1
9=	Washington Bullets	1

* *Teams separated by / indicate change of franchise: they have won the championship under both names*
# *Now the Sacramento Kings*
+ *Now the Atlanta Hawks*

A CENTURY OF PRO BASKETBALL

The National Basketball League (NBL), founded in 1898, was the first professional league in the world. Although similar games had been played for centuries, the modern game of basketball had been invented just eight years earlier by Canadian physical education teacher Dr. James A. Naismith (1861–1939) at the International YMCA College at Springfield, Massachusetts, as a game that could be played indoors during the winter. Peach baskets were originally used, but were replaced by metal rings with netting. In 1949 the NBL merged with the Basketball Association of America to create the National Basketball Association (NBA). Basketball is today reckoned to be the world's most popular indoor sport.

RUGBY LEAGUE & UNION

TOP 10

SCORING TEAMS IN THE RUGBY LEAGUE CHALLENGE CUP FINALS*

	Team	Points
1	Wigan	406
2	Leeds	239
3	St. Helens	179
4	Widnes	158
5	Huddersfield	130
6	Warrington	129
7	Hull	128
8	Wakefield Trinity	118
9	Halifax	110
10	Bradford	91

* *Including the two-stage finals during World War II*

TOP 10

HIGHEST-WINNING SCORES IN BRITISH RUGBY LEAGUE HISTORY

	Match (winners first)	Date	Competition	Score
1	Huddersfield *vs.* Blackpool	26 Nov 1994	Regal Trophy	142–4
2	Barrow *vs.* Nottingham	27 Nov 1994	Regal Trophy	138–0
3	Huddersfield *vs.* Swinton Park Rangers	28 Feb 1914	Challenge Cup	119–2
4	Wigan *vs.* Flimby and Fothergill	15 Feb 1925	Challenge Cup	116–0
5	St. Helens *vs.* Carlisle	14 Sep 1986	Lancashire Cup	112–0
6=	St. Helens *vs.* Trafford Borough	15 Sep 1991	Lancashire Cup	104–12
6=	Keighley *vs.* Highfield	23 Apr 1995	Division 2	104–4
8	Leeds *vs.* Coventry	12 Apr 1913	League	102–0
9	Hull Kingston Rovers *vs.* Nottingham City	19 Aug 1990	Yorkshire Cup	100–6
10	Doncaster *vs.* Highfield	20 Mar 1994	Division 2	96–0

The highest score in the First Division is Leeds' 90–0 victory over Barrow on 11 February 1990. Huddersfield had held the record score in British Rugby League for more than 80 years until 1994; in that year they beat their own record by a staggering 23 points. Remarkably, Barrow also broke the old record the very next day when they notched up 138 points against Nottingham. Their winning margin, of 138 points, is identical to the winning margin of Huddersfield against Blackpool.

TOP 10

WINNERS OF THE RUGBY LEAGUE CHALLENGE CUP

	Club	Years	Wins
1	Wigan	1924–95	16
2	Leeds	1910–78	10
3	Widnes	1930–84	7
4=	Huddersfield	1913–53	6
4=	St. Helens	1956–96	6
6=	Wakefield Trinity	1909–63	5
6=	Warrington	1905–74	5
6=	Halifax	1903–87	5
9=	Bradford Northern	1906–49	4
9=	Castleford	1935–86	4

The first Challenge Cup final, then known as the Northern Union Cup, was held at Headingley, Leeds, on 24 April 1897, with Batley the first winners, beating St. Helens 10–3 in front of a crowd of 13,492. When Wigan were eliminated by Salford in 1996, it ended Wigan's eight year run without defeat in the Challenge Cup. The last team to beat them before Salford was Oldham, in 1987.

TOP 10

RUGBY LEAGUE TEAMS*

	Club	Titles
1	Wigan	66
2	Leeds	35
3	St. Helens	34
4	Widnes	27
5	Huddersfield	26
6	Bradford Northern	23
7	Warrington	22
8	Oldham	21
9=	Wakefield Trinity	18
9=	Hull	18
9=	Hull Kingston Rovers	18

* *To end of 1996 season*

This list is based on the number of wins in the major competitions: Challenge Cup, Regal/John Player Trophy, Divisional Premierships, Championship play-off (1906–73), Divisions 1 and 2 (since 1973), Division 3 (1993), and the Lancashire/Yorkshire Cup.

TOP 10

POINTS SCORERS IN THE SUPER LEAGUE

	Club	Points
1	St. Helens	950
2	Wigan	902
3	Bradford Bulls	767
4	Halifax	667
5	London Broncos	611
6	Sheffield	599
7	Warrington	569
8	Leeds	555
9	Castleford Tigers	548
10	Oldham Bears	473

Rugby League took on a new look in 1996 as it moved away from its traditional winter-sport roots to become a summer game. The Super League was also introduced in 1996, with St. Helens its first champions.

SCORES IN THE 1995 RUGBY UNION WORLD CUP

	Winners/loser	Round	Score
1	New Zealand *vs.* Japan	Pool C	145–17
2	Scotland *vs.* Ivory Coast	Pool D	89–0
3	Wales *vs.* Japan	Pool C	57–10
4	France *vs.* Ivory Coast	Pool D	54–18
5	Ireland *vs.* Japan	Pool C	50–28
6	New Zealand *vs.* Scotland	Quarter-final	48–30
7	New Zealand *vs.* England	Semi-final	45–29
8	England *vs.* Western Samoa	Pool B	44–22
9	New Zealand *vs.* Ireland	Pool C	43–19
10=	Australia *vs.* Romania	Pool A	42–3
10=	Western Samoa *vs.* Italy	Pool B	42–18
10=	South Africa *vs.* Western Samoa	Quarter-final	42–14

The 1st World Cup was launched in 1987 and played jointly in Australia and New Zealand. Sixteen nations competed in the final stages with New Zealand beating France 29–9 in the final at Auckland. Four years later, the British Isles and France were joint hosts of the final stages, with Twickenham staging the final (in which England lost 12–6 to Australia). The 1995 tournament, also contested by 16 teams, was played exclusively in South Africa.

BIGGEST WINS IN THE RUGBY UNION INTERNATIONAL CHAMPIONSHIP

	Match (winners first)	Venue	Year	Score
1	Wales *vs.* France	Swansea	1910	49–14
2	France *vs.* Scotland	Paris	1997	47–20
3	England *vs.* Ireland	Twickenham	1997	46–6
4=	France *vs.* Ireland	Paris	1996	45–10
4=	France *vs.* Ireland	Paris	1996	45–10
6	France *vs.* Ireland	Paris	1992	44–12
7	England *vs.* Scotland	Twickenham	1997	41–13
8	England *vs.* France	Paris	1914	39–13
9	Scotland *vs.* Ireland	Murrayfield	1997	38–10
10	England *vs.* France	Twickenham	1911	37–0

This Top 10 is based on the winning team's scores, not the margin of victory. However, where two nations share the highest score, then margin of victory is used to separate them. The biggest victory by margin is England's 46–6 win over Ireland at Twickenham in 1997.

INDIVIDUAL POINTS SCORERS IN ONE RUGBY UNION WORLD CUP TOURNAMENT

	Player/country	Year	Points
1	Grant Fox, New Zealand	1987	126
2	Gavin Hastings, Scotland	1995	104
3	Thierry Lacroix, France	1995	103
4	Andrew Mehrtens, New Zealand	1995	84
5	Michael Lynagh, Australia	1987	82
6	Rob Andrew, England	1995	70
7	Ralph Keyes, Ireland	1991	68
8	Michael Lynagh, Australia	1991	66
9	Gavin Hastings, Scotland	1987	62
10	Gavin Hastings, Scotland	1991	61

POINTS SCORERS IN A RUGBY UNION INTERNATIONAL CHAMPIONSHIP SEASON

	Player/country	Year	Points
1	Jonathan Webb, England	1992	67
2	Paul Grayson, England	1996	64
3	Simon Hodgkinson, England	1991	60
4	Gavin Hastings, Scotland	1995	56
5	Jean-Patrick Lescarboura, France	1984	54
6	Rob Andrew, England	1995	53
7=	Ollie Campbell, Ireland	1983	52
7=	Gavin Hastings, Scotland	1986	52
7=	Paul Thorburn, Wales	1986	52
7=	Paul Grayson, England	1997	52

BIGGEST TEST WINS BY RUGBY UNION'S BRITISH LIONS

	Opponents	Test/year	Score
1	Australia	2nd Test 1966	31–0
2	South Africa	2nd Test 1974	28–9
3	South Africa	3rd Test 1974	26–9
4=	Australia	2nd Test 1950	24–3
4=	Australia	2nd Test 1959	24–3
6	South Africa	1st Test 1955	23–22
7	South Africa	3rd Test 1938	21–16
8	New Zealand	2nd Test 1993	20–7
9	Australia	2nd Test 1989	19–12
10	Australia	3rd Test 1989	19–18

This Top 10 is based on the most points scored by the Lions, not the greatest margin of victory, their record for which is their 31–0 win over Australia in 1966.

SOCCER – THE WORLD CUP

HIGHEST-SCORING WORLD CUP FINALS

	Year	Games	Goals	Average per game
1	1954	26	140	5.38
2	1938	18	84	4.66
3	1934	17	70	4.11
4	1950	22	88	4.00
5	1930	18	70	3.88
6	1958	35	126	3.60
7	1970	32	95	2.96
8	1982	52	146	2.81
9=	1962	32	89	2.78
9=	1966	32	89	2.78

HIGHEST-SCORING MATCHES IN THE FINAL STAGES OF THE WORLD CUP

	Match/year	Score
1	Austria *vs.* Switzerland, 1954	7–5
2=	Brazil *vs.* Poland, 1938	6–5
2=	Hungary *vs.* W. Germany, 1954	8–3
2=	Hungary *vs.* El Salvador, 1982	10–1
5	France *vs.* Paraguay, 1958	7–3
6=	Hungary *vs.* South Korea, 1954	9–0
6=	W. Germany *vs.* Turkey, 1954	7–2
6=	France *vs.* W. Germany, 1958	6–3
6=	Yugoslavia *vs.* Zaïre, 1974	9–0
10=	Italy *vs.* USA, 1934	7–1
10=	Sweden *vs.* Cuba, 1938	8–0
10=	Uruguay *vs.* Bolivia, 1950	8–0
10=	England *vs.* Belgium, 1954	4–4
10=	Portugal *vs.* North Korea, 1966	5–3

GOAL SCORERS IN THE FINAL STAGES OF THE WORLD CUP

	Player/country/years	Goals
1	Gerd Müller (W. Germany), 1970–74	14
2	Just Fontaine (France), 1958	13
3	Pelé (Brazil), 1958–70	12
4	Sandor Kocsis (Hungary), 1954	11
5=	Helmut Rahn (W. Germany), 1954–58	10
5=	Teófilio Cubillas (Peru), 1970–78	10
5=	Grzegorz Lato (Poland), 1974–82	10
5=	Gary Lineker (England), 1986–90	10
9=	Leónidas da Silva (Brazil), 1934–38	9
9=	Ademir Marques de Menezes (Brazil), 1950	9
9=	Vavà (Brazil), 1958–62	9
9=	Eusébio (Portugal), 1966	9
9=	Uwe Seeler (W. Germany), 1958–70	9
9=	Jairzinho (Brazil), 1970–74	9
9=	Paolo Rossi (Italy), 1978–82	9
9=	Karl-Heinz Rummenigge (W. Germany), 1978–86	9

COUNTRIES THAT HAVE PLAYED THE MOST MATCHES IN THE FINAL STAGES OF THE WORLD CUP

	Country	Tournaments	Matches played
1=	Brazil	15	73
1=	Germany/West Germany	13	73
3	Italy	13	61
4	Argentina	11	52
5	England	9	41
6=	Uruguay	9	37
6=	Spain	9	37
6=	Sweden	9	37
9=	France	9	34
9=	USSR/Russia	8	34

HOST COUNTRIES IN THE WORLD CUP

	Host	Year	Final Standing
1=	Uruguay	1930	Winners
1=	Italy	1934	Winners
1=	England	1966	Winners
1=	West Germany	1974	Winners
1=	Argentina	1978	Winners
6=	Brazil	1950	Runners-up
6=	Sweden	1958	Runners-up
8=	Chile	1962	Third
8=	Italy	1990	Third
10=	France	1938	Last 8
10=	Switzerland	1954	Last 8
10=	Mexico	1970	Last 8
10=	Mexico	1986	Last 8

Spain in 1982 (last 12) and the US in 1994 (last 16) are the only two host countries not to have reached the last eight.

LEAST-SUCCESSFUL COUNTRIES IN THE WORLD CUP

	Country	Tournaments	Matches played	won
1	Bulgaria	5	16	0
2	South Korea	4	11	0
3=	El Salvador	2	6	0
3=	Bolivia	3	6	0
5	Republic of Ireland	1	5	0
6	Egypt	2	4	0
7=	Canada	1	3	0
7=	Greece	1	3	0
7=	Haiti	1	3	0
7=	Iraq	1	3	0
7=	New Zealand	1	3	0
7=	United Arab Emirates	1	3	0
7=	Zaïre	1	3	0

THE WORLD CUP

aunched in 1930, credit for the inauguration of the tournament goes to former FIFA president Jules Rimet, who lent his name to the trophy, which was first won by Uruguay on home soil. Thirteen countries competed in the first tournament, in marked contrast to the 176 countries attempting to qualify for the 1998 tournament in France. The most dominant nation has been Brazil, winning the first of their four trophies in 1958. After winning the title for the 3rd time in 1970 they became the permanent holders of the Jules Rimet trophy. Four years later, West Germany became the first nation to lift the new FIFA World Cup trophy.

FIRST WORLD CUP WINNERS
The Uruguayan team won the inaugural World Cup in 1930, held on home soil in Montevideo, with a 4–2 victory over neighbours Argentina.

TOP 10

COUNTRIES IN THE WORLD CUP*

	Country	Win	R/u	3rd	4th	Total
1	Germany/W. Germany	3	3	2	1	26
2	Brazil	4	1	2	1	24
3	Italy	3	2	1	1	21
4	Argentina	2	2	-	-	14
5	Uruguay	2	-	-	2	10
6	Sweden	-	1	2	1	8
7=	Czechoslovakia	-	2	-	-	6
7=	Hungary	-	2	-	-	6
7=	Netherlands	-	2	-	-	6
10=	England	1	-	-	1	5
10=	France	-	-	2	1	5

* *Based on 4 pts for winning the tournament, 3 pts for runner-up, 2 pts for 3rd place, and 1 pt for 4th, up to and including 1994 World Cup*

GARY'S HAT TRICK
England appeared destined to exit the 1986 World Cup finals in Mexico until Gary Lineker scored three goals against Poland.

PELÉ THE CONQUEROR
Pelé, considered the world's greatest player, is seen here in action in what is regarded as the greatest ever World Cup final, Brazil vs. Italy, 1970.

GERMAN WIN
Victory for West Germany over Argentina in 1990 was sweet revenge for their defeat four years earlier.

CYCLING

T O P 1 0

MOST SUCCESSFUL OLYMPIC CYCLING COUNTRIES

	Country	gold	Medals silver	bronze	total
1	France	32	18	21	71
2	Italy	30	15	6	51
3	Great Britain	8	21	16	45
4	Germany/W Germany	7	12	14	33
5	Netherlands	10	12	5	27
6	USSR/Russia	12	5	9	26
7	Belgium	6	6	9	21
8=	Denmark	6	7	7	20
8=	Australia	5	7	8	20
10=	East Germany	7	6	4	17
10=	USA	4	4	9	17

Although it is the most successful country, France has not won a gold medal since Daniel Morelon won the sprint title in 1972.

T O P 1 0

LONGEST *TOURS DE FRANCE*

	Year	Winner/nationality	Stages	Distance km	miles
1	1926	Lucien Buysse (Belgium)	17	5,745	3,570
2	1919	Firmin Lambot (Belgium)	15	5,560	3,455
3	1911	Gustave Garrigou (France)	15	5,544	3,445
4	1920	Philippe Thys (Belgium)	15	5,503	3,419
5	1921	Léon Scieur (Belgium)	15	5,484	3,408
6	1925	Ottavio Bottecchia (Italy)	18	5,430	3,374
7	1924	Ottavio Bottecchia (Italy)	15	5,427	3,372
8	1914	Philippe Thys (Belgium)	15	5,414	3,364
9	1913	Philippe Thys (Belgium)	15	5,387	3,347
10	1923	Henri Pélissier (France)	15	5,386	3,347

The *Tour de France* is considered both the most important cycle stage race and the sporting event that attracts the largest live audience in the world. It was founded in 1903 by Henri Desgrange, a cyclist who was the first holder of the world one-hour record. He later became editor of the specialist cycling newspaper *L'Auto*, and the race was originally staged to publicize it. The first race covered 2,428 km/1,510 miles and was held over six extremely long stages, some of which involved riding through the night. The inaugural race was won by an Italian-born but naturalized Frenchman, a chimney sweep called Maurice Garin, who won by a remarkable 2 hours 49 minutes, the biggest-ever winning margin in the race. The longest post-war race was in 1948, when Italy's Gino Bartali won the 4,922-km/3,058-mile race. The shortest-ever race was the second *Tour*, which took place in 1904 and measured just 2,388 km/1,484 miles. The winner was Henri Cornet of France.

T O P 1 0

CYCLISTS WITH THE MOST CLASSIC RACE WINS

	Cyclist/country	Wins
1	Eddy Merckx (Belgium)	38
2	Bernard Hinault (France)	23
3	Fausto Coppi (Italy)	20
4	Kacqiues Anquetil (France)	19
5=	Alfredo Binda (Italy)	14
5=	Roger De Vlaeminck (Belgium)	14
7	Rik van Looy (Belgium)	13
8=	Gino Bartali (Italy)	12
8=	Felice Gimondi (Italy)	12
10=	Rik van Steenbergen (Belgium)	11
10=	Sean Kelly (Ireland)	11

The classic races are the three major tours of France, Italy, and Spain, the *Grand Prix des Nations*, the World Championship Road Race, and other prestigious road races including the Paris–Brussels, Paris–Roubaix, and the Tour of Lombardy.

T O P 1 0

COUNTRIES WITH MOST *TOUR DE FRANCE* WINNERS

	Country	Winners
1	France	36
2	Belgium	18
3=	Italy	8
3=	Spain	8
5	Luxembourg	4
6	USA	3
7=	Switzerland	2
7=	Netherlands	2
9=	Denmark	1
9=	Ireland	1

In 1991 Brazil became the 19th nation to win a stage in the tour.

TOP 10

POINTS-SCORERS IN THE 1996 MOUNTAIN BIKE WORLD CUP

	Cyclist/country	Points*
1	Christophe Dupouey (France)	373
2	Thomas Frischknecht (Switzerland)	357
3	Miguel Martinez (France)	321
4	Hubert Pallhuber (Italy)	302
5	Alessandro Fontana (Italy)	291
6	Lennie Kristensen (Denmark)	288
7	Rune Hoydahl (Norway)	266
8	Mike Kluge (Germany)	264
9	David Baker (UK)	262
10	Bart Brentjens (Netherlands)	244

* *Total scored in Men's Cross-Country events only in 10 locations*

TOP 10

TOUR DE FRANCE WINS

	Cyclist/country	Wins
1=	Jacques Anquetil (France)	5
1=	Eddy Merckx (Belgium)	5
1=	Bernard Hinault (France)	5
1=	Miguel Indurain (Spain)	5
5=	Philippe Thys (Belgium)	3
5=	Louison Bobet (France)	3
5=	Greg LeMond (USA)	3
8=	Lucien Petit-Breton (France)	2
8=	Firmin Lambot (Belgium)	2
8=	Ottavio Bottecchia (Italy)	2
8=	Nicholas Frantz (Luxemburg)	2
8=	André Leducq (France)	2
8=	Antonin Magne (France)	2
8=	Gino Bartali (Italy)	2
8=	Sylvere Maës (Belgium)	2
8=	Fausto Coppi (Italy)	2
8=	Bernard Thevenet (France)	2
8=	Laurent Fignon (France)	2

ON YOUR BIKE

Perhaps because its introduction was gradual and informal, rather than based on a single invention, the precise origin of the mountain bike is hotly debated, but it seems probable that it dates from 1973. In that year a group of cycling enthusiasts in Cupertino, California, USA, began customizing road cycles to use them off-road. Shortly afterwards, another group of road-race devotees in Marin County, California, known as the Canyon Gang, started riding off-road in the Mt. Tamalpais area, using bicycles with balloon tyres. Influenced by contact with the Cupertino group, they and other followers made further modifications to their bikes, progressively establishing the features that have since become familiar as mountain biking has become an internationally popular recreation and sport.

25 YEARS AGO · YEARS AGO · YEARS AGO · YEARS AGO

TOP 10

FASTEST AVERAGE WINNING SPEEDS IN THE *TOUR DE FRANCE*

	Winner/country/year	Average speed kph	mph
1	Bjarne Rijs (Denmark), 1996	39.969	24.841
2	Miguel Indurain (Spain), 1992	39.504	24.551
3	Miguel Indurain (Spain), 1995	39.193	24.359
4	Pedro Delgado (Spain), 1988	39.142	24.322
5	Miguel Indurain (Spain), 1991	39.021	24.247
6	Greg LeMond (USA), 1990	38.933	24.192
7	Miguel Indurain (Spain), 1993	38.709	24.058
8	Miguel Indurain (Spain), 1994	38.383	23.855
9	Bernard Hinault (France), 1981	37.844	23.515
10	Greg LeMond (USA), 1989	37.818	23.499

TOP 10

TOURS DE FRANCE WITH THE MOST FINISHERS

	Year	Starters	Finishers
1	1991	198	158
2	1990	198	156
3	1988	198	151
4	1989	198	148
5	1985	180	144
6	1993	180	136
7	1987	207	135
8	1986	210	132
9	1992	198	130
10	1996	198	129

MOTOR RACING

DRIVERS WITH THE MOST GRAND PRIX WINS

	Driver/country	Years	Wins
1	Alain Prost (France)	1981–93	51
2	Ayrton Senna (Brazil)	1985–93	41
3	Nigel Mansell (UK)	1985–94	31
4	Jackie Stewart (UK)	1965–73	27
5=	Jim Clark (UK)	1962–68	25
5=	Niki Lauda (Austria)	1974–85	25
7	Juan Manuel Fangio (Argentina)	1950–57	24
8	Nelson Piquet (Brazil)	1980–91	23
9	Michael Schumacher (Germany)	1992–96	22
10	Damon Hill (UK)	1993–96	21

MANUFACTURERS WITH THE MOST WORLD TITLES

	Manufacturer	Titles
1=	Ferrari	8
1=	Williams	8
3	Lotus	7
4	McLaren	6
5=	Brabham	2
5=	Cooper	2
7=	BRM	1
7=	Matra	1
7=	Tyrrell	1
7=	Vanwall	1
7=	Benetton	1

McLaren had their 104th win in 1993 when Ayrton Senna won at Monaco. The McLaren team was first formed in 1963 by New Zealander Bruce McLaren and ventured into Formula One in 1966. McLaren's first Grand Prix did not come until the 1968 Belgian Grand Prix. The team suffered a great loss in 1970 when McLaren was killed during a training session at Goodwood.

RACING RIVALS
At the end of the 1996 season, just one win separated the new World Champion Damon Hill (right) and Michael Schumacher (left).

DRIVERS WITH THE MOST GRAND PRIX POINTS

	Driver/country	Years	Points
1	Alain Prost (France)	1980–93	798.5
2	Ayrton Senna (Brazil)	1985–94	614
3	Nelson Piquet (Brazil)	1978–91	485.5
4	Nigel Mansell (UK)	1980–94	482
5	Niki Lauda (Austria)	1971–85	420.5
6	Michael Schumacher (Germany)	1991–96	361
7	Jackie Stewart (UK)	1965–73	360
8	Gerhard Berger (Austria)	1984–95	338
9	Damon Hill (UK)	1993-96	326
10	Carlos Reutemann (Argentina)	1972–82	310

By coming into the list at No.9, Damon Hill has pushed his father Graham into 11th place and off the list for the first time. The World Drivers' Championship was launched in 1950 and over the years the format has changed, allowing, in many cases, for only a certain number of successful drives to be taken into consideration.

BRITISH DRIVERS WITH THE MOST GRAND PRIX WINS

	Driver	Years	Wins
1	Nigel Mansell	1985–94	31
2	Jackie Stewart	1965–73	27
3	Jim Clark	1962–68	25
4	Damon Hill	1993–96	21
5	Stirling Moss	1955–61	16
6	Graham Hill	1962–69	14
7	James Hunt	1975–77	10
8=	Tony Brooks	1957–59	6
8=	John Surtees	1963–67	6
10	John Watson	1976–83	5

DRIVERS WITH THE MOST WINS IN A SEASON

	Driver/country	Season	Wins
1	Nigel Mansell (UK)	1992	9
2=	Ayrton Senna (Brazil)	1988	8
2=	Michael Schumacher (Germany)	1994	8
2=	Michael Schumacher (Germany)	1995	8
2=	Damon Hill (UK)	1996	8
6=	Jim Clark (UK)	1963	7
6=	Alain Prost (France)	1984	7*
6=	Alain Prost (France)	1988	7*
6=	Alain Prost (France)	1993	7
6=	Ayrton Senna (Brazil)	1991	7

* Did not win world title that year

In 1988 the Marlboro-McLaren pair of Ayrton Senna and Alain Prost completely dominated the Grand Prix scene by winning 15 of the 16 rounds between them. The only one they did not win was the Italian Grand Prix at Monza, which was won by the Austrian Gerhard Berger in a Ferrari.

DRIVERS WITH THE MOST WORLD TITLES

Driver/country	Titles	Driver/country	Titles
1 Juan Manuel Fangio (Argentina)	5	**3=** Jackie Stewart (UK)	3
2 Alain Prost (France)	4	**8=** Alberto Ascari (Italy)	2
3= Jack Brabham (Australia)	3	**8=** Jim Clark (UK)	2
3= Niki Lauda (Austria)	3	**8=** Graham Hill (UK)	2
3= Nelson Piquet (Brazil)	3	**8=** Emerson Fittipaldi (Brazil)	2
3= Ayrton Senna (Brazil)	3	**8=** Michael Schumacher (Germany)	2

YOUNGEST WORLD CHAMPIONS OF ALL TIME

Driver/country	Year	Age* yrs	Age* mths
1 Emerson Fittipaldi (Brazil)	1972	25	9
2 Michael Schumacher (Germany)	1994	25	10
3 Niki Lauda (Austria)	1975	26	7
4 Jim Clark (UK)	1963	27	7
5 Jochen Rindt (Austria)	1970	28	6
6 Ayrton Senna (Brazil)	1988	28	7
7= James Hunt (UK)	1976	29	2
7= Nelson Piquet (Brazil)	1981	29	2
9 Mike Hawthorn (UK)	1958	29	6
10 Jody Scheckter (South Africa)	1979	29	8

* If a driver can appear twice, only his youngest age is considered

OLDEST WORLD CHAMPIONS OF ALL TIME

Driver/country	Year	Age* yrs	Age* mths
1 Juan Manuel Fangio (Argentina)	1957	46	2
2 Giuseppe Farina (Italy)	1950	43	11
3 Jack Brabham (Australia)	1966	40	6
4 Graham Hill (UK)	1968	39	9
5 Mario Andretti (USA)	1978	38	8
6 Alain Prost (France)	1993	38	7
7 Nigel Mansell (UK)	1992	37	11
8 Damon Hill (UK)	1996	36	1
9 Niki Lauda (Austria)	1984	35	8
10 Nelson Piquet (Brazil)	1987	35	3

* If a driver can appear twice, only his oldest age is considered

THE WORLD LAND SPEED RECORD

The first world land speed record was set 100 years ago, on 18 December 1898, when at Achères, France, Count Gaston de Chasseloup-Laubat drove a Jeantaud to a then staggering speed of 62.78 km/h/39.24 mph. Concerned that the sales of his vehicles would be affected, Belgian car manufacturer Camille Jenatzy set about smashing the record himself, which he did on 17 January 1899, taking it to 66.27 km/h/ 41.42 mph. Both men each broke the record on two further occasions before 1899 was out, and by the end of the year it had reached 105.26 km/h/65.79 mph. The record was held until 1902, when Leon Serpollet attained 120.09 km/h/ 75.06 mph at Nice. The psychologically important mph "barriers" were then progressively broken: 100 mph in 1904, 200 mph in 1927, 300 mph in 1935, 400 mph in 1963, 500 mph in 1964, and 600 mph in 1965. A century after the first land speed record was set, it stands at 1,013.47 km/h/ 633.47 mph.

MANUFACTURERS WITH THE MOST GRAND PRIX WINS

Manufacturer	Years	Wins
1 Ferrari	1951–96	108
2 McLaren	1968–93	104
3 Williams	1979–96	95
4 Lotus	1960–87	79
5 Brabham	1964–85	35
6 Benetton	1986–95	25
7 Tyrrell	1971–83	23
8 BRM	1959–72	17
9 Cooper	1958–67	16
10 Renault	1979–83	15

CAR RACING

FASTEST WINNING SPEEDS OF THE INDIANAPOLIS 500

	Driver*	Car	Year	Speed km/h	mph
1	Arie Luyendyk (Netherlands)	Lola-Chevrolet	1990	299.307	185.984
2	Rick Mears	Chevrolet-Lumina	1991	283.980	176.457
3	Bobby Rahal	March-Cosworth	1986	274.750	170.722
4	Emerson Fittipaldi (Brazil)	Penske-Chevrolet	1989	269.695	167.581
5	Rick Mears	March-Cosworth	1984	263.308	163.612
6	Mark Donohue	McLaren-Offenhauser	1972	262.619	162.962
7	Al Unser, Jr.	March-Cosworth	1987	260.995	162.175
8	Tom Sneva	March-Cosworth	1983	260.902	162.117
9	Gordon Johncock	Wildcat-Cosworth	1982	260.760	162.029
10	Al Unser	Lola-Cosworth	1978	259.689	161.363

* All US drivers unless otherwise stated

The first Indianapolis 500, known affectionately as the "Indy", was held on Memorial Day, 30 May 1911, and was won by Ray Harroun driving a bright yellow 447-cubic inch six-cylinder Marmon Wasp at an average speed of 120.060 km/h/74.602 mph. The race takes place over 200 laps of the 2½-mile Indianapolis Raceway, which from 1927 to 1945 was owned by the World War I flying ace Eddie Rickenbacker. Over the years the speed has steadily increased: Harroun's race took 6 hours 42 minutes 6 seconds to complete, while Arie Luyendyk's record-breaking win was achieved in just 2 hours 18 minutes 18.248 seconds.

WINNERS OF THE INDIANAPOLIS 500 WITH THE HIGHEST STARTING POSITIONS

	Driver	Year	Starting position
1=	Ray Harroun	1911	28
1=	Louis Meyer	1936	28
3	Fred Frame	1932	27
4	Johnny Rutherford	1974	25
5=	Kelly Petillo	1935	22
5=	George Souders	1927	22
7	L.L. Corum and Joe Boyer	1924	21
8=	Frank Lockart	1926	20
8=	Tommy Milton	1921	20
8=	Al Unser, Jr.	1987	20

Of the 75 winners of the Indianapolis 500, 44 have started from a position between 1 and 5 on the starting grid. This Top 10 lists those winners who started the race from farthest back in the starting lineup.

MONEY-WINNERS AT THE INDIANAPOLIS 500 IN 1996

	Driver	Car	Total prizes ($)
1	Buddy Lazier	Reynard/Ford Cosworth	1,367,854
2	Davy Jones	Lola/Mercedes Illmor	632,503
3	Richie Hearn	Reynard/Ford Cosworth	375,203
4	Alessandro Zampedri	Lola/Ford Cosworth	270,853
5	Roberto Guerrero	Reynard/Ford Cosworth	315,503
6	Eliseo Salazar	Lola/Ford Cosworth	226,653
7	Danny Ongais	Lola/Menard V6	228,253
8	Hideshi Matsuda	Lola/Ford Cosworth	233,953
9	Robbie Buhl	Lola/Ford Cosworth	195,403
10	Scott Sharp	Lola/Ford Cosworth	202,053

Drivers are ranked here according to their finishing order, but as the list indicates, prize money – which in 1996 totalled $8,114,600 – does not follow precisely, varying according to such designations as first using a particular brand of tyre. Even losers can be high-earners in the Indy: Johnny Unser, who finished in 33rd and last position earned $143,953. The only woman in the race, Lyn St. James, was placed 14th in the money-winners with $182,603.

DRIVERS WITH THE MOST WINSTON CUP TITLES

	Driver	Years	Victories	Titles
1=	Richard Petty	1964–79	200	7
1=	Dale Earnhardt*	1980–94	68	7
3=	Lee Petty	1954–59	54	3
3=	David Pearson	1966–69	106	3
3=	Cale Yarborough	1976–78	83	3
3=	Darrell Waltrip*	1981–85	84	3
7=	Herb Thomas	1951–53	49	2
7=	Tim Flock	1952–55	40	2
7=	Buck Baker	1956–57	46	2
7=	Ned Jarrett	1961–65	50	2
7=	Joe Weatherly	1962–63	24	2

* Still driving at the end of the 1995 season

The Winston Cup is a season-long series of races organized by the National Association for Stock Car Auto Racing, Inc. (NASCAR). Races, which take place over enclosed circuits, are among the most popular car races in the US. The series started in 1949 as the Grand National series, but changed its title to the Winston Cup in 1970.

FASTEST WINNING SPEEDS OF THE DAYTONA 500

	Driver*	Car	Year	Speed km/h	mph
1	Buddy Baker	Oldsmobile	1980	285.823	177.602
2	Bill Elliott	Ford	1987	283.668	176.263
3	Bill Elliott	Ford	1985	277.234	172.265
4	Richard Petty	Buick	1981	273.027	169.651
5	Derrike Cope	Chevrolet	1990	266.766	165.761
6	A.J. Foyt, Jr.	Mercury	1972	259.990	161.550
7	Richard Petty	Plymouth	1966	258.504	160.627#
8	Davey Allison	Ford	1992	257.913	160.260
9	Bobby Allison	Ford	1978	257.060	159.730
10	LeeRoy Yarborough	Ford	1967	254.196	157.950

* All drivers from the US
# Race reduced to 797 km/495 miles

First held in 1959, the Daytona 500 is raced every February at the Daytona International Speedway, Daytona Beach, Florida. One of the most prestigious races of the NASCAR season, it covers 200 laps of the 2½-mile high-banked oval circuit. The race has produced its share of exciting racing, as in 1988 when Bobby Allinson, the winner in 1978 and 1982, driving a Buick, beat his son Davey Allison in a Ford into 2nd place by a margin of just two car lengths. The fastest speed recorded in this Top 10, that of Buddy Baker in 1980, also produced the shortest full-length race time, of 2 hrs 48 min 55 secs, compared with the slowest-ever winning time of 4 hrs 30 min in 1960, when the race was won by Junior Johnson in a Chevrolet at an average speed of 200.750 km/h/124.740 mph.

SLOWEST WINNING SPEEDS OF THE INDIANAPOLIS 500

	Winner/year	Average speed km/h	mph
1	Ray Harroun, 1911	120.060	74.602
2	Jules Goux, 1913	122.202	75.933
3	Joe Dawson, 1912	126.686	78.719
4	Rene Thomas, 1914	132.735	82.474
5	Dario Resta, 1916	135.187	84.001
6	Howard Wilcox, 1919	141.703	88.050
7	Gaston Chevrolet, 1920	142.617	88.618
8	Ralph DePalma, 1915	143.296	89.040
9	Tommy Milton, 1921	144.231	89.621
10	Tommy Milton, 1923	146.376	90.954

The speed of the Indianapolis 500 has steadily increased. The 100 mph (161 km/h) barrier was broken in 1930 by Billy Arnold, who won at an average speed of 100.448 mph (161.655 km/h).

NASCAR MONEY-WINNERS OF ALL TIME*

	Driver	Total prizes ($)
1	Dale Earnhardt	28,617,845
2	Bill Elliott	16,591,529
3	Darrell Waltrip	15,391,155
4	Terry Labonte	15,049,797
5	Rusty Wallace	14,788,069
6	Mark Martin	12,234,017
7	Ricky Rudd	11,871,803
8	Jeff Gordon	11,074,328
9	Geoff Bodine	10,733,939
10	Sterling Martin	9,288,581

* Up to and including April 6th, 1997 Interstate Batteries 500 race in Fort Worth, TX

Source: NASCAR (National Association for Stock Car Auto Racing, Inc.)

CART DRIVERS WITH THE MOST RACE WINS

	Driver/race career	Wins
1	A.J. Foyt, Jr. (1960-1981)	67
2	Mario Andretti (1965-1993)	52
3	Al Unser (1965-1987)	39
4	Bobby Unser (1966-1981)	35
5	Michael Andretti (1986-1996)	35
6	Al Unser Jr. (1984-1995)	31
7	Rick Mears (1978-1991)	29
8	Johnny Rutherford (1965-1986)	27
9	Roger Ward (1953-1966)	26
10	Gordon Johncock (1965-1983)	25

Source: Championship Auto Racing Teams

LAST DRIVERS KILLED DURING THE INDIANAPOLIS 500

	Driver	Year
1	Swede Savage	1973
2=	Eddie Sachs	1964
2=	Dave MacDonald	1964
4	Pat O'Connor	1958
5	Bill Vukovich Sr.	1955
6	Carl Scarborough	1953
7	Shorty Cantlon	1947
8	Floyd Roberts	1939
9	Clay Weatherly	1935
10=	Mark Billman	1933
10=	Lester Spangle	1933

WINTER SPORTS

ALPINE SKIING WORLD CUP TITLES – MEN

	Name/country	Years	Titles
1	Marc Girardelli (Luxembourg)	1985–93	5
2=	Gustavo Thoeni (Italy)	1971–75	4
2=	Pirmin Zurbriggen (Switzerland)	1984–90	4
4=	Ingemar Stenmark (Sweden)	1976–78	3
4=	Phil Mahre (USA)	1981–83	3
6=	Jean Claude Killy (France)	1967–68	2
6=	Karl Schranz (Austria)	1969–70	2
8=	Piero Gross (Italy)	1974	1
8=	Peter Lüscher (Switzerland)	1979	1
8=	Andreas Wenzel (Leichtenstein)	1980	1
8=	Paul Accola (Switzerland)	1992	1
8=	Kjetil Andre Aaamodt (Norway)	1994	1
8=	Alberto Tomba (Italy)	1995	1

The Alpine Skiing World Cup was launched as an annual event in 1967. Points are awarded for performances over a series of selected races, which are held during the winter months at meetings worldwide.

ALPINE SKIING WORLD CUP TITLES – WOMEN

	Name/country	Years	Titles
1	Annemarie Moser-Pröll (Austria)	1971–79	6
2=	Vreni Schneider (Switzerland)	1989–95	3
2=	Petra Kronberger (Austria)	1990–92	3
4=	Nancy Greene (Canada)	1967–68	2
4=	Hanni Wenzel (Liechtenstein)	1978–80	2
4=	Erika Hess (Switzerland)	1982–84	2
4=	Michela Figini (Switzerland)	1985–88	2
4=	Maria Walliser (Switzerland)	1986–87	2
9=	Gertrude Gabl (Austria)	1969	1
9=	Michèle Jacot (France)	1970	1
9=	Rosi Mittermeier (West Germany)	1976	1
9=	Lise-Marie Morerod (Switzerland)	1977	1
9=	Marie-Thérèse Nadig (Switzerland)	1981	1
9=	Tamara McKinney (USA)	1983	1
9=	Anita Wachter (Austria)	1993	1
9=	Kajta Seizinger (Germany)	1996	1

WINTER OLYMPIC MEDAL-WINNING NATIONS

	Country	G	S	B	Total
1	Russia/ Former USSR	99	71	71	241
2	Norway	73	77	64	214
3	USA	53	55	39	147
4	Austria	36	48	44	128
5	West Germany/ Germany	45	43	37	125
6	Finland	36	45	42	123
7	East Germany	39	36	35	110
8	Sweden	39	26	34	99
9	Switzerland	27	29	29	85
10	Italy	25	21	21	67

Norway headed this list for many years, but in recent times the strength of the Soviets in all sports, including winter sports, has seen them ascend to the top Winter Olympic medal-winning nation. Great Britain is well down the list in 15th place, but in recent games has produced memorable moments thanks to Torvill and Dean, John Curry, and Robin Cousins. Britain's finest hour, and one of the biggest upsets in Winter Olympic history, occurred at Innsbruck in 1964, when Anthony Nash and Robin Dixon won the two-man bob event.

DOWNHILL RACER
Ski races have been held since the last century, but have developed as major Olympic and World events in the 20th century along with the international growth of interest in the sport.

TOP 10

WORLD AND OLYMPIC FIGURE SKATING TITLES – MEN

	Skater/country	Years	Titles
1	Ulrich Salchow (Sweden)	1901–11	11
2	Karl Schäfer (Austria)	1930–36	9
3	Dick Button (USA)	1948–52	7
4	Gillis Grafstrom (Sweden)	1920–29	6
5=	Hayes Jenkins (USA)	1953–56	5
5=	Scott Hamilton (USA)	1981–84	5
7=	Willy Bockl (Austria)	1925–28	4
7=	David Jenkins (USA)	1957–60	4
7=	Ondrej Nepela (Czechoslovakia)	1971–73	4
7=	Kurt Browning (Canada)	1989–93	4

TOP 10

WORLD AND OLYMPIC FIGURE SKATING TITLES – WOMEN

	Skater/country	Years	Titles
1	Sonja Henie (Norway)	1927–36	13
2=	Carol Heiss (USA)	1956–60	6
2=	Herma Planck Szabo (Austria)	1922–26	6
2=	Katarina Witt (East Germany)	1984–88	6
5=	Lily Kronberger (Hungary)	1908–11	4
5=	Sjoukje Dijkstra (Netherlands)	1962–64	4
5=	Peggy Fleming (USA)	1966–68	4
8=	Meray Horvath (Hungary)	1912–14	3
8=	Tenley Albright (USA)	1953–56	3
8=	Annett Poetzsch (East Gemany)	1978–80	3
8=	Beatrix Schuba (Austria)	1971–72	3
8=	Barbara Ann Scott (Canada)	1947–48	3
8=	Kristi Yamaguchi (USA)	1991–92	3
8=	Madge Sayers (UK)	1906–08	3

TOP 10

OLYMPIC BOBSLEIGHING NATIONS

	Country	G	S	B	Total
1	Switzerland	9	8	8	25
2	Germany/West Germany	4	5	6	15
3	USA	5	4	5	14
4	East Germany	5	6	2	13
5	Italy	3	4	3	10
6=	Austria	1	2	0	3
6=	UK	1	1	1	3
6=	Former USSR	1	0	2	3
9	Belgium	0	1	1	2
10=	Canada	1	0	0	1
10=	Romania	0	0	1	1

TOP 10

WINNERS OF WORLD ICE DANCE TITLES

	Skater/country	Years	Titles
1=	Alexsandr Gorshkov (USSR)	1970–76	6
1=	Lyudmila Pakhomova (USSR)	1970–76	6
3=	Lawrence Demmy (UK)	1951–55	5
3=	Jean Westwood (UK)	1951–55	5
5=	Courtney Jones (UK)	1957–60	4
5=	Eva Romanova (Czechoslovakia)	1962–65	4
5=	Pavel Roman (Czechoslovakia)	1963–65	4
5=	Diane Towler (UK)	1966–69	4
5=	Bernard Ford (UK)	1966–69	4
5=	Jayne Torvill (UK)	1981–84	4
5=	Christopher Dean (UK)	1981–84	4
5=	Natalya Bestemianova (USSR)	1985–88	4
5=	Andrei Bukin (USSR)	1985–88	4
5=	Oksana Gritschuk (Rus)	1994–97	4
5=	Yevgeniy Platov (Rus)	1994-97	4

TOP 10

FASTEST WINNING TIMES OF THE IDITAROD DOG SLED RACE

	Winner/year	day	Time hr	min	sec
1	Doug Swingley, 1995	9	2	42	19
2	Jeff King, 1996	9	5	43	19
3	Martin Buser, 1997	9	8	30	45
4	Martin Buser, 1994	10	13	02	39
5	Jeff King, 1993	10	15	38	15
6	Martin Buser, 1992	10	19	17	15
7	Susan Butcher, 1990	11	01	53	28
8	Susan Butcher, 1987	11	02	05	13
9	Joe Runyan, 1989	11	05	24	34
10	Susan Butcher, 1988	11	11	41	40

Source: Iditarod Trail Committee

The race, which has been held annually since 1973, stretches from Anchorage to Nome, Alaska, covering 1,864 km/ 1,158 miles. Iditarod is a deserted mining village along the route, and the race commemorates an emergency operation in 1925 to get medical supplies to Nome following a diphtheria epidemic.

ON THE WATER

FASTEST WINNING TIMES OF THE OXFORD AND CAMBRIDGE BOAT RACE

	Year	Winner	Time
1	1984	Oxford	16.45
2	1976	Oxford	16.58
3	1991	Oxford	16.59
4	1985	Oxford	17.11
5	1990	Oxford	17.15
6=	1974	Oxford	17.35
6=	1988	Oxford	17.35
8	1992	Oxford	17.48
9	1948	Cambridge	17.50
10=	1971	Cambridge	17.58
10=	1986	Cambridge	17.58

The Boat Race was first rowed at Henley in 1829. The course from Putney to Mortlake (6.78 km/4 miles 374 yards) has been used since 1843 – although the race was rowed in the opposite direction in 1846, 1856, and 1863. There were two races in 1849, and the race has been rowed annually since 1856 except during the two world wars. Cambridge has won the race 70 times and still holds the record for the longest unbroken sequence of 13 wins from 1924 to 1936. Oxford has won on 68 occasions, and there was one dead-heat in 1877. The heavier crew has won the race on 79 occasions, the lighter crew has won 53 races, and the crews have weighed the same four times (1870, 1876, 1890, and 1980). Cambridge sank in 1859 and 1978 and Oxford in 1925; both crews sank in 1912 and Oxford won when the race was rowed again a week later; Oxford sank near the start in 1951 and Cambridge won the re-row two days later. The most successful Boat Race oarsman is Boris Rankov; he won six races with Oxford. C.R.W. Tottenham coxed Oxford to five successive victories.

WINNERS OF THE MOST MEN'S WORLD WATER-SKIING TITLES

	Skier/nationality	Total wins
1	Patrice Martin (France)	8
2	Sammy Duval (USA)	6
3=	Alfredo Mendoza (USA)	5
3=	Mike Suyderhoud (USA)	5
3=	Bob La Point (USA)	5
6=	George Athans (Canada)	3
6=	Guy de Clercq (Belgium)	3
6=	Wayne Grimditch (USA)	3
6=	Mike Hazelwood (GB)	3
6=	Ricky McCormick (USA)	3
6=	Billy Spencer (USA)	3
6=	Andy Mapple (GB)	3

POWERBOAT OWNERS WITH MOST RACE WINS

	Owner	Years	Wins
1	Bernie Little*	1966–97	104
2	Bill Muncey	1976–81	29
3	Joe & Lee Schoenith	1952–72	27
4	Ole Bardahl	1958–68	27
5	Dave Heerensperger	1968–82	25
6	Fran Muncey	1982–88	24
7	Willard Rhodes	1956–63	18
8	Steve Woomer*	1984–96	14
9	Bill Waggoner	1956–59	12
10	George Simon	1955–76	12

* Active at 1 June 1997

WINNERS OF THE MOST WOMEN'S WORLD WATER-SKIING TITLES

	Skier/nationality	Total
1	Liz Shetter (*née* Allen) (USA)	11
2	Willa McGuire (*née* Worthington) (USA)	8
3	Cindy Todd (USA)	7
4	Deena Mapple (*née* Brush) (USA)	6
5=	Marina Doria (Swi)	4
5=	Natalya Ponomaryeva (*née* Rumyantseva) (USSR)	4
7=	Maria Victoria Carrasco (Ven)	3
7=	Tawn Larsen (USA)	3
7=	Helena Kjellander (Swe)	3
10=	Leah Marie Rawls (USA)	2
10=	Vickie Van Hook (USA)	2
10=	Sylvie Hulseman (Lux)	2
10=	Jeanette Brown (USA)	2
10=	Jeanette Stewart-Wood (GB)	2
10=	Christy Weir (USA)	2
10=	Evie Wolford (USA)	2
10=	Kim Laskoff (USA)	2
10=	Dany Duflot (Fra)	2
10=	Ana Marie Carasco (Ven)	2
10=	Nancie Rideout (USA)	2
10=	Renate Hansluvka (Aut)	2
10=	Karen Neville (Aus)	2

Stewart-Wood is the only British woman to win a world title.

T O P 1 0

OLYMPIC YACHTING COUNTRIES

	Country	Medals			
		gold	silver	bronze	total
1	USA	15	13	11	39
2	Great Britain	15	8	8	31
3	Sweden	9	11	9	29
4	Norway	14	11	2	27
5	France	9	6	9	24
6	Denmark	8	8	3	19
7	West Germany	5	5	6	16
8	USSR	4	5	4	13
9	Holland	4	4	4	12
10=	Australia	3	1	4	8
10=	Italy	2	1	5	8
10=	Finland	1	1	6	8
10=	New Zealand	5	1	2	8

Yachting has provided one of the Olympics' most durable competitors: Paul Elvström of Denmark. The first person to win gold medals at four consecutive games (1948–60), he went on to compete in a further four Games in 1968, 1972, 1984, and 1988, when he was partnered by his daughter in the Tornado class.

T O P 1 0

SURFERS IN THE WORLD, 1996*

1 Kelly Slater (USA)

2 Shane Beschen (USA)

3 Sunny Garcia (Hawaii)

4 Luke Egan (Australia)

5 Kaipo Jaquias (Hawaii)

6 Taylor Know (USA)

7 Kalani Robb (Hawaii)

8 Matt Hoy (Australia)

9 Michael Rommelse (Australia)

10 Rob Machado (USA)

* *According to the Association of Surfing Professionals*

T O P 1 0

OLYMPIC ROWING COUNTRIES

	Country	Medals			
		gold	silver	bronze	total
1	USA	30	20	15	65
2	East Germany	33	7	8	48
3	USSR	12	20	11	43
4	West Germany	17	12	12	41
5	Great Britain	16	15	6	37
6	Italy	12	10	8	30
7	France	4	13	9	26
8=	Romania	8	6	6	20
8=	Switzerland	4	7	9	20
10	Canada	3	8	8	19

A member of the winning US eights team at the 1924 Paris Olympics was Benjamin Spock, who later became famous as the "baby expert", and whose book *The Common Sense Book of Baby and Child Care* has sold more than 39,200,000 copies worldwide.

T O P 1 0

OLYMPIC CANOEING COUNTRIES

	Country	Medals			
		gold	silver	bronze	total
1	USSR	29	13	9	51
2	Hungary	7	19	16	42
3	Germany/ West Germany	8	14	10	32
4	East Germany	14	7	9	30
5	Romania	9	9	11	29
6	Sweden	13	8	2	23
7	France	1	5	10	16
8	Austria	3	6	5	14
9	Canada	3	6	4	13
10	Bulgaria	3	3	6	12

Canoeing has been an official Olympic sport since 1936, although it was first seen as a demonstration sport 12 years earlier. Great Britain has never won an Olympic canoeing medal.

THIS SPORTING LIFE

TV AUDIENCES OF ALL TIME
FOR SPORTS EVENTS IN THE US

	Programme	Date	TV households total	%
1	Super Bowl XVI (San Francisco *vs.* Cincinnati)	24 Jan 1982	40,020,000	49.1
2	Super Bowl XVII (Washington *vs.* Miami)	30 Jan 1983	40,500,000	48.6
3	XVII Winter Olympics	23 Feb 1994	45,690,000	48.5
4	Super Bowl XX (Chicago *vs.* New England)	26 Jan 1986	41,490,000	48.3
5	Super Bowl XII (Dallas *vs.* Denver)	15 Jan 1978	34,410,000	47.2
6	Super Bowl XIII (Dallas *vs.* Pittsburgh)	21 Jan 1979	35,090,000	47.1
7=	Super Bowl XVIII (LA Raiders *vs.* Washington)	22 Jan 1984	38,800,000	46.4
7=	Super Bowl XIX (San Francisco *vs.* Miami)	20 Jan 1985	39,390,000	46.4
9	Super Bowl XIV (LA Rams *vs.* Pittsburgh)	20 Jan 1980	35,330,000	46.3
10	Super Bowl XXI (Giants *vs.* Denver)	25 Jan 1987	40,030,000	45.8

Copyright © 1997 Nielsen Media Research

"TV households" indicates the number of households with TV sets: population growth and the acquisition of sets steadily increase this figure, so recent events attract higher audiences. Super Bowl XXX on 28 January 1996 attracted the greatest number of individual viewers of any US TV programme ever, but a rating of only 41.3 keeps it outside this Top 10.

HIGHEST-EARNING SPORTSMEN* IN THE WORLD

	Name	Sport	Income 1996 ($)
1	Mike Tyson	Boxing	75,000,000
2	Michael Jordan	Basketball	52,600,000
3	Michael Schumacher (Germany)	Motor racing	33,000,000
4	Shaquille O'Neal	Basketball	24,400,000
5	Emmitt Smith	Football	16,500,000
6	Evander Holyfield	Boxing	15,500,000
7	Andre Agassi	Tennis	15,200,000
8	Arnold Palmer	Golf	15,100,000
9	Dennis Rodman	Basketball	12,900,000
10	Patrick Ewing	Basketball	12,400,000

* All from the US unless otherwise stated
Used by permission of Forbes Magazine

PARTICIPATION SPORTS,
GAMES, AND PHYSICAL
ACTIVITIES IN THE US

	Activity	Participants*
1	Exercise walking	70,794,000
2	Swimming	60,277,000
3	Fishing	51,992,000
4	Cycling	49,818,000
5	Exercising with equipment	43,784,000
6	Camping	42,932,000
7	Bowling	37,356,000
8	Billiards/pool	34,000,000
9	Basketball	28,191,000
10	Boating	26,400,000

* On more than one occasion
Source: National Sporting Goods Association

Perhaps surprisingly, this survey indicated that the national game of baseball as a participation sport scored relatively low, with only 15,096,000 followers.

PARTICIPATION SPORTS, GAMES,
AND PHYSICAL ACTIVITIES IN THE UK

	Activity	Percentage participating females	males
1	Walking	37	45
2	Snooker, pool, and billiards	5	21
3	Swimming	16	15
4	Cycling	7	14
5=	Darts	3	9
5=	Golf	2	9
5=	Weightlifting and training	3	9
8	Soccer	0	9
9	Running, jogging, etc.	2	7
10	Keep-fit and yoga	17	6

Based on interviews conducted in 1993–94, the percentages represent those who had participated in the activity in question during the four weeks prior to the interview. In that period, 72 per cent of men and 57 per cent of women had engaged in at least one sporting or physical activity.

THE 10
MOST COMMON SPORTING INJURIES

	Common name	Medical term
1	Bruise	Soft tissue contusion
2	Sprained ankle	Sprain of the lateral ligament
3	Sprained knee	Sprain of the medial collateral ligament
4	Low back strain	Lumbar joint dysfunction
5	Hamstring tear	Muscle tear of the hamstring
6	Jumper's knee	Patella tendinitis
7	Achilles tendinitis	Tendinitis of the Achilles tendon
8	Shin splints	Medial periostitis of the tibia
9	Tennis elbow	Lateral epicondylitis
10	Shoulder strain	Rotator cuff tendinitis

THE 10
WORST DISASTERS AT SPORTS VENUES IN THE 20TH CENTURY

	Location	Disaster	Date	No. killed
1	Hong Kong Jockey Club	Stand collapse and fire	26 Feb 1918	604
2	Lenin Stadium, Moscow, Russia	Crush in football stadium	20 Oct 1982	340
3	Lima, Peru	Football stadium riot	24 May 1964	320
4	Sinceljo, Colombia	Bullring stand collapse	20 Jan 1980	222
5	Hillsborough, Sheffield, UK	Crush in football stadium	15 Apr 1989	96
6	Guatemale City, Guatelama	Stampede in football stadium	16 Oct 1996	83
7	Le Mans, France	Racing car crash	11 Jun 1955	82
8	Katmandu, Nepal	Stampede in football stadium	12 Mar 1988	80
9	Buenos Aires, Argentina	Riot in football stadium	23 May 1968	73
10	Ibrox Park, Glasgow, UK	Barrier collapse in football stadium	2 Jan 1971	66

Before the Ibrox Park disaster, the worst accident at a British stadium was caused by the collapse of a stand at Burnden Park, Bolton, on 9 March 1946, which left 33 dead and 400 injured. If stunt-flying is included as a "sport", the worst airshow disaster of all time occurred at the Ramstein US base, Germany, on 28 August 1988, when three fighters collided, one of them crashing into the crowd, leaving 70 dead and 150 injured. Such tragedies are not an exclusively modern phenomenon: during the reign of Roman Emperor Antoninus Pius (AD 138–161), a stand at the Circus Maximus collapsed killing 1,162 spectators.

TOP 10
CATEGORIES OF ATHLETES WITH THE LARGEST* HEARTS

1	*Tour de France* cyclists
2	Marathon runners
3	Rowers
4	Boxers
5	Sprint cyclists
6	Middle-distance runners
7	Weightlifters
8	Swimmers
9	Sprinters
10	Decathletes

* *Based on average medical measurements*

The size of the heart of a person who engages regularly in a demanding sport enlarges according to the strenuousness involved in participating in the sport.

TOP 10
MOST EFFECTIVE KEEP-FIT ACTIVITIES

1	Swimming
2	Cycling
3	Rowing
4	Gymnastics
5	Judo
6	Dancing
7	Football
8	Jogging
9	Walking (briskly)
10	Squash

These sports and activities are the best means of building stamina and strength, and of increasing suppleness.

TOP 10
FILMS WITH SPORTING THEMES

	Film/year	Sport
1	*Days of Thunder* (1990)	Stock car racing
2	*Rocky IV* (1985)	Boxing
3	*Rocky III* (1982)	Boxing
4	*Rocky* (1976)	Boxing
5	*A League of Their Own* (1992)	Baseball
6	*Rocky II* (1979)	Boxing
7	*Tin Cup* (1979)	Golf
8	*White Men Can't Jump* (1992)	Basketball
9	*Field of Dreams* (1989)	Baseball
10	*Chariots of Fire* (1973)	Athletics

Led by superstar Sylvester Stallone's *Rocky* series, the boxing ring, a natural source of drama and thrills, dominates Hollywood's most successful sports-based epics. Baseball is a popular follow-up.

THE GOOD & THE BAD

TOP 10

COUNTRIES WITH THE LOWEST CRIME RATES

	Country	Reported crime rate per 100,000 population
1	Togo	11.0
2	Nepal	13.0
3	Guinea	18.4
4=	Congo	32.0
4=	Niger	32.0
6	Mali	33.0
7	Burkina Faso	41.0
8	Bangladesh	64.0
9	Côte d'Ivoire	67.0
10	Burundi	84.0

There are just 13 countries in the world with reported crime rates of fewer than 100 per 100,000 inhabitants; the other three are Burundi (87.0), Syria (89.0), and Ethiopia (94.0). It should be noted, however, that these figures are based on reported crimes. For propaganda purposes, many countries do not publish accurate figures, while in certain countries crime is so common and law enforcement so inefficient or corrupt that countless incidents are unreported.

UNDER ARREST
World crime rates reflect lawlessness but also police efficiency and public faith in the force's competence to deal with criminals.

THE 10

COUNTRIES WITH THE HIGHEST CRIME RATES

	Country	Reported crime rate per 100,000 population
1	Suriname	17,819
2	St Kitts and Nevis	15,468
3	New Zealand	14,496
4	Sweden	13,750
5	Canada	13,297
6	Gibraltar	12,581
7	US Virgin Islands	10,441
8	Denmark	10,339
9	Netherlands	10,181
10	Guam	10,080
	England and Wales	*9,880*
	USA	*5,278*

An appearance in this list does not necessarily confirm these as the most crime-ridden countries, since (as with the comparative list of The 10 Countries with the Lowest Crime Rates) the rate of reporting relates closely to such factors as confidence in local law enforcement authorities. However, a rate of approximately 1,000 per 100,000 may be considered average, so those countries in this Top 10 are well above it.

THE 10

COUNTRIES WITH MOST BURGLARIES

	Country	Annual burglaries per 100,000 population
1	Netherlands	3,803.0
2	US Virgin Islands	3,183.7
3	New Zealand	2,942.3
4	England and Wales	2,401.0
5	Denmark	2,381.0
6	Germany	2,039.4
7	Antigua and Barbuda	1,984.4
8	Australia	1,962.8
9	Bermuda	1,949.2
10	Finland	1,921.9
	USA	*987.6*

THE 10

COUNTRIES WITH MOST CAR THEFTS

	Country	Annual thefts per 100,000 population
1	Switzerland	1,520.0*
2	Australia	1,005.5
3	England and Wales	992.8
4	US Virgin Islands	954.0
5	New Zealand	905.4
6	Sweden	748.0
7	France	648.5
8	Denmark	619.7
9	Italy	566.6
10	USA	560.5

* *Including motorcycles and bicycles*

CAR CRIME
Although motor manufacturers are fitting increasingly sophisticated security measures, robbers continue to view cars as easy targets, and thefts of and from cars continue to grow.

THE 10

MOST COMMON OFFENCES IN ENGLAND AND WALES IN 1995

	Offence	No. offenders found guilty
1	Motoring offences	653,600
2	Summary offences (other than motoring)	410,000
3	Theft and handling stolen goods	116,100
4	Other offences	42,200
5	Burglary	35,300
6	Violence against the person	29,100
7	Drug offences	31,600
8	Fraud and forgery	17,200
9	Criminal damage	9,600
10	Robbery	5,200
	Total (indictable 302,200/ summary 1,052,400)	*1,354,600*

This list includes both indictable offences (those normally calling for a trial before a jury) and summary offences (usually tried before a magistrates' court). In the latter category, motoring offences comprise the largest proportion, but other offences are less precisely itemized and hence appear in official statistics under a general heading.

THE 10

FBI "MOST WANTED" FUGITIVES

Fugitive/crime

1 Lamen Khalifa Fhimah (b. 4 April 1956, Libya)

He is wanted for blowing up a PanAm flight over Lockerbie, 1988. Up to $4,000,000 reward.

2 Victor Manuel Gerena (b. 24 June 1958, USA)

Gerena is wanted for bank and armed robbery.

3 Glen Stewart Godwin (b. 26 June 1958, USA)

Godwin escaped from Folsom State Prison.

4 Mir Aimal Kansi (b. 10 February 1964, Pakistan)

He is wanted for the murder of two and injury to three in a shooting at CIA Headquarters, Langley, Virginia.

5 Abdel Basset Ali Al-Megrahi (b. 1 April 1952, Libya)

Al-Megrahi is wanted for the blowing up of a PanAm flight over Lockerbie, 1988.

Fugitive/crime

6 Agustin Vasquez-Mendoza (b. 1 October 1969, Mexico)

He is wanted for murder of a Drug Enforcement Administration Special Agent. $50,000 reward.

7 Thang Thanh Nguyen (b. 20 March 1969, Vietnam)

Nguyen is wanted for murder, attempted murder, burglary, and robbery.

8 David Alex Alvarez (b. 23 February 1967, USA)

Alverez is wanted for multiple homicide.

9 Arthur Lee Washington, Jr. (b. 30 November 1949, USA)

He is charged the with the attempted murder of a State Trooper.

10 Donald Eugene Webb (b. 14 July 1931, USA)

Webb is wanted for the murder of a police chief, and attempted burglary.

The FBI's "10 Most Wanted Fugitives" was first published on 14 March 1950. The lists are not ranked and have been listed here in alphabetical order. The criteria used for selection are that the individual must have a lengthy record of committing serious crimes and/or be considered a particularly dangerous menace to society, and it must be believed that the nationwide publicity given by the program can be of assistance in apprehending the fugitive.

POLICE, COURTS & PRISONS

US CITIES WITH THE MOST POLICE OFFICERS

	City	Officers
1	New York City	37,450
2	Chicago, Illinois	13,344
3	Los Angeles, California	8,363
4	Philadelphia, Pennsylvania	6,376
5	Houston, Texas	5,170
6	Detroit, Michigan	3,819
7	Washington, D.C.	3,671
8	Baltimore, Maryland	3,110
9	Dallas, Texas	2,833
10	Phoenix, Arizona	2,183

MOST COMMON REASONS FOR HIRING PRIVATE DETECTIVES

1	Tracing debtors
2	Serving writs
3	Locating assets
4	Assessing accident cases
5	Tracing missing persons
6	Insurance claims
7	Matrimonial
8	Countering industrial espionage
9	Criminal cases
10	Vetting personnel

COUNTRIES WITH THE MOST POLICE OFFICERS

	Country	Population per police officer
1	Angola	14*
2	Kuwait	80
3	Nicaragua	90*
4	Brunei	100
5=	Nauru	110
5=	Cape Verde	110
7=	Antigua and Barbuda	120
7=	Mongolia	120
7=	Seychelles	120
10=	Iraq	140
10=	United Arab Emirates	140
	USA	318
	UK	420

* Including civilian militia

Police personnel figures generally include only full-time paid officials, and exclude clerical and volunteer staff. However, there are variations around the world in the way in which these categories are defined.

COUNTRIES WITH THE FEWEST POLICE OFFICERS

	Country	Population per police officer
1	Maldives	35,710
2	Canada	8,640
3	Rwanda	4,650
4	Côte d'Ivoire	4,640
5	The Gambia	3,310
6	Benin	3,250
7	Madagascar	2,900
8	Central African Republic	2,740
9	Bangladesh	2,560
10	Niger	2,350 *

* Including paramilitary forces

The saying "there's never a policeman when you need one" is nowhere truer than in the countries appearing in this list, where the police are remarkably thin on the ground. There are various possible and contradictory explanations for these ratios: countries may be so law-abiding that there is simply no need for large numbers of police officers, or a force may be so underfunded and inefficient as to be completely irrelevant.

THE CITY'S FINEST
New York's police force is by far the largest of any US city.

THE 10

LARGEST FEDERAL CORRECTIONAL INSTITUTIONS IN THE US

	Institute	Location	Rated capacity
1	Federal Correctional Institution	Fort Dix, New Jersey	3,683
2	Federal Correctional Institution (Low and Medium Security)	Coleman, Florida	2,682
3	Federal Correctional Institution	Beaumont, Texas	1,536
4	US Penitentiary	Atlanta, Georgia	1,429
5	Federal Detention Center	Miami, Florida	1,259
6	US Penitentiary	Leavenworth, Kansas	1,201
7	Federal Correctional Institution	Beckley, West Virginia	1,152
8	Federal Medical Center	Fort Worth, Texas	1,132
9	Federal Medical Center	Lexington, Kentucky	1,106
10	Federal Correctional Institution	Milan, Michigan	1,065

Source: Bureau of Federal Prisons

THE 10

US STATES WITH THE MOST PRISON INMATES, 1980/1996

	State	1980	1996
1	California	24,569	142,814
2	Texas	29,892	129,937
3	New York	21,815	68,721
4	Florida	20,735	64,332
5	Ohio	13,489	45,314
6	Michigan	15,124	41,884
7	Illinois	11,899	38,373
8	Georgia	12,178	34,808
9	Pennsylvania	8,171	33,939
10	North Carolina	15,513	30,671
	US total:	*329,821*	*1,112,448*

In mid-1996 there were 1,019,281 prisoners in state prisons and 93,167 in federal institutions in the US. At the time of this census, a further 518,492 prisoners were held in local jails. The state with the fewest prisoners over the same period was North Dakota, with 253 in 1980 and 640 in 1996. The nationwide prison population in 1991 was more than three times greater than that in 1980, but that of certain states increased to an even greater extent: California's, for example, grew more than fivefold. The rate of incarceration in 1996 is equivalent to 615 prisoners for every 100,000 of the US population – in 1980 the rate was 146 per 100,000. Extrapolating from these figures, and keeping in mind population projections for the coming decades, readers may wish to indulge in the mathematical exercise of calculating the year in which the entire US population will be in jail.

THE 10

US STATES WITH THE HIGHEST RATE OF PRISON INCARCERATION

	State	Prisoners per 100,000 mid-1996*
1	Texas	659
2	Louisiana	611
3	Oklahoma	580
4	South Carolina	540
5	Nevada	493
6	Alabama	487
7	Mississippi	486
8	Arizona	481
9	Georgia	468
10	Florida	448

* Prisoners with a sentence of more than one year per 100,000 residents

The rate for the District of Columbia is 1,444 per 100,000, but is distorted by the fact that the DC prison and local jail systems are integrated. The state with the lowest rate of incarcerations is North Dakota, with 640 prisoners, equivalent to a rate of 90 per 100,000 residents.

TOP 10

PRISON INDUSTRIES IN ENGLAND AND WALES

	Industry	Workshop places
1	Textiles	2,426
2	Tailoring/shirts	2,257
3	Contract services	1,779
4	Laundries	1,082
5	Engineering	780
6	Woodwork	758
7	Weaving	334
8	Printing and binding	286
9	Footwear/leatherwork	266
10	Others*	210

* Including concrete and plastic moulding, brushmaking, computer-aided drafting, etc.

Sewing mailbags is perhaps the best known of prison industries, but has been replaced by ever more sophisticated activities that are increasingly encouraged – "purposeful activity" (including vocational and other courses) of 24.9 hours a week per prisoner is the official target. The value of goods and services currently produced is £55,000,000 per annum, from which prisoners earn on average £6.00 a week.

MASS MURDER

Serial killers are mass murderers who kill repeatedly, often over long periods, in contrast to the so-called "spree killers" who have been responsible for single occasion massacres, usually with guns, and other perpetrators of single outrages, often by means of bombs, resulting in multiple deaths. Because of the time-spans involved and the secrecy surrounding the horrific crimes of multiple killers, it is almost impossible to calculate the precise numbers of their victims. This is especially true of poisoners in the years before forensic science was developed, since establishing the cause of death was so imprecise. The tallies of murders attributed to the criminals listed here should therefore be taken as "best estimates" based on the most reliable evidence available, but such is the magnitude of the crimes of some of these killers that some of the figures may be underestimates.

THE 10
MOST PROLIFIC POISONERS IN THE WORLD*

Poisoner	Victims
1 Susannah Olah	up to 100
2 Gesina Margaretha Gottfried	at least 30
3 Hélène Jegado	23
4 Mary Ann Cotton	20
5= Dr William Palmer	14
5= Sadamichi Hirasawa	14
7= Johann Otto Hoch	at least 12
7= Marie Becker	12
9 Lydia Sherman	at least 11
10= Amy Archer-Gilligan	at least 5
10= Dr Thomas Neill Cream	5
10= Herman Billik	5

* Prior to 1950 and excluding poisoners where evidence is so confused with legend (such as that surrounding the Borgia family) as to be unreliable

THE 10
MOST PROLIFIC MURDERESSES IN THE WORLD

Murderess	Victims
1 Countess Erszébet Báthory	up to 650

In the period up to 1610 in Hungary, Báthory (1560–1614), known as "Countess Dracula" – later the title of a 1970 Hammer horror film about her life and crimes – was alleged to have murdered between 300 and 650 girls (her personal list of 610 victims was described at her trial) in the belief that drinking their blood would prevent her from ageing. She was eventually arrested in 1611. Tried and found guilty, she died on 21 August 1614 walled up in her own castle at Csejthe.

Murderess	Victims
2 Susannah Olah	up to 100

At the age of 40, Susi Olah, a 40-year-old nurse and midwife, arrived at Nagzrev, a Hungarian village. Over the next few years she "predicted" the demise of anything up to 100 people, who subsequently met their deaths as a result of arsenic poisoning. Many inhabitants believed the woman who came to be nicknamed the "Angel-maker" had prophetic powers, but her victims ranged from newborn and handicapped children to elderly people and the husbands of many of the local women – in most cases with the full complicity of their relatives. When the law finally caught up with her in 1929, she committed suicide.

Murderess	Victims
3 Delfina and Maria de Jesús Gonzales	at least 91

After abducting girls to work in their Mexican brothel, Rancho El Angel, as many as 80 of them, and an unknown number of their customers, were murdered and buried in the grounds by the Gonzales sisters, who in 1964 were sentenced to 40 years imprisonment.

Murderess	Victims
4 Bella Poulsdatter Sorensen Gunness	42

Bella or Belle Gunness (1859–1908?), a Norwegian-born immigrant to the US, is believed to have murdered her husband Peter Gunness for his life insurance (she claimed that an axe had fallen from a shelf and on to his head). After this she lured between 16 and 28 suitors through "lonely hearts" advertisements, as well as numerous others – a total of as many as 42 – to her Laporte, Indiana farm, where she murdered them. On 28 April 1908 her farm was burned to the ground. A headless corpse found in the ruins was declared to be Gunness, killed along with her three children by her accomplice Ray Lamphere, but it seems probable that she faked her own death and disappeared.

Murderess	Victims
5 Gesina Margaretha Gottfried	at least 30

Having poisoned her first husband and two children with arsenic in 1815, German murderess Gesina Mittenberg killed both her parents by the same method and then her next husband, Gottfried, whom she married on his deathbed, thereby inheriting his fortune. As her income dwindled, she carried out an extensive series of murders, including those of her brother, a creditor, and most of the family of a Bremen wheelwright called Rumf, for whom she worked as a housekeeper. Rumf himself became suspicious, and in 1828 Gottfried was arrested. After a trial at which she admitted to more than 30 murders, she was executed.

Murderess	Victims
6 Jane Toppan	30

Boston-born Nora Kelley, also known as Jane Toppan (1854–1938), was the daughter of Peter Kelley, who ended his days in a lunatic asylum, and she herself was almost certainly insane. She trained as a nurse, and within a few years, after numerous patients in her care had died, their bodies were exhumed and revealed traces of morphine and atropine poisoning. It seems probable, according to both evidence and her own confession, that she killed as many as 30 victims. She died in an asylum on 17 August 1938, at the age of 84.

Murderess	Victims
7 Hélène Jegado	23

Jegado was a French housemaid who was believed to have committed some 23 murders by arsenic. She was tried at Rennes in 1851, found guilty, and guillotined in 1852.

Murderess	Victims
8 Genene Jones	21

In 1984 Jones was found guilty of killing a baby at the San Antonio, Texas, hospital at which she worked as a nurse, by administering the drug succinylcholine. She was sentenced to 99 years in prison. Jones had been dismissed from the previous hospital at which she had worked after up to 20 babies in her care had died of suspicious, and some authorities linked her with as many as 42 deaths.

Murderess	Victims
9 Mary Ann Cotton	20

Cotton (1832–73), a one-time nurse, is generally held to be Britain's worst mass murderer. Over a 20-year period, it seems probable that she disposed of 14–20 victims, including two husbands, children, and stepchildren, by arsenic poisoning. She was hanged at Durham Prison on 24 March 1873, five days after giving birth.

Murderess	Victims
10 Waltraud Wagner	15

Wagner was the ringleader but only one of four nurses found guilty of causing numerous deaths through deliberate drug overdoses and other means at the Lainz hospital, Vienna, in the late 1980s – between 42 and possibly as many as several hundred patients became the victims of the Wagner "death squad", for which she was sentenced to life imprisonment on charges that included 15 counts of murder and 17 of attempted murder.

THE 10

MOST PROLIFIC SERIAL KILLERS* OF THE 20th CENTURY

	Serial killer	Victims
1	Pedro Alonzo (or Armando) López	over 300

Following his 1980 capture López, known as the "Monster of the Andes", led police to 53 graves, but probably murdered more than 300 young girls in Columbia, Ecuador, and Peru. He was sentenced to life imprisonment.

	Serial killer	Victims
2	Henry Lee Lucas	over 200

The subject of the film, Henry, Portrait of a Serial Killer, Lucas (b. 1937) may have committed 200 or more murders, many of them in partnership with Ottis Toole. He admitted in 1983 to 360 and was convicted of 11, and is currently on Death Row in Huntsville.

	Serial killer	Victims
3	Delfina and Maria de Jesús Gonzales	at least 91

(See The 10 Most Prolific Murderesses in the World, No. 3)

	Serial killer	Victims
4	Bruno Lüdke	86

Lüdke (b. 1909) was a German who confessed to murdering 86 women between 1928 and 29 January 1943. Declared insane, he was incarcerated in a Vienna hospital where he was subjected to medical experiments, apparently dying on 8 April 1944 after a lethal injection.

	Serial killer	Victims
5	Daniel Camargo Barbosa	71

Coincidentally, eight years after the arrest of Pedro López in Ecuador, Barbosa was captured following a similar series of horrific murders of children – a probable total of 71 victims, for which he was sentenced to just 16 years.

	Serial killer	Victims
6	Kampatimar Shankariya	70

Caught after a two-year spree during which he killed as many as 70 times, Shankariya was hanged in Jaipur, India, on 16 May 1979.

	Serial killer	Victims
7	Randolph Kraft	67

From 1972 until his arrest on 14 May 1983, Kraft is thought to have murdered 67 men.

	Serial killer	Victims
8	Dr Marcel André Henri Félix Petiot	63

Dr Marcel Petiot admitted to 63 murders during World War II. It is probable that they were wealthy Jews whom he robbed.

	Serial killer	Victims
9	Donald Harvey	58

Working in hospitals, Harvey is believed to have murdered some 58 patients.

	Serial killer	Victims
10	Andrei Chikatilo	52

Russia's worst serial killer was convicted in Rostov-on-Don in 1992 of killing 52 women and children between 1978 and 1990.

* Including only individual and partnership murderers

THE 10

WORST GUN MASSACRES* OF ALL TIME

	Perpetrator/location/date	Victims
1	Woo Bum Kong, Sang-Namdo, South Korea, 28 April 1982	57

Off-duty policeman Woo Bum Kong (or Wou Bom-Kon), 27, went on a drunken rampage with rifles and hand grenades, killing 57 and injuring 38 before blowing himself up.

	Perpetrator/location/date	Victims
2	Martin Bryant, Port Arthur, Tasmania, Australia, 28 April 1996	35

Bryant used a rifle in a horrific spree that began in a restaurant and ended with a siege in a guesthouse which he set on fire before being captured by police.

	Perpetrator/location/date	Victims
3	Baruch Goldstein, Hebron, Occupied West Bank, Israel, 25 February 1994	29

Goldstein, a 42-year-old US immigrant doctor, carried out a gun massacre of Palestinians at prayer at the Tomb of the Patriarchs before being beaten to death by the crowd.

	Perpetrator/location/date	Victims
4=	James Oliver Huberty, San Ysidro, California, USA, 18 July 1984	22

Huberty opened fire in a McDonald's, killing 21 before being shot dead by a SWAT marksman. A further 19 were wounded, including one who died the following day.

	Perpetrator/location/date	Victims
4=	George Jo Hennard, Killeen, Texas, USA, 16 October 1991	22

Hennard drove his pick-up truck through the window of Luby's Cafeteria and, in 11 minutes, killed 22 with semi-automatic pistols.

	Perpetrator/location/date	Victims
6	Thomas Hamilton, Dunblane, Stirling, UK, 13 March 1996	17

Hamilton, 43, shot 16 children and a teacher in Dunblane Primary School before killing himself in the UK's worst shooting incident.

	Perpetrator/location/date	Victims
7=	Charles Joseph Whitman, Austin, Texas, USA, 31 July–1 August 1966	16

Whitman killed his mother and wife on 31 July 1996. The following day he ascended to the observation deck of the campus tower at the University of Texas, from where he shot 14 and wounded 34 before being shot dead by police officer Romero Martinez.

	Perpetrator/location/date	Victims
7=	Michael Ryan, Hungerford, Berkshire, UK, 19 August 1987	16

Ryan, 26, shot 14 dead and wounded 16 others (two of whom later died) before shooting himself.

	Perpetrator/location/date	Victims
7=	Ronald Gene Simmons, Russellville, Arkansas, USA, 28 December 1987	16

Simmons' total included 14 family members.

	Perpetrator/location/date	Victims
10=	Wagner von Degerloch, Muehlhausen, Germany, 3–4 September 1913	14

Wagner von Degerloch murdered his wife and children before embarking on a shooting spree.

	Perpetrator/location/date	Victims
10=	Patrick Henry Sherrill, Edmond, Oklahoma, USA, 20 August 1986	14

Sherrill, aged 44, shot 14 dead and wounded six others at the post office where he worked.

	Perpetrator/location/date	Victims
10=	Christian Dornier, Luxiol, Doubs, France, 12 July 1989	14

Dornier went on a rampage leaving 14 dead.

	Perpetrator/location/date	Victims
10=	Marc Lépine, Université de Montreal, Quebec, Canada, 6 December 1989	14

Lépine went on a rampage, firing only at women, then shot himself.

* By individuals, excluding terrorist and military actions; totals exclude perpetrator

MURDER FILE

THE 10

COUNTRIES WITH THE HIGHEST MURDER RATES

	Country	Murders p.a. per 100,000 population
1	Swaziland	87.8
2	Lesotho	51.1
3	Colombia	40.5
4	Sudan	30.5
5	Philippines	30.1
6	Guatemala	27.4
7	French Guyana	27.2
8	Nauru	25.0
9	Aruba	24.9
10	Puerto Rico	24.1
	USA	*9.0*
	England and Wales	*1.3*

The incidence of murder is affected by inter-tribal conflicts in Africa and by drug-related killings in Colombia.

MURDER BY NUMBERS

As the lists on these pages indicate, there are countries with worse murder rates (numbers of victims as a ratio of population) than the US, but nowhere in the world has as many murders each year. This has not always been so: in 1900 there were just 230 murders, a rate of 1.2 per 100,000 inhabitants. The number grew steadily, first exceeding 1,000 in 1906, when there were 1,310 cases, and first topping 10,000 in 1930 (10,331). By 1933 gangland violence pushed the figure up to an all-time peak of 12,124 and a rate of 9.7 per 100,000. This number was not exceeded until 1967, when 13,425 murders were recorded, but a further increase since then means that in 1994 there were 23,305 murders in the US, a rate of 9.0 per 100,000.

THE 10

MOST COMMON MURDER WEAPONS AND METHODS IN THE US

	Weapon/method	Victims 1995
1	Handguns	11,198
2	Knives or cutting instruments	2,538
3	"Personal weapons" (hands, feet, fists, etc.)	1,182
4	Shotguns	917
5	Blunt objects (hammers, clubs, etc.)	904
6	Firearms (type not stated)	892
7	Rifles	637
8	Strangulation	232
9	Explosives	190
10	Fire	166

In 1995 "other weapons or weapons not stated" were used in 960 murders. The number of deaths from explosives increased dramatically from the 10 incidents recorded in the previous year. This was a consequence of the bombing of the Federal Building, Oklahoma City, on 19 April 1995, in which 169 people were killed. Relatively less common methods included asphyxiation (135 cases), drowning (29), and poisoning (12). The total number of murders for the year amounted to 20,043 – equivalent to one person in every 13,162. The total number of murders committed has escalated dramatically during the 20th century, although the order of the weapons has not changed much in recent years. Perhaps most surprisingly, the proportion of killings involving firearms has scarcely changed at all – and has even gone down compared with the figures for the early years of the century.

THE 10

MOST COMMON MURDER WEAPONS AND METHODS IN ENGLAND AND WALES

	Weapon/method	Victims 1995
1	Sharp instrument	251
2	Hitting and kicking	113
3	Blunt instrument	85
4	Strangulation and asphyxiation	84
5	Shooting	70
6	Burning	38
7	Poison and drugs	20
8	Motor vehicle	7
9	Drowning	3
10	Explosives	1

According to Home Office statistics, there were 699 homicides in 1995 in England and Wales (474 male and 225 female victims). In addition to those in the list, the apparent method in a further 17 incidents is described as "other", and in 10 cases as "unknown". This represents a nine per cent increase on the previous year (from 639), although it should be noted that some offences first recorded as homicides were later reclassified. The number of victims first exceeded the 400 mark in 1952; there were 500 in 1974, and 600 in 1979. The use of certain types of weapon has also varied disproportionately. Contrary to press reports suggesting the contrary, killings involving guns have actually declined from a 1987 peak of 78, while homicides caused by sharp instruments have become more widespread, in 1995 accounting for 36 per cent of all killings. Based on the 1995 statistic, however, England and Wales (Scotland classifies its homicides according to a different system, which makes it misleading to compare the numbers) are still relatively safe countries: the odds of being murdered in England and Wales are one in 73,589. One is almost six times as likely to be a victim in the US.

THE 10
WORST STATES FOR MURDER IN THE US

	State	Firearms used	Total murders
1	California	2,593	3,531
2	Texas	1,143	1,642
3	New York	1,012	1,522
4	Florida	615	1,037
5	Illinois*	601	810
6	Michigan	559	791
7	Louisiana	568	715
8	Pennsylvania	476	677
9	North Carolina	448	671
10	Georgia	454	649

* Provisional figures

THE 10
WORST CITIES FOR MURDER IN THE US

	City	Murders (1996)*
1	New York	507
2	Chicago	383
3	Los Angeles	370
4	Philadelphia	209
5	Detroit	201
6	Washington, DC	199
7	Baltimore	165
8	New Orleans	155
9	Houston	134
10	Dallas	114

* Provisional figures

TOP 10
RELATIONSHIPS OF MURDER VICTIMS TO PRINCIPAL SUSPECTS IN THE US

	Relationship	Victims
1	Acquaintance	6,125
2	Stranger	2,888
3	Wife	823
4	Friend	733
5	Girlfriend	525
6	Husband	346
7	Son	326
8	Boyfriend	228
9	Daughter	212
10	Neighbour	173

THE 10
WORST METROPOLITAN AREAS FOR VIOLENT CRIME*

	Metropolitan area	Violent crimes per 1,000 people (1995)
1	Miami-Dade	18.9
2=	Los Angeles-Long Beach	14.2
2=	Gainesville	14.2
4=	New York	13.9
4=	Baton Rouge	13.9
6	Baltimore	13.4
7=	New Orleans	13.3
7=	Lawton, OK	13.3
9	Sioux City	12.7
10	Memphis	12.5

* Murder, rape, aggravated assault, and robbery

TOP 10
RELATIONSHIPS OF MURDER VICTIMS TO PRINCIPAL SUSPECTS IN ENGLAND AND WALES

	Relationship	Victims 1995
1	Male friend or acquaintance	155
2	Male stranger	144
3	Current or former wife, female cohabitant, or lover	93
4	Current or former husband, male cohabitant, or lover	38
5	Female friend or acquaintance	36
6	Son	32
7	Female stranger	25
8	Daughter	21
9	Father	15
10	Mother	10

In addition to these offences, Home Office statistics record that in 1995 14 homicide victims were unspecified males and 4 were female family members.

THE 10
WORST YEARS FOR GUN MURDERS IN THE US

	Year	Victims
1	1993	16,136
2	1994	15,546
3	1992	15,489
4	1991	14,373
5	1980	13,650
6	1990	13,035
7	1981	12,523
8	1974	12,474
9	1975	12,061
10	1989	11,832

CAPITAL PUNISHMENT

INSTRUMENT OF EXECUTION
Harold P. Brown and electrical pioneer Thomas Alva Edison's chief electrician Dr. A.E. Kennelly jointly take the credit for inventing the electric chair, first used to execute murderer William Kemmler in 1890.

10 US EXECUTION FIRSTS

1 First to be hanged

John Billington, for the shooting murder of John Newcomin in Plymouth, Massachusetts, 30 September 1630.

2 First to be hanged for witchcraft

Achsah Young, in Massachusetts on 27 May 1647. Eighty-year-old Giles Cory became the last man to be pressed to death (for refusing to plead on charges of witchcraft) in Salem, Massachusetts, on 19 September 1692; the last executions for witchcraft (of eight women) also took place at Salem on 22 September 1692.

3 First to be hanged for treason

Jacob Leisler, for insurrection against New York Governor Francis Nicholson, in City Hall Park, New York, 16 May 1691.

4 First to be hanged for slave trading

Captain Nathaniel Gordon (technically hanged for piracy, which included slave trading) was executed at the Tombs Prison, New York, 21 February 1862.

5 First civilian to be hanged for treason

William Bruce Mumford, for tearing down the American flag in New Orleans, 7 June 1862.

6 First man to be electrocuted

William Kemmler (alias John Hart), for murder, at Auburn Prison, New York, 6 August 1890.

7 First woman to be electrocuted

Martha M. Place, for murder, at Sing Sing Prison, New York, 20 March 1899.

8 First to be executed in the gas chamber

Gee Jon, for murder, in Carson City, Nevada, 8 February 1924.

9 First to be electrocuted for treason

Julius and Ethel Rosenberg, at Sing Sing Prison, New York, 19 June 1953.

10 First to be executed by lethal injection

Charles Brooks, for murder, at the Department of Corrections, Huntsville, Texas, 6 December 1982.

THE 10
FIRST COUNTRIES TO ABOLISH CAPITAL PUNISHMENT

	Country	Abolished
1	Russia	1826
2	Venezuela	1863
3	Portugal	1867
4=	Brazil	1882
4=	Costa Rica	1882
6	Ecuador	1897
7	Panama	1903
8	Norway	1905
9	Uruguay	1907
10	Colombia	1910
	UK	*1965*

Some countries abolished capital punishment in peacetime only, or for all crimes except treason, although several countries later reinstated the penalty.

THE 10
LAST PEOPLE EXECUTED AT THE TOWER OF LONDON

1 Wilhelm Johannes Roos   30 Jul 1915

Roos was a Dutchman who posed as a cigar salesman and sent coded messages to a firm in Holland detailing ship movements in British ports. Roos was the 3rd spy of World War I to be executed at the Tower of London. He was shot.

2 Haike Marinus Petrus Janssen   30 Jul 1915

An accomplice of Roos who used the same methods. The two were tried together and executed the same day. Janssen was shot 10 minutes after Roos, at 6.10 am.

3 Ernst Waldemar Melin   10 Sep 1915

A German spy who was shot after General Court Martial during World War I.

4 Agusto Alfredo Roggen   17 Sep 1915

A German who attempted to escape the death penalty by claiming to be Uruguayan. He was found guilty of spying on the trials of a new torpedo at Loch Lomond, then sending the information in invisible ink.

5 Fernando Buschman   19 Oct 1915

Posing as a Dutch violinist, he spied while offering entertainment at Royal Navy bases.

6 Georg T. Breeckow   26 Oct 1915

Posing as an American (Reginald Rowland) with a forged passport, he was caught when he sent a parcel containing secret messages, but addressed in German style, with country and town name preceding that of the street.

7 Irving Guy Ries   27 Oct 1915

A German commercial traveller who was sentenced to death on spying charges.

8 Albert Meyer   2 Dec 1915

Like Ries, Meyer was a German spy posing as a commercial traveller.

9 Y.L. Zender-Hurwitz   11 Apr 1916

A spy of Peruvian descent charged with sending information to Germany about British troop movements, for which he received a salary of £30 a month.

10 Josef Jakobs   15 Aug 1941

A German army sergeant who was caught when he parachuted into England wearing civilian clothes and carrying an identity card in the name of James Rymer. Following General Court Martial, he was shot at 7.15 am – the only spy executed at the Tower during the course of World War II.

THE 10

US STATES WITH THE MOST PRISONERS ON DEATH ROW

	State	Prisoners under death sentence
1	California	420
2	Texas	404
3	Florida	362
4	Pennsylvania	196
5	Ohio	155
6	Illinois	154
7	Alabama	143
8	North Carolina	139
9	Oklahoma	129
10	Arizona	117

* As at 31 December 1995
Source: Department of Justice

THE 10

US STATES WITH THE MOST WOMEN ON DEATH ROW

	State	No. under death sentence*
1	California	7
2	Texas	6
3=	Florida	5
3=	Oklahoma	5
5=	Alabama	4
5=	Illinois	4
5=	Pennsylvania	4
8=	Missouri	2
8=	North Carolina	2
10=	Arizona	1
10=	Idaho	1
10=	Louisiana	1
10=	Mississippi	1
10=	Nevada	1
10=	Tennessee	1

* As at 14 May 1996

THE 10

US STATES WITH THE MOST EXECUTIONS

	State	Method now in force	Executed 1930–95
1	Texas	Lethal injection	401
2	Georgia	Electrocution	386
3	New York	Lethal injection	329
4	California	Lethal gas	294
5	North Carolina	Lethal gas or injection	271
6	Florida	Electrocution	206
7	Ohio	Electrocution	172
8	South Carolina	Electrocution	167
9	Mississippi	Lethal injection*	158
10	Louisiana	Lethal injection	155

* Lethal gas if sentenced prior to 1 July 1984
Source: Department of Justice

THE 10

FIRST ELECTROCUTIONS AT SING-SING PRISON, NEW YORK

	Name	Electrocuted
1	Harris A. Smiler	7 Jul 1891
2	James Slocum	7 Jul 1891
3	Joseph Wood	7 Jul 1891
4	Schihick Judigo	7 Jul 1891
5	Martin D. Loppy	7 Dec 1891
6	Charles McElvaine	8 Feb 1892
7	Jeremiah Cotte	28 Mar 1892
8	Fred McGuire	19 Dec 1892
9	James L. Hamilton	3 Apr 1893
10	Carlyle Harris	8 May 1893

The electric chair was installed in Sing-Sing Prison, New York, in 1891, just a year after it was first used to execute William Kemmler at Auburn Prison, also in New York State. By the end of the 19th century, 29 inmates had been executed by this means (including the first female, 44-year-old Martha M. Place, on 20 March 1899).

THE 10

YEARS WITH THE MOST EXECUTIONS IN THE US*

	Year	Executions
1	1935	199
2	1936	195
3	1938	190
4	1934	168
5=	1933	160
5=	1939	160
7	1930	155
8=	1931	153
8=	1947	153
10	1937	147

* All offences, 1930 to 1995

The total number of executions in the US fell below three figures for the first time this century in 1952, when 82 prisoners were executed, and below double figures in 1965, with seven executions. Only one prisoner was executed in 1966, in 1977 (when Gary Gilmore became the first for 10 years to receive the death penalty), and in 1981. There were no executions at all between 1968 and 1976, but double figures were recorded again in 1984 (21 executions) and in all subsequent years.

THE 10

LAST MEN HANGED FOR MURDER IN THE UK

	Name	Hanged
1	John Robson Welby	13 Aug 1964
2	Peter Anthony Allen	13 Aug 1964
3	Dennis Whitty	17 Dec 1963
4	Russell Pascoe	17 Dec 1963
5	Henry Burnett	15 Aug 1963
6	James Smith	28 Nov 1962
7	Oswald Grey	20 Nov 1962
8	James Hanratty	4 Apr 1962
9	Hendryk Niemasz	8 Sep 1961
10	Samuel McLaughlin	25 Jul 1961

WORLD WAR I

LARGEST ARMED FORCES OF WORLD WAR I

	Country	Personnel*
1	Russia	12,000,000
2	Germany	11,000,000
3	British Empire#	8,904,467
4	France	8,410,000
5	Austria–Hungary	7,800,000
6	Italy	5,615,000
7	USA	4,355,000
8	Turkey	2,850,000
9	Bulgaria	1,200,000
10	Japan	800,000

* Total at peak strength
\# Including Australia, Canada, India, New Zealand, South Africa, and other countries in the Commonwealth

COUNTRIES SUFFERING THE GREATEST MILITARY LOSSES IN WORLD WAR I

	Country	Killed
1	Germany	1,773,700
2	Russia	1,700,000
3	France	1,357,800
4	Austria–Hungary	1,200,000
5	British Empire	908,371
6	Italy	650,000
7	Romania	335,706
8	Turkey	325,000
9	USA	116,516
10	Bulgaria	87,500

The number of battle fatalities and deaths from other causes among military personnel varied enormously: Romania's death rate was highest at 45 per cent and Japan's 0.04 per cent among the lowest.

WAR DEAD
The carnage of trench warfare in particular resulted in as many as 8,545,800 military casualties during World War I.

FIGHTING FORCE
More Russian troops served in World War I than those of any other nation, with one in seven killed and one in five taken prisoner.

COUNTRIES SUFFERING THE GREATEST MERCHANT SHIPPING LOSSES IN WORLD WAR I

	Country	Vessels sunk number	tonnage
1	UK	2,038	6,797,802
2	Italy	228	720,064
3	France	213	651,583
4	USA	93	372,892
5	Germany	188	319,552
6	Greece	115	304,992
7	Denmark	126	205,002
8	Netherlands	74	194,483
9	Sweden	124	192,807
10	Spain	70	160,383

COUNTRIES WITH THE MOST PRISONERS OF WAR, 1914–18

	Country	Prisoners		Country	Prisoners
1	Russia	2,500,000	6	Turkey	250,000
2	Austria–Hungary	2,200,000	7	British Empire	191,652
3	Germany	1,152,800	8	Serbia	152,958
4	Italy	600,000	9	Romania	80,000
5	France	537,000	10	Belgium	34,659

AMERICA'S TOP AIR ACE DIES

Edward ("Eddie") Rickenbacker first established his reputation in the US as a champion motor-racing driver. A visit to England in 1917 encouraged his interest in flying, and when the US entered World War I Rickenbacker enlisted and trained as a pilot. On 19 March 1918 Rickenbacker took part in the first-ever US patrol over enemy lines, and on 29 April shot down his first aircraft. A month later, with five kills to his credit, he became an acknowledged "ace", eventually achieving a total of 26 kills and winning the US Congressional Medal of Honor. Rickenbacker also saw service during World War II. He died in Zurich, Switzerland, on 23 July 1973 at the age of 82.

TOP 10

BRITISH AND COMMONWEALTH AIR ACES OF WORLD WAR I

	Pilot	Nationality	Kills claimed
1	Edward Mannock	British	73
2	William Avery Bishop	Canadian	72
3	Raymond Collishaw	Canadian	62
4	James Thomas Byford McCudden	British	57
5=	Anthony Wetherby Beauchamp-Proctor	South African	54
5=	Donald MacLaren	Canadian	54
7=	William George Barker	Canadian	52
7=	Philip Fletcher Fullard	British	52
9	R.S. Dallas	Australian	51
10	George Edward Henry McElroy	Irish	49

TOP 10

US AIR ACES OF WORLD WAR I

	Pilot*	Kills claimed
1	Edward Vernon Rickenbacker	26
2	William C. Lambert	22
3=	August T. Iaccaci	18
3=	Frank Luke, Jr.	18
5=	Frederick W. Gillet	17
5=	Gervais Raoul Lufbery	17
7=	Howard A. Kuhlberg	16
7=	Oren J. Rose	16
9	Clive W. Warman	15
10=	David Endicott Putnam	13
10=	George Augustus Vaughan, Jr.	13

* *Includes American pilots flying with RAF and French flying service*

The term "ace" was first used during World War I for a pilot who had brought down at least five enemy aircraft. The first-ever reference in print to an air "ace" appeared in an article in *The Times* (14 September 1917), which described Raoul Lufbery as "the 'ace' of the American Lafayette Flying Squadron". The names of French pilots who achieved this feat were recorded in official communiqués, but although US and other pilots followed the same system, the British definition of an "ace" varied from three to ten aircraft and was never officially approved, remaining an informal concept during both world wars.

TOP 10

GERMAN AIR ACES OF WORLD WAR I

	Pilot	Kills claimed
1	Manfred von Richthofen	80
2	Ernst Udet	62
3	Erich Loewenhardt	53
4	Werner Voss	48
5=	Bruno Loerzer	45
5=	Fritz Rumey	45
7	Rudolph Berthold	44
8	Paul Bäumer	43
9	Josef Jacobs	41
10=	Oswald Boelcke	40
10=	Franz Büchner	40
10=	Lothar Freiherr von Richthofen	40

The claims of top World War I ace Rittmeister Manfred, Baron von Richthofen of 80 kills has been disputed, since only 60 of them have been completely confirmed. Richthofen, known as the "Red Baron" and leader of the so-called "Flying Circus" (because the aircraft were painted in distinctive bright colours), shot down 21 Allied fighters in the month of April 1917.

TOP 10

FRENCH AIR ACES OF WORLD WAR I

	Pilot	Kills claimed
1	Capitaine René P. Fonck	75
2	Capitaine George M.L.J. Guynemer	54
3	Lieutenant Charles E.J.M. Nungesser	45
4	Capitaine Georges F. Madon	41
5	Lieutenant Maurice Boyau	35
6	Lieutenant Jean-Pierre L. Bourjade	28
7	Capitaine Armand Pinsard	27
8=	Sous-Lieutenant René Dorme	23
8=	Lieutenant Gabriel Guérnin	23
8=	Sous-Lieutenant Claude M. Haegelen	23

WORLD WAR II

154

FIRST COUNTRIES TO DECLARE WAR IN WORLD WAR II

	Declaration	Date
1=	UK on Germany	3 Sep 1939
1=	Australia on Germany	3 Sep 1939
1=	New Zealand on Germany	3 Sep 1939
1=	France on Germany	3 Sep 1939
5	South Africa on Germany	6 Sep 1939
6	Canada on Germany	9 Sep 1939
7	Italy on UK and France	10 Jun 1940
8	France on Italy	11 Jun 1940
9=	Japan on USA, UK, Australia, Canada, New Zealand, and South Africa	7 Dec 1941
9=	UK on Finland, Hungary, and Romania	7 Dec 1941

The last of these declarations took place on the day of the Japanese attack on Pearl Harbor, as a result of which the US (as well as the UK and Free France) declared war on Japan the next day. On 11 December 1941, Germany and Italy declared war on the US, followed the same day by a counter-declaration by the US. Further declarations followed right up to 1945, some even in the closing months of the war. Italy, for example, declared war on Japan as late as 14 July 1945.

SHIP OF STATE
One of the largest battleships in service during World War II, the 270-m/887-ft USS New Jersey *last saw action in the Gulf War of 1990.*

COUNTRIES SUFFERING THE GREATEST MILITARY LOSSES IN WORLD WAR II

	Country	Killed
1	USSR	13,600,000
2	Germany	3,300,000
3	China	1,324,516
4	Japan	1,140,429
5	British Empire (of which UK	357,116 264,000)
6	Romania	350,000
7	Poland	320,000
8	Yugoslavia	305,000
9	USA	292,131
10	Italy	279,800

COUNTRIES SUFFERING THE GREATEST CIVILIAN LOSSES IN WORLD WAR II

	Country	Killed
1	China	8,000,000
2	USSR	6,500,000
3	Poland	5,300,000
4	Germany	2,350,000
5	Yugoslavia	1,500,000
6	France	470,000
7	Greece	415,000
8	Japan	393,400
9	Romania	340,000
10	Hungary	300,000

LARGEST ARMED FORCES OF WORLD WAR II

	Country	Personnel		Country	Personnel
1	USSR	12,500,000	6	UK	4,683,000
2	USA	12,364,000	7	Italy	4,500,000
3	Germany	10,000,000	8	China	3,800,000
4	Japan	6,095,000	9	India	2,150,000
5	France	5,700,000	10	Poland	1,000,000

LARGEST BATTLESHIPS OF WORLD WAR II

	Battleship	Country	Status	Length m	ft	Tonnage
1=	*Musashi*	Japan	Sunk 25 Oct 1944	263	862	72,809
1=	*Yamato*	Japan	Sunk 7 Apr 1945	263	862	72,809
3=	*Iowa*	USA	Still in service with US Navy	270	887	55,710
3=	*Missouri*	USA	Still in service with US Navy	270	887	55,710
3=	*New Jersey*	USA	Still in service with US Navy	270	887	55,710
3=	*Wisconsin*	USA	Still in service with US Navy	270	887	55,710
7=	*Bismarck*	Germany	Sunk 27 May 1941	251	823	50,153
7=	*Tirpitz*	Germany	Sunk 12 Nov 1944	251	823	50,153
9=	*Jean Bart*	France	Survived war, later scrapped	247	812	47,500
9=	*Richelieu*	France	Survived war, later scrapped	247	812	47,500

FAST AND FURIOUS
More than 20,000 of the fast and highly manoeuvrable Spitfire fighter planes were built during the course of World War II.

TOP 10

FASTEST FIGHTER AIRCRAFT OF WORLD WAR II

	Aircraft	Country	Maximum speed km/h	mph
1	Messerschmitt *Me 163*	Germany	959	596
2	Messerschmitt *Me 262*	Germany	901	560
3	Heinkel *He 162A*	Germany	890	553
4	*P-51-H Mustang*	USA	784	487
5	Lavochkin *La11*	USSR	740	460
6	*Spitfire XIV*	UK	721	448
7	Yakovlev *Yak-3*	USSR	719	447
8	*P-51-D Mustang*	USA	708	440
9	*Tempest VI*	UK	705	438
10	Focke-Wulf *Fw 190D*	Germany	700	435

THE 10

MOST HEAVILY BLITZED CITIES IN THE UK

	City	Major raids	Tonnage of high explosive
1	London	85	23,949
2	Liverpool/Birkenhead	8	1,957
3	Birmingham	8	1,852
4	Glasgow/Clydeside	5	1,329
5	Plymouth/Devonport	8	1,228
6	Bristol/Avonmouth	6	919
7	Coventry	2	818
8	Portsmouth	3	687
9	Southampton	4	647
10	Hull	3	593

TOP 10

US AIR ACES OF WORLD WAR II

	Pilot	Kills claimed
1	Maj. Richard I. Bong	40
2	Maj. Thomas B. McGuire	38
3	Cdr. David S. McCampbell	34
4=	Col. Francis S. Gabreski	28
4=	Lt–Col. Gregory Boyington	28*
6=	Maj. Robert S. Johnson	27
6=	Col. Charles H. MacDonald	27
8=	Maj. George E. Preddy	26
8=	Maj. Joseph J. Foss	26
10	Lt. Robert M. Hanson	25

* Also 6.5 kills in the Korean War

TOP 10

BRITISH AND COMMONWEALTH AIR ACES OF WORLD WAR II

	Pilot	Nationality	Kills claimed
1	Sqd. Ldr. Marmaduke Thomas St. John Pattle	South African	over 40
2	Gp. Capt. James Edgar "Johnny" Johnson	British	33.91
3	Wng. Cdr. Brendan "Paddy" Finucane	Irish	32
4	Flt. Lt. George Frederick Beurling	Canadian	31.33
5	Wng. Cdr. John Randall Daniel Braham	British	29
6	Gp. Capt. Adolf Gysbert "Sailor" Malan	South African	28.66
7	Wng. Cdr. Clive Robert Caldwell	Australian	28.50
8	Sqd. Ldr. James Harry "Ginger" Lacey	British	28
9	Sqd. Ldr. Neville Frederick Duke	British	27.83
10	Wng. Cdr. Colin F. Gray	New Zealander	27.70

BATTLES & MEDALS

THE AMERICAN CIVIL WAR
More than 50,000 died in the Battle of Gettysburg, Pennsylvania, on 1–3 July 1863, the site of which is now preserved as a National Battlefield. The action was the bloodiest of the Civil War, itself the second worst in US history.

THE 10

LONGEST WARS OF ALL TIME

	War	Combatants	Dates	Duration (years)
1	Hundred Years War	France *vs.* England	1338–1453	115
2=	Wars of the Roses	Lancaster *vs.* York	1455–1485	30
2=	Thirty Years War	Catholic *vs.* Protestant	1618–1648	30
4	Peloponnesian War	Peloponnesian League (Sparta, Corinth, etc.) *vs.* Delian League (Athens, etc.)	431–404 BC	27
5=	First Punic War	Rome *vs.* Carthage	264–241 BC	23
5=	Napoleonic Wars	France *vs.* other European countries	1792–1815	23
7=	Greco-Persian Wars	Greece *vs.* Persia	499–478 BC	21
7=	Second Great Northern War	Russia *vs.* Sweden and Baltic states	1700–21	21
9	Vietnam War	South Vietnam (with US support) *vs.* North Vietnam	1957–1975	18
10	Second Punic War	Rome *vs.* Carthage	218–201 BC	17

It may be argued that the total period of the Crusades (Christianity *vs.* Islam) constitutes one long single conflict spanning a total of 195 years from 1096 to 1291, rather than a series of nine short ones, in which case it ranks as the longest war ever. Similarly, if all the Punic Wars between 264 and 146 BC are taken as one, they would rank second at 118 years. The War of the Spanish Succession (1701–14) is the only other major conflict to have lasted more than 10 years, with the War of the Austrian Succession (1740–48), the American War of Independence (1775–83) and Chinese-Japanese War (1937–45) each lasting eight years.

THE 10

FIRST NATIONAL BATTLEFIELDS IN THE US

	National Battlefield/ battle	Established
1	Chickamauga and Chattanooga, Georgia/ Tennessee, Sep 19–20, 1863	Aug 19, 1890
2	Antietam, Maryland, Sep 17, 1862	Aug 30, 1890
3	Shiloh, Tennessee, Apr 6–7, 1862	Dec 27, 1894
4	Gettysburg, Pennsylvania, Jul 1–3, 1863	Feb 11, 1895
5	Vicksburg, Mississippi, Jan 9–Jul 4, 1863	Feb 21, 1899
6	Big Hole, Montana, Aug 9, 1877	Jun 23, 1910
7	Guilford Courthouse, North Carolina, Mar 15, 1781	Mar 2, 1917
8	Kennesaw Mountain, Georgia, Jun 20–Jul 2, 1864	Apr 22, 1917
9	Moores Creek, North Carolina, Feb 27, 1776	Jun 2, 1926
10	Petersburg, Virginia, Jun 15, 1864– Apr 3, 1865	Jul 3, 1926

* *Dates include those for locations originally assigned other designations but later authorized as National Battlefields, National Battlefield Parks, and National Military Parks*

There are in all 24 National Battlefields, National Battlefield Parks, and National Military Parks, but just one National Battlefield Site, Brices Cross Roads, Mississippi (the scene of a Civil War engagement on June 10, 1864; the site was established on February 21, 1929). The earliest battle to be so commemorated is Fort Necessity, Pennsylvania (July 3, 1754; National Battlefield established March 4, 1931), the site of the opening hostility in the French and Indian War, in which the militia led by George Washington, then a 22-year-old Lt.-Colonel, was defeated and captured.

T O P 1 0

US MEDAL OF HONOR CAMPAIGNS

	Campaign	Years	Medals awarded
1	Civil War	1861–65	1,520
2	World War II	1941–45	433
3	Indian Wars	1861–98	428
4	Vietnam War	1965–73	238
5	Korean War	1950–53	131
6	World War I	1917–18	123
7	Spanish–American War	1898	109
8	Philippines/Samoa	1899–1913	91
9	Boxer Rebellion	1900	59
10	Veracruz	1914	55

The Congressional Medal of Honor, the USA's highest military award, was first issued in 1863. In addition to the medal itself, recipients receive such benefits as a $400 per month pension for life, free air travel, and the right to be buried in the Arlington National Cemetery. Past winners of the award include William "Buffalo Bill" Cody, who received it in 1872. His medal was revoked in 1917 when a new ruling stipulated that recipients had to have been serving members of the military, but it was reinstated in 1989.

T H E 1 0

20TH-CENTURY WARS WITH THE MOST MILITARY FATALITIES

	War/years	Approximate no. of fatalities
1	World War II (1939–45)	15,843,000
2	World War I (1914–18)	8,545,800
3	Korean War (1950–53)	1,893,100
4=	Sino-Japanese War (1937–41)	1,000,000
4=	Biafra–Nigeria Civil War (1967–70)	1,000,000
6	Spanish Civil War (1936–39)	611,000
7	Vietnam War (1965–73)	546,000
8=	India–Pakistan War (1947)	200,000
8=	Soviet invasion of Afghanistan (1979–89)	200,000
8=	Iran–Iraq War (1980–88)	200,000

The statistics of warfare have always been an imperfect science. Not only are battle deaths seldom recorded accurately, but figures are often deliberately inflated by both sides in a conflict. For political reasons and to maintain morale, each is anxious to enhance reports of its military success and low casualty figures, so that often quite contradictory reports of the same battle may be issued. These figures thus represent military historians' "best guesses".

T O P 1 0

NATIONALITIES OF VC WINNERS DURING WORLD WAR II

	Nationality	VCs
1	British and Irish	109
2	Australian	19
3	Indian	17
4	Canadian	13
5	Nepalese (Gurkha)	10
6	New Zealander	8
7	South African	3
8=	Danish	1
8=	Fijian	1
8=	Rhodesian	1

Of the total of 182 Victoria Crosses awarded during World War II, 88 were awarded posthumously.

T O P 1 0

MOST AWARDED BRITISH MEDALS

	Medal	Total awarded*
1	Military Medal	132,045
2	Military Cross	48,459
3	Distinguished Conduct Medal	29,227
4	Distinguished Flying Cross	22,249
5	Distinguished Service Order	16,838
6	Distinguished Service Medal	11,249
7	Distinguished Flying Medal	6,959
8	Distinguished (formerly Conspicuous) Service Cross	6,617
9	Indian Meritorious Service Medal#	5,814
10	Indian Distinguished Service Medal	5,611

* To end of 1979, excluding bars and foreign awards

\# Awarded 1917–25 only

WAR WOUNDED
As well as innumerable military personnel and civilians who were injured and killed, more than 30 million military fatalities have resulted from 20th-century conflicts.

MODERN MILITARY

TOP 10

COUNTRIES WITH THE LARGEST DEFENCE BUDGETS

	Country	Budget ($)
1	USA	267,900,000,000
2	China	52,840,000,000
3	Russia	48,000,000,000
4	Japan	46,800,000,000
5	France	37,200,000,000
6	Germany	33,600,000,000
7	UK	33,200,000,000
8	Italy	20,000,000,000
9	South Korea	15,600,000,000
10	Saudi Arabia	13,900,000,000

The so-called "peace dividend" – the savings made as a consequence of the end of the Cold War between the West and the former Soviet Union – means that both the numbers of personnel and the defence budgets of many countries have been cut. That of the USA has gone down from its 1989 peak of $303.6 billion.

TOP 10

LARGEST ARMED FORCES IN THE WORLD

	Country	Estimated active forces			
		Army	Navy	Air Force	Total
1	China	2,200,000	265,000	470,000	2,935,000
2	USA	495,000	426,700	388,200	1,483,800 *
3	Russia	460,000	190,000	145,000	1,270,000 #
4	India	980,000	110,000	55,000	1,145,000
5	North Korea	923,000	46,000	85,000	1,054,000
6	South Korea	548,000	60,000	52,000	660,000
7	Turkey	525,000	51,000	63,000	639,000
8	Pakistan	520,000	22,000	45,000	587,000
9	Vietnam	500,000	42,000	15,000	572,000
10	Iran	345,000	18,000	30,000	513,000 +
	UK	*113,000*	*48,000*	*65,000*	*226,000*

* *Includes 173,900 Marine Corps*
\# *Includes Strategic Deterrent Forces, Paramilitary, National Guard, etc*
+ *Includes 120,000 Revolutionary Guards*

In addition to the active forces listed here, many of the world's foremost military powers have considerable reserves on standby. South Korea's has been estimated at some 4,500,000, Vietnam's at 3–4,000,000, and China's 1,200,000. Russia's has steadily dwindled as a result both of the end of the Cold War and its current economic problems. China is also notable for having a massive arsenal of military equipment at its disposal, including some 8,000 tanks, 4,600 fighter aircraft, and 1,225 bombers and ground attack aircraft.

TOP 10

COUNTRIES WITH THE HIGHEST PER CAPITA DEFENCE EXPENDITURE

	Country	Expenditure per capita, 1995 ($)
1	Kuwait	2,091
2	Singapore	1,349
3	Israel	1,279
4	USA	1,056
5	United Arab Emirates	1,044
6	Oman	978
7	Brunei	909
8	Norway	863
9	France	826
10	Switzerland	720

TOP 10

ARMS IMPORTERS IN THE WORLD

	Country	Annual imports ($)
1	Saudi Arabia	5,200,000,000
2	Libya	1,800,000,000
3	Egypt	1,500,000,000
4	USA	1,100,000,000
5=	Israel	1,000,000,000
5=	South Korea	1,000,000,000
7	Turkey	950,000,000
8	Japan	650,000,000
9	Angola	600,000,000
10	Spain	525,000,000
	UK	*200,000,000*

TOP 10

COUNTRIES WITH THE HIGHEST MILITARY/ CIVILIAN RATIO

	Country	Military personnel per 10,000 population
1	Russia	833
2	North Korea	435
3	United Arab Emirates	357
4	Israel	303
5	Syria	286
6	Jordan	217
7	Qatar	213
8	Bahrein	189
9	Iraq	175
10	Armenia	167
	USA	*56*
	UK	*39*

TOP 10

RANKS OF THE US NAVY, ARMY, AND AIR FORCE

	Navy	Army	Air Force
1	Fleet Admiral	General	General
2	Admiral	Lieutenant-General	Lieutenant-General
3	Vice-Admiral	Major-General	Major-General
4	Rear-Admiral (Upper Half)	Brigadier-General	Brigadier-General
5	Rear-Admiral (Lower Half)	Colonel	Colonel
6	Captain	Lieutenant-Colonel	Lieutenant-Colonel
7	Commodore	Major	Major
8	Lieutenant-Commander	Captain	Captain
9	Lieutenant	First Lieutenant	First Lieutenant
10	Lieutenant (Junior Grade)	Second Lieutenant	Second Lieutenant

STORMIN' NORMAN'S DESERT VICTORY
General Norman Schwarzkopf acknowledges applause during a special meeting of the US Congress after his return from the Gulf War. He declared, "It's a great day to be a soldier and a great day to be an American."

TOP 10

RANKS OF THE ROYAL NAVY, ARMY, AND ROYAL AIR FORCE

	Royal Navy	Army	Royal Air Force
1	Admiral	General	Air Chief Marshal
2	Vice-Admiral	Lieutenant-General	Air Marshal
3	Rear-Admiral	Major-General	Air Vice-Marshal
4	Commodore	Brigadier	Air Commodore
5	Captain	Colonel	Group Captain
6	Commander	Lieutenant-Colonel	Wing Commander
7	Lieutenant-Commander	Major	Squadron Leader
8	Lieutenant	Captain	Flight Lieutenant
9	Sub-Lieutenant	Lieutenant	Flying Officer
10	Acting Sub-Lieutenant	Second Lieutenant	Pilot Officer

In February 1996 the three most senior ranks in all three services – Admiral of the Fleet, Field Marshal, and Marshal of the Royal Air Force – were abolished, in the cases of the first two ending a tradition that dates back several centuries. The names given to some ranks date back to medieval times – in the case of Admiral of the Fleet, for example, its earliest use in English has been dated to *c.* 1425, while Admiral was used even earlier to mean a prince or other military ruler in the service of a Sultan. The first recorded use of General was in 1576, and it appeared in Shakespeare's plays soon afterwards. The term Brigadier dates from 1678, and Field Marshall first appeared in print in 1736, when the Duke of Argyll and the Earl of Orkney were both appointed as Field Marshalls of the British army. Some terms have parallels in the US military, but with certain differences: in the Royal navy, for example, the rank of Commodore, first recorded in 1695, is a temporary one applied to senior officers in command of detached squadrons, and is divided into two classes, the upper of which receives pay equivalent to that of a Rear-Admiral and has a captain under him, while the second class does not. Since 1862, in the US navy, a commodore may command a naval division or station, or a first-class warship.

TOP 10

COUNTRIES WITH THE LARGEST UN PEACEKEEPING FORCES*

	Country	Troops
1	Pakistan	1,725
2	Bangladesh	1,155
3	Russian Federation	1,114
4	Jordan	1,101
5	Poland	1,094
6	India	1,082
7	Canada	1,067
8	Brazil	1,014
9	Finland	910
10	Austria	865

* As of 31 March 1997

United Nations peacekeeping forces are established by the UN Security Council. Although most UN member states provide troops, troops are most frequently drawn from neutral or non-aligned members.

WORLD RELIGIONS

THE WAY OF BUDDHA
*Originating in India in the 6th century BC,
Buddhism's quest for enlightenment and its
espousal of peace and tolerance have contributed
to its appeal throughout Asia and beyond.*

TOP 10

ORGANIZED RELIGIONS IN THE WORLD

	Religion	Members
1	Christianity	1,927,953,000
2	Islam	1,099,634,000
3	Hinduism	780,547,000
4	Buddhism	323,894,000
5	Sikhism	19,161,000
6	Judaism	14,117,000
7	Confucianism	5,254,000
8	Baha'ism	6,104,000
9	Jainism	4,886,000
10	Shintoism	2,844,000

This list excludes the followers of various
tribal and folk religions, new religions, and
shamanism, which together total almost
500,000,000. There are also perhaps more
than 800,000,000 people who may be
classified as "non-religious" (having no
interest in religion of any persuasion), and
a further 220,000,000 atheists (opposed to
religion of any kind, or followers of
alternative, non-religious philosophies).

TOP 10

LARGEST BUDDHIST POPULATIONS IN THE WORLD

	Location	Total Buddhist population
1	China	102,000,000
2	Japan	89,650,000*
3	Thailand	55,480,000
4	Vietnam	49,690,000
5	Myanmar (Burma)	41,610,000
6	Sri Lanka	12,540,000
7	South Korea	10,920,000
8	Taiwan	9,150,000
9	Cambodia	9,130,000
10	India	7,000,000

* Including many who also practise Shintoism

TOP 10

LARGEST JEWISH POPULATIONS IN THE WORLD

	Location	Total Jewish population
1	USA	5,602,000
2	Israel	4,390,000
3	Russia	1,450,000
4	France	640,000
5	Canada	350,000
6	UK	320,000
7	Argentina	250,000
8	Brazil	150,000
9	Australia	92,000
10	South Africa	70,000

The Diaspora, or scattering of Jewish
people, has been in progress for
nearly 2,000 years, and as a
result Jewish communities
are found in virtually every
country in the world.

TOP 10

LARGEST CHRISTIAN POPULATIONS IN THE WORLD

	Location	Total Christian population
1	USA	224,457,000
2	Brazil	139,000,000
3	Mexico	86,210,000
4	Germany	67,170,000
5	Philippines	63,470,000
6	UK	51,060,000
7	Italy	47,690,000
8	France	44,150,000
9	Nigeria	38,180,000
10	Russia	37,400,000

It is difficult to put a precise figure on
nominal membership of a religion (declared
religious persuasion) rather than active
participation (regular attendance at a place of
worship). It was claimed, for example, that
out of the total US population of
248,709,873 (according to the 1990 Census),
62.86 per cent were active members of a
religious organization including
non-Christian groups, whereas this Top 10
asserts a nominal figure for Christians alone
that is equivalent to almost 90 per cent of
the country's current population.

PRACTISING THE JEWISH FAITH
*The prayer shawl (tallith), skull cap
(yarmulke), branched candlestick (menorah),
and Hebrew Bible are all important in the
practice of Judaism.*

THE BLUE MOSQUE
The superbly decorated Blue Mosque in Istanbul, Turkey, is one of the great centres of the Muslim faith. Islam, the world's fastest-growing religion, has almost 800 million followers in the Top 10 countries alone.

T O P 1 0

LARGEST MUSLIM POPULATIONS IN THE WORLD

	Location	Total Muslim population
1	Indonesia	170,310,000
2	Pakistan	136,000,000
3	Bangladesh	106,050,000
4	India	103,000,000
5	Turkey	62,410,000
6	Iran	60,790,000
7	Egypt	53,730,000
8	Nigeria	47,720,000
9	Algeria	27,910,000
10	Morocco	26,900,000

T O P 1 0

LARGEST HINDU POPULATIONS IN THE WORLD

	Location	Total Hindu population			Location	Total Hindu population
1	India	751,000,000		6	Malaysia	1,400,000
2	Nepal	17,380,000		7	USA	910,000
3	Bangladesh	12,630,000		8	Mauritius	570,000
4	Sri Lanka	2,800,000		9	South Africa	420,000
5	Pakistan	2,120,000		10	UK	410,000

T O P 1 0

COUNTRIES MOST VISITED BY POPE JOHN PAUL II*

	Country	Visits
1=	Poland	5
1=	France	5
1=	USA#	5
4	Spain	4
5=	Kenya	3
5=	Mexico	3
5=	Brazil	3
5=	Ivory Coast	3
9=	Argentina, Australia, Austria, Belgium, Benin, Canada, Dominican Republic, Guinea, Papua New Guinea, Peru, Philippines, Portugal, South Korea, Switzerland, Uruguay, West Germany, Zaïre	2

* To the end of 1996
\# Includes a 1984 stopover in Alaska

After taking office as Pope in 1978, John Paul II broke with papal tradition completely and embarked on an extensive series of travels. Prior to these trips, only one Pope had ever travelled outside Italy (Paul VI went to Israel in 1964).

T O P 1 0

RELIGIOUS AFFILIATIONS IN THE US

	Affiliation	Members
1	Protestant	105,939,000
2	Roman Catholic	52,259,000
3	Eastern Orthodox	5,631,000
4	Jewish	5,602,000
5	Muslim	5,100,000
6	Anglican	2,350,000
7	Hindu	910,000
8	Buddhist	780,000
9	Baha'i	300,000
10	Sikh	190,000

T O P 1 0

RELIGIOUS GROUPS IN THE UK

	Group	Members
1	Roman Catholic	2,000,000
2	Anglican	1,700,000
3	Presbyterian	1,100,000
4	Muslim	600,000
5	Methodist	400,000
6=	Orthodox	300,000
6=	Sikh	300,000
8=	Baptist	200,000
8=	Mormon	200,000
10=	Hindu	100,000
10=	Jewish	100,000

THE BIBLE

NAMES MOST MENTIONED IN THE BIBLE

	Name	OT*	NT*	Total
1	Jesus (984)/ Christ (576)	0	1,560	1,560
2	David	1,005	59	1,064
3	Moses	767	80	847
4	Jacob	350	27	377
5	Aaron	347	5	352
6	Solomon	293	12	305
7=	Joseph	215	35	250
7=	Abraham	176	74	250
9	Ephraim	182	1	183
10	Benjamin	162	2	166

* *Occurrences in verses in the King James Bible (Old and New Testaments), including possessive uses, such as "John's"*

In addition to these personal names, "God" is referred to on 4,105 occasions (2,749 Old Testament; 1,356 New Testament). The name Judah also appears 816 times, but the total includes references to the territory as well as the individual with that name. At the other end of the scale, there are many names that – perhaps fortunately – appear only once or twice, among them Berodach-baladan and Tilgath-pilneser. The most mentioned place names produce few surprises, with Israel heading the list (2,600 references), followed by Jerusalem (814), Egypt (736), Babylon (298), and Assyria (141). Heaven is referred to 440 times in both the Old and New Testaments.

ANIMALS MOST MENTIONED IN THE BIBLE

	Animal	OT*	NT*	Total
1	Sheep	155	45	200
2	Lamb	153	35	188
3	Lion	167	9	176
4	Ox	156	10	166
5	Ram	165	0	165
6	Horse	137	27	164
7	Bullock	152	0	152
8	Ass	142	8	150
9	Goat	131	7	138
10	Camel	56	6	62

* *Occurrences in verses in the King James Bible (Old and New Testaments), including plurals*

The sheep are sorted from the goats in this Top 10, in a menagerie of the animals considered most significant in biblical times, either economically or symbolically (as in the many references to the lion's strength). A number of generic terms are also found in abundance: beast (a total of 337 references), cattle (153), fowl (90), fish (56), and bird (41). Some creatures are mentioned only once, in *Leviticus* 11, which contains a list of animals that are considered "unclean" – the weasel, chameleon, and tortoise, for example – and are never referred to again. Though Egypt may have suffered a plague of frogs, just 14 appear in the Bible, along with just three spiders and two mice.

LONGEST WORDS IN THE BIBLE

	Word*	Letters
1=	covenantbreakers (NT only)	16
1=	evilfavouredness	16
1=	lovingkindnesses	16
1=	unprofitableness	16
1=	unrighteousness (and NT)	16
1=	uprightreousness	16
7=	acknowledgement	15
7=	administrations (NT only)	15
7=	bloodyguiltness	15
7=	confectionaries	15
7=	fellowdisciples (NT only)	15
7=	fellowlabourers (NT only)	15
7=	interpretations	15
7=	kneadingtroughs	15
7=	notwithstanding (and NT)	15
7=	prognosticators	15
7=	righteousnesses	15
7=	stumblingblocks	15
7=	threshingfloors	15

* *All Old Testament only (King James version) unless otherwise stated*

GIDEONS INTERNATIONAL

If you have ever wondered where the bibles that are found in hotel rooms the world over come from, the answer dates back to as long ago as 1898, when travelling salesman John H. Nicholson and his colleague Sam Hill stayed at the Central Hotel Boscobel, Wisconsin, USA, and there decided to establish an association of Christian businessmen. Their avowed aim was to "put the word of God into the hands of the unconverted", which they proposed to achieve by placing bibles in hotel rooms, hospitals, prisons, and other suitable locations. A century later Gideons International continues to distribute a total of more than 16,000,000 bibles a year throughout the world.

TOP 10

LONGEST NAMES OF PEOPLE AND PLACES IN THE BIBLE

	Name	Letters
1	Mahershalalhashbaz (Isaiah's son)	18
2=	Bashanhavothjair (alternative name of Argob)	16
2=	Chepharhaammonai (Ammonite settlement)	16
2=	Chusharishathaim (king of Mesopotamia)	16
2=	Kibrothhattaavah (desert encampment of Israelites)	16
2=	Selahammahlekoth (stronghold in Maon)	16
7=	Abelbethmaachah (town near Damascus)	15
7=	Almondiblathaim (stopping-place of Israelites)	15
7=	Apharsathchites (Assyrian nomadic group)	15
7=	Berodachbaladan/Merodachbaladan (king of Babylon)	15
7=	Helkathhazzurim (a battlefield)	15
7=	Ramathaimzophin (town where Samuel was born)	15
7=	Tilgathpilneser (king of Assyria)	15
7=	Zaphnathpaaneah (name given to Joseph by Pharaoh)	15

TOP 10

WORDS MOST MENTIONED IN THE BIBLE

	Word	OT*	NT*	Total
1	The	52,948	10,976	63,924
2	And	40,975	10,721	51,696
3	Of	28,518	6,099	34,617
4	To	10,207	3,355	13,562
5	That	9,152	3,761	12,913
6	In	9,767	2,900	12,667
7	He	7,348	3,072	10,420
8	For	6,690	2,281	8,971
9	I	6,669	2,185	8,854
10	His	7,036	1,437	8,473

* *Occurrences in verses in the King James Bible (Old and New Testaments)*

A century before computers were invented, Thomas Hartwell Horne (1780–1862), a dogged biblical researcher, undertook a manual search of biblical word frequencies and concluded that "and" appeared a total of 35,543 times in the Old Testament and 10,684 times in the New Testament. He was fairly close on the latter – but he clearly missed quite a few in the Old Testament, as a recent computer search of the King James Bible indicates.

THE 10

COMMANDMENTS

1 Thou shalt have no other gods before me.

2 Thou shalt not make unto thee any graven image.

3 Thou shalt not take the name of the Lord thy God in vain.

4 Remember the sabbath day, to keep it holy.

5 Honour thy father and thy mother.

6 Thou shalt not kill.

7 Thou shalt not commit adultery.

8 Thou shalt not steal.

9 Thou shalt not bear false witness against thy neighbour.

10 Thou shalt not covet thy neighbour's house, thou shalt not covet thy neighbour's wife, nor his manservant, nor his maidservant, nor his ox, nor his ass, nor any thing that is thy neighbour's.

Exodus 20 iii (King James Version)

TOP 10

CROPS MOST MENTIONED IN THE BIBLE

	Crop	OT*	NT*	Total
1	Corn	86	11	97
2	Fig	45	21	66
3	Olive	42	19	61
4	Wheat	40	12	52
5	Grape	46	3	49
6	Barley	43	3	46
7	Pomegranate	33	0	33
8	Raisin	9	7	16
9	Apple	11	0	11
10	Bean	6	0	6

* *Occurrences in verses in the King James Bible (Old and New Testaments), including plurals*

DISASTERS

THE 10

WORST RAIL DISASTERS IN THE WORLD

Location/date/incident	No. killed
1 Bagmati River, India, 6 June 1981	c. 800

The carriages of a train travelling from Samastipur to Banmukhi in Bihar plunged off a bridge over the river Bagmati near Mansi – when the driver braked, apparently to avoid hitting a sacred cow. Although the official death toll was said to have been 268, many authorities have claimed that the train was so massively overcrowded that the actual figure was in excess of 800, making it probably the worst rail disaster of all time.

Location/date/incident	No. killed
2 Chelyabinsk, Russia, 3 June 1989	up to 800

Two Trans-Siberian passenger trains, going to and from the Black Sea, were destroyed when liquid gas from a nearby pipeline exploded.

Location/date/incident	No. killed
3 Guadalajara, Mexico, 18 January 1915	over 600

A train derailed on a steep incline, but political strife in the country meant that full details of the disaster were suppressed.

Location/date/incident	No. killed
4 Modane, France, 12 December 1917	573

A troop-carrying train ran out of control and was derailed. It was probably overloaded, and as many as 1,000 people may have died.

Location/date/incident	No. killed
5 Balvano, Italy, 2 March 1944	521

A heavily-laden train stalled in the Armi Tunnel, and many passengers asphyxiated.

Location/date/incident	No. killed
6 Torre, Spain, 3 January 1944	over 500

A double collision and fire in a tunnel resulted in many deaths. Like the disaster at Balvano two months later, wartime secrecy prevented full details from being published.

Location/date/incident	No. killed
7 Awash, Ethiopia, 13 January 1985	428

A derailment hurled a train into a ravine.

Location/date/incident	No. killed
8 Cireau, Romania, 7 January 1917	374

An overcrowded passenger train crashed into a military train and was derailed.

Location/date/incident	No. killed
9 Quipungo, Angola, 31 May 1993	355

A train was derailed by UNITA guerrilla action.

Location/date/incident	No. killed
10 Sangi, Pakistan, 4 January 1990	306

A diverted train resulted in a fatal collision.

Casualty figures for rail accidents are often extremely imprecise, especially during wartime – and no fewer than half of the 10 worst disasters occurred during the two World Wars. Further vague incidents, such as one at Kalish, Poland, in December 1914, for example, with "400 dead", one in November 1918 at Norrköpping, Sweden, alleged to have killed 300, and certain other similarly uncertain cases have been omitted.

SCENE OF THE ACCIDENT
Some of the worst rail accidents in both the US and UK occurred when signalling and safety equipment were less sophisticated than they are today.

WORST RAIL DISASTERS IN THE US

Location/date/incident	No. killed
1 Nashville, Tennessee, 9 July 1918	101

On the Nashville, Chattanooga, and St. Louis Railway, a head-on collision resulted in a death-toll that remains the worst in US history, with 171 injured.

2 Brooklyn, New York, 2 November 1918	97

A subway train was derailed in the Malbone Street tunnel.

3= Eden, Colorado, 7 August 1904	96

A bridge washed away during a flood smashed Steele's Hollow Bridge as the "World's Fair Express" was crossing.

3= Wellington, Washington, 1 March 1910	96

An avalanche swept two trains into a canyon.

5 Bolivar, Texas, 8 September 1900	85

A train travelling from Beaumont encountered the hurricane that destroyed Galveston, killing 6,000. Attempts to load the train on to a ferry were abandoned, and when it tried to return it was destroyed by the storm.

6 Woodbridge, New Jersey, 6 February 1951	84

A Pennsylvania Railroad train crashed while speeding through a sharply curving detour.

7 Chatsworth, Illinois, 10 August 1887	82

A trestle bridge caught fire and collapsed as the Toledo, Peoria, & Western train was passing over. As many as 372 were injured.

8 Ashtabula, Ohio, 29 December 1876	80

A bridge collapsed in a snow storm, and the Lake Shore train fell into the Ashtabula river. The death toll may have been as high as 92.

9= Frankford Junction, Pennsylvania, 6 September 1943	79

This was Pennsylvania's worst railway accident since that at Camp Hill on 17 July 1856, which resulted in the deaths of 66 school children on a church picnic outing.

9= Richmond Hill, New York, 22 November 1950	79

A Long Island Railroad commuter train rammed into the rear of another, leaving 79 dead and 363 injured.

WORST RAIL DISASTERS IN THE UK

Location/date/incident	No. killed
1 Quintinshill near Gretna Green, 22 May 1915	227

A troop train carrying 500 members of the 7th Royal Scots Regiment collided head-on with a passenger train. Barely a minute later, the Scottish express, drawn by two engines and weighing a total of 600 tonnes, ploughed into the wreckage. The 15 coaches of the troop train, 195 m/640 yards long, were so crushed that they ended up just 61 m/200 ft long. The gas-lit troop train then caught fire. Since their records were destroyed in the blaze, the actual number of soldiers killed was never established. It was probably 215, as well as two members of the train's crew, eight in the express and two in the local train – a total of 227 killed, and 246 injured, many very seriously. An enquiry established that the accident was caused by the negligence of the signalmen, George Meakin and James Tinsley, who were convicted of manslaughter and jailed.

2 Harrow and Wealdstone Station, 8 October 1952	122

In patchy fog Robert Jones, the relief driver of the Perth to Euston sleeping-car express, pulled by the City of Glasgow, failed to see a series of signal lights warning him of danger, and at 8.19 am collided with the waiting Watford to Euston train. Seconds later, the Euston to Liverpool and Manchester express hit the wreckage of the two trains. The casualties were 112 killed instantly, 10 who died later, and 349 injured.

3 Lewisham, South London, 4 December 1957	90

A steam and an electric train collided in fog. The disaster was made worse by the collapse of a bridge on to the wreckage.

4 Tay Bridge, Scotland, 28 December 1879	80

As the North British mail train passed over it during a storm, the bridge collapsed, killing all 75 passengers and the crew of five. The bridge – the longest in the world at that time – had only been opened on 31 May the previous year, and Queen Victoria had crossed it in a train soon afterwards. The locomotive was salvaged from the bed of the Tay several months later. It had surprisingly little damage, and was repaired. It continued in service until 1919.

5 Armagh, Northern Ireland, 12 June 1889	78

A Sunday school excursion train with 940 passengers stalled on a hill. When 10 carriages were uncoupled, they ran backwards and collided with a passenger train, killing 78 (claims of 300 deaths have not been substantiated) and leaving 250 injured.

6 Hither Green, South London, 5 November 1967	49

The Hastings to Charing Cross train was derailed by a broken track. As well as those killed, 78 were injured, 27 of them seriously.

7= Bourne End, Hertfordshire, 30 September 1945	43

Travelling at about 50 mph, the Perth to Euston express sped through a crossover with a 20 mph speed restriction imposed during engineering works, and was derailed. Its coaches plunged down an embankment.

7= Moorgate Station, London, 28 February 1975	43

A tube ran into the wall at the end of the tunnel, killing 43 and injuring 74 in London Transport's worst rail disaster.

9 Castlecary, Scotland, 10 December 1937	35

The Edinburgh to Glasgow train ran into a stationary train and rode over the top of it.

10= Shipton near Oxford, 24 December 1874	34

The Paddington to Birkenhead train plunged over the embankment after a carriage wheel broke, killing 34 and badly injuring 65.

10= Clapham Junction, London, 12 December 1988	34

The 7.18 Basingstoke to Waterloo train, carrying 906 passengers, stopped at signals outside Clapham Junction; the 6.30 train from Bournemouth ran into its rear, and an empty train from Waterloo hit the wreckage, leaving 33 dead (and one who died later) and 111 injured.

OFF THE RAILS
Rail passengers are not always as lucky as those who miraculously escaped when this carriage failed to plunge over a viaduct.

ROAD TRANSPORT DISASTERS

THE 10
WORST MOTOR VEHICLE AND ROAD DISASTERS IN THE WORLD

	Location/date/incident	No. killed
1	Afghanistan, 3 November 1982	2,000+

Following a collision with a Soviet army truck, a petrol tanker exploded in the 2.7-km/1.7-mile long Salang Tunnel. Some authorities estimate that the death toll could be as high as 3,000.

2	Colombia, 7 August 1956	1,200

Seven army ammunition trucks exploded at night in the centre of the city of Cali, destroying eight city blocks.

3	Thailand, 15 February 1990	150+

A dynamite truck exploded.

4	Nepal, 23 November 1974	148

Hindu pilgrims were killed when a suspension bridge over the River Mahahali collapsed.

5	Egypt, 9 August 1973	127

A bus drove into an irrigation canal.

6	Togo, 6 December 1965	125+

Two lorries collided with a group of dancers during a festival at Sotouboua.

7	Spain, 11 July 1978	120+

A liquid gas tanker exploded in a camping site at San Carlos de la Rapita.

8	South Korea, 28 April 1995	110

An underground explosion destroyed vehicles and caused about 100 cars and buses to plunge into the pit it created.

9	The Gambia, 12 November 1992	c. 100

A bus full of passengers plunged into a river when its brakes failed.

10	Kenya, early December 1992	nearly 100

A bus carrying 112 passengers skidded, hit a bridge, and plunged into a river.

The worst-ever motor racing accident occurred on 13 June 1955, at Le Mans, France, when French driver Pierre Levegh's Mercedes-Benz 300 SLR went out of control, hit a wall, and exploded in mid-air, showering wreckage into the crowd and killing a total of 82.

THE 10
MOST ACCIDENT-PRONE CAR COLOURS IN THE UK

	Colour	Accidents per 10,000 cars of each colour
1	Black	179
2	White	160
3	Red	157
4	Blue	149
5	Grey	147
6	Gold	145
7	Silver	142
8	Beige	137
9	Green	134
10=	Brown	133
10=	Yellow	133

Figures released by the Department of Transport appeared to refute the notion that white cars were safest. These statistics were disputed by some car manufacturers, insurance companies, and psychologists who pointed out that the type of vehicle and age and experience of drivers were equally salient factors, and until further surveys are conducted it would perhaps be misleading to consider one colour "safer" than another.

THE 10
AGE GROUPS MOST VULNERABLE TO ROAD ACCIDENTS IN GREAT BRITAIN

	Age group	Killed or seriously injured (1995)
1	20–24	44,756
2	15–19	39,108
3	25–29	38,736
4	30–34	31,528
5	35–39	22,441
6	10–14	19,222
7	40–44	17,771
8	45–49	16,562
9	5–9	13,674
10	50–54	12,718

THE 10
WORST YEARS FOR FATAL MOTOR VEHICLE ACCIDENTS IN THE US

	Year	Fatalities per 100,000,000 VMT*	Total deaths#
1	1972	4.3	54,589
2	1973	4.1	54,052
3	1969	5.0	53,543
4	1968	5.2	52,725
5	1970	4.7	52,627
6	1971	4.5	52,542
7	1979	3.3	51,093
8	1980	3.3	51,091
9	1966	5.5	50,894
10	1967	5.3	50,724

* *Vehicle Miles of Travel*
\# *Traffic fatalities occurring within 30 days of accident*

THE 10
WORST YEARS FOR ROAD FATALITIES IN GREAT BRITAIN

	Year	No. killed
1	1941	9,169
2	1940	8,609
3	1939	8,272
4	1966	7,985
5	1965	7,952
6	1964	7,820
7	1972	7,763
8	1971	7,699
9	1970	7,499
10	1973	7,406

Road fatalities were first recorded in Great Britain in 1873, when there were about 1,500 out of a population of over 23,000,000; most of these accidents involved horses and horse-drawn vehicles. The first road deaths due to cars occurred in 1896 but were actually outnumbered by those involving cyclists until 1906, when deaths caused by motor vehicles exceeded 100 for the first time.

DEATH ON THE ROAD

As the number of vehicles on the world's roads has increased, so have fatalities resulting from traffic accidents. Based on the total number of deaths, the US tops the list, but not because American drivers are any less careful than those of other countries. The US has more vehicles that collectively travel greater distances than any other country on the Earth, and when these factors are taken into account the rate of fatal accidents is actually much lower than in many countries. On the basis of deaths per 100 million vehicle miles, the US has just 1.8, while South Korea, for example, has a rate of 46.9 – or 26 times as many – implying that driving habits and road conditions play very significant roles.

FLAG OF INCONVENIENCE
Until 1896 British drivers had to warn of their presence by waving a red flag.

THE 10

COUNTRIES WITH THE HIGHEST NUMBER OF ROAD DEATHS

	Country	Total deaths*
1	USA	41,465
2	Thailand	15,176
3	Japan	10,649
4	South Korea	10,087
5	Germany	9,814
6	France	8,533
7	Brazil	6,759
8	Poland	6,744
9	Italy	6,578
10	Spain	6,378

* In latest year for which figures are available

Despite increasing numbers of vehicles on British roads, the UK's record has slowly improved, with 3,598 fatalities in 1996 – a figure comparable to those of the 1920s.

SCENE OF THE ACCIDENT
Car crashes in the US kill more than 40,000 people every year.

AFTER THE EVENT
Firefighters are called on to rescue crash victims and to clear up after road accidents.

CRASH TEST DUMMY
Car manufacturers undertake research to improve the safety of their vehicles.

MARINE DISASTERS

WORST MARINE DISASTERS OF THE 20TH CENTURY

	Vessel	Date	Approx. no. killed
1	*Wilhelm Gustloff*	30 January 1945	up to 7,700

This German liner, laden with refugees, was torpedoed off Danzig by a Soviet submarine, S-13. The precise death toll remains uncertain, but it is thought to be in the range of 5,348–7,700.

2	*Goya*	16 April 1945	6,500

A German ship carrying evacuees from Danzig was torpedoed in the Baltic near Cape Rixhöft.

3	Unknown vessel	November 1947	over 6,000

An unidentified Chinese troopship carrying Nationalist soldiers from Manchuria sank off Yingkow. The exact date is unknown.

4	*Cap Arcona*	3 May 1945	4,650

A German ship carrying concentration camp survivors was bombed and sunk by British aircraft in Lübeck harbour.

5	*Lancastria*	17 June 1940	4,000

A British troop ship sank off St. Nazaire.

6	*Yamato*	7 April 1945	3,033

The Japanese battleship sank off Kyushu Island.

7	*Dona Paz*	20 December 1987	up to 3,000

The ferry Dona Paz *was struck by oil tanker MV Victor in the Tabias Strait, Philippines.*

8	*Kiangya*	3 December 1948	over 2,750

An overloaded steamship carrying refugees struck a Japanese mine off Woosung, China.

9	*Thielbeck*	3 May 1945	2,750

A refugee ship sank during the British bombardment of Lübeck harbour in the closing weeks of World War II.

10	*Arisan Maru*	24 October 1944	1,790

A Japanese vessel carrying American prisoners-of-war was torpedoed by a US submarine in the South China Sea.

Due to a reassessment of the death tolls in some World War II marine disasters, the most famous of all, the sinking of the *Titanic* (the British liner that struck an iceberg in the North Atlantic on 15 April 1912 and went down with the loss of 1,517 lives), no longer ranks in this list. However, the *Titanic* tragedy remains one of the worst-ever peacetime disasters, along with such notable incidents as that involving the *General Slocum*, an excursion liner that caught fire in the port of New York on 15 June 1904 with the loss of 1,021. Among other disasters occurring during wartime are the sinking of the British cruiser *HMS Hood* by the German battleship *Bismarck* in the Denmark Strait on 24 May 1941, with 1,418 killed; the torpedoing by German submarine *U-20* of the British passenger liner *Lusitania* on 7 May 1915, with the loss of 1,198 civilians; and the accidental sinking by a US submarine of *Rakuyo Maru*, a Japanese troopship carrying Allied prisoners of war, on 12 September 1944, killing some 1,141.

WORST SUBMARINE DISASTERS OF ALL TIME
(Excluding those as a result of military action)

	Submarine	Date	No. killed
1	*Le Surcourf*	18 February 1942	159

The French submarine was accidentally rammed by a US merchant ship.

2	*Thresher*	10 April 1963	129

The three-year-old US nuclear submarine, worth $45,000,000, sank in the North Atlantic, 350 km/220 miles east of Boston, USA.

3	*I-12*	January 1945	114

The Japanese submarine sank in the Pacific in unknown circumstances.

4	*I-174*	3 April 1944	107

A Japanese submarine sank in the Pacific in unknown circumstances.

5	*I-26*	October 1944	105

This Japanese submarine sank east of Leyte, cause and date unknown.

6	*I-169*	4 April 1944	103

A Japanese submarine flooded and sank while in harbour at Truk.

7	*I-22*	October 1942	100

A Japanese submarine sank off the Solomon Islands, exact date unknown.

8=	*Seawolf*	3 October 1944	99

A US submarine was sunk in error by USS Rowell off Morotai.

8=	*Thetis*	13 March 1943	99

The British submarine sank on 1 June 1939 during trials in Liverpool Bay, with civilians on board. Her captain and three crew members escaped. Thetis was later salvaged and renamed Thunderbolt. *She was sunk by an Italian ship with the loss of 63 lives.*

8=	*Scorpion*	21 May 1968	99

This US nuclear submarine was lost in the North Atlantic, south-west of the Azores. The wreck was located on 31 October of that year.

The loss of the *Thresher* is the worst accident ever involving a nuclear submarine. It sank while undertaking tests off the US coast and was located by the bathyscaphe *Trieste*. The remains of the submarine were scattered over the ocean floor at a depth of 2,560 m/ 8,400 ft. The cause of the disaster remains a military secret.

CLEANING UP
*Around two million tonnes of oil are spilled
into the seas every year, damaging the
environment. Seabirds suffer because they
are unable to clean oil from their feathers.*

THE 10

WORST PASSENGER FERRY DISASTERS OF THE 20TH CENTURY

	Ferry/location/date	Approx. no. killed
1	*Dona Paz*, Philippines, 20 December 1987	up to 3,000
2	*Neptune*, Haiti, 17 February 1992	1,800
3	*Toya Maru*, Japan, 26 September 1954	1,172
4	*Don Juan*, Philippines, 22 April 1980	over 1,000
5	*Estonia*, Baltic Sea, 28 September 1994	909
6	*Samia*, Bangladesh, 25 May 1986	600
7	*MV Bukoba*, Tanzania, 21 May 1996	549
8	*Salem Express*, Egypt, 14 December 1991	480
9	*Tampomas II*, Indonesia, 27 January 1981	431
10	*Nam Yung Ho*, South Korea, 15 December 1970	323

THE 10

WORST OIL TANKER SPILLS OF ALL TIME

	Tanker	Location	Date	Approx. spillage (tonnes)
1	*Atlantic Empress* and *Aegean Captain*	Trinidad	19 July 1979	300,000
2	*Castillio de Bellver*	Cape Town, South Africa	6 August 1983	255,000
3	*Olympic Bravery*	Ushant, France	24 January 1976	250,000
4	*Showa-Maru*	Malacca, Malaya	7 June 1975	237,000
5	*Amoco Cadiz*	Finistère, France	16 March 1978	223,000
6	*Odyssey*	Atlantic, off Canada	10 November 1988	140,000
7	*Torrey Canyon*	Scilly Isles, UK	18 March 1967	120,000
8	*Sea Star*	Gulf of Oman	19 December 1972	115,000
9	*Irenes Serenada*	Pilos, Greece	23 February 1980	102,000
10	*Urquiola*	Corunna, Spain	12 May 1976	101,000

The grounding of the *Exxon Valdez* in Prince William Sound, Alaska, USA, on 24 March 1989 ranks outside the 10 worst spills at about 35,000 tonnes of oil spilled, but resulted in major ecological damage. All the accidents in this Top 10 were caused by collision, grounding, fire, or explosion, but worse tanker oil spills have been caused by military action. Between January and June 1942, for example, German U-boats torpedoed a number of tankers off the east coast of the US with a loss of some 600,000 tonnes of oil, and in June 1991, during the Gulf War, various tankers were sunk in the Persian Gulf, spilling a total of more than 1,000,000 tonnes of oil.

THE SINKING OF *LA BOURGOGNE*

One of the 10 worst marine disasters of the 19th century occurred on 4 July 1898, when *La Bourgogne*, a French steamliner, collided with the British sailing vessel *Cromartyshire* off Sable Island, Nova Scotia. *La Bourgogne* had set out from New York. Despite dense fog, the ship continued to maintain a high speed and was sailing off course when she was struck. The unwritten rule that the safety of women and children should be put first, was ignored as crew members shamelessly pushed passengers overboard as they scrambled into the remaining lifeboats, with the result that 560 lives were lost. Of the 165 survivors, some 100 were French crewmen; only one woman passenger was saved.

100 YEARS AGO

AIR DISASTERS

T H E 1 0

WORST AIR DISASTERS IN THE WORLD

	Incident	Killed
1	27 March 1977, Tenerife, Canary Islands	583

Two Boeing 747s (Pan Am and KLM, carrying 364 passengers with 16 crew, and 230 passengers with 11 crew, respectively) collided and caught fire on the runway of Los Rodeos airport after the pilots received incorrect control-tower instructions.

	Incident	Killed
2	12 August 1985, Mt. Ogura, Japan	520

A JAL Boeing 747 on an internal flight from Tokyo to Osaka crashed, killing all but four on board in the worst-ever disaster involving a single aircraft.

	Incident	Killed
3	12 November 1996, Charkhi Dadrio, India	349

Soon after taking off from New Delhi's Indira Gandhi International Airport, a Saudi Airways Boeing 747 collided with a Kazakh Airlines Ilyushin IL-76 cargo aircraft on its descent and exploded, killing all 312 on the Boeing and 37 on the Ilyushin in the world's worst mid-air crash.

	Incident	Killed
4	3 March 1974, Paris, France	346

A Turkish Airlines DC-10 crashed at Ermenonville, north of Paris, immediately after take-off for London, with many English rugby supporters among the dead.

	Incident	Killed
5	23 June 1985, off the Irish coast	329

An Air India Boeing 747, on a flight from Vancouver to Delhi, exploded in mid-air, perhaps as a result of a terrorist bomb.

	Incident	Killed
6	19 August 1980, Riyadh, Saudi Arabia	301

A Saudia (Saudi Arabian) Airlines Lockheed TriStar caught fire during an emergency landing.

	Incident	Killed
7	8 January 1996, Kinshasa, Zaïre	300

A Zaïrean Antonov-32 cargo plane crashed shortly after take-off, killing shoppers in a city-centre market in Kinshasa. The final death toll has not yet been officially announced.

	Incident	Killed
8	3 July 1988, off the Iranian coast	290

An Iran Air A300 Airbus was shot down in error by a missile fired by the USS Vincennes.

	Incident	Killed
9	25 May 1979, Chicago, USA	273

The worst air disaster in the US occurred when an engine fell off a DC-10 as it took off from Chicago's O'Hare airport. The aircraft plunged out of control, killing all 271 on board and two on the ground.

	Incident	Killed
10	21 December 1988, Lockerbie, Scotland, UK	270

Pan Am Flight 103 from London Heathrow to New York exploded in mid-air as a result of a terrorist bomb, killing 243 passengers, 16 crew, and 11 on the ground in the UK's worst-ever air disaster.

Five further air disasters have resulted in the deaths of more than 250 people: on 1 September 1983 a Korean Air Lines Boeing 747 that had strayed into Soviet airspace was shot down with the loss of 269 lives; on 26 April 1994 a China Airlines Airbus A300-600 crashed while landing, killing 264; on 11 July 1991 at Jeddah, Saudi Arabia, a DC-8 crashed on take-off killing 261; on 28 November 1979 a DC-10 crashed killing 257 passengers and crew; and on 12 December 1985 a DC-8 crashed killing all 256 on board.

T H E 1 0

WORST AIR COLLISIONS IN THE WORLD

	Incident	Killed
1	12 November 1996, Charkhi Dadrio, India	349

(See The 10 Worst Air Disasters in the World, No. 3.)

	Incident	Killed
2	10 September 1976, Near Gaj, Yugoslavia	177

A British Airways Trident and a Yugoslav DC-9 collided, killing all 176 on board and a woman on the ground.

	Incident	Killed
3	11 August 1979, Near Dneprodzerzhinsk, Ukraine, USSR	173

Two Soviet Tupolev-134 Aeroflot airliners collided in mid air.

	Incident	Killed
4	30 July 1971, Morioko, Japan	162

An air collision occurred between an All Nippon Boeing 727 and Japanese Air Force F-86F. The student pilot and instructor in the fighter survived, but were both were found guilty of negligence and jailed.

	Incident	Killed
5	22 December 1992, near Souq as-Sabt, Libya	157

A Libyan Boeing 747 and a Libyan air force MiG-23 fighter collided. The fighter crew reportedly ejected to safety, but all passengers and crew on the airliner were killed.

	Incident	Killed
6	25 September 1978, San Diego, California, USA	144

A Pacific Southwest Boeing 727 collided in the air with a Cessna 172 light aircraft with a student pilot, killing 135 in the airliner, two in the Cessna, and seven on the ground.

	Incident	Killed
7	16 December 1960, New York City, USA	135

A United Airlines DC-8, with 77 passengers and a crew of seven, and a TWA Super Constellation, with 39 passengers and four crew, collided in a snowstorm. The DC-8 crashed in Brooklyn killing eight on the ground; the Super Constellation crashed in Staten Island harbour, killing all passengers and crew on board.

	Incident	Killed
8	8 February 1993, Tehran, Iran	132

As it took off, a passenger aircraft carrying pilgrims was struck by a military aircraft, causing it to crash and killing all on board.

	Incident	Killed
9	30 June 1956, Grand Canyon, Arizona, USA	128

A United Airlines DC-7 and a TWA Super Constellation collided in the air, killing all passengers and crew on board both airliners, in the worst civil aviation disaster to that date, and the first ever commercial aviation accident with more than 100 fatalities.

	Incident	Killed
10	1 February 1963, Ankara, Turkey	104

A Middle East Airlines Viscount 754 and a Turkish Air Force C-47 collided and plunged on to the city. All 14 on the airliner, three in the fighter, and 87 on the ground were killed by the crash and fire that followed.

The first air collision resulting in the deaths of more than 50 people occurred on 1 November 1949, when a Bolivian Air Force P-38 fighter collided with an Eastern Air Lines DC-4 as they came in to land at Washington, DC. In the collision the pilot of the P-38 and all 55 on board the airliner were killed, making this the worst air disaster in the US up to that date. Although air traffic control, radar, and communications equipment have greatly improved since that disaster, the volume of air traffic has vastly increased, and the mid-air collision of two aircraft remains one of the major hazards of modern aviation.

THE 10

WORST AIRSHIP DISASTERS IN THE WORLD

Incident	Killed
1 4 April 1933, off the Atlantic coast, USA	73

US Navy airship Akron *crashed into the sea in a storm, leaving only three survivors in the world's worst airship tragedy.*

2 21 December 1923, over the Mediterranean	52

French airship Dixmude *is assumed to have been struck by lightning, broken up, and crashed into the sea. Wreckage, believed to be from the airship, was found off Sicily 10 years later.*

3 5 October 1930, near Beauvais, France	50

British airship R101 crashed into a hillside, leaving 48 dead, with two dying later, and six saved.

4 24 August 1921, off the coast near Hull, UK	44

Airship R38, sold by the British Government to the US and renamed USN ZR-2, broke in two on a training and test flight.

5 6 May 1937, Lakehurst, New Jersey, USA	36

German Zeppelin Hindenburg *caught fire when mooring.*

6 21 February 1922, Hampton Roads, Virginia, USA	34

Roma, *an Italian airship bought by the US Army, crashed killing all but 11 people on board.*

7 17 October 1913, Berlin, Germany	28

German airship LZ18 crashed after engine failure during a test flight at Berlin-Johannisthal.

8 30 March 1917, Baltic Sea	23

German airship SL9 was struck by lightning on a flight from Seerappen to Seddin and crashed into the sea.

9 3 September 1915, mouth of the River Elbe, Germany	19

German airship L10 was struck by lightning and plunged into the sea.

10= 9 September 1913, off Heligoland	14

German Navy airship L1 crashed into the sea, leaving six survivors out of the 20 on board.

10= 3 September 1925, Caldwell, Ohio, USA	14

US dirigible Shenandoah, *the first airship built in the US and the first to use safe helium instead of inflammable hydrogen, broke up in a storm, scattering sections over many miles of the Ohio countryside.*

From its earliest years, the history of the airship has been a mixture of triumphs and disasters. Following a series of accidents in the 1920s, the world's largest airship, the 237-m/777-ft British-built *R101*, crashed in France, broke in two, and burst into flames. Britain's interest in airships promptly ended, as did that of the US after the loss of the *Akron* less than three years later. Germany's enthusiasm lasted until 1937, when the 245-m/803.8-ft *Hindenburg* arrived at Lakehurst, New Jersey, after a three-day trip from Frankfurt. As she moored, she caught fire and turned into an inferno, the last moments of which remain among the most haunting sights ever captured on newsreel, with commentator Herb Morrison describing the horrific scene through floods of tears.

THE 10

WORST AVIATION DISASTERS WITH GROUND FATALITIES

Incident	Ground fatalities
1 8 January 1996, Kinshasa, Zaïre	300

(See The 10 Worst Air Disasters in the World, No. 7.)

2 24 December 1966, Dar Nang, South Vietnam	107

A Canadair CL-44 crash-landed onto a village.

3 1 February 1963, Ankara, Turkey	87

A Vickers Viscount 754 and a Turkish Air Force Douglas C-47 collided and fell into the city.

4 16 March 1969, Maracaibo, Venezuela	71

A DC-9 crashed onto the city after hitting power lines.

5 4 October 1992, Amsterdam, Netherlands	70

An El Al cargo plane crashed into a suburban apartment block.

6 28 August 1988, Ramstein US base, Germany	67

Three fighters in an Italian aerobatic team collided, one of them crashing into the crowd, leaving 70 dead (including the three pilots) and 150 spectators injured.

7 24 July 1938, Campo de Marte, Bogota, Colombia	53

A low-flying stunt plane crashed into a stand, broke up, and hurled blazing wreckage into the crowd.

8 23 August 1944, Freckelton, Lancashire, UK	51

A B-24 bomber crashed onto a school.

9 3 September 1989, Near Havana, Cuba	34

An Ilyushin Il-62M crashed and exploded on take-off.

10 22 October 1996, Manta, Ecuador	30

A Boeing 707 crashed into a residential area.

DOWN IN FLAMES
Overweight and unstable, British airship R101 crashed en route for India and was engulfed in a fireball when its 141,585 cu m/ 5,000,000 cu ft of hydrogen exploded, killing all but six on board.

MANMADE & OTHER DISASTERS

WORST MINING DISASTERS IN THE WORLD

	Location/date	Killed
1	Hinkeiko, China, 26 April 1942	1,549
2	Courrières, France, 10 March 1906	1,060
3	Omuta, Japan, 9 November 1963	447
4	Senghenydd, UK, 14 October 1913	439
5	Coalbrook, South Africa, 21 January 1960	437
6	Wankie, Rhodesia, 6 June 1972	427
7	Dharbad, India, 28 May 1965	375
8	Chasnala, India, 27 December 1975	372
9	Monongah, USA, 6 December 1907	362
10	Barnsley, UK, 12 December 1866	361 *

* *Including 27 killed the following day while searching for survivors*

A mining disaster at the Fushun mines, Manchuria, China, in February 1931 may have resulted in up to 3,000 deaths, but information was suppressed by the Chinese government. Soviet security was also responsible for obscuring details of an explosion at the East German Johanngeorgendstadt uranium mine on 29 November 1949, when as many as 3,700 may have died. The two worst disasters both resulted from underground explosions, and the large numbers of deaths among mine workers resulted from that cause, and from asphyxiation by poisonous gases. Among the most tragic disasters of this century, that at Aberfan, Wales, on 20 October 1966, was a mine disaster that affected the community rather than the miners. Waste from the local mine had been building up for many years to become a heap some 244 m/800 ft in height. Weakened by the presence of a spring, a huge volume of slurry suddenly flowed down and engulfed the local school, killing 144, of whom 116 were children.

WORST COMMERCIAL AND INDUSTRIAL DISASTERS*

	Location/incident	Date	Killed
1	Bhopal, India (methyl isocyanate gas escape at Union Carbide plant)	3 December 1984	over 2,500
2	Seoul, Korea (collapse of department store)	29 June 1995	640
3	Oppau, Germany (explosion at chemical plant)	21 September 1921	561
4	Mexico City, Mexico (explosion at PEMEX gas plant)	20 November 1984	540
5	Brussels, Belgium (fire in L'Innovation department store)	22 May 1967	322
6	Guadalajara, Mexico (explosions after gas leak into sewers)	22 April 1992	230
7	São Paulo, Brazil (fire in Joelma bank and office building)	1 February 1974	227
8	Bangkok, Thailand (fire engulfed a four-storey doll factory)	10 May 1993	187
9	North Sea (Piper Alpha oil rig explosion and fire)	6 July 1988	173
10	New York City (fire in Triangle Shirtwaist Factory)	25 March 1911	145

* *Including industrial sites, factories, offices, and stores; excluding military, mining, marine, and other transport disasters*

Officially, the meltdown of the nuclear reactor at Chernobyl, Ukraine, on 26 April 1986 caused the immediate death of 31 people. However, it has been suggested that by 1992 some 6,000 to 8,000 people had died as a direct result of radioactive contamination, a toll that will continue to increase for many years to come.

WORST FIRES IN THE WORLD*

	Location/incident	Date	Killed
1	Kwanto, Japan (following earthquake)	1 September 1923	60,000
2	London, UK (London Bridge)	July 1212	3,000 #
3	Peshtigo, Wisconsin, USA (forest)	8 October 1871	2,682
4	Santiago, Chile (church of La Compañía)	8 December 1863	2,500
5	Chungking, China (docks)	2 September 1949	1,700
6	Constantinople, Turkey (city fire)	5 June 1870	900
7	Cloquet, Minnesota, USA (forest)	12 October 1918	800
8	Mandi Dabwali, India (school tent)	23 December 1995	over 500
9	Hinckley, Minnesota, USA (forest)	1 September 1894	480
10	Hoboken, New Jersey, USA (docks)	30 June 1900	326

* *Excluding sports and entertainment venues, mining disasters, and the results of military action*
# *Burned, crushed, and drowned in ensuing panic*

Historically, city fires have caused the greatest loss of life. In 1212 about 3,000 were thought to have died when London Bridge caught fire. However, while the Great Fire of London of 1666 resulted in great material damage, there were just eight fatalities.

THE 10

WORST EXPLOSIONS IN THE WORLD*

	Location/incident	Date	Killed#
1	Lanchow, China (arsenal)	26 October 1935	2,000
2	Halifax, Nova Scotia (ammunition ship *Mont Blanc*)	6 December 1917	1,635
3	Memphis, Tennessee, USA (*Sultana* boiler explosion)	27 April 1865	1,547
4	Bombay, India (ammunition ship *Fort Stikine*)	14 April 1944	1,376
5	Cali, Colombia (ammunition trucks)	7 August 1956	1,200
6	Salang Tunnel, Afghanistan (petrol tanker collision)	2 November 1982	over 1,100
7	Chelyabinsk, USSR (liquid gas beside railway)	3 June 1989	up to 800
8	Texas City, Texas, USA (ammonium nitrate on *Grandcamp* freighter)	16 April 1947	752
9	Oppau, Germany (chemical plant)	21 September 1921	561
10	Mexico City, Mexico (PEMEX gas plant)	20 November 1984	540

* *Excluding mining disasters, and terrorist and military bombs*
# *All these "best estimate" figures should be treated with caution, since – as with fires and shipwrecks – body counts are notoriously unreliable*

MEXICO CITY GAS EXPLOSION
The PEMEX gas plant explosion of 20 November 1984 in Mexico City, Mexico, which left 540 dead, is not only one of the worst industrial disasters, but also one of the worst explosions of modern times.

THE 10

MOST COMMON CAUSES OF INJURY AT WORK IN THE UK

	Cause	Fatalities	Injuries*
1	Injured while handling, lifting, or carrying	0	45,518
2	Slip, trip, or fall on same level	2	32,255
3	Struck by moving (including flying or falling) object	25	20,475
4	Fall from height	50	13,108
5	Struck against something fixed or stationary	1	9,029
6	Contact with moving machinery	17	7,554
7	Exposure to, or contact with, harmful substance	6	3,998
8	Struck by moving vehicle	39	3,828
9	Injured by an animal	2	863
10	Contact with electricity	11	820
	Total (including causes not listed above)	208	146,375

* *Resulting in work absence of more than three days, employees only (excluding self-employed), 1995–96*

THE 10

COMMONEST CAUSES OF FATAL ACCIDENT IN THE HOME IN THE UK

	Accident	Killed
1	Unspecified falls	1,261
2	Poisoning/inhalation	512
3	Fall from stairs	490
4	Uncontrolled fire	430
5	Foreign body	243
6	Fall between two levels	139
7	Fall on same level	75
8	Suffocating/choking	71
9	Drowning	61
10	Fall from building	54
	Total (including causes not in Top 10)	3,569

174 NATURAL DISASTERS

WORST AVALANCHES AND LANDSLIDES OF THE 20th CENTURY*

	Location	Incident	Date	Estimated no. killed
1	Yungay, Peru	Landslide	31 May 1970	17,500
2	Italian Alps	Avalanche	13 December 1916	10,000
3	Huarás, Peru	Avalanche	13 December 1941	5,000
4	Nevada Huascaran, Peru	Avalanche	10 January 1962	3,500
5	Medellin, Colombia	Landslide	27 September 1987	683
6	Chungar, Peru	Avalanche	19 March 1971	600
7	Rio de Janeiro, Brazil	Landslide	11 January 1966	550
8=	Northern Assam, India	Landslide	15 February 1949	500
8=	Grand Riviere du Nord, Haiti	Landslide	13/14 November 1963	500
10	Blons, Austria	Avalanche	11 January 1954	411

* *Excluding those where most deaths resulted from flooding, earthquakes, etc. associated with landslides*

The worst incident of all, the destruction of Yungay, Peru, in May 1970, was only part of a much larger cataclysm that left a total of up to 70,000 dead. Following an earthquake and flooding, the town was wiped out by an avalanche that left just 2,500 survivors out of a population of 20,000. Similar incidents, in which the avalanche was a contributor in a series of disasters, include that at Khansou, China, on 16 December 1920, when a total of 180,000 were killed from the combined effects of earthquake, a massive landslide, and winter weather after their homes were destroyed.

THE WRATH OF THE VOLCANO
There are perhaps more than 500 currently active volcanoes in the world, with as many as 2,500 that have been active in recorded history. Fortunately, most do not endanger human life, but the attractions of farming on rich volcanic soil mean that settlements have sometimes fallen victim to major eruptions.

WORST TSUNAMIS OF THE 20th CENTURY

	Locations affected/date	Estimated no. killed
1	Agadir, Morocco,* 29 Feb 1960	12,000
2=	Philippines, 17 Aug 1976	5,000
2=	Chile/Pacific islands/Japan, 22 May 1960	5,000
4	Japan/Hawaii, 2 Mar 1933	3,000
5	Japan,* 21 Dec 1946	1,088
6	Japan, 1944	998
7	Colombia, 12 Dec 1979	500
8	Lomblem Island, Indonesia, 22 Jul 1979	700
9	Hawaii/Aleutians/California, 1 Apr 1946	173
10	Alaska/Aleutians/California,* 27 Mar 1964	122

* *Combined effect of earthquake and tsunamis*

Tsunamis (from the Japanese *tsu* [port] and *nami* [wave]) are powerful waves caused by undersea disturbances such as earthquakes or volcanic eruptions. Tsunamis can be so intense that they frequently cross entire oceans, devastating islands and coastal regions in their paths.

WORST FLOODS AND STORMS OF THE 20th CENTURY

	Location	Date	Estimated no. killed
1	Huang Ho River, China	August 1931	3,700,000
2	Bangladesh	13 November 1970	300–500,000
3	Henan, China	1939	more than 200,000
4	Chang Jiang River, China	September 1911	100,000
5	Bengal, India	15–16 November 1942	40,000
6	Bangladesh	1–2 June 1965	30,000
7	Bangladesh	28–29 May 1963	22,000
8	Bangladesh	11–12 May 1965	17,000
9	Morvi, India	11 August 1979	5,000–15,000
10	Hong Kong	18 September 1906	10,000

THE AFTERMATH OF AN EARTHQUAKE
Even though instruments can now detect impending seismic activity, there is rarely sufficient time for inhabitants of areas prone to earthquakes to evacuate their homes. In densely populated cities that are prone to earthquakes, thousands of people can be caught unawares, resulting in many catastrophes.

T H E   1 0

WORST EARTHQUAKES OF THE 20th CENTURY

	Location	Date	Estimated no. killed
1	Tang-shan, China	28 July 1976	242,419
2	Nanshan, China	22 May 1927	200,000
3	Kansu, China	16 December 1920	180,000
4	Messina, Italy	28 December 1908	160,000
5	Tokyo/Yokohama, Japan	1 September 1923	142,807
6	Kansu, China	25 December 1932	70,000
7	Callejon de Huaylas, Peru	31 May 1970	66,800
8	Quetta, India*	30 May 1935	50–60,000
9	Armenia	7 December 1988	over 55,000
10	Iran	21 June 1990	over 40,000

* Now Pakistan

There are some discrepancies between the "official" death tolls in many of the world's worst earthquakes and the estimates of other authorities: a figure of 750,000 is sometimes quoted for the Tang-shan earthquake of 1976, for example, and totals ranging from 58,000 to 250,000 are given for the quake that devastated Messina in 1908. Several other earthquakes in China and Turkey have resulted in deaths of 100,000 or more.

T H E   1 0

WORST VOLCANIC ERUPTIONS OF THE 20th CENTURY

	Location/date	Estimated no. killed
1	Mt. Pelée, Martinique, 8 May 1902	up to 40,000

After lying dormant for centuries, Mt. Pelée began to erupt in April 1902. Assured that there was no danger, the 30,000 residents of the main city, St. Pierre, stayed in their homes and were there on 8 May when the volcano burst apart at 7.30 am and showered the port with molten lava, ash, and gas, destroying all life and property.

2	Nevado del Ruiz, Colombia, 13 November 1985	22,940

The Andean volcano gave warning signs of erupting, but by the time it was decided to evacuate the local inhabitants, it was too late. The hot steam, rocks, and ash ejected from Nevado del Ruiz melted its icecap, resulting in a mudslide that completely engulfed the town of Armero.

3	Keluit, Java, 19 May 1919	5,110

One of the most remarkable of all volcanic eruptions on record, water pouring from Keluit's crater lake drowned inhabitans on the lower slopes.

4	Santa Maria, Guatemala, 24 October 1902	4,500

Some 1,500 died as a direct consequence of the volcanic eruption, and a further 3,000 as a result of its after effects.

5	Mt. Lamington, New Guinea, 21 January 1951	2,942

Mt. Lamington erupted with hardly any warning, with a huge explosion that was heard up to 320 km/200 miles away.

6	El Chichón, Mexico, 29 March 1982	1,879

Of these, 1,755 people were reported missing and 124 confirmed killed.

7	Lake Nyos, Cameroon, 21 August 1986	more than 1,700

A volcano erupted beneath the lake, and gases killed sleeping villagers.

8	La Soufriere, St. Vincent, 7–8 May 1902	1,565

The day before the cataclysmic eruption of Mt. Pelée (No. 1), La Soufriere erupted and engulfed the local inhabitants in ash flows.

9	Merapi, Java, 18 December 1931	1,369

In addition to the human casualties, 2,140 cattle were killed.

10	Taal, Philippines, 30 January 1911	1,335

Taal has erupted frequently, with the 1911 incident the worst of several during this century.

SPITTING FIRE AND BRIMSTONE
Red hot lava (liquid rock) shoots out of a volcano in a curtain of fire. Severe volcanic eruptions in the past have destroyed entire communities and killed thousands of people.

CULTURE & LEARNING

WILLIAM SHAKESPEARE

TOP 10

COUNTRIES WITH MOST CHILDREN AT PRIMARY SCHOOL

	Country	Primary-school children*
1	China	154,529,000
2	India	109,043,663
3	USA	33,410,000
4	Brazil	30,520,748
5	Indonesia	29,598,790
6	Pakistan	16,722,000
7	Nigeria	16,191,000
8	Mexico	14,468,700
9	Bangladesh	14,202,000
10	Philippines	10,731,453
	UK	*4,997,700*

* *In latest year for which information is available*

Absentees from this list include such countries as Japan: even though its population is greater than that of Mexico, its low birth rate means that it has little over half as many children at primary school.

TOP 10

MOST EXPENSIVE PUBLIC SCHOOLS IN THE UK*

	Public school	Boarding fees per annum (£)
1	Winchester College, Hampshire	13,944
2	Harrow School, Middlesex	13,830
3	Millfield, Somerset	13,785
4	Bedales School, Hampshire	13,647
5	Roedean School, East Sussex	13,635
6	Tonbridge School, Kent	13,620
7	Westminster School, London	13,530
8	Cobham Hall, Kent	13,500
9	King's School, Kent	13,440
10	Marlborough College, Wiltshire	13,425

* *Excluding specialist schools for the disabled, music schools, and religious schools, some of which are more expensive than these*

Inflation has affected school fees along with other consumer expenditure. A decade ago, Winchester's fees stood at £6,999; 50 years ago, it was £245. Today, more than 20 British independent schools charge annual tuition fees in excess of £13,000.

TOP 10

COUNTRIES WITH THE HIGHEST RATIO OF UNIVERSITY STUDENTS

	Country	University students per 100,000
1	Canada	7,197
2	USA	5,653
3	New Zealand	4,232
4	South Korea	4,208
5	Puerto Rico	4,091
6	Norway	3,883
7	Finland	3,757
8	Peru	3,465
9	France	3,414
10	Spain	3,335
	UK	*2,406*

TOP 10

LARGEST UNIVERSITIES IN THE US

	University*/location	Enrolments (1995–96)
1	Ohio State University, Columbus, Ohio	48,676
2	University of Texas, Austin, Texas	47,905
3	Arizona State University, Tempe, Arizona	42,040
4	Texas A&M University, College Station, Texas	41,790
5	Michigan State University, East Lansing, Michigan	40,647
6	Pennsylvania State, University Park, Pennsylvania	39,646
7	University of Florida, Gainesville, Florida	39,439
8	University of Wisconsin, Madison, Wisconsis	37,890
9	University of Minnesota, Minneapolis, Minnesota	36,995
10	University of Michigan, Ann Arbor, Michigan	36,687

* Four-year colleges only

Source: National Center For Education Statistics, US Department of Education

TOP 10

COUNTRIES WITH THE LONGEST SCHOOL YEARS

	Country	School year (days)
1	China	251
2	Japan	243
3	Korea	220
4	Israel	215
5=	Germany	210
5=	Russia	210
7	Switzerland	207
8=	Netherlands	200
8=	Scotland (England 192)	200
8=	Thailand	200

TOP 10

LARGEST UNIVERSITIES IN THE UK*

	University (founded)	Full-time students#
1	London (1836)	69,560
2	Manchester Metropolitan (1992)	19,706
3	De Montfort (Leicester) (1992)	18,392
4	Leeds (1904)	17,197
5	Manchester (1851)	16,990
6	Sheffield (1905)	15,911
7	Nottingham Trent (1992)	15,730
8	Edinburgh (1583)	15,455
9	Oxford (1249)	15,156
10	Birmingham (1900)	15,105

* Excluding Open University
# Undergraduates and post-graduates

As a result of the recent elevation of polytechnics to university status, several "new" large universities have arrived in the Top 10. One effect of this has been that Cambridge, Britain's second oldest university (founded in 1284), no longer makes the list.

GRADUATION DAY
Education to university level for a high proportion of a country's population has long been the goal of most industrialized countries, and is increasingly the aspiration of developing countries.

THE 10

COUNTRIES WITH THE LOWEST LITERACY RATES IN THE WORLD

	Country	Literacy per cent
1	Niger	13.6
2	Burkina Faso	19.2
3	Eritrea	20.0
4	Mali	31.0
5	Sierra Leone	31.4
6	Afghanistan	31.5
7	Senegal	33.1
8	Burundi	35.3
9	Ethiopia	35.5
10	Guinea	35.9

* Total of males and females aged over 15 who can read

While most Western countries report literacy rates of virtually 100 per cent, this list represents 10 countries where, on average, fewer than one person in three is able to read. Even within countries with these low levels of literacy, there are disparities between males and females, with the females often receiving inferior education. In Niger, for example, as few as 6.6 per cent, or one woman in 15, are regarded as literate.

LIBRARIES OF THE WORLD

LARGEST REFERENCE LIBRARIES IN THE WORLD

	Library	Location	Founded	Books
1	Library of Congress	Washington, DC, USA	1800	29,000,000
2	British Library	London, UK	1753*	20,303,000
3	Harvard University Library	Cambridge, Massachusetts, USA	1638	13,369,855
4	Russian State Library#	Moscow, Russia	1862	11,750,000
5	New York Public Library	New York City, USA	1848✚	11,661,064★
6	Yale University Library	New Haven, Connecticut, USA	1701	9,758,341
7	Biblioteca Academiei Romane	Bucharest, Romania	1867	9,397,260
8	Bibliothèque Nationale	Paris, France	1480	9,000,000
9	University of Illinois	Urbana, Illinois, USA	1867	8,840,362
10	University of Califonia	Berkeley, Califonia, USA	1868	8,462,123

* Founded as part of the British Museum 1753; became an independent body 1973
# Founded as Rumyantsev Library; formerly State V.I. Lenin Library
✚ Astor Library founded 1 February 1848; consolidated with Lenox Library and Tilden Trust to form New York Public Library in 1895
★ Reference holdings only, excluding books in lending library branches

RUSSIAN STATE LIBRARY
Formerly the Lenin Library, this huge building, designed by V.A. Shchuko and V.G. Gel'freytch, was begun in 1928 and completed in the 1950s.

COUNTRIES WITH MOST PUBLIC LENDING LIBRARIES

	Country	Libraries
1	Former USSR	208,146
2	UK	23,678
3	Germany	18,868
4	USA	15,870
5	Romania	7,227
6	Canada	6,157
7	Cuba	4,671
8	Spain	3,635
9	France	2,640
10	Mexico	2,269

The very high figure reported by UNESCO for the former Soviet Union's public libraries may owe more to the propaganda value attached to cultural status than to reality. National literary traditions play a major role in determining the ratio of libraries to population. The people of Japan, for example, do not customarily borrow books, and consequently the country has only 1,950 public libraries, whereas Australia, with a strong literary heritage but only one-seventh the population of Japan, has almost as many libraries (1,904), while Finland, which has a population of little over one-twenty-fifth that of Japan, has 1,429 libraries.

FIRST 10 PUBLIC LIBRARIES IN THE US

	Library	Founded
1	Peterboro Public Library, Peterboro, New Hampshire	1833
2	New Orleans Public Library, New Orleans, Louisiana	1843
3	Boston Public Library, Boston, Massachusetts	1852
4	Public Library of Cincinnati and Hamilton County, Cincinnati, Ohio	1853
5	Springfield City Library, Springfield, Massachusetts	1857
6	Worcester Public Library, Worcester, Massachusets	1859
7	County Library, Portland, Oregon	1864
8=	Detroit Public Library, Detroit, Michigan	1865
8=	St Louis Public Library, St Louis, Missouri	1865
10	Atlanta-Fulton Public Library, Atlanta, Georgia	1867

TOP 10

LARGEST PUBLIC LIBRARIES IN THE US

	Library/no. of branches	Location	Founded	Books
1	New York Public Library (The Branch Libraries) (82)	New York City	1895*	11,661,064#
2	Public Library of Cincinnati and Hamilton County (41)	Cincinnati, Ohio	1853	8,268,543
3	Queens Borough Public Library (62)	Jamaica, New York	1896	7,963,171
4	Free Library of Philadelphia (52)	Philadelphia, Pennsylvania	1891	7,881,335
5	Chicago Public Library (81)	Chicago, Illinois	1872	7,095,735
6	Boston Public Library (26)	Boston, Massachusetts	1852	6,704,883
7	Houston Public Library (37)	Houston, Texas	1901	6,551,173
8	Carnegie Library of Pittsburgh (18)	Pittsburgh, Pennsylvania	1895	6,526,198
9	County of Los Angeles Public Library (147)	Los Angeles, California	1872	6,404,353
10	Brooklyn Public Library (59)	Brooklyn, New York	1896	6,134,045

* Astor Library founded 1 February 1848; consolidated with Lenox Library and Tilden Trust to form New York Public Library in 1895
 # Lending library and reference library holdings available for loan

STUDENT IN UNIVERSITY LIBRARY

TOP 10

LARGEST REFERENCE LIBRARIES IN THE UK*

	Library	Location	Founded	Books
1	British Library	London	1753	20,303,000
2	National Library of Scotland	Edinburgh	1682	6,979,000
3	Bodleian Library	Oxford	1602	5,900,000
4	University of Cambridge Library	Cambridge	c.1400	4,728,419
5	National Library of Wales	Aberystwyth	1907	3,678,000
6	John Rylands University Library of Manchester	Manchester	1972*	3,600,000
7	University of Leeds	Leeds	1904	2,501,770
8	University of Edinburgh	Edinburgh	1583	2,324,648
9	University of Birmingham	Birmingham	1900	2,055,000
10	University of Liverpool	Liverpool	1903	1,401,108

* In 1972 the John Rylands Library (founded 1900) was amalgamated with Manchester University Library (1851)

In addition to the books held by these libraries, many have substantial holdings of manuscripts, periodicals, and other printed material. The annual growth of five of the institutions listed here is increased by the law under which one copy of every book that is published in the UK must be deposited within a month of publication with each of five "copyright deposit libraries": the British Library, National Library of Scotland, Bodleian Library, University of Cambridge, and the National Library of Wales, together with Trinity College, Dublin.

THE 10

FIRST PUBLIC LIBRARIES IN THE UK

	Library	Founded
1	Manchester Free Library	1852
2	Liverpool	1852
3	Sheffield	1856
4	Birmingham	1860
5	Cardiff	1862
6	Nottinghamshire	1868
7	Dundee	1869
8	Glasgow (Mitchell Library)	1874
9	Aberdeen	1884
10	Edinburgh	1890

Various specialist institutions, such as theological libraries, existed in Britain as early as the 17th century, and were joined in the 19th by other that charged a small fee. Following the 1850 Public Libraries Act, the Manchester Free Library was the country's first free municipally supported lending library open to the public.

WORD POWER

LONGEST WORDS IN THE *OXFORD ENGLISH DICTIONARY*

	Word (first used)	Letters
1	Pneumonoultramicroscopicsilico-volcanoconiosis (1936)	45
2	Supercalifragilisticexpialidocious (1964)	34
3	Pseudopseudohypoparathyroidism (1952)	30
4=	Floccinaucinihilipilification (1741)	29
4=	Triethylsulphonemethylmethane (19??)	29
6=	Antidisestablishmentarianism (1923)	28
6=	Hepaticocholangiogastrostomy (1933)	28
6=	Octamethylcyclotetrasiloxane (1946)	28
6=	Tetrachlorodibenzoparadioxin (1959)	28
10=	Radioimmunoelectrophoresis (1962)	26
10=	Radioimmunoelectrophoretic (1962)	26

Words that are hyphenated, including such compound words as "transformational-generative" and "tristhio-dimethyl-benzaldehyde", have not been included. Only one unhyphenated word did not quite make it into the Top 10, the 25-letter psychophysicotherapeutics. After this, there is a surprisingly large number of words containing 20 to 24 letters (pneumonoence-phalographic, pneumonoventriculography, psychoneuroendocrinology, radioimmuno-precipitation, spectrophotofluorometric, thyroparathyroidectomize, hypergamma-globulinaemia, hypergammaglobulinaemic, roentgenkymographically, tribothermo-luminescence, photomorphogenetically, honorificabilitudinity and immuno-sympathectomized, for example) – few of which are ever used by anyone except scientists and crossword compilers. Supercalifragilisticexpialidocious was popularized by the song of this title in the film *Mary Poppins* (1964) where it is used to mean "wonderful", but it originally appeared in 1949 in an unpublished song in which it was spelled "supercalafaja-listickespialadojus" – which has 32 letters.

MOST COMMON WORDS IN ENGLISH

	Spoken English	Written English
1	the	the
2	and	of
3	I	to
4	to	in
5	of	and
6	a	a
7	you	for
8	that	was
9	in	is
10	it	that

Various surveys have been conducted to establish the most common words in spoken English of various types, from telephone conversations to broadcast commentaries. Beyond this Top 10, various other words, such as "yes" and "well", also appear with far greater frequency in everyday speech than in the comparative list of the most common words in written English, which is based on a survey of newspaper usage.

MOST COMMONLY MISSPELLED ENGLISH WORDS

1	consensus
2	innovate
3	practice/practise
4	facsimile
5	instalment
6	supersede
7	fulfil
8	withhold
9	occurred
10	possession

This list is based on the mistakes most frequently made by entrants for the Royal Society of Arts Examinations Board's Spelltest for Officeworkers.

MOST USED LETTERS IN WRITTEN ENGLISH

	i	ii
1	e	e
2	t	t
3	a	a
4	o	i
5	i	n
6	n	o
7	s	s
8	r	h
9	h	r
10	l	d

Column i is the order as indicated by a survey across approximately 1,000,000 words appearing in a wide variety of printed texts, ranging from newspapers to novels. Column ii is the order estimated by Samuel Morse, the inventor in the 1830s of Morse Code, based on his calculations of the respective quantities of type used by a printer. The number of letters in the printer's type trays ranged from 12,000 for "e" to 4,400 for "d", with only 200 pieces of type for "z".

WORDS WITH MOST MEANINGS IN THE OXFORD ENGLISH DICTIONARY

	Word	Meanings
1	Set	464
2	Run	396
3	Go	368
4	Take	343
5	Stand	334
6	Get	289
7	Turn	288
8	Put	268
9	Fall	264
10	Strike	250

MOST WIDELY SPOKEN LANGUAGES IN THE WORLD

	Language	Approx. no. of speakers
1	Chinese (Mandarin)	960,000,000
2	English	470,000,000
3	Hindustani	418,000,000
4	Spanish	381,000,000
5	Russian	288,000,000
6	Arabic	218,000,000
7	Bengali	196,000,000
8	Portuguese	182,000,000
9	Malay-Indonesian	155,000,000
10	Japanese	126,000,000

According to 1994 estimates by Sidney S. Culbert of the University of Washington, in addition to those languages appearing in this Top 10, there are only three other languages that are spoken by more than 100,000,000 individuals: French (124,000,000), German (121,000,000), and Urdu (102,000,000). A further 12 languages are spoken by between 50,000,000 and 100,000,000 people.

COUNTRIES WITH THE MOST ENGLISH-LANGUAGE SPEAKERS

	Country	Approx. no. of speakers
1	USA	226,710,000
2	UK	56,990,000
3	Canada	17,916,000
4	Australia	15,316,000
5	South Africa	3,600,000
6	Irish Republic	3,340,000
7	New Zealand	3,244,000
8	Jamaica	2,370,000
9	Trinidad and Tobago	1,218,000
10	Guyana	748,000

MOST WIDELY SPOKEN LANGUAGES IN THE US

	Language	Approx. no. of speakers*
1	English	198,601,000
2	Spanish	17,339,000
3	French	1,702,000
4	German	1,547,000
5	Italian	1,309,000
6	Chinese	1,249,000
7	Tagalog	843,000
8	Polish	723,000
9	Korean	626,000
10	Vietnamese	507,000

Based on most recent Census (1990)

MOST STUDIED FOREIGN LANGUAGES IN THE US*

	Language	Registrations
1	Spanish	533,944
2	French	272,472
3	German	133,348
4	Italian	49,699
5	Japanese	45,717
6	Russian	44,626
7	Latin	28,178
8	Chinese	19,490
9	Ancient Greek	16,401
10	Hebrew	12,995 [#]

In US Institutions of Higher Education

Comprises 5,724 registrations in Biblical Hebrew and 7,271 in Modern Hebrew

These figures are from the most recent survey conducted by the Modern Language Association of America from colleges and universities in the fall of 1990, which indicated a total of 1,184,100 foreign language registrations, the highest enrollment ever recorded by the surveys.

MOST WIDELY SPOKEN LANGUAGES IN THE EC

	Language	Approx. no. of speakers*
1	German	86,562,000
2	English	59,735,000
3	French	58,084,000
4	Italian	55,320,000
5	Spanish (Castilian)	31,398,000
6	Dutch	20,711,000
7	Portuguese	10,622,000
8	Greek	10,411,000
9	Swedish	8,207,000
10	Catalan	5,120,000

* As a "first language", including speakers resident in EC countries other than those where it is the main language, such as German-speakers living in France

MOST STUDIED FOREIGN LANGUAGES IN THE UK

	Language
1	French
2	Spanish
3	Arabic
4	Chinese (Mandarin)
5	German
6	Italian
7	Russian
8	Japanese
9	Dutch
10	Portuguese

This ranking is based on language courses studied by students at the School of Languages at the University of Westminster (formerly the Polytechnic of Central London), which is the largest single source of language teaching in the state sector throughout the whole of Europe. The school offers courses in 28 different languages.

BOOKS & READERS

TOP 10

MOST ANTHOLOGIZED ENGLISH-LANGUAGE POEMS

	Poem/poet	Appearances*
1	*The Tyger*, William Blake (1757–1827)	62
2	*Dover Beach*, Matthew Arnold (1822–88)	61
3	*Kubla Khan*, Samuel Taylor Coleridge (1722–1834)	58
4	*La belle dame sans merci*, John Keats (1795–1821)	52
5	*To Autumn*, John Keats	50
6	*Pied Beauty*, Gerard Manley Hopkins (1844–89)	49
7	*Sir Patrick Spens*, Unknown (early Scottish)	48
8	*Stopping by Woods on a Snowy Evening*, Robert Frost (1874–1963)	56
9	*To the Virgins, to Make Much of Time*, Robert Herrick (1591–1674)	55
10	*That Time of Year Thou Mayst in Me Behold*, William Shakespeare (1564–1616)	51

* *In anthologies listed in* Granger's Index to Poetry

TOP 10

MOST TRANSLATED AUTHORS IN THE WORLD

	Author	Translations
1	V.I. Lenin (1870–1924)	3,842
2	Agatha Christie (1890–1976)	1,904
3	Jules Verne (1828–1905)	1,856
4	William Shakespeare (1564–1616)	1,689
5	Enid Blyton (1897–1968)	1,582
6=	Leo Tolstoy (1828–1910)	1,429
6=	Charles Perrault (1628–1703)	1,429
8	Georges Simenon (1903–89)	1,392
9	Karl Marx (1818–83)	1,312
10	Fyodor Dostoevski (1821–81)	1,202

TOP 10

MOST POPULAR ENGLISH-LANGUAGE POEMS*

	Poem/poet
1	*If*, Rudyard Kipling (1865–1936)
2	*The Lady of Shallot*, Alfred, Lord Tennyson (1809–92)
3	*The Listener*, Walter de la Mare (1873–1956)
4	*Not Waving but Drowning*, Stevie Smith (1902–71)
5	*Daffodils*, William Wordsworth (1770–1850)
6	*To Autumn*, John Keats (1795–1821)
7	*The Lake Isle of Innisfree*, W.B. Yeats (1864–1939)
8	*Dulce et Decorum*, Wilfred Owen (1893–1918)
9	*Ode to a Nightingale*, John Keats
10	*He Wishes for the Cloths of Heaven*, W.B. Yeats (1865–1939

* *Based on a survey conducted in the UK on National Poetry Day, 1995*

TOP 10

TYPES OF BOOK MOST PUBLISHED IN THE UK

	Subject	Titles published 1996
1	Fiction	9,209
2	Children's	8,045
3	Economics	4,519
4	History	4,348
5	Religion	4,331
6	Social sciences	4,068
7	Medicine	3,964
8	School textbooks	3,629
9	Computers	3,515
10	Biography	3,292

TOP 10

MOST PUBLISHED AUTHORS OF ALL TIME

	Author	Nationality
1	William Shakespeare (1564–1616)	British
2	Charles Dickens (1812–70)	British
3	Sir Walter Scott (1771–1832)	British
4	Johann Goethe (1749–1832)	German
5	Aristotle (384–322 BC)	Greek
6	Alexandre Dumas (*père*) (1802–70)	French
7	Robert Louis Stevenson (1850–94)	British
8	Mark Twain (1835–1910)	American
9	Marcus Cicero (106–43 BC)	Roman
10	Honoré de Balzac (1799–1850)	French

This Top 10 is based on a search of a major US library computer database. Citations, which include books by and about the author, total more than 15,000 for Shakespeare.

THE BIRDS OF AMERICA
John James Audubon's sumptuous collection of over 400 large coloured engravings was sold for $3,600,000 in 1989.

TOP 10

BOOK-PRODUCING COUNTRIES IN THE WORLD

	Country	Titles published*
1	UK	101,504
2	China	73,923
3	Germany	62,277
4	USA	49,276
5	France	45,379
6	Japan	42,245
7	Spain	37,325
8	Italy	26,620
9	South Korea	25,017
10	Russia	22,028

* Total of new titles, new editions, and reprints in latest year for which figures are available

TOP 10

BOOK MARKETS IN THE WORLD

	Country	Annual book sales ($)
1	USA	25,490,000,000
2	Japan	10,467,000,000
3	Germany	9,962,000,000
4	UK	3,651,000,000
5	France	3,380,000,000
6	Spain	2,992,000,000
7	South Korea	2,805,000,000
8	Brazil	2,526,000,000
9	Italy	2,246,000,000
10	China	1,760,000,000

Source: Euromonitor

TOP 10

MOST EXPENSIVE BOOKS AND MANUSCRIPTS EVER SOLD AT AUCTION

	Book/manuscript/sale	Price (£)*
1	*The Codex Hammer*, Christie's, New York, 11 November 1994	19,230,000 ($30,800,000)
2	*The Gospels of Henry the Lion*, c. 1173–75, Sotheby's, London, 6 December 1983	7,400,000
3	*The Gutenberg Bible*, 1455, Christie's, New York, 22 October 1987	2,934,131 ($5,390,000)
4	*The Northumberland Bestiary*, c. 1250–60, Sotheby's, London, 29 November 1990	2,700,000
5	Autographed manuscript of nine symphonies by Wolfgang Amadeus Mozart, c. 1773–74, Sotheby's, London, 22 May 1987	2,350,000
6	John James Audubon's *The Birds of America*, 1827–38, Sotheby's, New York, 6 June 1989	2,292,993 ($3,600,000)
7	*The Bible in Hebrew*, Sotheby's, London, 5 December 1989	1,850,000
8	*The Monypenny Breviary*, illuminated manuscript, c. 1490–95, Sotheby's, London, 19 June 1989	1,700,000
9	*The Hours and Psalter of Elizabeth de Bohun*, Countess of Northampton, c. 1340–45, Sotheby's, London, 21 June 1988	1,400,000
10	*Schumann's Second Symphony*, Sotheby's, London, 1 December 1994	1,350,000

* Excluding premiums

TOP 10

MOST POPULAR BOOKS IN THE UK*

	Author	Date of book	Book
1	J.R.R. Tolkien (British, 1892–1973)	1954–55	*The Lord of the Rings*
2	George Orwell (British, 1903–50)	1949	*Nineteen Eighty-four*
3	George Orwell	1945	*Animal Farm*
4	James Joyce (Irish, 1882–1941)	1922	*Ulysses*
5	Joseph Heller (American, 1923–)	1961	*Catch 22*
6	J.D. Salinger (American, 1919–)	1951	*The Catcher in the Rye*
7	Harper Lee (American, 1928–)	1969	*To Kill a Mockingbird*
8	Gabriel García Márquez (Colombian, 1928–)	1967	*One Hundred Years of Solitude*
9	John Steinbeck (American, 1902–68)	1939	*The Grapes of Wrath*
10	Irvine Welsh (British, 1958–)	1993	*Trainspotting*

* Based on a survey conducted by Waterstone's and Channel 4's Book Choice, 1996

WORLD BESTSELLERS

ESSENTIAL READING
Popularly known as "The Thoughts of Chairman Mao" and the "Little Red Book", this work by Chinese Communist Party leader Mao Tse-tung (1893–1976) was a summary of the strict doctrine through which China was controlled for many years. Since the book's possession was mandatory during the so-called Cultural Revolution that began in 1966, it inevitably became a bestseller, while photographs and films of frenzied crowds brandishing copies remain vivid images of the political fervour of that era.

TOP 10

BESTSELLING BOOKS OF ALL TIME

Title	No. sold
1 The Bible	6,000,000,000

No one really knows how many copies of the Bible have been printed, sold, or distributed. The Bible Society's attempt to calculate the number printed between 1816 and 1975 produced the figure of 2,458,000,000. A more recent survey, for the years up to 1992, put it closer to 6,000,000,000 in more than 2,000 languages and dialects.

2 *Quotations from Chairman Mao Tse-tung (Little Red Book)*	800,000,000

Chairman Mao's Little Red Book *could scarcely fail to become a bestseller: between the years 1966 and 1971 it was compulsory for every Chinese adult to own a copy. It was both sold and distributed to the people of China – although what proportion voluntarily bought it must remain open to question. Some 100,000,000 copies of his* Poems *were also disseminated.*

3 *American Spelling Book* by Noah Webster	100,000,000

First published in 1783, this reference book by the American man of letters Noah Webster (1758–1843) remained a bestseller in the US throughout the 19th century.

4 *The Guinness Book of Records*	79,000,000*

First published in 1955, The Guinness Book of Records *stands out as the greatest contemporary publishing achievement. There have now been 40 editions in the UK alone.*

5 *The McGuffey Readers* by William Holmes McGuffey	60,000,000

Published in numerous editions from 1853, some authorities have put the total sales of these educational textbooks as high as 122,000,000.

6 *A Message to Garcia* by Elbert Hubbard	40–50,000,000

Now forgotten, Hubbard's polemic on the subject of labour relations was published in 1899 and within a few years had achieved these phenomenal sales, largely because many American employers purchased bulk supplies to distribute to their employees.

7 *World Almanac*	over 40,000,000*

Having been published annually since 1868 (with a break from 1876 to 1886), this wide-ranging reference book has remained a constant bestseller ever since.

8 *The Common Sense Book of Baby and Child Care* by Dr. Benjamin Spock	over 39,200,000

Dr. Spock's 1946 manual became the bible of infant care for subsequent generations of parents. Most of the sales have been of the paperback edition of the book.

9 *The Valley of the Dolls* by Jacqueline Susann	30,000,000

This tale of sex, violence, and drugs by Jacqueline Susann (1921–74), first published in 1966, is perhaps surprisingly the world's bestselling novel.

10 *In His Steps: "What Would Jesus Do?"* by Rev. Charles Monroe Sheldon	28,500,000

Although virtually unknown today, American clergyman Charles Sheldon (1857–1946) achieved fame and fortune with this 1896 instructive religious treatise on moral dilemmas.

* *Aggregate sales of annual publication*

It is extremely difficult to establish precise sales of contemporary books and virtually impossible to do so with books published long ago. How many copies of the complete works of Shakespeare or Conan Doyle's Sherlock Holmes books have been sold in countless editions? The publication of variant editions, translations, and pirated copies all affect the global picture, and few publishers or authors are willing to expose their royalty statements to public scrutiny. As a result, this Top 10 list offers no more than the "best guess" at the great bestsellers of the past, and it may well be that there are many other books with a valid claim to a place in it.

THE BESTSELLING CHILDREN'S AUTHORS IN THE WORLD

René Goscinny and Albert Uderzo

René Goscinny (1926–77) and Albert Uderzo (b. 1927) created the comic-strip character Astérix the Gaul in 1959. They produced 30 books with total sales of some 250,000,000 copies.

Hergé

Georges Rémi (1907–83), the Belgian author–illustrator who wrote under the pen name Hergé, created the comic-strip character Tintin in 1929. Tintin appeared in book form from 1948 onwards. He achieved worldwide popularity, and the books have been translated into about 45 languages and dialects. Total sales are believed to be at least 160,000,000.

Enid Blyton

With sales of her Noddy books exceeding 60,000,000 copies, and with more than 700 children's books to her name (UNESCO calculated that there were 974 translations of her works in the 1960s alone), total sales of her works are believed to be over 100,000,000, making her the bestselling English language author of the 20th century.

Dr. Seuss

His books in the US Top 10 alone total about 30,000,000 copies. To this must be added those titles that have sold fewer than 5,000,000 in the US and all foreign editions of all his books, suggesting total sales of more than 100,000,000.

Beatrix Potter

The Tale of Peter Rabbit (1902) was one of a series of books, the cumulative total sales of which probably exceed 50,000,000.

Lewis Carroll

Total world sales of all editions of Carroll's two classic children's books, Alice's Adventures in Wonderland and Alice Through the Looking Glass, are incalculable. However, just these two books probably place Lewis Carroll among the 20 bestselling children's authors of all time.

Rev. W. (Wilbert Vere) Awdry

Collectively, the various Thomas the Tank Engine books which the Rev. Awdry began writing in 1946 have sold over 50,000,000 copies. Sales of the books have been enhanced in recent years, along with the popularity of videos of the stories and associated products.

Mark Twain

Book sales in the US were not accurately recorded prior to 1895, but it is probable that Twain's The Adventures of Tom Sawyer and The Adventures of Huckleberry Finn may each have sold more than 20,000,000 copies.

Judy Blume

Several of American author Judy Blume's novels, including Are You There God, It's Me, Margaret, and Tales of a Fourth-Grade Nothing have sold more than 5,000,000 copies in the US alone, implying substantial cumulative sales of her many popular books.

Roald Dahl

British writer Roald Dahl has been popular the world over since James and the Giant Peach was first published in 1961. Sales of that novel, and others, including Charlie and the Chocolate Factory, The B.F.G., and Matilda have been further enhanced through the release of animated and live-action films.

It is impossible to make a definitive list of the bestselling children's books in the world. However, based on total sales of their entire output, the authors above have produced titles that have been bestsellers – especially those in numerous translations – over a long period of time.

ASTÉRIX THE GAUL
Astérix was created by René Goscinny and Albert Uderzo in 1959. The stories of the intrepid Gauls and their victories over the invading Romans have enthralled readers for almost 40 years.

THE WORLD'S BESTSELLING FICTION

Author	Title
Richard Bach	*Jonathan Livingstone Seagull*
William Blatty	*The Exorcist*
Peter Benchley	*Jaws*
Erskine Caldwell	*God's Little Acre*
Harper Lee	*To Kill a Mockingbird*
Colleen McCullough	*The Thorn Birds*
Grace Metalious	*Peyton Place*
Margaret Mitchell	*Gone with the Wind*
George Orwell	*Animal Farm*
Mario Puzo	*The Godfather*
J.D. Salinger	*The Catcher in the Rye*
Erich Segal	*Love Story*
Jacqueline Susann	*Valley of the Dolls*
J.R.R. Tolkein	*The Hobbit*

As with the bestselling books of all time, it is virtually impossible to arrive at a definitive list of fiction bestsellers that encompasses all permutations including hardback and paperback editions, book club sales, and translations, and takes account of the innumerable editions of earlier classics such as *Robinson Crusoe* or the works of Jane Austen, Charles Dickens, or popular foreign authors such as Jules Verne. Although only Jacqueline Susann's *The Valley of the Dolls* appears in the all-time list, and publishers' precise sales data remains tantalizingly elusive (it has been said that the most widely published fiction is publishers' own sales figures), there are many other novels that must be close contenders for this list. It seems certain that all the titles in this list have sold in excess of 10,000,000 copies in hardback and paperback worldwide.

ENGLISH-LANGUAGE BESTSELLERS

T O P 1 0
LONGEST-RUNNING BESTSELLERS IN THE UK

	Title	Author/publication*	Appearances#
1	*A Brief History of Time*	Stephen Hawking (H; 1988)	237
2	*The Country Diary of an Edwardian Lady*	Edith Holden (H; 1977)	183
3	*Complete Hip and Thigh Diet*	Rosemary Conley (P; 1989)	169
4	*A Year in Provence*	Peter Mayle (P; 1990)	165✛
5	*Delia Smith's Complete Illustrated Cookery Course*	Delia Smith (H; 1989)	142
6	*Life on Earth*	David Attenborough (H; 1979)	139
7	*Delia Smith's Complete Cookery Course*	Delia Smith (H; 1986)	127
8	*Wild Swans*	Jung Chang (P; 1993)	124
9	*Delia Smith's Summer Collection*	Delia Smith (H; 1993)	121
10	*The Secret Diary of Adrian Mole, Aged 13¾*	Sue Townsend (P; 1983)	119

* H = *hardback*, P = *paperback*
\# *Based on number of appearances in the* Sunday Times *bestseller lists 14 Apr1974 to 24 Mar 1996*
✛ *Includes appearances of TV tie-in paperback edition*

T O P 1 0
BESTSELLING HARDBACK NOVELS OF 1996 IN THE UK

	Title/author	Sales
1	*The Fourth Estate,* Jeffrey Archer	128,290
2	*Evening Class,* Maeve Binchy	117,905
3	*Appassionata,* Jilly Cooper	115,902
4	*To the Hilt,* Dick Francis	108,879
5	*Hogfather,* Terry Pratchett	100,562
6	*Executive Orders,* Tom Clancy	93,976
7	*Cause of Death,* Patricia Cornwell	90,234
8	*The Runaway Jury,* John Grisham	74,739
9	*Death is Now My Neighbour,* Colin Dexter	74,705
10	*Icon,* Frederick Forsyth	64,671

Source: Bookwatch

T O P 1 0
BESTSELLING PAPERBACK BOOKS OF 1996 IN THE UK

	Title/author	Sales
1	*The Horse Whisperer,* Nicholas Evans	406,521
2	*Sophie's World,* Jostein Gaarder	393,850
3	*The Rainmaker,* John Grisham	387,194
4	*High Fidelity,* Nick Hornby	358,627
5	*Behind the Scenes at the Museum,* Kate Atkinson	352,086
6	*Coming Home,* Rosamund Pilcher	325,031
7	*Notes From a Small Island,* Bill Bryson	321,629
8	*From Potter's Field,* Patricia Cornwell	320,342
9	*A Ruthless Need,* Catherine Cookson	280,126
10	*The Best of Friends,* Joanna Trollope	254,910

T O P 1 0
BESTSELLING CHILDREN'S BOOKS OF 1996 IN THE UK

	Title/author	Sales
1	*The Beano Book*	237,232
2	*Goosebumps: It Came from Beneath the Sink,* R.L. Stine	90,018
3	*X Files: X Marks the Spot,* Les Martin	88,243
4	*James and the Giant Peach,* Roald Dahl	59,669
5	*Goosebumps: The Barking Ghost,* R.L. Stine	55,484
6	*Horrible Histories: The Terrible Tudors,* Terry Deary	49,903
7	*Goosebumps: Ghost Beach,* R.L. Stine	49,543
8	*Goosebumps: The Horror at Camp Jellyjam,* R.L. Stine	48,795
9	*The Very Hungry Caterpillar,* Eric Carle	47,517
10	*Babe (The Sheep-Pig),* Dick King-Smith	46,883

T O P 1 0

BESTSELLING COOKERY BOOKS IN THE UK

	Title	Author	Estimated sales*
1	Delia Smith's Complete Illustrated Cookery Course	Delia Smith	2,500,000 #
2	Delia Smith's Winter Collection	Delia Smith	1,800,000
3	Delia Smith's Summer Collection	Delia Smith	1,400,000
4	Madhur Jaffrey's Indian Cookery	Madhur Jaffrey	800,000
5	Ken Hom's Chinese Cookery	Ken Hom	700,000
6	Sarah Brown's Vegetarian Kitchen	Sarah Brown	550,000
7	Crank's Recipe Book	Kay Canter	500,000
8=	Hamlyn's New All-colour Cookbook	Hamlyn (pub.)	350,000
8=	Delia Smith's Christmas#	Delia Smith	350,000
10	Floyd on France	Keith Floyd	300,000

* Excluding book club sales   # All formats

T O P 1 0

NOVELS OF THE 1990s IN THE UK

	Title	Author	Sales*
1	Jurassic Park	Michael Crichton	769,981
2	The Chamber	John Grisham	760,495
3	The Client	John Grisham	722,195
4	Bravo Two Zero	Andy McNab	715,406
5	The Glass Lake	Maeve Binchy	683,270
6	Schindler's Ark/List	Thomas Keneally	601,308
7	Polo	Jilly Cooper	597,562
8	The Negotiator	Frederick Forsyth	553,380
9	The Man Who Made Husbands Jealous	Jilly Cooper	526,591
10	As the Crow Flies	Jeffrey Archer	515,867

* Publisher's declared first-year sales

T O P 1 0

HARDBACK FICTION BESTSELLERS OF 1996 IN THE US

	Title/author	Sales
1	The Runaway Jury, John Grisham	2,775,000
2	Executive Orders, Tom Clancy	2,371,602
3	Desperation, Stephen King	1,542,077
4	Airframe, Michael Crichton	1,487,494
5	The Regulators, Richard Bachman	1,200,000
6=	Malice, Danielle Steel	1,150,000
6=	Silent Honor, Danielle Steel	1,150,000
8	Primary Colors, Anonymous (Joe Klein)	972,385
9	Cause of Death, Patricia Cornwell	920,403
10	The Tenth Insight, James Redfield	892,687

Source: Publishers Weekly

MICHAEL CRICHTON
US author Michael Crichton's Jurassic Park has remained at the top of the list of bestselling novels of the 1990s in the UK, with sales of over three-quarters of a million copies.

T O P 1 0

HARDBACK NON-FICTION BESTSELLERS OF 1996 IN THE US

	Title/author	Sales
1	Make the Connection, Oprah Winfrey & Bob Greene	2,302,697
2	Men Are from Mars, Women Are from Venus, John Gray	1,485,089
3	The Dilbert Principle, Scott Adams	1,319,507
4	Simple Abundance, Sarah Ban Breathnach	1,087,149
5	The Zone, Barry Sears with Bill Lawren	930,311
6	Bad As I Wanna Be, Dennis Rodman	800,000
7	In Contempt, Christopher Darden	752,648
8	A Reporter's Life, Walter Cronkhite	673,591
9	Dogbert's Top Secret Management Handbook, Scott Adams	652,085
10	My Sergei: A Love Story, Ekaterina Gordeeva with E.M. Swift	563,567

Source: Publishers Weekly

LITERARY PRIZES

THE 10

LAST WINNERS OF THE PULITZER PRIZE FOR FICTION

	Author/novel	Year
1	Richard Ford, *Independence Day*	1996
2	Carol Shields, *The Stone Diaries*	1995
3	E. Annie Proulx, *The Shipping News*	1994
4	Robert Olen Butler, *A Good Scent from a Strange Mountain: Stories*	1993
5	Jane Smiley, *A Thousand Acres*	1992
6	John Updike, *Rabbit at Rest*	1991
7	Oscar Hijuelos, *The Mambo Kings Play*	1990
8	Anne Tyler, *Breathing Lessons*	1989
9	Toni Morrison, *Beloved*	1988
10	Peter Taylor, *A Summons to Memphis*	1987

THE 10

LAST BOOKER PRIZE WINNERS

	Author/novel	Year
1	Graham Swift, *Last Orders*	1996
2	Pat Barker, *The Ghost Road*	1995
3	James Kelman, *How Late It Was, How Late*	1994
4	Roddy Doyle, *Paddy Clarke Ha Ha Ha*	1993
5=	Michael Ondaatje, *The English Patient*	1992
5=	Barry Unsworth, *Sacred Hunger*	1992
7	Ben Okri, *Famished Road*	1991
8	A.S. Byatt, *Possession: A Romance*	1990
9	Kazuo Ishiguro, *The Remains of the Day*	1989
10	Peter Carey, *Oscar and Lucinda*	1988

TOP 10

LITERARY PRIZES AND AWARDS IN THE UK

	Prize/award	Category	Total value (£)
1	David Cohen British Literature Prize	"Lifetime's achievement" award of £30,000 plus £10,000 to enable the writer to produce new work	40,000
2	Orange Prize for Fiction	Best fiction title by a woman	30,000
3	Whitbread Book of the Year	Books by residents of the UK or Ireland; first prize £23,000 (plus three other prizes of £2,000)	29,000
4	Eric Gregory Award	For poets under 30; total shared	28,000
5=	NCR Book Award for Non-fiction	Best non-fiction book	25,000
5=	Betty Trask Awards	First novel of a traditional or romantic nature by authors under 35; total shared	25,000
5=	Wellcome Trust Prize	Previously unpublished science writer	25,000
5=	Wolfson History Prizes	Historical works	25,000
8=	Booker Prize	Best novel in English	20,000
8=	Science Book Prizes	For science books; adult and junior categories	20,000
10	Commonwealth Writers' Prize	A work of fiction be a Commonwealth citizen: first prize £10,000 (plus £3,000 for best first published book, and four regional prizes of £1,000 each)	17,000

While the Booker Prize attracts the most publicity, there are numerous other valuable literary prizes awarded in the UK. Those that are not exclusively British, and writing bursaries awarded to enable writers to survive while working on their books, are not included. The newly established David Cohen British Literature Prize was first awarded in 1993 (to V.S. Naipaul). In addition, there are many other awards of £10,000 or less – some for as little as £100 or just a certificate or gift, such as the bronze eggs given to winners of the Mother Goose Award or the diamond dagger received by Crime Writers' Association Award winners.

THE 10

LAST WINNERS OF HUGO AWARDS FOR BEST SCIENCE FICTION NOVEL

	Author/novel	Year
1	Lois McMaster Bujold, *Mirror Dance*	1995
2	Kim Stanley Robinson, *Green Mars*	1994
3	Vernor Vinge, *A Fire Upon the Deep*	1993
4	Connie Willis, *Doomsday Book*	1993
5	Lois McMaster Bujold, *Barrayar*	1992
6	Lois McMaster Bujold, *The Vor Game*	1991
7	Dan Simmons, *Hyperion*	1990
8	C.J. Cherryh, *Cyteen*	1989
9	David Brin, *The Uplift War*	1988
10	Orson Scott Card, *Speaker for the Dead*	1987

Hugo Awards for science fiction novels, short stories and other fiction and non-fiction works are presented by the World Science Fiction Society. They were established in 1953 as "Science Fiction Achievement Awards for the best science fiction writing". The prize in the Awards' inaugural year was presented to Alfred Bester for *The Demolished Man*.

T O P 1 0

FIRST WINNERS OF THE "ODDEST TITLE AT THE FRANKFURT BOOK FAIR" COMPETITION

	Title	Year
1	*Proceedings of the Second International Workshop on Nude Mice*	1978
2	*The Madam as Entrepreneur: Career Management in House Prostitution*	1979
3	*The Joy of Chickens*	1980
4	*Last Chance at Love – Terminal Romances*	1981
5	Judges split between *Population and Other Problems* and *Braces Owners Manual*	1982
6	*The Theory of Lengthwise Rolling*	1983
7	*The Book of Marmalade: Its Antecedents, Its History and Its Role in the World Today*	1984
8	*Natural Bust Enlargement with Total Mind Power: How to Use the Other 90 Per Cent of Your Mind to Increase the Size of Your Breasts*	1985
9	*Oral Sadism and the Vegetarian Personality*	1986
10	*Versailles: The View From Sweden*	1988

Every year since 1978 the Diagram Group and *The Bookseller* have organized a competition for the book title spotted at the Frankfurt Book Fair that "most outrageously exceeds all bounds of credibility". In 1987 the judges did not consider that the standard was sufficiently high, and no award was presented.

T H E 1 0

LAST WINNERS OF THE JOHN NEWBERY MEDAL

	Author/title	Year
1	Karen Cushman, *The Midwife's Apprentice*	1996
2	Sharon Creech, *Walk Two Moons*	1995
3	Lois Lowry, *The Giver*	1994
4	Cynthia Rylant, *Missing May*	1993
5	Phyllis Reynolds Naylor, *Shiloh*	1992
6	Jerry Spinelli, *Maniac Magee*	1991
7	Lois Lowry, *Number The Stars*	1990
8=	Paul Fleischman, *Joyful Noise*	1989
8=	Walter Myers, *Scorpions*	1989
10	R. Freedman, *Lincoln Photobiography*	1988

The John Newbery Medal is awarded annually for "the most distinguished contribution to American literature for children". Its first winner in 1923 was Hugh Lofting's *The Voyages of Doctor Dolittle*. The medal is named after John Newbery (1713–67), a London bookseller and publisher who specialized in children's books.

T H E 1 0

LAST RANDOLPH CALDECOTT MEDAL WINNERS

	Author/title	Year
1	Peggy Rathman, *Officer Buckle and Gloria*	1996
2	Eve Bunting (illustrated by David Diaz), *Smoky Night*	1995
3	Allen Say, *Grandfather's Journey*	1994
4	Emily McCully Honor, *Mirette on High Wire*	1993
5	David Weisner, *Tuesday*	1992
6	David Macauley, *Black & White*	1991
7	Ed Young, *Lon Po Po*	1990
8	Stephen Gammell, *Song & Dance Man*	1989
9	Jane Yolen (illustrated by John Schoenherr), *Owl Moon*	1988
10	Arthur Yorinks (illustrated by Richard Egielski), *Hey, Al*	1987

The Randolph Caldecott Medal, named after the English illustrator (1846–86), has been awarded annually since 1938 "to the artist of the most distinguished American picture book for children published in the United States during the preceding year". The winner in the debut year was Helen Dean Fish's *Animals Of The Bible*, illustrated by Dorothy P. Lethrop. In subsequent years many books have been honoured that have gone on to be regarded as modern clasics, among them Maurice Sendak's *Where The Wild Things Are*, the Medal winner in 1964.

T H E 1 0

LAST KATE GREENAWAY MEDAL WINNERS

	Artist/author/title	Year
1	P.J. Lynch (text Susan Wojciechowski), *The Christmas Miracle of Jonathan Toomey*	1995
2	Gregory Rogers (text Libby Hathorn), *The Way Home*	1994
3	Alan Lee (text Rosemary Sutcliff), *Black Ships Before Troy*	1993
4	Anthony Browne, *Zoo*	1992
5	Janet Ahlberg (text Allan Ahlberg), *The Jolly Christmas Postman*	1991
6	Gary Blythe (text Dyan Sheldon), *The Whales' Song*	1990
7	Michael Foreman, *War Boy: A Country Childhood*	1989
8	Barbara Firth (text Martin Waddell), *Can't You Sleep, Little Bear?*	1988
9	Adrienne Kennaway (text Mwenye Hadithi), *Crafty Chameleon*	1987
10	Fiona French, *Snow White in New York*	1986

The Kate Greenaway Medal, named after the English illustrator (1846–1901), has been awarded annually since 1956 for the most distinguished work in the illustration of children's books published in the United Kingdom.

THE PRESS

COUNTRIES WITH THE MOST DAILY NEWSPAPERS

	Country	No. of daily newspapers
1	India	2,300
2	USA	1,586
3	Turkey	399
4	Brazil	373
5	Germany	355
6	Russia	339
7	Mexico	292
8	Pakistan	274
9	Argentina	190
10	Spain	148
	UK	*101*

Certain countries have large numbers of newspapers, each serving relatively small areas and therefore with restricted circulations. The US is the most notable example with 1,586 daily newspapers, but only four of them with average daily sales of more than 1,000,000. The UK, with fewer individual newspapers, has five with circulations of over 1,000,000. If the table is arranged by total sales of daily newspapers per 1,000 inhabitants, the result – as seen below – is somewhat different:

	Country	Sales per 1,000 inhabitants
1	Hong Kong	822
2	Norway	607
3	Japan	577
4	Iceland	519
5	Finland	512
6	Sweden	511
7	Macau	510
8	South Korea	412
9	Austria	398
10	Russia	387
	UK	*383*
	USA	*240*

THE DAILY NEWS
Reading the newspaper has been an important part of everyday life for several hundred years.

ENGLISH-LANGUAGE DAILY NEWSPAPERS IN THE WORLD

	Newspaper/ founded/country	Average daily circulation
1	*The Sun,* 15 September 1964, UK	3,935,312
2	*The Mirror,* 2 November 1903, UK	2,370,891
3	*Daily Mail,* 4 May 1896, UK	2,126,637
4	*Wall Street Journal,* 8 July 1889, USA	1,837,194
5	*USA Today,* 15 September 1982, USA	1,662,060
6	*Daily Express,* 24 April 1900, UK	1,207,851
7	*Daily Telegraph,* 29 June 1855, UK	1,126,479
8	*New York Times,* 18 September 1851, USA	1,107,168
9	*Los Angeles Times,* 4 December 1881, USA	1,068,812
10	*Washington Post,* 6 December 1877, USA	818,231

Several long-established English-language dailies fail to make this Top 10: in the UK *The Times* has been published since 1 January 1785, while the *New York Post*, first published on 16 November 1801, holds the record as America's longest-running daily (the *Hartford Courant* was first issued as a weekly on 29 October 1764 but was not a daily until 1836).

BRITISH NATIONAL DAILY NEWSPAPERS

	Newspaper	Average daily sales (1996/97)
1	*The Sun*	3,935,312
2	*The Mirror*	2,370,891
3	*Daily Mail*	2,126,637
4	*Daily Express*	1,207,851
5	*Daily Telegraph*	1,126,479
6	*The Times*	772,317
7	*Daily Record* (Scotland)	702,470
8	*Daily Star*	660,033
9	*The Guardian*	401,853
10	*Financial Times*	303,977

The 11th bestselling daily newspaper in Great Britain is *The Independent,* with total average daily sales during this period of 256,161 copies. The combined sales of all the "quality" daily newspapers (*Daily Telegraph, The Guardian, The Times, The Independent,* and *Financial Times*) are more than 1,000,000 less than the average daily sales of *The Sun.*

BRITISH NATIONAL SUNDAY NEWSPAPERS

	Newspaper	Average sales per issue (1996/97)
1	*News of the World*	4,499,267
2	*Sunday Mirror*	2,330,617
3	*Mail on Sunday*	2,126,191
4	*The People*	2,003,611
5	*Sunday Times*	1,338,396
6	*Express on Sunday*	1,163,906
7	*Sunday Telegraph*	883,078
8	*The Observer*	457,986
9	*Sunday Sport*	284,913
10	*Independent on Sunday*	275,917

In April 1951 sales of the *News of the World* peaked at 8,480,878 copies, the highest ever circulation of any British newspaper.

TOP 10
GENERAL INTEREST MAGAZINES IN THE UK

	Magazine	Average sales per issue
1	*Sky TV Guide*	3,256,918
2	*What's on TV*	1,675,844
3	*Reader's Digest*	1,516,194
4	*Radio Times*	1,405,862
5	*TV Times*	981,811
6	*Cable Guide*	908,187
7	*Woman*	828,144
8	*Woman's Own*	808,311
9	*Woman's Weekly*	696,212
10	*Prima*	565,051

In 1916, American bank clerk DeWitt Wallace published a booklet called *Getting the Most Out of Farming*, which consisted of extracts from various US Government agricultural publications. While recovering after being wounded in France during the war, he contemplated applying the same principle to a general interest magazine. He published 5,000 copies of the first issue of *Reader's Digest* in February 1922. It was an enormous success, rapidly becoming America's bestselling monthly magazine.

TOP 10
SPECIALIST MAGAZINES IN THE UK

	Magazine	Average sales per issue
1	*AA Magazine*	3,981,939
2	*National Trust Magazine*	1,350,000
3	*Connections*	834,078
4	*Ford Magazine*	795,100
5	*Saga Magazine*	738,371
6	*Birds* (RSPB)	547,000
7	*Auto Trader* (combined, all editions)	401,753
8	*BBC Gardener's World*	293,041
9	*Top of the Pops*	292,824
10	*The Caravan Club Magazine*	285,262

TOP 10
CONSUMERS OF NEWSPRINT

	Country	Consumption per inhabitant		
		kg	lb	oz
1	Sweden	54.32	119	12
2	USA	47.633	105	0
3	Austria	46.271	102	0
4	Switzerland	46.235	101	15
5	Norway	42.654	94	1
6	Denmark	42.226	93	1
7	Australia	37.395	82	7
8	Hong Kong	36.500	80	8
9	Singapore	36.367	80	3
10	UK	32.243	71	1

National consumption of newsprint provides a measure of the extent of the newspaper sales in the Top 10 countries above.

BACK ISSUES

The oldest journal in print in the UK is the *Philosophical Transactions of the Royal Society*, which was first issued on 6 March 1665. *The Scots Magazine* (1739), *Archaeologia* (the journal of the Society of Antiquaries, 1770), and *Curtis's Botanical Magazine* (1787) have also all been published for more than 200 years. The medical journal *The Lancet* (1823) is the oldest British weekly publication. The oldest-established magazine in the US is the *Saturday Evening Post*, which was started in Philadelphia in 1821 by Samuel C. Atkinson and Charles Alexander (the often-stated claim that it was published as early as 1728 is unfounded). *Scientific American* began publication in New York on 28 August 1845, *Town & Country* in 1846, and *Harper's Magazine* in 1850 (then named *Harper's Monthly*). *Harper's Bazar* was first issued in 1867. After William Randoph Hearst bought it in 1913, he subtly changed its name by spelling *Bazaar* with a double "a".

HOT OFF THE PRESS
Huge quantities of newsprint are consumed to satisfy global demand, but increasingly large amounts are recycled.

TOP 10
BESTSELLING BRITISH COMICS OF ALL TIME

	Title	Published
1	*Beano*	1938–present
2	*Comic Cuts*	1890–1953
3	*Dandy*	1937–present
4	*Eagle*	1950–69; 1982–present
5	*Film Fun*	1920–62
6	*Illustrated Chips*	1890–1953
7	*Mickey Mouse Weekly*	1936–57
8	*Radio Fun*	1938–61
9	*Rainbow*	1914–56
10	*School Friend*	1950–65

Accurate circulation figures for British comics are hard to come by, but information supplied by the Association of Comics Enthusiasts indicates that all 10 comics listed (in alphabetical order) achieved very high circulation figures, *Eagle*, *Film Fun*, *Rainbow*, and *School Friend* all hitting 1,000,000 at their peak.

ART AT AUCTION

TOP 10

MOST EXPENSIVE PAINTINGS BY ANDY WARHOL

	Work/sale	Price (£)
1	*Marilyn X 100,* Sotheby's, New York, 17 November 1992	2,251,656 ($3,400,000)
2	*Shot Red Marilyn,* Christie's, New York, 3 May 1989	2,228,916 ($3,700,000)
3	*Shot Red Marilyn,* Christie's, New York, 2 November 1994	2,062,500 ($3,300,000)
4	*Marilyn Monroe, Twenty Times,* Sotheby's, New York, 10 November 1988	2,000,000 ($3,600,000)
5	*Liz,* Christie's, New York, 7 November 1989	1,297,468 ($2,050,000)
6	*Triple Elvis,* Sotheby's, New York, 8 November 1989	1,265,823 ($2,000,000)
7	*210 Coca-Cola bottles,* Christie's, New York, 5 May 1992	1,061,453 ($1,900,000)
8	*Ladies and Gentlemen, 1975,* Binoche et Godeau, Paris, 30 November 1989	1,030,397 (FF9,799,080)
9=	*The Last Supper,* Sotheby's, New York, 8 November 1989	1,012,658 ($1,600,000)
9=	*Race Riot,* Christie's, New York, 7 November 1989	1,012,658 ($1,600,000)

Born Andrew Warhola, Andy Warhol (1926–87) became one of the most famous American artists of all time through his leadership of the Pop Art movement. He typically featured images derived from popular culture, among them familiar brands, such as Campbell's soup cans, and portraits – often multiple images – of well-known celebrities from Marilyn Monroe to Mao Tse-Tung. He also produced graphic designs, including album covers for the Rolling Stones and others, and was a film-maker and magazine publisher.

TOP 10

MOST EXPENSIVE PAINTINGS BY PABLO PICASSO

	Work/sale	Price (£)
1	*Les Noces de Pierrette,* Binoche et Godeau, Paris, 30 November 1989	33,123,028 (FF315,000,000)
2	*Self Portrait: Yo Picasso,* Sotheby's, New York, 9 May 1989	26,687,116 ($43,500,000)
3	*Au Lapin Agile,* Sotheby's, New York, 15 November 1989	23,870,968 ($37,000,000)
4	*Acrobate et Jeune Arlequin,* Christie's, London, 28 November 1988	19,000,000
5	*Angel Fernandez de Soto,* Sotheby's, New York, 8 May 1995	18,045,500 ($28,152,500)
6	*Le Miroir,* Sotheby's, New York, 15 November 1989	15,483,872 ($24,000,000)
7	*Les Tuileries,* Christie's, London, 25 June 1990	12,500,000
8	*Maternité,* Christie's, New York, 14 June 1988	12,362,638 ($22,500,000)
9	*Le Miroir,* Christie's, New York, 7 November 1995	11,592,357 ($18,200,000)
10	*Mère et Enfant,* Sotheby's, New York, 15 November 1989	10,967,743 ($17,000,000)

By the late 1950s the Spanish painter Pablo Picasso (1881–1973) was already being hailed as the foremost artist of the 20th century. This was progressively reflected in the saleroom: when *Mère et Enfant* (*Mother and Child*) was sold in 1957 for $185,000 (then £66,071), it was the highest price ever paid for a painting during an artist's lifetime. The upward spiral continued with *Woman and Child at the Seashore*, sold in 1962 for £190,000. In 1981 Picasso's *Self Portrait: Yo Picasso* made £2,950,000 – a level considered astonishing at the time. The 8 May 1995 sale of the painting *Angel Fernandez De Soto* achieved the highest price for any painting sold at auction since 1990.

THE 10

FIRST PAINTINGS AUCTIONED FOR OVER $3M

	Work/artist/price	Sale date
1	*Portrait of Juan de Pareja,* Diego Rodriguez de Silva y Velásquez (Spanish; 1599–1660), Christie's, London, $5,524,000	27 Nov 1970
2	*The Death of Actaeon,* Titian (Italian; c. 1488–1576), Christie's, London, $4,036,000	25 Jun 1971
3	*The Resurrection,* Dirk Bouts (Dutch; 1400–75), Sotheby's, London, $3,740,000	16 Apr 1980
4	*Saltimbanque Seated with Arms Crossed,* Pablo Picasso (Spanish; 1881–1973), Sotheby's, New York, $3,000,000	12 May 1980
5	*Paysan en Blouse Bleu,* Paul Cézanne (French; 1839–1906), Christie's, New York, $3,900,000	13 May 1980
6	*Le Jardin du Poète, Arles,* Vincent van Gogh (Dutch; 1853–80), Christie's, New York, $5,200,000	13 May 1980
7	*Juliet and Her Nurse,* J.M.W. Turner (British; 1775–1851), Sotheby's, New York, $6,400,000	29 May 1980
8	*Samson and Delilah,* Sir Peter Paul Rubens (Flemish; 1577–1640), Christie's, London, $5,474,000	11 Jul 1980
9	*The Holy Family with Saints and Putti,* Nicolas Poussin (French; 1594–1665), Christie's, London, $3,564,000	10 Apr 1981
10	*Self Portrait: Yo Picasso,* Pablo Picasso, Sotheby's, New York, $5,300,000	21 May 1981

TOP 10

MOST EXPENSIVE PAINTINGS EVER SOLD AT AUCTION

Work/artist/sale	Price (£)
1 *Portrait of Dr. Gachet*, Vincent van Gogh (Dutch; 1853–80), Christie's, New York, 15 May 1990	44,378,696 ($75,000,000)

Both this painting and the one in the No. 2 position were bought by Ryoei Saito, head of Japanese Daishowa Paper Manufacturing.

2 *Au Moulin de la Galette*, Pierre-Auguste Renoir (French; 1841–1919), Sotheby's, New York, 17 May 1990	42,011,832 ($71,000,000)
3 *Les Noces de Pierrette*, Pablo Picasso (Spanish; 1881–1973), Binoche et Godeau, Paris, 30 November 1989	33,123,028 (F.Fr315,000,000)

The painting was sold by Swedish financier Fredrik Roos to Tomonori Tsurumaki, a property developer, who bid for it by telephone from Tokyo.

4 *Irises*, Vincent van Gogh, Sotheby's, New York, 11 November 1987	28,000,000 ($49,000,000)

After much speculation, its purchaser was confirmed as businessman Alan Bond. However, he was unable to pay for it in full, so its former status as the world's most expensive work of art has been disputed.

5 *Self Portrait: Yo Picasso*, Pablo Picasso, Sotheby's, New York, 9 May 1989	26,687,116 ($43,500,000)

Work/artist/sale	Price (£)
6 *Au Lapin Agile*, Pablo Picasso, Sotheby's, New York, 15 November 1989	23,870,968 ($37,000,000)

The painting depicts Picasso as a harlequin at the bar of the café Lapin.

7 *Sunflowers*, Vincent van Gogh, Christie's, London, 30 March 1987	22,500,000

At the time this was the most expensive picture ever sold.

8 *Portrait of Duke Cosimo I de Medici*, Jacopo da Carucci (Pontormo) (Italy; 1494–1556/7), Christie's, New York, 31 May 1989	20,253,164 ($32,000,000)

This is the record price paid for an Old Master – and the only one in this Top 10. It was bought by the J. Paul Getty Museum, Malibu, USA.

9 *Acrobate et Jeune Arlequin*, Pablo Picasso, Christie's, London, 28 November 1988	19,000,000

Until the sale of Yo Picasso, this held the world record for a 20th-century painting. It was bought by Mitsukoshi, a Japanese department store (in Japan, many major stores have important art galleries).

10 *Angel Fernandez De Soto*, Pablo Picasso, Sotheby's, New York, 8 May 1995	18,045,500 ($28,152,500)

This painting was sold by one Greek shipowner, George Embiricos, and bought by another, Stavros Niarchos.

TOP 10

MOST EXPENSIVE PAINTINGS BY WOMEN ARTISTS

Work/artist/sale	Price (£)
1 *In the Box*, Mary Cassatt (American; 1844–1926), Christie's, New York, 23 May 1988	2,450,331 ($3,700,000)
2 *The Conversation*, Mary Cassatt, Christie's, New York, 11 May 1988	2,180,850 ($4,100,000)
3 *Mother, Sara, and the Baby*, Mary Cassatt, Christie's, New York, 10 May 1989	2,147,239 ($3,500,000)
4 *Autoretrato con chango y loro*, Frida Kahlo (Mexican; 1907–54), Sotheby's, New York, 17 May 1995	1,847,134 ($2,900,000)
5 *Augusta Reading to Her Daughter*, Mary Cassatt, Sotheby's, New York, 9 May 1989	1,717,790 ($2,800,000)
6 *Young Lady in a Loge, Gazing to the Right*, Mary Cassatt, Sotheby's, New York, 10 November 1992	1,523,179 ($2,300,000)
7 *Sara Holding Her Dog*, Mary Cassatt, Sotheby's, New York, 11 November 1988	1,461,988 ($2,500,000)
8 *Adam et Eve*, Tamara de Lempicka (Polish; 1898–1980), Christie's, New York, 3 March 1994	1,208,054 ($1,800,000)
9 *Black Hollyhocks with Blue Larkspur*, Georgia O'Keeffe (American; 1887–1986), Sotheby's, New York, 3 December 1987	1,046,512 ($1,800,000)
10 *Madame H. de Fleury and Her Child*, Mary Cassatt, Sotheby's, New York, 25 May 1988	1,027,027 ($1,900,000)

RISING SUNFLOWERS
When it was sold in 1987 for £22,500,000, Vincent van Gogh's Sunflowers *(1888) almost tripled the world record price for a painting. One of several works in a series, its price is equivalent to £1,500,000 per sunflower.*

COLLECTABLES

MOST EXPENSIVE PIECES OF FURNITURE EVER SOLD AT AUCTION

Item/auction	Price (£)
1 18th-century "Badminton Cabinet", Christie's, London, 5 July 1990	8,580,000
2 1760s mahogany desk by John Goddard, Christie's, New York, 3 June 1989 ($12,100,000)	7,786,358
3 Mahogany and ebony chest of drawers by G. Benneman, probably for Queen Marie Antoinette, Ader Picard Tajan, Monaco, 11 November 1984 (FF 15,000,000)	1,277,357
4 *c.* 1760 George III ormolu-mounted mahogany dressing and writing commode attributed to John Channon, Christie's, London, 6 July 1989	1,100,000
5 1784 black-and-gold lacquer *secrétaire*, attributed to Adam Weisweiler, Sotheby's, London, 8 July 1983	990,000
6 Louis XV marquetry and ormolu corner cabinet by Dubois, Sotheby, Parke Bernet, Monte Carlo, 25 June 1979 (FF 7,600,000)	844,440
7 *c.* 1705 black japanned bureau-bookcase, formerly owned by Queen Mary, Christie's, New York, 18 October 1981 ($860,000)	463,666
8 Mahogany wing armchair by Thomas Affleck, Sotheby's, New York, 31 January 1987 ($2,700,000)	
9 George II bombe commode, Christie's, London, 7 July 1988	407,000
10 Louis XVI ormolu mounted ebony *bureau plat* and *cartonnier*, Sotheby, London, 13 December 1974	240,000

MOST COLLECTED POSTCARD THEMES

1 Street scenes (especially busy, turn-of-the-century subjects)

2 Social history

3 Greetings

4 Photographic nudes

5= Glamour (especially from Art Nouveau and Art Deco periods)

5= The *Titanic*

7 Cat illustrations (especially turn-of-the-century by Louis Wain and other artists)

8 Novelty subjects

9 World War I

10 Miscellaneous modern subjects

The first postcards appeared in Great Britain in 1870, but Post Office regulations meant that they were not illustrated until 1894, and it was another eight years before they were issued with the now familiar "divided back" so that the message and address could appear on the same side with a picture on the other. After this, the fashion for sending picture postcards took off and cartophily – postcard collecting – is today an internationally popular hobby, with rare and early examples often changing hands for considerable amounts.

MOST EXPENSIVE SCULPTURES BY AUGUSTE RODIN EVER SOLD AT AUCTION

Sculpture/sale	Price (£)
1 *Les Bourgeois de Calais grands modeles – Pierre de Wiessant Vetu*, Sotheby's, New York, 17 May 1990 ($3,900,000)	2,307,692
2 *Psyche regardant l'amour*, Sotheby's, New York, 8 November 1995 ($1,800,000)	1,146,497
3 *La fauness*, Christie's, New York, 11 May 1995 ($1,200,000)	764,331
4 *Le penseur*, Sotheby's, New York, 17 May 1990 ($1,050,000)	621,302
5 *Le penseur*, Christie's, New York, 10 May 1994 ($900,000)	600,000
6 *Eve*, Sotheby's, New York, 8 November 1994 ($925,000)	581,761
7 *Le penseur*, Sotheby's, New York, 13 November 1990 ($1,100,000)	558,376
8 Le penseur, Sotheby's, New York, 15 November 1989 ($825,000)	532,258
9 *Le penseur*, Sotheby's, New York, 8 November 1995 ($780,000)	496,815
10 *Le baiser*, Christie's, New York, 11 May 1995 ($775,000)	493,631

Auguste Rodin (1840–1917) was the foremost French sculptor of his day. He achieved international fame through such creations as *The Thinker* and *The Kiss*, which was commissioned by an American connoisseur Edward Perry Warren, and kept at his house in Lewes, England, until it was sold to the Tate Gallery, London. Bronze casts of Rodin's works mean that multiple copies exist of a number of them, including *The Burghers of Calais*, one of his most celebrated sculptures. A version of this sculpture heads this list, but it can also be seen in Calais and in Victoria Tower Gardens in London.

TOP 10

BESTSELLING POSTCARDS IN THE NATIONAL GALLERY, LONDON

1 Vincent van Gogh, *Sunflowers*, 1888

2 Vincent van Gogh, *A Cornfield, with Cypresses*, 1889

3 J. M. W. Turner, *The Fighting Téméraire Tugged to her Last Berth to be Broken Up*, before 1839

4 Claude Monet, *The Thames Below Westminster*, 1871

5 Georges Pierre Seurat, *Bathers, Asnières*, 1884

6 Pierre-Auguste Renoir, *The Umbrellas*, c. 1881–86

7 Henri Rousseau, *Tropical Storm with a Tiger*, 1891

8 Jan van Eyck, *The Marriage of Giovanni(?) Arnolfini and Giovanna Cenami (?)*, 1434

9 Claude Monet, *The Water-Lily Pond*, 1899

10 J. M. W. Turner, *Rain, Steam, and Speed – The Great Western Railway*, before 1844

TOP 10

MOST VALUABLE VANITY FAIR CARICATURES

	Subject	Profession	Caption	Date	Value (£)
1=	Lord Hawke	Cricketer	"Yorkshire Cricket"	24 Sep 1892	500
1=	Jack Hobbs	Cricketer	"A Tested Centurion"	7 Aug 1912	500
1=	Frederick Spofforth	Cricketer	"The Demon Bowler"	13 Jul 1878	500
4	Lord Harris	Cricketer	"Kent"	16 Jul 1881	485
5	Winston Churchill	Politician	"Winnie"	8 Mar 1911	450
6	Winston Churchill	Politician	"Winston"	27 Sep 1900	400
7=	W.S. Gilbert	Dramatist	"Patience"	21 May 1881	300
7=	Tod Sloane	Jockey	"An American Jockey"	25 May 1899	300
9=	William Gillette	Actor	"Sherlock Holmes"	27 Feb 1907	275
9=	Oscar Wilde	Writer	"Oscar"	24 May 1884	275

When Vanity Fair magazine was first published 1865 it contained popular coloured caricatures of men of the day, from sportsmen and soldiers to artists and royalty. They were produced initially by an Italian-born aristocrat Carlo Pellegrini, working under the pseudonym "Ape". He was briefly succeeded by James Tissot (pseudonym Coïdé), and then by Sir Leslie Ward, working under the name "Spy", whose caricatures appeared over a long period (1877–1909). Other contributors included Jean de Paleologu ("Pal"), Adriano Cecioni, Walter Sickert ("Sic"), and Max Beerbohm ("Max"). The individual elongated style of the Vanity Fair caricatures made them instantly recognizable, and they have become highly collectable. There is scarcely a solicitor's office in the UK that does not display one of an eminent judge or barrister. Cricketers are especially popular – outside this Top 10, W.G. Grace is much sought-after.

TOP 10

MOST EXPENSIVE SCIENTIFIC INSTRUMENTS EVER SOLD AT AUCTION BY CHRISTIES, UK

	Item/sale	Price (£)
1	Pair of globes, terrestrial and celestial, attributed to Gerard Mercator, 1579, 30 October 1991	1,023,000
2	Ptolemaic armillary sphere, c. 1579, 9 April 1997	771,500
3	Astrolabe by Ersamus Habermel, c. 1590, 11 October 1995	540,000
4	Astrolabe by Walter Arsenius, 1559, 29 September 1988	385,000
5	The Regiomontanus Astrolabe, 1462, 28 September 1989	209,000
6	Astrolabe quadrant by Christopher Schissler, 1576, 28 September 1989	187,000
7	Section of Difference Engine No.1 by Charles and Henry Prevost Babbage, 16 November 1995	176,750
8	Arithmometre (mechanical calculator) by Thomas de Colmar, 1848, 9 April 1997	166,500
9	Universal rectilinear dial by Erasmus Habermel, c. 1590, 27 September 1990	154,000
10	Astrolabe by George Hartman, 1581, 2 March 1995	88,750

ASTROLABE
This Flemish brass astrolabe, made by Walter Arsenius in 1599, held the world record for the highest price paid for a scientific instrument when it was sold in 1988 for £385,000.

MUSIC

TOP 10

SINGLES OF ALL TIME WORLDWIDE

	Title/artist	Sales exceed
1	*White Christmas,* Bing Crosby	30,000,000
2	*Rock Around the Clock,* Bill Haley & His Comets	17,000,000
3	*I Want to Hold Your Hand,* Beatles	12,000,000
4=	*It's Now or Never,* Elvis Presley	10,000,000
4=	*I Will Always Love You,* Whitney Houston	10,000,000
6=	*Hound Dog/Don't Be Cruel,* Elvis Presley	9,000,000
6=	*Diana,* Paul Anka	9,000,000
8=	*Hey Jude,* Beatles	8,000,000
8=	*I'm a Believer,* Monkees	8,000,000
8=	*(Everything I Do) I Do It For You,* Bryan Adams	8,000,000

Global sales are notoriously difficult to calculate, since for many decades very little statistical research on record sales was done in a large part of the world. "Worldwide" is thus usually taken to mean the known minimum "western world" sales.

TOP 10

SINGLES OF ALL TIME IN THE US

	Title/artist	Year
1	*White Christmas,* Bing Crosby	1942
2	*I Want to Hold Your Hand,* Beatles	1964
3	*Hound Dog/Don't Be Cruel,* Elvis Presley	1956
4	*It's Now or Never,* Elvis Presley	1960
5	*I Will Always Love You,* Whitney Houston	1992
6	*Hey Jude,* Beatles	1968
7	*We Are the World,* USA For Africa	1985
8	*Whoomp! There It Is,* Tag Team	1993
9	*Everything I Do (I Do It for You),* Bryan Adams	1991
10	*Macarena,* Los Del Rio	1996

TOP 10

SINGLES OF ALL TIME IN THE UK

	Title/artist	Year
1	*Do They Know It's Christmas?,* Band Aid	1984
2	*Bohemian Rhapsody,* Queen	1975/91
3	*Mull of Kintyre,* Wings	1977
4	*Rivers of Babylon/Brown Girl in the Ring,* Boney M	1978
5	*Relax,* Frankie Goes To Hollywood	1984
6	*She Loves You,* Beatles	1963
7	*You're the One That I Want,* John Travolta and Olivia Newton-John	1978
8	*Unchained Melody,* Robson Green and Jerome Flynn	1995
9	*Mary's Boy Child/Oh My Lord,* Boney M	1978
10	*I Just Called to Say I Love You,* Stevie Wonder	1984

BAND AID
George Michael, Bono, Freddie Mercury, and other international stars contributed to make Band Aid's 1984 single the UK's all-time bestseller.

I WANT TO HOLD YOUR HAND
The Beatles' smash hit became the bestselling record of the 1960s in the US, and the world's third most successful single ever.

TOP 10
SINGLES OF THE 1980s IN THE UK

	Title/artist	Year
1	*Do They Know It's Christmas?*, Band Aid	1984
2	*Relax*, Frankie Goes to Hollywood	1984
3	*I Just Called to Say I Love You*, Stevie Wonder	1984
4	*Two Tribes*, Frankie Goes to Hollywood	1984
5	*Don't You Want Me?*, The Human League	1981
6	*Last Christmas*, Wham!	1984
7	*Karma Chameleon*, Culture Club	1983
8	*Careless Whisper*, George Michael	1984
9	*The Power of Love*, Jennifer Rush	1985
10	*Come on Eileen*, Dexy's Midnight Runners	1982

Singles from the boom year of 1984 dominate this Top 10. Two of them are by newcomers Frankie Goes To Hollywood, and two by Wham!/George Michael. Stevie Wonder and Jennifer Rush, the sole US entrants, were the only Americans to have UK million-sellers during the 1980s.

TOP 10
SINGLES OF THE 1980s IN THE US

	Title/artist	Year
1	*We Are the World*, USA for Africa	1985
2	*Physical*, Olivia Newton-John	1981
3	*Endless Love*, Diana Ross and Lionel Richie	1981
4	*Eye of the Tiger*, Survivor	1982
5	*I Love Rock 'n' Roll*, Joan Jett & the Blackhearts	1982
6	*When Doves Cry*, Prince	1984
7	*Celebration*, Kool & the Gang	1981
8	*Another One Bites the Dust*, Queen	1980
9	*Wild Thing*, Tone Loc	1989
10	*Islands in the Stream*, Kenny Rogers and Dolly Parton	1983

TOP 10
SINGLES OF THE 1990s IN THE US TO DATE*

	Title/artist	Year
1	*I Will Always Love You*, Whitney Houston	1992
2	*Whoomp! There It Is*, Tag Team	1993
3	*Macarena*, Los Del Rio	1995
4	*Everything I Do (I Do It for You)*, Bryan Adams	1991
5	*Gangsta's Paradise*, Coolio featuring LV	1995
6	*Tha Crossroads*, Bone Thugs 'N Harmony	1996
7	*Fantasy*, Mariah Carey	1995
8	*Jump*, Kris Kross	1992
9	*Vogue*, Madonna	1990
10	*How Do U Want It/ California Love*, 2 Pac featuring Dr. Dre & Roger Troutman	1996

* Up to 31 December 1996

TOP 10
SINGLES OF THE 1990s IN THE UK TO DATE*

	Title/artist	Year
1	*Unchained Melody*, Robson Green and Jerome Flynn	1995
2	*Love is All Around*, Wet Wet Wet	1994
3	*Everything I Do (I Do It for You)*, Bryan Adams	1991
4	*I Will Always Love You*, Whitney Houston	1992
5	*Killing Me Softly*, Fugees	1996
6	*Wannabe*, Spice Girls	1996
7	*Gangsta's Paradise*, Coolio featuring LV	1995
8	*I Believe/Up On The Roof*, Robson Green & Jerome Flynn	1995
9	*Earth Song*, Michael Jackson	1995
10	*Spaceman*, Babylon Zoo	1996

* Up to 31 December 1996

THE GLITZ AND HITS OF 1973

The year 1973 marked the high-water of glam-pop, fashion hell, and early teen idols, and both the singles charts and television's *Top of the Pops* were accordingly resplendent with groups and artists with bouffant hair-styles, glitter make-up, spangly tops, flares and platform boots. Sweet, Suzi Quatro, Wizard, Slade, and Gary Glitter each had at least one UK No. 1 single during the year, as did American teenage heartthrobs David Cassidy and Donny Osmond. It was therefore ironic that the year's second biggest seller (after Gary Glitter's *I Love You Love Me*) was the strings-dominated instrumental *Eye Level* by the Simon Park Orchestra, popularized as the theme from the television series *Van Der Valk* starring Barry Foster.

25 YEARS AGO • YEARS AGO • YEARS AGO • YEARS AGO •

CHART TOPPERS

T H E 1 0

FIRST BRITISH GROUPS TO HAVE A NO. 1 HIT IN THE US

	Artist	Title	Date at No. 1
1	Tornados	*Telstar*	22 Dec 62
2	Beatles	*I Want to Hold Your Hand*	1 Feb 64
3	Animals	*House of the Rising Sun*	5 Sep 64
4	Manfred Mann	*Do Wah Diddy Diddy*	17 Oct 64
5	Freddie & The Dreamers	*I'm Telling You Now*	10 Apr 65
6	Wayne Fontana & The Mindbenders	*The Game of Love*	24 Apr 65
7	Herman's Hermits	*Mrs Brown You've Got a Lovely Daughter*	1 May 65
8	Rolling Stones	*(I Can't Get No) Satisfaction*	10 Jul 65
9	Dave Clark Five	*Over and Over*	25 Dec 65
10	Troggs	*Wild Thing*	30 Jul 66

It was not until 1977, when Manfred Mann's Earthband hit US No. 1 with *Blinded by the Light* that the number of British groups to top the American survey reached 20.

T H E 1 0

FIRST AMERICAN GROUPS TO HAVE A NO. 1 HIT IN THE UK

	Artist	Title	Date at No. 1
1	Bill Haley & His Comets	*Rock around the Clock*	12 Nov 55
2	Dream Weavers	*It's Almost Tomorrow*	17 Mar 56
3	Teenagers featuring Frankie Lymon	*Why Do Fools Fall in Love?*	21 Jul 56
4	Crickets	*That'll Be the Day*	2 Nov 57
5	Johnny Otis Show	*Ma, He's Making Eyes at Me*	4 Jan 58
6	Platters	*Smoke Gets in Your Eyes*	14 Mar 59
7	Marcels	*Blue Moon*	6 May 61
8	Highwaymen	*Michael*	7 Oct 61
9	B. Bumble & The Stingers	*Nut Rocker*	12 May 62
10	Supremes	*Baby Love*	14 Nov 64

Numbers two, three, five, and nine all scored higher on the UK chart than in their native country. Note that it took until the mid-1960s for an all-female US group to top the British chart.

T H E 1 0

FIRST FEMALE SINGERS TO HAVE A NO. 1 HIT IN THE US

	Artist	Title	Date at No. 1
1	Dinah Shore	*I'll Walk Alone*	5 Oct 44
2	Betty Hutton	*Doctor, Lawyer, Indian Chief*	21 Feb 46
3	Peggy Lee	*Mañana*	5 Mar 48
4	Margaret Whiting	*A Tree in the Meadow*	1 Oct 48
5	Evelyn Knight	*A Little Bird Told Me*	14 Jan 49
6	Teresa Brewer	*Music! Music! Music!*	10 Mar 50
7	Eileen Barton	*If I Knew You Were Comin', I'd Have Baked a Cake*	7 Apr 50
8	Patti Page	*The Tennessee Waltz*	22 Dec 50
9	Rosemary Clooney	*Come On-A My House*	20 Jul 51
10	Kay Starr	*Wheel of Fortune*	7 Mar 52

The American singles chart was inaugurated in 1940, so it can be seen that it took four years before a record by a female soloist headed it, and well over a decade before the ranks of distaff chart-toppers swelled to double figures. All the above women were Americans, as was Doris Day, who would be the 11th in this particular list. The 12th female singer to hit the top in the US was a British export in the shape of Vera Lynn, who dominated the US chart for nine weeks in mid-1952 with the number one hit *Auf Weiderseh'n Sweetheart*.

T H E 1 0

FIRST FEMALE SINGERS TO HAVE A NO. 1 HIT IN THE UK

	Artist	Title	Date at No. 1
1	Jo Stafford	*You Belong to Me*	9 Jan 53
2	Kay Starr	*Comes A-Long A-Love*	23 Jan 53
3	Lita Roza	*(How Much Is That) Doggie in the Window?*	17 Apr 53
4	Doris Day	*Secret Love*	16 Apr 54
5	Kitty Kallen	*Little Things Mean a Lot*	10 Sep 54
6	Vera Lynn	*My Son, My Son*	5 Nov 54
7	Rosemary Clooney	*This Ole House*	26 Nov 54
8	Ruby Murray	*Softly Softly*	19 Feb 55
9	Alma Cogan	*Dreamboat*	16 Jul 55
10	Anne Shelton	*Lay Down Your Arms*	22 Sep 56

The UK singles chart was launched in November 1952, and Jo Stafford's *You Belong to Me* was only the second single to reach No.1 on the chart. The females were actually briefly running ahead of their male counterparts in these early days, when Kay Starr's *Comes A-Long A-Love* became Britain's third chart-topper only a fortnight after Ms. Stafford's single. Lita Roza, covering a US No.1 by Patti Page, was the first British female artist to reach the summit, six months into the life of the chart.

T O P 1 0

SINGLES WITH MOST WEEKS AT NO. 1 IN THE US

	Title/artist	Year	Weeks at No. 1
1	*One Sweet Day*, Maria Carey and Boyz II Men	1995	16
2=	*I Will Always Love You*, Whitney Houston	1992	14
2=	*I'll Make Love to You*, Boyz II Men	1994	14
2=	*Macarena (Bayside Boys Mix)*, Los Del Rios	1995	14
5	*End of the Road*, Boyz II Men	1992	13
6=	*Don't Be Cruel/Hound Dog*, Elvis Presley	1956	11
6=	*I Swear*, All-4-One	1994	11
8=	*Cherry Pink and Apple Blossom White*, Perez Prado	1955	10
8=	*You Light Up My Life*, Debby Boone	1977	10
8=	*Physical*, Olivia Newton-John	1981	10

* *Based on* Billboard *charts*

This list covers the period from 1955 when *Billboard's* US Top 100 was inaugurated for singles. Long No. 1 runs were actually more commonplace in the pre-Rock 'n' Roll days of the 1940s and early 1950s when the market was generally slower-moving. Oddly enough, 1981 holds the record for the greatest number of singles (three) having runs of two months or more.

BOYZ II MEN
Boyz II Men, a Philadelphia R&B vocal quartet, are Motown's biggest-selling act of the 1990s by far, scoring three platinum singles within a period of 18 months.

T O P 1 0

SINGLES WITH MOST WEEKS AT NO. 1 IN THE UK

	Title/artist/year	Weeks at No. 1
1	*I Believe*, Frankie Laine (1953)	18
2	*Everything I Do (I Do It for You)*, Bryan Adams (1991)	16
3	*Love Is All Around*, Wet Wet Wet (1994)	15
4	*Bohemian Rhapsody*, Queen (1975 and 1991)	14
5	*Rose Marie*, Slim Whitman (1955)	11
6=	*Cara Mia*, David Whitfield (1954)	10
6=	*I Will Always Love You*, Whitney Houston (1993)	10
8=	*Diana*, Paul Anka (1957)	9
8=	*Here in My Heart*, Al Martino (1952)	9
8=	*Mull of Kintyre*, Wings (1977)	9
8=	*Oh Mein Papa*, Eddie Calvert (1954)	9
8=	*Secret Love*, Doris Day (1954)	9
8=	*Two Tribes*, Frankie Goes to Hollywood (1984)	9
8=	*You're the One That I Want*, John Travolta and Olivia Newton-John (1978)	9

The totals for the singles *I Believe* and *Bohemian Rhapsody* are the accumulation of more than one run at No. 1.

T O P 1 0

YOUNGEST SINGERS TO HAVE A NO. 1 SINGLE IN THE US*

	Artist/title	Age yrs	mths
1	Jimmy Boyd, *I Saw Mommy Kissing Santa Claus*	12	11
2	Stevie Wonder, *Fingertips*	13	2
3	Donny Osmond, *Go Away Little Girl*	13	9
4	Michael Jackson, *Ben*	13	11
5	Laurie London, *He's Got the Whole World in His Hands*	14	3
6	Little Peggy March, *I Will Follow Him*	15	1
7	Brenda Lee, *I'm Sorry*	15	7
8=	Paul Anka, *Diana*	16	1
8=	Tiffany, *I Think We're Alone Now*	16	1
10=	Little Eva, *The Loco-Motion*	17	1
10=	Lesley Gore, *It's My Party*	17	1

* *To 31 December 1996*

T O P 1 0

YOUNGEST SINGERS TO HAVE A NO. 1 SINGLE IN THE UK*

	Artist/title	Age yrs	mths
1	Little Jimmy Osmond, *Long Haired Lover from Liverpool*	9	8
2	Donny Osmond, *Puppy Love*	14	6
3	Helen Shapiro, *You Don't Know*	14	10
4	Paul Anka, *Diana*	16	0
5	Tiffany, *I Think We're Alone Now*	16	3
6	Nicole, *A Little Peace*	17	0
7	Glenn Medeiros, *Nothing's Gonna Change My Love*	18	0
8	Mary Hopkin, *Those Were the Days*	18	4
9	Cliff Richard, *Living Doll*	18	8
10	Adam Faith, *What Do You Want?*	19	5

* *To 31 December 1996*

GOLD & PLATINUM DISCS

TOP 10

ARTISTS WITH MOST PLATINUM ALBUMS IN THE US

Artist	Platinum albums
1 Barbra Streisand	22
2 Beatles	20
3 Elton John	19
4= Alabama	18
4= Neil Diamond	18
4= Elvis Presley	18
4= Rolling Stones	18
4= George Strait	18
9 Chicago	17
10= Willie Nelson	14
10= Prince	14

Source: RIAA, February 1997

This award, made by the Recording Industry Association of America (RIAA), the trade association of record companies in the US, confirms a minimum sale of 1,000,000 copies of an album.

TOP 10

ARTISTS WITH THE MOST GOLD ALBUMS IN THE US

Artist	Gold albums
1 Elvis Presley	46
2 Rolling Stones	36
3= Neil Diamond	32
3= Barbra Streisand	32
5 Elton John	31
6 Beatles	29
7= Bob Dylan	22
7= Kenny Rogers	22
7= Frank Sinatra	22
7= Willie Nelson	22

Source: RIAA, February 1997

This award confirms a minimum sale of 500,000 copies of an album. The RIAA began certification for gold records in 1958, when the Oklahoma Original Soundtrack was awarded the first such honor.

THE BIRTH OF THE LONG-PLAYER

A team of engineers at Columbia Records, led by Dr. Peter Goldmark (the inventor who had developed the first colour TV in 1940), developed the "long-player", a 12-inch micro-groove disc of non-breakable Vinylite, which was launched in 1948. It reproduced a clearer sound, turned at $33\frac{1}{3}$ revolutions per minute, and could accommodate up to 23 minutes per side of recording (compared with a maximum of 4 minutes per side on a 78-rpm record). It was unveiled to the trade in Atlantic City on 21 June, and then to the public on 21 July at the Waldorf-Astoria Hotel, New York City. The following year, RCA Victor introduced the smaller, five-minute 45-rpm vinyl record as hardware manufacturers began producing multi-speed turntables that could facilitate all three speeds. The initialization "LP" was the common term for the extended format, but "album" had usurped this role by the late 1970s.

50 YEARS AGO

TOP 10

GROUPS WITH THE MOST PLATINUM ALBUMS IN THE US

Group	Platinum albums
1 Beatles	20
2= Alabama	18
2= Rolling Stones	18
4 Chicago	17
5= Aerosmith	13
5= Rush	13
7= AC/DC	12
7= Pink Floyd	12
9= Kiss	11
9= Led Zeppelin	11
9= Van Halen	11

Source: RIAA; to February 1997

The official RIAA platinum certification, signifying one million US sales of an album, was introduced in 1976 in response to ever-increasing LP sales, though awards were also made retrospectively where appropriate – as here, to 1960s albums by the Beatles, Rolling Stones, and Led Zeppelin. The odd men out among the enduring rock bands in this list are clearly country music quartet Alabama, whose album career did not take off until 1980, but who have been consistently huge sellers in the country market ever since.

TOP 10

GROUPS WITH THE MOST GOLD ALBUMS IN THE US

Group	Gold albums
1 Rolling Stones	36
2 Beatles	29
3= Kiss	21
3= Rush	21
5= Alabama	20
5= Chicago	20
7 Jefferson Airplane/Starship*	18
8 Beach Boys	17
9= AC/DC	16
9= Pink Floyd	16

* Includes awards for Jefferson Airplane, Jefferson Starship, and Starship (the evolution of the band's name)

Source: RIAA; to February 1997

The RIAA introduced its gold certification for albums in 1958, originally awarding it to releases that generated a million dollars' worth of sales. When inflation eventually began to devalue this approach, the criteria were changed to recognize US sales of half a million instead, and this is still the basis on which these awards are made in the late 1990s. Naturally, every platinum album also receives a gold award when its sales pass the appropriate level.

TOP 10
MALE ARTISTS WITH THE MOST GOLD ALBUMS IN THE UK

	Artist	Gold albums
1	Elton John	18
2	Bob Dylan	16
3=	David Bowie	15
3=	Paul McCartney	15
3=	Rod Stewart	15
6=	Elvis Presley	14
6=	Cliff Richard	14
8	Prince	11
9	Bruce Springsteen	10
10	Eric Clapton	9

TOP 10
FEMALE ARTISTS WITH THE MOST GOLD ALBUMS IN THE UK

	Artist	Gold albums
1	Madonna	11
2	Kate Bush	8
3	Tina Turner	7
4=	Kylie Minogue	6
4=	Barbra Streisand	6
4=	Diana Ross	6
7=	Whitney Houston	5
7=	Gloria Estefan	5
7=	Mariah Carey	5
7=	Sade	5

ELTON JOHN
Britain's most successful solo artist ever in the US, Elton had his first US Top 10 hit in 1970 and followed it with 15 No. 1 records and 40 million-sellers over the next 24 years.

TOP 10
MALE ARTISTS WITH THE MOST PLATINUM ALBUMS IN THE UK

	Artist	Platinum albums
1	Elton John	12
2=	Bob Dylan	11
2=	David Bowie	11
4	Rod Stewart	7
5=	Elvis Presley	6
5=	Phil Collins	6
5=	Michael Jackson	6
5=	Cliff Richard	6
9=	Eric Clapton	5
9=	Bruce Springsteen	5

Longevity of appeal allies itself to consistently high sales, as this list of solidly-entrenched stars indicates. Any of these artists can reasonably expect to add further to their tally of 300,000-plus sellers – including the 20-years-dead Elvis!

TOP 10
FEMALE ARTISTS WITH THE MOST PLATINUM ALBUMS IN THE UK

	Artist	Platinum albums
1	Madonna	11
2	Tina Turner	6
3=	Gloria Estefan	4
3=	Kate Bush	4
3=	Enya	4
3=	Mariah Carey	4
7=	Whitney Houston	3
7=	Alison Moyet	3
7=	Celine Dion	3
7=	Janet Jackson	3

Every album released by Madonna since her 1984 debut has achieved (and in the cases of some releases, hugely exceeded) the 300,000-sale Platinum mark in the UK, representing consistency at a level unmatched by any other female performer.

THE 10
GROUPS WITH THE MOST PLATINUM ALBUMS IN THE UK

	Group	Platinum albums
1	The Beatles	17
2	Pink Floyd	16
3	Queen	14
4=	Genesis	10
4=	Led Zeppelin	10
6=	Abba	9
6=	Dire Straits	9
8=	Simon & Garfunkel	8
8=	U2	8
10=	The Police	7
10=	The Eurythmics	7

The Beatles were the first act in UK pop history to sell albums in quantities comparable to singles sales. Although this became commonplace in the 1970s, in 1963, when the average big-selling album might sell 50,000 copies, the Beatles' first album *Please Please Me* sold over 500,000 in nine months, while its follow-up *With The Beatles* exceeded that figure in its first week.

STAR SINGLES

TOP 10

BEATLES SINGLES IN THE UK

1	She Loves You	1963
2	I Want to Hold Your Hand	1963
3	Can't Buy Me Love	1964
4	I Feel Fine	1964
5	We Can Work It Out/Day Tripper	1965
6	Help!	1965
7	Hey Jude	1968
8	A Hard Day's Night	1964
9	From Me to You	1963
10	Hello Goodbye	1967

The Beatles' two bestselling UK singles, both from the late 1963 "Beatlemania" period, remain among the UK's all-time Top 10 singles 30 years later. Their sales towards the end of the 1960s were generally lower, although *Hey Jude* proved a match for the earlier mega-hits. Nos. 1 to 5 were all million-plus UK sellers.

TOP 10

QUEEN SINGLES IN THE UK

1	Bohemian Rhapsody	1975/1991
2	Under Pressure (with David Bowie)	1981
3	We Are the Champions	1977
4	Radio Ga-Ga	1984
5	Killer Queen	1974
6	I Want to Break Free	1984
7	Crazy Little Thing Called Love	1979
8	Somebody to Love	1976
9	A Kind of Magic	1986
10	Innuendo	1991

It was Freddie Mercury's death in 1991 that resulted in Queen achieving the UK's all-time, second-bestselling single with *Bohemian Rhapsody*, which topped 2,000,000 UK sales after it returned to No. 1 16 years after its original triumph. Queen's best-ever US seller, *Another One Bites the Dust* (1980), does not appear in this list, as it only reached No.7 in the UK.

THE ROLLING STONES IN CONCERT
One of the leading groups of the 1960s, the Rolling Stones still attract a huge following today. Their most recent "Voodoo Lounge World Tour" consisted of 123 concerts played worldwide on four continents. The tour grossed a total of $320 million, and is still the most successful tour by a rock band to date.

TOP 10

ROLLING STONES SINGLES IN THE UK

1	The Last Time	1965
2	(I Can't Get No) Satisfaction	1965
3	Honky Tonk Women	1969
4	It's All Over Now	1964
5	Get Off of My Cloud	1965
6	Paint It Black	1966
7	Jumpin' Jack Flash	1968
8	Little Red Rooster	1964
9	Miss You	1978
10	Brown Sugar	1971

The mid-1960s were the Stones' singles-selling heyday, when the first eight of these titles reached No. 1 in the UK. Though arguably the next most popular group to the Beatles for most of that decade, their sales nonetheless rarely approached those of the Fab Four: *The Last Time* only just outsold *A Hard Day's Night*, the Beatles' 8th most successful single.

TOP 10

GEORGE MICHAEL AND WHAM! SINGLES IN THE UK

1	Last Christmas (Wham!)	1984
2	Careless Whisper (Solo)	1984
3	Freedom (Wham!)	1984
4	Wake Me Up Before You Go-Go (Wham!)	1984
5	A Different Corner (Solo)	1985
6	I'm Your Man (Wham!)	1985
7	Bad Boys (Wham!)	1983
8	Don't Let the Sun Go Down on Me (with Elton John)	1991
9	The Edge of Heaven (Wham!)	1986
10	Young Guns (Go For It) (Wham!)	1982

By and large, George Michael's solo singles since the break-up of Wham! have not had the consistent success that the duo's records enjoyed (in the UK, anyway; the opposite is true in America). His two biggest-selling solo performances (Nos. 2 and 5 above) were both made while Wham! was still operating, and the only post-split recording here is not strictly a solo effort, but a live concert performance on which Elton John (the song's writer) guested.

TOP 10

MADONNA SINGLES IN THE UK

1	*Like a Virgin*	1984
2	*Into the Groove*	1985
3	*Papa Don't Preach*	1986
4	*Crazy for You*	1985
5	*Holiday*	1984
6	*True Blue*	1986
7	*Vogue*	1990
8	*La Isla Bonita*	1987
9	*Like a Prayer*	1989
10	*Who's That Girl?*	1987

The most successful chart artist of the 1980s, Madonna had scored 25 UK Top 10 hits, including seven No. 1s, by the end of the decade. Interestingly, her biggest seller, *Like a Virgin*, failed to make No. 1, being held at No. 3 over the Christmas period in 1984 by the gigantic sales of the Band Aid single and Wham!'s hit *Last Christmas*.

TOP 10

DIRE STRAITS SINGLES IN THE UK

1	*Private Investigations*	1982
2	*Walk of Life*	1986
3	*Money for Nothing*	1985
4	*Sultans of Swing*	1979
5	*Romeo and Juliet*	1981
6	*Twisting by the Pool*	1983
7	*Brothers in Arms*	1985
8	*So Far Away*	1985
9	*Your Latest Trick*	1986
10	*Calling Elvis*	1991

This is a band whose albums have always considerably outsold their singles; Dire Straits have amassed only 10 Top 30 hits (those in this list) in a career spanning almost 15 years. The first, *Sultans of Swing*, "slept" for a year on release until its US success prompted a reactivation in the UK. It is worth noting that half the songs here (Nos. 2, 3, 7, 8 and 9) are taken from the album *Brothers in Arms*, which has sold 3,000,000 copies in the UK.

TOP 10

ABBA SINGLES IN THE UK

1	*Dancing Queen*	1976
2	*Knowing Me, Knowing You*	1977
3	*Fernando*	1976
4	*Super Trouper*	1980
5	*The Name of the Game*	1977
6	*Take a Chance on Me*	1978
7	*Mamma Mia*	1975
8	*Money Money Money*	1976
9	*The Winner Takes It All*	1980
10	*Waterloo*	1974

Abba are one of the biggest singles-selling groups ever in the UK. Nine of these 10 records reached No. 1, and the top eight all sold in excess of 500,000 copies each. Their last year together (1982) showed a notable sales decline, at which point they split, either to pursue solo careers or other musical projects, such as the stage show *Chess*.

TOP 10

BEACH BOYS SINGLES IN THE UK

1	*Good Vibrations*	1966
2	*Sloop John B*	1966
3	*God Only Knows*	1966
4	*Do It Again*	1968
5	*Cottonfields*	1970
6	*I Get Around*	1964
7	*Then I Kissed Her*	1967
8	*Barbara Ann*	1966
9	*Break Away*	1969
10	*Lady Lynda*	1979

Good Vibrations was also a Top 20 hit when reissued a decade after its initial success, cementing its status as the Beach Boys' biggest UK seller by far. By contrast, the group's belated all-time US top-seller, 1988's *Kokomo*, was only a middling British success and registers nowhere near this Top 10 listing. The group were also co-vocalists on the Fat Boys' revival of *Wipe Out* in 1987; this single would appear at No. 8 if it was included here.

TOP 10

MICHAEL JACKSON SINGLES IN THE UK

1	*One Day in Your Life*	1981
2	*Billie Jean*	1983
3	*Say Say Say* (with Paul McCartney)	1983
4	*Don't Stop Till You Get Enough*	1979
5	*Beat It*	1983
6	*Rockin' Robin*	1972
7	*Black and White*	1991
8	*I Just Can't Stop Loving You*	1987
9	*Ben*	1972
10	*Heal the World*	1992

Despite the gigantic UK sales of Jackson's *Bad* and *Thriller* albums (or more likely, because of these successes), most of the singles taken from them – while being buoyant chart-riders – tended not to sell well enough to challenge some of his longer-term bestsellers such as *Ben* (which continued to sell thousands each year for the best part of a decade). The major irony in this list is the top seller, which was released by Motown many years after it was recorded, and quite a few years after Jackson had departed the label.

TOP 10

ELTON JOHN SINGLES IN THE UK

1	*Don't Go Breaking My Heart* (with Kiki Dee)	1976
2	*Sacrifice*	1990
3	*Rocket Man*	1972
4	*Nikita*	1985
5	*Crocodile Rock*	1972
6	*Daniel*	1973
7	*Song for Guy*	1978
8	*I Guess That's Why They Call It the Blues*	1983
9	*I'm Still Standing*	1983
10	*Passengers*	1984

WOMEN IN THE CHARTS

TOP 10

FEMALE SINGERS WITH THE MOST TOP 10 HITS IN THE US AND UK*

	Singer	Top 10 hits
1	Madonna	69
2	Janet Jackson (including three duets with Michael Jackson and two with Luther Vandross)	31
3=	Whitney Houston (including one duet with CeCe Winans)	29
3=	Diana Ross (including one duet each with Marvin Gaye and Lionel Richie)	29
5	Mariah Carey (including two duets with Boyz II Men and two with Luther Vandross)	27
6	Connie Francis	26
7	Olivia Newton-John (including two duets with John Travolta and one with ELO)	25
8	Donna Summer (including one duet with Barbra Streisand)	23
9	Aretha Franklin (including two duets with George Michael and one with Eurythmics)	22
10	Cher	20

* *To 31 December 1996*

TOP 10

FEMALE GROUPS OF ALL TIME IN THE US*

	Group	No. 1 hits	Top 10 hits	Top 20 hits
1	Supremes	12	20	2
2	Pointer Sisters	–	7	13
3	Expose	1	8	9
4=	McGuire Sisters	2	4	9
4=	Shirelles	2	6	7
6	TLC	–	7	7
7=	Bangles	2	5	6
7=	Martha & the Vandellas	–	6	7
9	Fontane Sisters	2	2	8
10	En Vogue	–	5	6

* *To 31 December 1996; ranked according to total number of Top 20 singles*

Source: The Popular Music Database

TOP 10

FEMALE GROUPS OF ALL TIME IN THE UK*

	Group	No. 1 hits	Top 10 hits	Top 20 hits
1	Supremes	1	13	18
2	Bananarama	—	10	15
3	Eternal	–	10	12
4	Three Degrees	1	5	7
5	Sister Sledge	1	4	7
6	Nolans	—	3	7
7	Salt N Pepa	–	4	5
8	Bangles	1	3	5
9	Pointer Sisters	—	2	5
10	Spice Girls	4	4	4

* *To 31 March 1997; ranked according to total number of Top 20 singles*

The Supremes also had three other Top 20 hits, not included here, in partnership with Motown male groups the Four Tops and Temptations. However, Bananarama's charity revival of *Help!*, shared with comediennes Dawn French and Jennifer Saunders, has been included since all the participants are female.

TOP 10

SINGLES BY FEMALE SINGERS IN THE US

	Single/singer
1	*I Will Always Love You*, Whitney Houston,
2	*Fantasy*, Mariah Carey
3	*Vogue*, Madonna
4	*Mr. Big Stuff*, Jean Knight
5	*You Light Up My Life*, Debby Boone
6	*Physical*, Olivia Newton-John
7	*I Will Survive*, Gloria Gaynor
8	*Hot Stuff*, Donna Summer
9	*Emotion*, Samantha Sang
10	*Mickey*, Toni Basil

Source: The Popular Music Database

TOP 10

SINGLES BY FEMALE SINGERS IN THE UK

	Single/singer	Year
1	*I Will Always Love You*, Whitney Houston	1992
2	*The Power of Love*, Jennifer Rush	1985
3	*Think Twice*, Celine Dion	1994
4	*Don't Cry for Me Argentina*, Julie Covington	1977
5	*Fame*, Irene Cara	1982
6	*Anyone Who Had a Heart*, Cilla Black	1964
7	*Feels Like I'm in Love*, Kelly Marie	1980
8	*Woman in Love*, Barbra Streisand	1980
9	*Nothing Compares 2 U*, Sinead O'Connor	1990
10	*Oooh Aah...Just a Little Bit*, Gina G	1996

Perhaps the most significant aspect of this list is how comparatively recent most of its entries are. Only two of these singles were released before 1980, and only Cilla Black's 1964 chart-topper is of real vintage.

TOP 10
YOUNGEST FEMALE SINGERS TO HAVE A NO. 1 SINGLE IN THE UK

	Singer	years	Age months	days
1	Helen Shapiro	14	10	13
2	Tiffany	16	3	28
3	Nicole	17	0	0
4	Sandie Shaw	17	7	26
5	Mary Hopkin	18	4	22
6	Sonia	18	5	9
7	Connie Francis	19	5	4
8	Kate Bush	19	7	12
9	Kylie Minogue	19	8	23
10	Ruby Murray	19	10	11

The ages shown are those of each artist on the publication date of the chart in which she achieved her first No. 1 single. All ten of these girls were still in their teens when they had their first taste of chart-topping glory.

TOP 10
OLDEST FEMALE SINGERS TO HAVE A NO. 1 SINGLE IN THE UK

	Singer	years	months	Age days
1	Cher	40	11	14
2	Barbra Streisand	38	6	1
3	Vera Lynn	35	7	16
4	Tammy Wynette	33	0	12
5	Kitty Kallen	32	3	16
6	Robin Beck	32	2	12
7	Jo Stafford	32	2	4
8	Charlene	32	0	25
9	Doris Day	32	0	13
10	Chaka Khan	31	7	18

The ages shown are those of each artist on the publication date of the chart in which her first No. 1 single reached the top. It is, of course, entirely possible that Vera Lynn, Jo Stafford, and Doris Day might have reached No. 1 at a younger age, had the UK charts existed before November 1952.

TOP 10
YOUNGEST FEMALE SINGERS TO HAVE A NO. 1 SINGLE IN THE US

	Singer	years	Age months	days
1	Little Peggy March	15	1	20
2	Brenda Lee	15	7	7
3	Tiffany	16	1	5
4	Lesley Gore	17	0	30
5	Little Eva	17	1	27
6	Shelley Fabares	18	2	19
7	Debbie Gibson	18	6	4
8	Joan Weber	18	?	?*
9	Lulu	19	11	18
10	Martika	20	2	4

*   Birthdate unknown, but was between 18 years and 6 months and 19 years

Source: The Popular Music Database

TOP 10
ALBUMS BY FEMALE GROUPS IN THE UK

	Album/group	Year
1	*Spice*, Spice Girls	1996
2	*Always and Forever*, Eternal	1993
3	*Power of a Woman*, Eternal	1995
4	*Different Light*, Bangles	1986
5	*20 Golden Greats*, Supremes	1977
6	*The Greatest Hits Collection*, Bananarama,	1988
7	*Greatest Hits*, Bangles	1980
8	*Everything*, Bangles	1980
9	*We Are Family*, Sister Sledge	1979
10	*Break Out*, Pointer Sisters	1984

All of the albums in this Top 10 were released within the last two decades, and the three biggest sellers of all within the last four years. Three of these groups – the Spice Girls, Eternal, and Bananarama – are British, the other four being American. Only the Bangles also played instruments while performing, all the other outfits being purely vocal groups.

TOP 10
SINGLES BY FEMALE GROUPS IN THE US

	Single/group
1	*Don't Let Go*, En Vogue
2	*Hold On*, En Vogue
3	*Whatta Man*, Salt N Pepa
4	*Expressions*, Salt N Pepa
5	*Push It*, Salt N Pepa
6	*Waterfall*, TLC
7	*Creep*, TLC
8	*Weak*, SWV
9	*Baby, Baby, Baby*, TLC
10	*Red Light Special*, TLC

Source: The Popular Music Database

TOP 10
SINGLES BY FEMALE GROUPS IN THE UK*

	Single/group	Year
1	*Wannabe*, Spice Girls	1996
2	*Say You'll Be There*, Spice Girls	1996
3	*2 Become 1*, Spice Girls	1996
4	*Frankie*, Sister Sledge	1985
5	*When Will I See You Again*, Three Degrees	1974
6	*Baby Love*, Supremes	1964
7	*I'm in the Mood for Dancing*, Nolans	1980
8	*Eternal Flame*, Bangles	1989
9	*Who Do You Think You Are/ Mama*, Spice Girls	1997
10	*Then He Kissed Me*, Crystals	1963

*   To 31 March 1997

Such has been the Spice Girls' impact on popular music that they have totally re-written the record book as far as successful girl-group singles are concerned, snatching the three all-time biggest sellers with their first three releases. The fourth, already the all-time No. 9, was still a Top 3 seller as this list was being compiled.

CHRISTMAS HITS

TOP 10

CHRISTMAS SINGLES OF ALL TIME IN THE UK

	Single/artist	Year
1	*Do They Know It's Christmas?*, Band Aid	1984
2	*Bohemian Rhapsody*, Queen	1975/1991
3	*Mull of Kintyre*, Wings	1977
4	*Mary's Boy Child/Oh My Lord*, Boney M	1978
5	*I Want to Hold Your Hand*, Beatles	1963
6	*Don't You Want Me*, The Human League	1981
7	*Last Christmas*, Wham!	1984
8	*I Feel Fine*, Beatles	1964
9	*We Can Work It Out/ Day Tripper*, Beatles	1965
10	*It's Now or Never*, Elvis Presley	1960

With Christmas being the traditional high-point of the year for UK record sales, it is not surprising that these Top 10 singles rank among Britain's top 30 sellers of all time. All were No. 1 hits at the time, apart from Wham's *Last Christmas*, which despite its enormous sales, was held at No. 2 in Christmas week of 1984 by the still bigger Band Aid single.

TOP 10

CHRISTMAS HITS OF THE 1950s IN THE UK

	Single/artist	Year
1	*Mary's Boy Child*, Harry Belafonte	1957
2	*Christmas Alphabet*, Dickie Valentine	1955
3	*Santo Natale*, David Whitfield	1954
4	*Santa Bring My Baby Back (To Me)*, Elvis Presley	1957
5	*The Little Drummer Boy*, The Beverley Sisters	1959
6	*I Saw Mommy Kissing Santa Claus*, Jimmy Boyd	1953
7	*Jingle Bell Rock*, Max Bygraves	1959
8	*Christmas Island*, Dickie Valentine	1956
9	*The Little Drummer Boy*, The Harry Simeone Chorale	1959
10	*Little Donkey*, The Beverley Sisters	1959

TOP 10

CHRISTMAS HITS OF THE 1970s IN THE UK

	Single/artist	Year
1	*Mary's Boy Child/Oh My Lord*, Boney M	1978
2	*Merry Christmas Everybody*, Slade	1973
3	*When a Child Is Born*, Johnny Mathis	1976
4	*Lonely This Christmas*, Mud	1974
5	*I Believe in Father Christmas*, Greg Lake	1975
6	*I Wish It Could Be Christmas Every Day*, Wizzard	1973
7	*Wombling Merry Christmas*, The Wombles	1974
8	*White Christmas*, Bing Crosby	1977
9	*Merry Xmas (War is Over)*, John Lennon	1972
10	*It's Gonna Be a Cold, Cold Christmas*, Dana	1975

TOP 10

CHRISTMAS HITS OF THE 1960s IN THE UK

	Single/artist	Year
1	*Little Donkey*, Nina & Frederick	1960
2	*Lonely Pup (in the Christmas Shop)*, Adam Faith	1960
3	*Pretty Paper*, Roy Orbison	1964
4	*Rockin' Around the Christmas Tree*, Brenda Lee	1962
5	*If Every Day Was Like Christmas*, Elvis Presley	1966
6	*Blue Christmas*, Elvis Presley	1964
7	*Merry Gentle Pops*, The Barron Knights	1965
8	*All I Want for Christmas is a Beatle*, Dora Bryan	1963
9	*Bambino*, The Springfields	1961
10	*Christmas Will Be Just Another Lonely Day*, Brenda Lee	1964

TOP 10

CHRISTMAS HITS OF THE 1980s IN THE UK

	Single/artist	Year
1	*Do They Know It's Christmas?*, Band Aid	1984
2	*Last Christmas*, Wham!	1984
3	*Mistletoe and Wine*, Cliff Richard	1988
4	*Do They Know It's Christmas?*, Band Aid 2	1989
5	*Stop the Cavalry*, Jona Lewie	1980
6	*Let's Party*, Jive Bunny	1989
7	*Merry Christmas Everyone*, Shakin' Stevens	1985
8	*Merry Xmas (War is Over)*, John Lennon	1980
9	*Blue Christmas (EP)*, Shakin' Stevens	1982
10	*Peace on Earth/The Little Drummer Boy*, David Bowie & Bing Crosby	1982

TOP 10

CHRISTMAS ALBUMS OF ALL TIME IN THE UK

Album/artist

1 *Now! – The Christmas Album*, Various

2 *It's Christmas*, Various

3 *The Best Christmas Album in the World...Ever!*, Various

4 *It's Christmas Time*, Various

5 *Elvis' Christmas Album*, Elvis Presley

6 *Phil Spector's Christmas Album*, Various

7 *The No. 1 Christmas Album*, Various

8 *12 Songs of Christmas*, Jim Reeves

9 *Together with Cliff Richard*, Cliff Richard

10 *Special Olympics – A Very Special Christmas*, Various

TOP 10

CHRISTMAS HITS WITH A CHRISTMAS SUBJECT IN THE UK

	Single/artist	Year
1	*Do They Know It's Christmas?*, Band Aid	1984
2	*Mary's Boy Child/Oh My Lord*, Boney M	1978
3	*Last Christmas*, Wham!	1984
4	*Merry Christmas Everybody*, Slade	1973
5	*Mary's Boy Child*, Harry Belafonte	1957
6	*White Christmas*, Bing Crosby	1977 *
7	*Mistletoe and Wine*, Cliff Richard	1988
8	*When a Child is Born*, Johnny Mathis	1976
9	*Happy Xmas (War is Over)*, John Lennon	1980 *
10	*Lonely This Christmas*, Mud	1974

* *Year of highest chart position*

Band Aid's *Do They Know It's Christmas?* has now sold over 3,500,000 copies in the UK alone. Slade's *Merry Christmas Everybody* has charted on eight seasonal occasions. Bing Crosby's *White Christmas* charted for the first time in the UK as late as 1977, a few weeks after the singer's death.

TOP 10

CHRISTMAS HITS WITH A NON-CHRISTMAS SUBJECT IN THE UK

	Single/artist	Year		Single/artist	Year
1	*Bohemian Rhapsody*, Queen	1975/1991	6	*We Can Work It Out/ Day Tripper*, Beatles	1965
2	*Mull of Kintyre*, Wings	1977	7	*It's Now or Never*, Elvis Presley	1960
3	*I Want to Hold Your Hand*, Beatles	1963	8	*Green, Green Grass of Home*, Tom Jones	1966
4	*Don't You Want Me*, Human League	1981	9	*Another Brick in the Wall, Part 2*, Pink Floyd	1979
5	*I Feel Fine*, Beatles	1964	10	*Long-Haired Lover from Liverpool*, Little Jimmy Osmond	1972

Chart history proves that it is actually more likely for a non-Christmas-themed single to be the No. 1 seller at Christmas, though only during one decade – the 1960s – were there no year-end chart-toppers at all with a Yule theme. This is why there is a slight '60s (and especially Beatles) bias evident in this Top 10. Note that the unseasonal *Bohemian Rhapsody* topped the Christmas charts in both 1975 and 1991.

"BEST SONG" OSCARS

THE 10

"BEST SONG" OSCAR WINNERS OF THE 1940s

	Song	Film
1940	When You Wish upon a Star	Pinocchio
1941	The Last Time I Saw Paris	Lady Be Good
1942	White Christmas	Holiday Inn
1943	You'll Never Know	Hello, Frisco, Hello
1944	Swinging on a Star	Going My Way
1945	It Might as Well Be Spring	State Fair
1946	On the Atchison, Topeka and Santa Fe	The Harvey Girls
1947	Zip-A-Dee-Doo-Dah	Song of the South
1948	Buttons and Bows	The Paleface
1949	Baby, It's Cold Outside	Neptune's Daughter

The first "Best Song" Oscar was won in 1934 by *The Continental* from the film *The Gay Divorcée*.

THE 10

"BEST SONG" OSCAR WINNERS OF THE 1950s

	Song	Film
1950	Mona Lisa	Captain Carey
1951	In the Cool, Cool, Cool of the Evening	Here Comes the Groom
1952	High Noon (Do Not Forsake Me, Oh My Darling)	High Noon
1953	Secret Love	Calamity Jane
1954	Three Coins in the Fountain	Three Coins in the Fountain
1955	Love Is a Many-splendored Thing	Love Is a Many-splendored Thing
1956	Whatever Will Be, Will Be (Que Sera, Sera)	The Man Who Knew Too Much
1957	All the Way	The Joker Is Wild
1958	Gigi	Gigi
1959	High Hopes	A Hole in the Head

THE 10

"BEST SONG" OSCAR WINNERS OF THE 1960s

	Song	Film
1960	Never on Sunday	Never on Sunday
1961	Moon River	Breakfast at Tiffany's
1962	Days of Wine and Roses	Days of Wine and Roses
1963	Call Me Irresponsible	Papa's Delicate Condition
1964	Chim Chim Cheree	Mary Poppins
1965	The Shadow of Your Smile	The Sandpiper
1966	Born Free	Born Free
1967	Talk to the Animals	Dr. Doolittle
1968	The Windmills of Your Mind	The Thomas Crown Affair
1969	Raindrops Keep Falling on My Head	Butch Cassidy and the Sundance Kid

French crooner Sacha Distel's cover version of the 1969 Oscar-winner charted no less than five times in the UK, all in 1970.

THE 10

"BEST SONG" OSCAR WINNERS OF THE 1970s

	Song	Film
1970	For All We Know	Lovers and Other Strangers
1971	Theme from "Shaft"	Shaft
1972	The Morning After	The Poseidon Adventure
1973	The Way We Were	The Way We Were
1974	We May Never Love Like This Again	The Towering Inferno
1975	I'm Easy	Nashville
1976	Evergreen	A Star Is Born
1977	You Light up My Life	You Light up My Life
1978	Last Dance	Thank God It's Friday
1979	It Goes Like It Goes	Norma Rae

Barbra Streisand became the first artist since Frank Sinatra to win two Oscar song awards in the same decade. Her two award-winners were *The Way We Were* and *Evergreen*, both of which went on to become huge international hits.

THE 10

"BEST SONG" OSCAR WINNERS OF THE 1980s

	Song	Film
1980	Fame	Fame
1981	Up Where We Belong	An Officer and a Gentleman
1982	Arthur's Theme (Best That You Can Do)	Arthur
1983	Flashdance	Flashdance
1984	I Just Called to Say I Love You	The Woman in Red
1985	Say You, Say Me	White Nights
1986	Take My Breath Away	Top Gun
1987	(I've Had) The Time of My Life	Dirty Dancing
1988	Let the River Run	Working Girl
1989	Under the Sea	The Little Mermaid

Award winners of the 1990s are: 1990, *Sooner or Later (I Always Get My Man)* from *Dick Tracy*; 1991, *Beauty and the Beast*; 1992, *Whole New World* from *Aladdin*; 1993, *Streets of Philadelphia* from *Philadelphia*; 1994, *Can You Feel the Love Tonight* from *The Lion King*; 1995, *Colors of the Wind* from *Pocahontas*; and 1996, *You Must Love Me* from *Evita*.

THE BEST AND WORST

Although the first Oscars were presented during the last days of silent films, since 1934 the writers of lyrics and music have been honoured at the annual Academy Awards ceremony with Oscars for "Best Song". This accolade has sometimes coincided with a song's commercial success – Debbie Boone's recording of the 1977 winner *You*

Light Up My Life was also the bestselling single of the year in the US. However, a number of winners have been perversely at odds with the musical taste of the period. The whimsical *Talk to the Animals* (from the 1967 film *Doctor Dolittle*) not only failed to achieve chart success, but was honoured at a time when the Beatles were dominating the charts.

SAMMY CAHN
The lyricist Sammy Cahn (1913–93) won his 1st Oscar in 1954 for Three Coins in the Fountain.

TOP 10
ARTISTS WITH MOST "BEST SONG" OSCAR NOMINATIONS

	Artist	Wins	Years	Nominations
1	Sammy Cahn	4	1942–75	26
2	Johnny Mercer	4	1938–71	18
3=	Paul Francis Webster	3	1944–76	16
3=	Alan and Marilyn Bergman	2	1968–95	16
5	James Van Heusen	4	1944–68	14
6=	Henry Warren	3	1935–57	11
6=	Henry Mancini	2	1961–86	11
6=	Ned Washington	1	1940–61	11
9=	Sammy Fain	2	1937–77	10
9=	Leo Robin	1	1934–53	10
9=	Jule Styne	1	1940–68	10

It was not until the 7th year of the Awards, in 1934, that the category of "Best Song" was added to the other accolades bestowed on the previous year's films.

MOON RIVER
Henry Mancini wrote the award-winning music for Moon River *(from* Breakfast at Tiffany's*).*

THOROUGHLY MODERN MILLIE
This 1967 film starring Julie Andrews added to the tally of best-song nominations achieved by Sammy Cahn and James Van Heusen.

THE THOMAS CROWN AFFAIR
The Windmills of Your Mind *from Steve McQueen's 1968 film won the Bergmans their 1st Oscar.*

BARBRA STREISAND
Barbra Streisand had a hit in 1973 with the Bergman's Oscar-winning The Way We Were.

MUSIC AWARDS

ARTISTS WITH MOST GRAMMY AWARDS

	Artist	Awards
1	Sir George Solti	31
2	Quincy Jones	26
3	Vladimir Horowitz	25
4=	Henry Mancini	20
4=	Stevie Wonder	20
6	Pierre Boulez	17
7	Leonard Bernstein	16
7=	John T. Williams	16
9=	Aretha Franklin	15
9=	Itzhak Perlman	15

The Grammy Awards ceremony has been held annually in the US since its inauguration on 4 May 1959, and the awards are considered to be the most prestigious in the music industry. The proliferation of classical artists in this Top 10 (not least, conductor Sir George Solti) is largely attributable to the large number of classical award categories at the Grammys, which latterly have been overshadowed by the rise of pop and rock. Grammy winners are selected annually by the 7,000-member Recording Academy of NARAS (the National Academy of Recording Arts & Sciences).

FIRST INDUCTEES INTO THE ROCK 'N' ROLL HALL OF FAME

1	Chuck Berry
2	James Brown
3	Ray Charles
4	Sam Cooke
5	Fats Domino
6	Everly Brothers
7	Buddy Holly
8	Jerry Lee Lewis
9	Elvis Presley
10	Little Richard

These seminal artists were all inducted at the first ceremony which took place on 23 January 1986 at the Waldorf-Astoria Hotel, New York. While only 10 performing artists were inducted, two non-performing Rock 'n' Roll pioneers were also recipients: DJ Alan Freed and Sun record label owner Sam Phillips. Three official "Early Influence" inductions were also confirmed at this inaugural dinner: Robert Johnson, Jimmie Rodgers, and Jimmy Yancey.

ARTISTS WITH MOST BRIT AWARDS

	Artist	Awards
1	Annie Lennox	7
2=	Phil Collins	6*
2=	Prince	6#
4=	Michael Jackson	5
4=	George Michael	5+
6=	Blur	4
6=	Oasis	4
6=	Take That	4
9=	Dire Straits	3
9=	Trevor Horn	3
9=	R.E.M.	3
9=	Seal	3
9=	Lisa Stansfield	3
9=	David A. Stewart	3
9=	Paul Young	3

* *Includes award for Best Film Soundtrack (1989, for* Buster *Original Soundtrack)*
# *Includes award for Best Film Soundtrack (1990, for* Batman *Original Soundtrack)*
+ *Includes two awards with Wham! (1985 and 1986)*

FIRST GRAMMY RECORDS OF THE YEAR

	Record	Artist	Year
1	*Nel Blu Dipinto di Blu (Volare)*	Domenico Modugno	1958
2	*Mack the Knife*	Bobby Darin	1959
3	*Theme From a Summer Place*	Percy Faith	1960
4	*Moon River*	Henry Mancini	1961
5	*I Left My Heart in San Francisco*	Tony Bennett	1962
6	*The Days of Wine and Roses*	Henry Mancini	1963
7	*The Girl from Ipanema*	Stan Getz & Astrud Gilberto	1964
8	*A Taste of Honey*	Herb Alpert & the Tijuana Brass	1965
9	*Strangers in the Night*	Frank Sinatra	1966
10	*Up Up and Away*	5th Dimension	1967

COUNTRIES WITH MOST WINS AT THE EUROVISION SONG CONTEST

	Country	Years	Wins
1	Ireland	1970, 1980, 1987, 1992, 1993, 1994, 1996	7
2=	France	1958, 1960, 1962, 1969*, 1977	5
2=	Luxembourg	1961, 1965, 1972, 1973, 1983	5
2=	UK	1967, 1969*, 1976, 1981, 1997	5
5	Netherlands	1957, 1959, 1969*, 1975	4
6	Sweden	1974, 1984, 1991	3
7=	Israel	1978, 1979	2
7=	Italy	1964, 1990	2
7=	Spain	1968, 1969*	2
7=	Switzerland	1956, 1988	2

* *All four countries tied as winners in 1969*

THE 10

FIRST RECIPIENTS OF THE BRITS "OUTSTANDING CONTRIBUTION TO BRITISH MUSIC" AWARD

	Artist	Date
1	John Lennon	24 Feb 82
2	Beatles	8 Feb 83
3	George Martin	21 Feb 84
4	Police	11 Feb 85
5	Wham! and Elton John	10 Feb 86
6	Eric Clapton	9 Feb 87
7	Who	8 Feb 88
8	Cliff Richard	13 Feb 89
9	Queen	9 Feb 90
10	Status Quo	10 Feb 91

The Outstanding Contribution Award is the highest honour given by the Brits Awards committee, which inaugurated the annual ceremony in 1982 at Grosvenor House Hotel, London. In 1992 the award name was changed, for that year only, to "Special Tribute" in recognition of the contribution and life of Queen's Freddie Mercury, who had died on 24 November 1991.

THE 10

LAST WINNERS OF THE BRIT AWARD FOR BEST VIDEO*

Year	Video/artist
1997	*Say You'll Be There* (Spice Girls)
1996	*Wonderwall* (Oasis)
1995	*Parklife* (Blur)
1994	*Pray* (Take That)
1993	*Stay* (Shakespears Sister)
1992	*Killer* (Seal)
1991	*A Little Time* (The Beautiful South)
1990	*Lullaby* (The Cure)
1989	*Smooth Criminal* (Michael Jackson)
1988	*True Faith* (New Order)

* Now "Best Video by a British Artist"

THE 10

LAST WINNERS OF THE BRIT AWARD FOR BEST BRITISH MALE SOLO ARTIST

Year	Artist
1997	George Michael
1996	Paul Weller
1995	Paul Weller
1994	Sting
1993	Mick Hucknall
1992	Seal
1991	Elton John
1990	Phil Collins
1989	Phil Collins
1988	George Michael

THE 10

LAST WINNERS OF THE BRIT AWARD FOR BEST SINGLE BY A BRITISH ARTIST

Year	Single/artist
1997	*Wannabe* (Spice Girls)
1996	*Back for Good* (Take That)
1995	*Parklife* (Blur)
1994	*Pray* (Take That)
1993	*Could It Be Magic* (Take That)
1992	*These Are the Days of Our Lives* (Queen)
1991	*Enjoy the Silence* (Depeche Mode)
1990	*Another Day in Paradise* (Phil Collins)
1989	*Perfect* (Fairground Attraction)
1988	*Never Gonna Give You Up* (Rick Astley)

THE 10

LAST WINNERS OF THE BRIT AWARD FOR BEST BRITISH FEMALE SOLO ARTIST

Year	Artist
1997	Gabrielle
1996	Annie Lennox
1995	Eddie Reader
1994	Dina Carroll
1993	Annie Lennox
1992	Lisa Stansfield
1991	Lisa Stansfield
1990	Annie Lennox
1989	Annie Lennox
1988	Alison Moyet

THE 10

LAST WINNERS OF THE BRIT AWARD FOR BEST ALBUM*

Year	Album/artist
1997	*Everything Must Go* (Manic Street Preachers)
1996	*(What's the Story) Morning Glory* (Oasis)
1995	*Parklife* (Blur)
1994	*Connected* (Stereo MCs)
1993	*Diva* (Annie Lennox)
1992	*Seal* (Seal)
1991	*Listen Without Prejudice, Vol. 1* (George Michael)
1990	*The Raw and the Cooked* (Fine Young Cannibals)
1989	*First of a Million Kisses* (Fairground Attraction)
1988	*Nothing Like the Sun* (Sting)

* Now "Best Album by a British Artist"

The Brits, organized annually by the British Phonographic Industry, celebrated their 10th anniversary in 1992 when Seal won an unprecedented three trophies.

MUSIC IN THE SALEROOM

T O P 1 0

MOST EXPENSIVE MUSIC MANUSCRIPTS EVER SOLD AT AUCTION

	Manuscript/sale	Price (£)*
1	Nine symphonies by Wolfgang Amadeus Mozart, Sotheby's, London, 22 May 1987	2,350,000
2	Schumann's *Second Symphony*, Sotheby's, London, 1 December 1994	1,350,000
3	Ludwig van Beethoven's *Piano Sonata in E Minor*, Opus 90, Sotheby's, London, 6 December 1991	1,000,000
4=	Robert Schumann's *Piano Concerto in A Minor*, Opus 54, Sotheby's, London, 22 November 1989	800,000
4=	Wolfgang Amadeus Mozart's *Fantasia in C Minor* and *Sonata in C Minor*, Sotheby's, London, 21 November 1990	800,000
6	Joseph Haydn's *Four String Quartets*, Opus 50, Sotheby's, London, 18 May 1995	600,000
7	Ludwig van Beethoven's first movement of the *Sonata for Violoncello and Piano in A Major*, Opus 69, Sotheby's, London, 17 May 1990	480,000
8	Johann Sebastian Bach's *Cantata No. 2*, Sotheby's, London, 15 May 1996	450,000
9	Johann Sebastian Bach's cantata *Auf Christi Himmelfahrt allein*, Sotheby's, London, 22 November 1989	390,000
10	Igor Stravinsky's *Rite of Spring*, Sotheby's, London, 11 November 1982	300,000

* 'Hammer prices', excluding premiums

T O P 1 0

MOST EXPENSIVE MUSICAL INSTRUMENTS EVER SOLD AT AUCTION

	Instrument/sale	Price (£)*
1	"Mendelssohn" Stradivarius violin, Christie's, London, 21 November 1990	902,000
2	"Cholmondley" Stradivarius violoncello, Sotheby's, London, 22 June 1988	682,000
3	Acoustic guitar owned by David Bowie, Paul McCartney, and George Michael, Christie's, London, 18 May 1994	220,000
4	Jimi Hendrix's Fender Stratocaster electric guitar, Sotheby's, London, 25 April 1990	198,000
5	Steinway grand piano, decorated by Lawrence Alma-Tadema and Edward Poynter for Henry Marquand, 1884–87, Sotheby Parke Bernet, New York, 26 March 1980	163,500 ($390,000)
6	Verne Powell platinum flute, Christie's, New York, 18 October 1986	126,200 ($187,000)
7	Charlie Parker's Grafton Saxophone, Christie's, London, 8 September 1994	93,500
8	Two-manual harpsichord by Andreas Ruckers of Antwerp, 1623, Sotheby's, London, 8 November 1995	89,500
9	Flemish single-manual harpsichord by Johan Daniel Dulken of Antwerp, 1755, Sotheby's, London, 27 March 1990	82,280
10	One-keyed ebony "Quantz" flute made for Frederick the Great of Prussia, *c.* 1750, Sotheby's, Baden-Baden, 10 October 1995	57,600

* Including 10 per cent buyer's premium, where appropriate

T O P 1 0

MOST EXPENSIVE ITEMS OF ROCK STARS' CLOTHING EVER SOLD AT AUCTION IN THE UK

	Item/sale	Price (£)*
1	Jimi Hendrix's orange floral velvet jacket, Bonham's, London, 18 August 1994	38,000
2	Elvis Presley's one-piece "Shooting Star" stage outfit, *c.* 1972, Phillips, London, 24 August 1988	28,600
3	John Lennon's black leather jacket, *c.* 1960–62, Christie's, London, 7 May 1992	24,200
4	Jimi Hendrix's peacock feather waistcoat, 1967–68, Sotheby's, London 13 September 1995	24,150
5	Jimi Hendrix's striped wool jacket, Bonham's, London, 18 August 1994	23,000
6	Four "super hero"-style costumes worn by glam rock group Kiss in the film *Kiss Meets the Phantom* (1978), Christie's, London, 14 May 1993	20,900

	Item/sale	Price (£)*
7	John Lennon's tan suede jacket, 1965, worn for the Beatles' *Rubber Soul* album cover, Christie's, London, 25 May 1995	20,250#
8	Jimi Hendrix's psychedelic "poppy" jacket, Bonham's, London, 18 August 1994	20,000
9	Jimi Hendrix's green velvet double-breasted jacket, Bonham's, London, 18 August 1994	19,000
10	John Lennon's "Happi" coat, 1966, given to him by Japanese Airlines during the Beatles' trip to Japan, Christie's, London, 7 September 1995	18,000#

* Including 10 per cent buyer's premium unless otherwise noted
# Including 12.5 per cent buyer's premium

JOHN LENNON'S ROCK 'N' ROLLS ROYCE
*The former Beatle's multi-coloured Phantom V became
the most expensive used car ever sold when it was acquired
by Jim Pattison, Chairman of the Expo '86 World Fair.*

T O P   1 0

MOST EXPENSIVE ITEMS OF POP MEMORABILIA EVER SOLD AT AUCTION*

	Item/sale	Price (£)#
1	John Lennon's 1965 Rolls-Royce Phantom V touring limousine, finished in psychedelic paintwork, Sotheby's, New York, 29 June 1985	1,768,462 ($2,299,000)
2	Acoustic guitar owned by David Bowie, Paul McCartney, and George Michael, Christie's, London, 18 May 1994	220,000
3	Jimi Hendrix's Fender Stratocaster electric guitar, Sotheby's, London, 25 April 1990	198,000
4	Paul McCartney's handwritten lyrics for *Getting Better*, 1967, Sotheby's, London, 14 September 1995	161,000
5	Buddy Holly's Gibson acoustic guitar, *c.* 1945, in a tooled leather case made by Holly, Sotheby's, New York, 23 June 1990	139,658 ($242,000)
6	John Lennon's 1970 Mercedes-Benz 600 Pullman four-door limousine, Christie's, London, 27 April 1989	137,500
7	Elvis Presley's 1963 Rolls-Royce Phantom V touring limousine, Sotheby's, London, 28 August 1986	110,000
8	Elvis Presley's 1942 Martin D-18 guitar (used to record his first singles, 1954–56), Red Baron Antiques, Atlanta, Georgia, 3 October 1991. The same guitar was resold by Christie's, London, 14 May 1993	106,825 ($180,000) 99,000
9	Charlie Parker's Grafton saxophone, Christie's, London, 8 September 1994	93,500
10	Recording of 16-year-old John Lennon singing at a 1957 church fête in Liverpool, Sotheby's, London, 15 September 1994	78,500

* *Excluding rock stars' clothing – see opposite*
\# *Including 10 per cent buyer's premium, where appropriate*

Pioneered particularly by Sotheby's in London, pop memorabilia has become big business – especially if it involves personal association with mega-stars such as the Beatles. A Rickenbacker guitar autographed by all four members was sold by Bonhams Tokyo on 22 March 1997 for £76,000/$118,788 and would be in 10th place if Charlie Parker's saxophone is eliminated as belonging to the jazz, rather than "pop", genre. The painted bass drumskin featured on the album sleeve of *Sgt. Pepper's Lonely Hearts Club Band* made £52,100/$80,755 at Sotheby's, London, on 15 September 1994, and even such items as the Liverpool birthplace of Ringo Starr, the barber's shop mentioned in the Beatles song *Penny Lane*, and a door from John Lennon's house have been offered for sale as artefacts from the archaeology of the Beatles. Latterly, items associated with Buddy Holly have become similarly collectable – his Fender Stratocaster electric guitar was sold at Sotheby's, New York, on 23 June 1990 for £63,481/$110,000, and his spectacles at the same sale for £30,000/$45,100. In some instances items have been re-auctioned by a sequence of celebrity owners to raise money for charities (the guitar at No. 2 in this list is in this category). Beyond this Top 10, high prices have also been paid for other musical instruments once owned by notable rock stars, such as a guitar belonging to John Entwistle of the Who and pianos that were formerly owned by Paul McCartney and John Lennon.

CLASSICAL & OPERA

WOLFGANG AMADEUS MOZART
Considered by many the greatest musical genius of all time, Mozart died at the age of just 35 after a lifetime devoted to composing and performing.

TOP 10

MOST PROLIFIC CLASSICAL COMPOSERS*

	Composer/nationality	Hours
1	Joseph Haydn (1732–1809), Austrian	340
2	George Handel (1685–1759), German/English	303
3	Wolfgang Amadeus Mozart (1656–91), Austrian	202
4	Johann Sebastian Bach (1685–1750), German	175
5	Franz Schubert (1797–1828), German	134
6	Ludwig van Beethoven (1770–1827), German	120
7	Henry Purcell (1659–95), English	116
8	Giuseppe Verdi (1813–1901), Italian	87
9	Antonín Dvořák (1841–1904), Czechoslovakian	79
10=	Franz Liszt (1811–86), Hungarian	76
10=	Peter Tchaikovsky (1840–93), Russian	76

* Based on a survey conducted by Classical Music *magazine*

TOP 10

LARGEST OPERA HOUSES IN THE WORLD

	Opera house	Location	seating	Capacity standing	Total
1	The Metropolitan Opera	New York, USA	3,800	265	4,065
2	Cincinnati Opera	Cincinnati, USA	3,630	–	3,630
3	Lyric Opera of Chicago	Chicago, USA	3,563	–	3,563
4	San Francisco Opera	San Francisco, USA	3,176	300	3,476
5	The Dallas Opera	Dallas, USA	3,420	–	3,420
6	Canadian Opera Company	Toronto, Canada	3,167	–	3,167
7	Los Angeles Music Center Opera	Los Angeles, USA	3,098	–	3,098
8	San Diego Opera	San Diego, USA	2,992	84	3,076
9	Seattle Opera	Seattle, USA	3,017	–	3,017
10	L'Opéra de Montréal	Montreal, Canada	2,874	–	2,874

TOP 10

OPERAS MOST FREQUENTLY PERFORMED AT THE ROYAL OPERA HOUSE, COVENT GARDEN, 1833–1996

	Opera	Composer	First performance	Total
1	*La Bohème*	Giacomo Puccini	2 October 1897	526
2	*Carmen*	Georges Bizet	27 May 1882	495
3	*Aïda*	Giuseppe Verdi	22 June 1876	471
4	*Faust*	Charles Gounod	18 July 1863	428
5	*Rigoletto*	Giuseppe Verdi	14 May 1853	423
6	*Don Giovanni*	Wolfgang Amadeus Mozart	17 April 1834	386
7	*Tosca*	Giacomo Puccini	12 July 1900	383
8	*La Traviata*	Giuseppe Verdi	25 May 1858	369
9	*Norma*	Vincenzo Bellini	12 July 1833	353
10	*Madama Butterfly*	Giacomo Puccini	10 July 1905	342

THE SYDNEY OPERA HOUSE

Plans to put Sydney on the world opera map began in 1957 when Danish architect Jørn Utzon won the international design competition. Although he later resigned from the project, the building was eventually constructed on Bennelong Point, Sydney Harbour, Australia. The first performance took place on 28 September 1973, but the Opera House was officially opened by Queen Elizabeth II on 20 October 1973. The art complex's distinctive sail-like roofs comprise 2,194 pre-cast concrete sections weighing 27,230 tonnes. Although considered controversial at the time, within 25 years the Opera House has become the internationally recognized symbol of its city.

25 YEARS AGO

THE 10

LAST WINNERS OF THE "BEST CLASSICAL ALBUM" GRAMMY AWARD

Year	Composer/title/conductor/orchestra
1996	Claude Debussy, *La Mer*, Pierre Boulez, Cleveland Orchestra
1995	Béla Bartók, *Concerto for Orchestra; Four Orchestral Pieces, Op. 12*, Pierre Boulez, Chicago Symphony Orchestra
1994	Béla Bartók, *The Wooden Prince*, Pierre Boulez, Chicago Symphony Orchestra and Chorus
1993	Gustav Mahler, *Symphony No. 9*, Leonard Bernstein, Berlin Philharmonic Orchestra
1992	Leonard Bernstein, *Candide*, Leonard Bernstein, London Symphony Orchestra
1991	Charles Ives, *Symphony No. 2 (and Three Short Works)*, Leonard Bernstein, New York Philharmonic Orchestra
1990	Béla Bartók, *Six String Quartets*, Emerson String Quartet
1989	Giuseppi Verdi, *Requiem and Operatic Choruses*, Robert Shaw, Atlanta Symphony Orchestra
1988	*Horowitz In Moscow*, Vladimir Horowitz
1987	*Horowitz: The Studio Recordings, New York*, Vladimir Horowitz

TOP 10

CLASSICAL ALBUMS OF ALL TIME IN THE UK

	Album	Artist
1	*The Essential Pavarotti*	Luciano Pavarotti
2	*The Three Tenors Concert*	Carreras, Domingo, Pavarotti
3	*Vivaldi: The Four Seasons*	Nigel Kennedy/ECO
4	*The Essential Mozart*	Various
5	*Essential Opera*	Various
6	*The Three Tenors – In Concert 1994*	Carreras, Domingo, Pavarotti, Mehta
7	*Mendelssohn/Bruch: Violin Concertos*	Nigel Kennedy/ECO
8	*Brahms: Violin Concerto*	Nigel Kennedy/LPO
9	*Górecki: Symphony No. 3*	London Sinfonia/David Zinman
10	*The Essential Pavarotti 2*	Luciano Pavarotti

Sales of classical music boomed at the end of the 1980s and into the 1990s. This was largely a result of a select band of superstars, such as the Three Tenors and young-gun violinist Nigel Kennedy.

THE 10

LAST WINNERS OF THE "BEST OPERA RECORDING" GRAMMY AWARD

Year	Composer/title/principal soloists
1996	Hector Berlioz, *Les Troyens*, Charles Dutoit
1995	Carlisle Floyd, *Susannah*, Jerry Hadley, Samuel Ramey, Cheryl Studer, Kenn Chester
1994	George Handel, *Semele*, Kathleen Battle, Marilyn Horne, Samuel Ramey, Sylvia McNair, Michael Chance
1993	Richard Strauss, *Die Frau Ohne Schatten*, Placido Domingo, Jose Van Dam, Hildegard Behrens
1992	Richard Wagner, *Götterdämmerung*, Hildegard Behrens, Ekkehard Wlashiha
1991	Richard Wagner, *Das Rheingold*, James Morris, Kurt Moll, Christa Ludwig
1990	Richard Wagner, *Die Walküre*, Gary Lakes, Jessye Norman, Kurt Moll
1989	Richard Wagner, *Lohengrin*, Placido Domingo, Jessye Norman, Eva Randova
1988	Richard Strauss, *Ariadne Auf Naxos*, Anna Tomowa-Sintow, Katleen Battle, Agnes Baltsa, Gary Lakes
1987	Leonard Bernstein, *Candide*, Ernie Mills, David Eisler, John Lankston

STAGE, SCREEN & BROADCASTING

TOP 10

LONGEST-RUNNING SHOWS ON BROADWAY

	Show	Performances
1	*A Chorus Line* (1975–90)	6,137
2	*Cats* (1982–)	6,081*
3	*Oh! Calcutta!* (1976–89)	5,959
4	*Les Misérables* (1987–)	4,183*
5	*The Phantom of the Opera* (1988–)	3,889*
6	*42nd Street* (1980–89)	3,486
7	*Grease* (1972–80)	3,388
8	*Fiddler on the Roof* (1964–72)	3,242
9	*Life with Father* (1939–47)	3,224
10	*Tobacco Road* (1933–41)	3,182

* *Still running; total at 30 April 1997*

TOP 10

LONGEST-RUNNING SHOWS IN THE UK

	Show	Performances
1	*The Mousetrap* (1952–)	18,357*
2	*No Sex, Please – We're British* (1971–81; 1982–86; 1986–87)	6,761
3	*Cats* (1981–)	6,527*
4	*Starlight Express* (1984–)	5,321*
5	*Les Misérables* (1985–)	4,599*
6	*The Phantom of the Opera* (1986–)	4,244*
7	*Oliver!* (1960–69)	4,125
8	*Oh! Calcutta!* (1970–80)	3,918
9	*Jesus Christ, Superstar* (1972–80)	3,357
10	*Evita* (1978–86)	2,900

* *Still running; total at 31 December 1996*

TOP 10

LONGEST-RUNNING COMEDIES IN THE UK

	Show	Performances
1	*No Sex, Please – We're British* (1971–80; 1982–86; 1986–87)	6,761
2	*Run for Your Wife* (1983–91)	2,638
3	*There's a Girl in My Soup* (1966–69; 1969–72)	2,547
4	*Pyjama Tops* (1969–75)	2,498
5	*Worm's Eye View* (1945–51)	2,245
6	*Boeing Boeing* (1962–63; 1965–67)	2,035
7	*Blithe Spirit* (1941–42; 1942; 1942–46)	1,997
8	*Dirty Linen* (1976–80)	1,667
9	*Reluctant Heroes* (1950–54)	1,610
10	*Seagulls over Sorrento* (1950–54; 1954)	1,551

TOP 10

LONGEST-RUNNING MUSICALS ON BROADWAY

	Show	Performances
1	*A Chorus Line* (1975–90)	6,137
2	*Cats* (1982–)	6,081*
3	*Les Misérables* (1987–)	4,183*
4	*The Phantom of the Opera* (1988–)	3,889*
5	*42nd Street* (1980–89)	3,486
6	*Grease* (1972–80)	3,388
7	*Fiddler on the Roof* (1964–72)	3,242
8	*Hello Dolly!* (1964–71)	2,844
9	*My Fair Lady* (1956–62)	2,717
10	*Annie* (1977–83)	2,377

* Still running; total at 30 April 1997

TOP 10

LONGEST-RUNNING MUSICALS IN THE UK

	Show	Performances
1	*Cats* (1981–)	6,527*
2	*Starlight Express* (1984–)	5,321*
3	*Les Misérables* (1985–)	4,599*
4	*The Phantom of the Opera* (1986–)	4,244*
5	*Oliver!* (1960–69)	4,125
6	*Jesus Christ, Superstar* (1972–80)	3,357
7	*Miss Saigon* (1989–)	3,083*
8	*Evita* (1978–86)	2,900
9	*The Sound of Music* (1961–67)	2,386
10	*Salad Days* (1954–60)	2,283

* Still running; total at 31 December 1996

On 12 May 1989 *Cats* became the longest continuously-running musical in British theatre history, and on 26 January 1996, with its 6,138th performance, became the longest-running musical of all time in either the West End or on Broadway, beating the previous record holder, *A Chorus Line*, which closed on Broadway in 1990 after a total of 6,137 performances.

LORD OF THE MUSICAL

As the lists on these pages testify, Andrew Lloyd Webber, who was born on 22 March 1948, has come to dominate the London and New York stages with some of the most successful and longest-running musicals of all time. His first musical was *Joseph and the Amazing Technicolor Dreamcoat*, which had its debut in 1968. This was followed by a dozen further productions, with *Cats*, *Starlight Express*, *The Phantom of the Opera*, *Jesus Christ, Superstar*, and *Evita* being numbered among the Top 10 musicals of all time in London. Lloyd Webber while he became the first person ever to have three musicals running simultaneously on both sides of the Atlantic. In 1997 he became a peer, taking the title Lord Lloyd-Webber of Sydmonton.

TOP 10

LONGEST-RUNNING NON-MUSICALS ON BROADWAY

	Show	Performances
1	*Oh! Calcutta!* (1976–89)	5,959
2	*Life with Father* (1939–47)	3,224
3	*Tobacco Road* (1933–41)	3,182
4	*Abie's Irish Rose* (1922–27)	2,327
5	*Deathtrap* (1978–82)	1,792
6	*Gemini* (1977–81)	1,788
7	*Harvey* (1944–49)	1,775
8	*Born Yesterday* (1946–49)	1,642
9	*Mary, Mary* (1961–64)	1,572
10	*Voice of the Turtle* (1943–48)	1,558

More than half the longest-running non-musical shows on Broadway began their runs before World War II; the others all predate the 1970s, before the long-running musical dominated the Broadway stage. Off Broadway, these records have all been broken by *The Drunkard*, which was performed at the Mart Theatre, Los Angeles, from 6 July 1933 to 6 September 1953, and then re-opened with a musical adapation and continued its run from 7 September 1953 until 17 October 1959.

ANDREW LLOYD WEBBER
In a career spanning 30 years, originally in partnership with lyricist Tim Rice, Andrew Lloyd Webber has composed the music for and produced some of the most successful shows in theatre history.

TOP 10

LONGEST-RUNNING NON-MUSICALS IN THE UK

	Show	Performances
1	*The Mousetrap* (1952–)	18,357*
2	*No Sex, Please – We're British* (1971–80; 1982–86; 1986–87)	6,761
3	*Oh! Calcutta!* (1970–80)	3,918
4	*Run for Your Wife* (1983–91)	2,638
5	*There's a Girl in My Soup* (1966–69; 1969–72)	2,547
6	*Pyjama Tops* (1969–75)	2,498
7	*Sleuth* (1970–75)	2,359
8	*Worm's Eye View* (1945–51)	2,245
9	*Boeing Boeing* (1962–63; 1965–67)	2,035
10	*Blithe Spirit* (1941–42; 1942; 1942–46)	1,997

* Still running; total at 31 December 1996

THE IMMORTAL BARD

THE 10

FIRST PLAYS BY SHAKESPEARE

	Play	Approx. year written
1	Titus Andronicus	1588–90
2	Love's Labour's Lost	1590
3	Henry VI, Parts I–III	1590–91
4=	The Comedy of Errors	1591
4=	Richard III	1591
4=	Romeo and Juliet	1591
7	The Two Gentlemen of Verona	1592–93
8	A Midsummer Night's Dream	1593–94
9	Richard II	1594
10	King John	1595

Precise dating of Shakespeare's plays is difficult. Contemporary records of early performances are rare, and only half the plays were published before Shakespeare died in 1616. Even these were much altered from the originals. It was only after 1623, when the "Folios" were published, that the complete works of Shakespeare were published progressively.

TOP 10

MOST DEMANDING SHAKESPEAREAN ROLES

	Role	Play	Lines
1	Hamlet	Hamlet	1,422
2	Falstaff	Henry IV, Parts I and II	1,178
3	Richard III	Richard III	1,124
4	Iago	Othello	1,097
5	Henry V	Henry V	1,025
6	Othello	Othello	860
7	Vincentio	Measure for Measure	820
8	Coriolanus	Coriolanus	809
9	Timon	Timon of Athens	795
10	Antony	Antony and Cleopatra	766

Hamlet's role comprises 11,610 words – over 36 per cent of the total number of lines spoken in the play, but if multiple plays are considered he is beaten by Falstaff who, as well as appearing in Henry IV, Parts I and II, also appears in The Merry Wives of Windsor in which he has 436 lines. His total of 1,614 lines would thus make him the most talkative of all Shakespeare's characters.

TOP 10

WORDS MOST USED BY SHAKESPEARE

	Word	Frequency
1	the	27,457
2	and	26,285
3	I	21,206
4	to	19,938
5	of	17,079
6	a	14,675
7	you	14,326
8	my	13,075
9	that	11,725
10	in	11,511

In his complete works, William Shakespeare wrote a total of 884,647 words – 118,406 lines comprising 31,959 separate speeches. He used a total vocabulary of 29,066 different words, some – such as "America" – appearing only once (The Comedy of Errors, III.ii). At the other end of the scale, this Top 10 accounts for all those words that he used on more than 10,000 occasions. Perhaps surprisingly, their relative frequency is not dissimilar to what we might encounter in modern usage.

10 ACTORS WHO HAVE PLAYED HAMLET

1 Sarah Bernhardt

French actress, appeared as Hamlet at the Adelphi Theatre, London, in 1899, and in a French silent film version in 1900.

2 Edwin Booth

American actor, opened as Hamlet in the USA in 1864 for a record run.

3 Kenneth Brannagh

Brannagh took the title role as well as directing the 1996 film of the play.

4 Richard Burton

British actor, appeared in the role at the Old Vic in 1953 and on film in 1964.

5 Richard Chamberlain

American actor previously best known for his TV role as Dr. Kildare, appeared in a television version of Hamlet in 1970.

6 Mel Gibson

American film actor, appeared in the 1991 film directed by Franco Zeffirelli.

7 Stacy Keach

American film actor, made his stage debut in 1964 in a New York production of Hamlet.

8 Laurence Olivier

British actor, appeared in both the title role and directed the 1948 film, the first British production to win a "Best Picture" Oscar.

9 Innokenti Smoktunovski

Russian actor, starred in a 1964 Soviet film of Hamlet, translated by Doctor Zhivago author Boris Pasternak.

10 Nicol Williamson

British actor, starred in the 1969 film, with pop singer Marianne Faithfull as Ophelia.

TOP 10

FILMS OF SHAKESPEARE'S PLAYS

1	Romeo and Juliet	1996
2	Romeo and Juliet	1968
3	Much Ado About Nothing	1993
4	Hamlet	1990
5	Henry V	1989
6	Hamlet	1996
7	Richard III	1995
8	Othello	1995
9	The Taming of the Shrew	1967
10	Hamlet	1948

The romantic appeal of Romeo and Juliet has ensured its place in this list, with, respectively, those directed by Baz Luhrmann and Franco Zeffirelli.

T O P 1 0

MOST-FILMED SHAKESPEARE PLAYS

1	*Hamlet*
2	*Romeo and Juliet*
3	*Macbeth*
4	*A Midsummer Night's Dream*
5	*Julius Caesar*
6	*Othello*
7	*Richard III*
8	*Henry V*
9	*The Merchant of Venice*
10	*Antony and Cleopatra*

Counting modern versions, including those in foreign languages, but discounting made-for-TV films, parodies and stories derived from the plays, it appears that *Hamlet* is the most-filmed of all Shakespeare's works, with some 70 releases to date, while *Romeo and Juliet* has been re-made on at least 40 occasions.

T O P 1 0

MOST PRODUCED PLAYS BY SHAKESPEARE*

	Play	Productions
1	*Twelfth Night*	74
2	*Hamlet*	73
3=	*As You Like It*	72
3=	*The Taming of the Shrew*	72
5	*Much Ado about Nothing*	68
6	*The Merchant of Venice*	67
7	*A Midsummer Night's Dream*	66
8	*Macbeth*	60
9	*The Merry Wives of Windsor*	58
10	*Romeo and Juliet*	55

* To 1 January 1997

This list is based on an analysis of Shakespearean plays produced between 31 December 1878 and 1 January 1997 at Stratford-upon-Avon and by the Royal Shakespeare Company in London; it therefore provides a reasonably accurate picture of his most popular plays.

T O P 1 0

LONGEST PLAYS BY SHAKESPEARE

	Play	Lines
1	*Hamlet*	3,901
2	*Richard III*	3,886
3	*Coriolanus*	3,820
4	*Cymbeline*	3,813
5	*Othello*	3,672
6	*Antony and Cleopatra*	3,630
7	*Troilus and Cressida*	3,576
8	*Henry VIII*	3,450
9	*Henry V*	3,368
10	*The Winter's Tale*	3,354

TO BE OR NOT TO BE, THAT IS THE QUESTION
Mel Gibson, of Mad Max *and* Lethal Weapon *fame, surprised his fans and critics alike with his masterful portrayal of Hamlet in the 1991 big-screen version of William Shakespeare's longest play. Hamlet is the most demanding of Shakespearean roles for an actor.*

FILM HITS & MISSES

In previous editions of The Top Ten of Everything, *the relative success of the films that appear in the lists was measured by the rental income earned by the US and Canadian distributors. However, while this remains a valid way of comparing the success of films over long periods of time, film has become an international medium, and nowadays many Hollywood films earn more outside the US than within it. The decision has therefore been taken to base the film lists on worldwide box-office income. This revision means that certain films that have gone on to achieve greater global than domestic success will appear at a higher ranking than in previous editions of* The Top Ten of Everything.

TOP 10

HIGHEST-GROSSING FILMS OF ALL TIME

	Film	Year	Total gross ($) USA	Overseas	World
1	Jurassic Park	1993	356,839,725	556,000,000	912,839,725
2	Independence Day	1996	306,153,456	491,800,000	797,953,456
3	The Lion King	1994	312,855,561	459,000,000	771,855,561
4	Star Wars	1977/97	459,095,451	281,000,000	740,095,451
5	E.T.: The Extra-Terrestrial	1982	399,804,539	301,600,000	701,404,539
6	Forrest Gump	1994	329,690,974	344,100,000	673,790,974
7	Home Alone	1990	285,016,000	248,000,000	533,016,000
8	Terminator 2: Judgement Day	1991	204,446,562	310,000,000	514,446,562
9	Ghost	1990	217,631,306	290,000,000	507,631,306
10	The Empire Strikes Back	1980/97	288,801,028	206,800,000	495,601,028

TOP 10

FILM SEQUELS OF ALL TIME

	Film series	Years
1	Star Wars/The Empire Strikes Back/Return of the Jedi	1977–97
2	Raiders of the Lost Ark/Indiana Jones and the Temple of Doom/Indiana Jones and the Last Crusade	1981–89
3	Batman /Batman Returns/Batman Forever	1989–95
4	Home Alone 1–2	1990–92
5	Star Trek I–VI/Generations/First Contact	1979–96
6	Jaws I–IV	1975–87
7	Beverly Hills Cop I–III	1984–94
8	Back to the Future I–III	1985–90
9	Die Hard 1–2/Die Hard: With a Vengeance	1988–95
10	Terminator/Terminator 2: Judgment Day	1984–91

Based on total earnings of the original film and all its sequels up to 1997, the *Star Wars* trilogy stands head and shoulders above the rest, having grossed more than $1.6 billion around the world. All the other films in this Top 10 have achieved global earnings of more than $500,000,000 each, and have made almost $9 billion between them.

TOP 10

FILM OPENINGS OF ALL TIME IN THE US

	Film	Release	Opening weekend gross ($)
1	Batman Forever	16 Jun 1995	52,784,000
2	Independence Day	3 Jul 1996	50,228,000
3	Jurassic Park	12 Jun 1993	50,159,000
4	Batman Returns	19 Jun 1992	47,721,000
5	Batman	23 Jun 1989	42,708,000
6	Twister	10 May 1996	41,059,000
7	The Lion King	15 Jun 1994	40,888,000
8	Ace Ventura: When Nature Calls	10 Nov 1995	37,804,000
9	Interview with the Vampire	11 Nov 1994	36,390,000
10	Star Wars: Special Edition	31 Jan 1997	35,907,000

FILM BLOCKBUSTERS OF 1973

Based on worldwide box office income, *The Exorcist* was the most successful film of 1973. This influential horror movie was nominated for "Best Picture" Oscar, but the award was won by the second commercial success of the year, *The Sting* – for his role in which Robert Redford was nominated as "Best Actor". *Live and Let Die*, the ninth James Bond film, was the third highest-earning film of the year, principally from its popularity outside the US. The film that ranked fourth among the year's high earners was George Lucas's *American Graffiti*, in which Harrison Ford made an early career appearance, heralding the beginning of the partnership that was to produce the successful *Star Wars* and *Indiana Jones* trilogies.

TOP 10

HIGHEST-GROSSING FILMS OF 1996 IN THE US

	Film	Box office gross ($)		Film	Box office gross ($)
1	Independence Day	306,153,456	6	Ransom	124,641,941
2	Twister	241,717,524	7	The Birdcage	123,939,840
3	Mission: Impossible	180,943,675	8	A Time to Kill	108,706,165
4	The Rock	134,067,443	9	Phenomenon	104,464,977
5	The Nutty Professor	128,810,418	10	101 Dalmatians	104,111,652

TOP 10

HIGHEST-GROSSING FILMS OF ALL TIME IN THE UK

	Film	Year	Approx. gross (£)
1	Jurassic Park	1993	47,100,000
2	Independence Day	1996	36,700,000
3	Four Weddings and a Funeral	1994	27,800,000
4	Ghost	1990	23,300,000
5	The Lion King	1994	23,100,000
6	Toy Story	1995	22,100,000
7	E.T.: The Extra Terrestrial	1983	21,700,000
8	Crocodile Dundee	1987	21,500,000
9	Mrs. Doubtfire	1994	21,200,000
10	Robin Hood: Prince of Thieves	1991	20,500,000

Inevitably, bearing inflation in mind, the top-grossing films of all time are releases from the 1980s and 1990s.

COSTLY COSTNER
With estimates varying from $150 to $175 million, Waterworld, *produced by and starring Kevin Costner, is believed to have been the most expensive film ever made, but its substantial earnings outside the US have rescued it from the status of "flop".*

TOP 10

MOST EXPENSIVE FILMS EVER MADE

	Film*	Year	Estimated cost ($)
1	Waterworld	1995	160,000,000
2	True Lies	1994	110,000,000
3	Cutthroat Island	1996	105,000,000
4	Inchon (US/Korea)	1981	102,000,000
5	War and Peace (USSR)	1967	100,000,000
6	Terminator 2: Judgment Day	1991	95,000,000
7	Total Recall	1990	85,000,000
8	The Last Action Hero	1993	82,500,000
9=	Batman Returns	1992	80,000,000
9=	Superman II	1980	80,000,000

* All US-made unless otherwise stated

TOP 10

BIGGEST FILM FLOPS OF ALL TIME

	Film	Year	Estimated loss ($)
1	Cutthroat Island	1995	94,000,000
2	The Adventures of Baron Münchhausen	1988	48,100,000
3	Ishtar	1987	47,300,000
4	Hudson Hawk	1991	47,000,000
5	Inchon	1981	44,100,000
6	The Cotton Club	1984	38,100,000
7	Santa Claus – The Movie	1985	37,000,000
8	Heaven's Gate	1980	34,200,000
9	Billy Bathgate	1991	33,000,000
10	Pirates	1986	30,300,000

FILMS OF THE DECADES

FILMS OF THE 1930s

1	Gone with the Wind*	1939
2	Snow White and the Seven Dwarfs	1937
3	The Wizard of Oz	1939
4	The Woman in Red	1935
5	King Kong	1933
6	San Francisco	1936
7=	Mr. Smith Goes to Washington	1939
7=	Lost Horizon	1937
7=	Hell's Angels	1930
10	Maytime	1937

* Winner of "Best Picture" Academy Award

Both *Gone with the Wind* and *Snow White and the Seven Dwarfs* have generated more income than any other pre-war film. However, if the income of *Gone with the Wind* was adjusted to allow for inflation in the period since its release, it could be regarded as the most successful film ever.

THE WONDERFUL WIZARD OF OZ
Although held to an honourable third place by blockbusters Gone with the Wind *and* Snow White and the Seven Dwarfs, The Wizard of Oz *was one of the most popular films of the 1930s.*

FILMS OF THE 1940s

1	Bambi	1942
2	Pinocchio	1940
3	Fantasia	1940
4	Cinderella	1949
5	Song of the South	1946
6	The Best Years of Our Lives*	1946
7	The Bells of St. Mary's	1945
8	Duel in the Sun	1946
9	Mom and Dad	1944
10	Samson and Delilah	1949

* Winner of "Best Picture" Academy Award

With the top four films of the decade classic Disney cartoons, the 1940s may truly be regarded as the "golden age" of the animated film. The genre was especially appealing in this era of colourful escapism after the drabness of the war years. The cumulative income of a selection of the Disney cartoons has increased as a result of their systematic re-release in the cinema and on video.

FILMS OF THE 1950s

1	Lady and the Tramp	1955
2	Peter Pan	1953
3	Ben-Hur*	1959
4	The Ten Commandments	1956
5	Sleeping Beauty	1959
6	Around the World in 80 Days*	1956
7=	The Robe	1953
7=	The Greatest Show on Earth*	1952
9	The Bridge on the River Kwai*	1957
10	Peyton Place	1957

* Winner of "Best Picture" Academy Award

While the popularity of animated films continued with *Lady and the Tramp*, *Peter Pan*, and *Sleeping Beauty*, the 1950s was outstanding as the decade of the "big" picture. Not only were many of the most successful films enormous in terms of cast and scale, but also the magnitude of the subjects they tackled. Three of these very popular films were major biblical epics.

FILMS OF THE 1960s

1	101 Dalmatians	1961
2	The Jungle Book	1967
3	The Sound of Music*	1965
4	Thunderball	1965
5	Goldfinger	1964
6	Doctor Zhivago	1965
7	You Only Live Twice	1967
8	The Graduate	1968
9	Mary Poppins	1964
10	Butch Cassidy and the Sundance Kid	1969

* Winner of "Best Picture" Academy Award

During the 1960s the growth in popularity of soundtrack record albums and featured singles often matched the commercial success of the films from which they were derived. Four of these Top 10 films of the decade were avowed musicals, while all – with the possible exception of *Thunderball* – had a high musical content.

TOP 10

FILMS OF THE 1970s

1	Star Wars	1977/97
2	Jaws	1975
3	Close Encounters of the Third Kind	1977/80
4	Moonraker	1979
5	The Spy Who Loved Me	1977
6	The Exorcist	1973
7	The Sting*	1973
8	Grease	1978
9	The Godfather*	1972
10	Saturday Night Fever	1977

* Winner of "Best Picture" Academy Award

In the 1970s the arrival of the two prodigies, Steven Spielberg and George Lucas, set the scene for the high-adventure blockbusters which have continued to dominate films ever since. Lucas directed his first science-fiction film, *THX 1138*, in 1970 and went on to write and direct *Star Wars*. Spielberg directed *Jaws* and wrote and directed *Close Encounters of the Third Kind*.

TOP 10

FILMS OF THE 1980s

1	E.T.: The Extra-Terrestrial	1982
2	Indiana Jones and the Last Crusade	1989
3	Batman	1989
4	Rain Man	1988
5	Return of the Jedi	1983
6	Raiders of the Lost Ark	1981
7	The Empire Strikes Back	1980
8	Who Framed Roger Rabbit?	1988
9	Back to the Future	1985
10	Top Gun	1986

The 1980s was clearly the decade of the adventure film, with George Lucas and Steven Spielberg continuing to assert their control of Hollywood, dominating this Top 10 between them, with Lucas as producer of nos. 5 and 7 and Spielberg director of 1, 2, 6, 8, and 9. Paradoxically, despite their colossal box office success, they consistently failed to match this with an Academy Award for "Best Picture".

TOP 10

FILMS OF THE 1990s TO DATE

1	Jurassic Park	1993
2	Independence Day	1996
3	The Lion King	1994
4	Forrest Gump*	1994
5	Home Alone	1990
6	Terminator 2: Judgement Day	1991
7	Ghost	1990
8	Twister	1996
9	Aladdin	1992
10	Pretty Woman	1990

* Winner of "Best Picture" Academy Award

All 10 of these films of the present decade have earned more than $400,000,000 each around the world, as have four further films, *Mission: Impossible*, *Dances with Wolves*, *The Bodyguard*, and *Mrs. Doubtfire*. *Jurassic Park* has earned more than $900,000,000 at the box office.

ALMOST A VICTORY
The colossal success of Independence Day, *in which the Earth's conquest by aliens is averted, makes it a close second to the 1990s' top money earner,* Jurassic Park.

FILM GENRES

TOP 10

COP FILMS

1	Die Hard with a Vengeance	1995
2	The Fugitive	1993
3	Basic Instinct	1992
4	Se7en	1995
5	Beverly Hills Cop	1984
6	Beverly Hills Cop II	1987
7	Speed	1994
8	Heat	1995
9	Lethal Weapon 2	1989
10	Lethal Weapon 3	1993

Although films in which one of the central characters is a policeman have never been among the most successful films of all time, many have earned respectable amounts at the box office. Both within and outside this Top 10, they are divided between those with a comic slant, such as the two *Beverly Hills Cop* films, and darker police thrillers, such as *Basic Instinct*. Films featuring FBI and CIA agents have been excluded from the reckoning, hence eliminating blockbusters such as *The Silence of the Lambs*.

TOP 10

SCIENCE-FICTION AND FANTASY FILMS

1	Jurassic Park	1993
2	Independence Day	1996
3	Star Wars	1977
4	E.T.: The Extra-Terrestrial	1982
5	Terminator 2: Judgement Day	1991
6	Ghost	1990
7	The Empire Strikes Back	1980
8	Return of the Jedi	1983
9	Batman	1989
10	Back to the Future	1985

The first seven films are also the all-time Top 10, and all 10 among the 33 most successful films ever, having earned over $348,000,000 each from worldwide box office income. Four further films in this genre have each earned more than $200,000,000: *Batman Forever* (1995), *Close Encounters of the Third Kind* (1977/80), *Ghostbusters* (1984), and *Batman Returns* (1992).

TOP 10

WAR FILMS

1	Schindler's List	1993
2	Platoon	1986
3	Good Morning, Vietnam	1987
4	Apocalypse Now	1979
5	M*A*S*H	1970
6	Patton	1970
7	The Deer Hunter	1978
8	Full Metal Jacket	1987
9	Midway	1976
10	The Dirty Dozen	1967

This list excludes films with military, rather than war, themes, such as *A Few Good Men* (1992), *The Hunt for Red October* (1990), *Crimson Tide* (1995), and *An Officer and a Gentleman* (1982), which would have been in the top five; and *Top Gun* (1986), which would top the list, just beating *Rambo: First Blood 2* (1985), a post-Vietnam action film.

TOP 10

COMEDY FILMS

1	Forrest Gump	1994
2	Home Alone	1990
3	Ghost	1990
4	Pretty Woman	1990
5	Mrs. Doubtfire	1993
6	Flintstones	1995
7	Who Framed Roger Rabbit	1988
8	Beverly Hills Cop	1984
9	Beverly Hills Cop II	1987
10	Look Who's Talking	1989

Forrest Gump accelerated to the head of this list as the most succesful comedy of all time. The two *Beverly Hills Cop* films are regarded by some critics and film buffs as "action thrillers" rather than comedies. If they are excluded, Nos. 9 and 10 become *Coming to America* (1988) and *Home Alone 2: Lost in New York* (1992).

TOP 10

DISASTER FILMS

1	Twister	1996
2	Die Hard with a Vengeance	1995
3	Apollo 13	1995
4	Outbreak	1995
5	Die Hard	1988
6	Die Hard 2	1990
7	The Towering Inferno	1975
8	Airport	1970
9	The Poseidon Adventure	1972
10	Earthquake	1974

Disasters involving blazing buildings, natural disasters such as earthquakes, tidal waves, train and air crashes, sinking ships, and terrorist attacks have long been a staple of Hollywood films – and now, with *Twister*, *Apollo 13*, and *Outbreak*, tornadoes, exploding space capsules, and killer viruses may be added to the genre.

TOP 10

FILMS IN WHICH THE STAR WEARS DRAG

	Film/year	Star
1	Mrs. Doubtfire (1994)	Robin Williams
2	The Bird Cage (1996)	Nathan Lane
3	Tootsie (1983)	Dustin Hoffman
4	Under Siege (1992)	Gary Busey
5	The Rocky Horror Picture Show (1974)	Tim Curry
6	The Crying Game (1993)	Jaye Davidson
7	Psycho (1960)	Anthony Perkins
8	Dressed to Kill (1980)	Michael Caine
9	Some Like It Hot (1959)	Tony Curtis/ Jack Lemmon
10	La Cage aux Folles (1979)	Michel Serrault

TOP 10

WESTERN FILMS

1	Dances with Wolves	1990
2	Maverick	1994
3	Unforgiven	1992
4	Butch Cassidy and the Sundance Kid	1969
5	Jeremiah Johnson	1972
6	How the West Was Won	1962
7	Young Guns	1988
8	Young Guns II	1990
9	Pale Rider	1985
10=	Bronco Billy	1980
10=	Little Big Man	1970

Clint Eastwood is in the unusual position of directing and starring in a film that has forced another of his own films out of this Top 10, since the success of *Unforgiven* has ejected *The Outlaw Josey Wales* (1976). Although it has a Western setting, *Back to the Future, Part III* (1990) is essentially a science-fiction film; if included, it would be in 5th position. According to some criteria, *The Last of the Mohicans* (1992) qualifies as a Western; if included, it would be at No. 6.

TOP 10

HORROR FILMS

1	Jurassic Park	1993	6	The Exorcist	1973
2	Jaws	1975	7	Mary Shelley's Frankenstein	1994
3	Interview With the Vampire	1994	8	The Amityville Horror	1979
4	Jaws II	1978	9	Aliens	1986
5	Bram Stoker's Dracula	1992	10	Poltergeist	1982

THE BOND DYNASTY
Pierce Brosnan (right) is the sixth, and current, actor to play James Bond on film. Sean Connery in Dr. No *was the first, followed by David Niven in* Casino Royale. *George Luzenby played Bond only once, in* On Her Majesty's Secret Service. *He was followed by Roger Moore, who played Bond in seven films before handing over to Timothy Dalton in 1987.*

TOP 10

JAMES BOND FILMS

	Film/year	Bond actor
1	Goldeneye (1995)	Pierce Brosnan
2	Moonraker (1979)	Roger Moore
3	Never Say Never Again (1983)	Sean Connery
4	For Your Eyes Only (1981)	Roger Moore
5	The Living Daylights (1987)	Timothy Dalton
6	The Spy Who Loved Me (1977)	Roger Moore
7	Octopussy (1983)	Roger Moore
8	Licence to Kill (1990)	Timothy Dalton
9	A View to a Kill (1985)	Roger Moore
10	Thunderball (1965)	Sean Connery

OSCAR WINNERS – FILMS

GOLDEN IDOL
Standing 34-cm (13½-in) high, the gold-plated "Oscar" was reputedly named for his resemblance to a film librarian's Uncle Oscar.

FILMS NOMINATED FOR THE MOST OSCARS

(Oscar® is a registered trade mark of the Academy of Motion Picture Arts and Sciences)

	Film	Year	Awards	Nominations
1	*All about Eve*	1950	6	14
2=	*Gone with the Wind*	1939	8	13
2=	*From Here to Eternity*	1953	8	13
2=	*Mary Poppins*	1964	5	13
2=	*Who's Afraid of Virginia Woolf?*	1966	5	13
2=	*Forrest Gump*	1994	6	13
7=	*Mrs. Miniver*	1942	6	12
7=	*The Song of Bernadette*	1943	4	12
7=	*Johnny Belinda*	1948	1	12
7=	*A Streetcar Named Desire*	1951	4	12
7=	*On the Waterfront*	1954	8	12
7=	*Ben-Hur*	1959	11	12
7=	*Becket*	1964	1	12
7=	*My Fair Lady*	1964	8	12
7=	*Reds*	1981	3	12
7=	*Dances with Wolves*	1990	7	12
7=	*Schindler's List*	1993	7	12
7=	*The English Patient*	1996	9	12

While *Johnny Belinda* and *Becket* at least had the consolation of winning once out of their 12 nominations, both *The Turning Point* (1977) and *The Color Purple* (1985) suffered the ignominy of receiving 11 nominations without a single win.

FILMS TO WIN MOST OSCARS

	Film	Year	Awards
1	*Ben-Hur*	1959	11
2	*West Side Story*	1961	10
3=	*Gigi*	1958	9
3=	*The Last Emperor*	1987	9
3=	*The English Patient*	1996	9
6=	*Gone with the Wind*	1939	8
6=	*From Here to Eternity*	1953	8
6=	*On the Waterfront*	1954	8
6=	*My Fair Lady*	1964	8
6=	*Cabaret*	1972	8
6=	*Gandhi*	1982	8
6=	*Amadeus*	1984	8

THE STORY OF "OSCAR"

The Academy of Motion Picture Arts and Sciences, founded 4 May 1927, proposed improving the image of the film industry by issuing "awards for merit or distinction". The award took the form of a statuette – a gold-plated, nude male figure clutching a sword and standing on a reel of film with five holes, each representing a branch of the Academy. It was simply called "the statuette" until 1931, when Academy librarian Margaret Herrick commented, "It looks like my Uncle Oscar!". The name stuck as a universally recognized symbol of excellence in film-making.

HIGHEST-EARNING "BEST PICTURE" OSCAR WINNERS

1	*Forrest Gump*	1994
2	*Dances with Wolves*	1990
3	*Rain Man*	1988
4	*Schindler's List*	1993
5	*Braveheart*	1995
6	*Gone with the Wind*	1939
7	*The Sound of Music*	1965
8	*The Sting*	1973
9	*The Godfather*	1972
10	*Platoon*	1986

THE 10

"BEST PICTURE" OSCAR WINNERS OF THE 1930s

1930	All Quiet on the Western Front
1931	Cimarron
1932	Grand Hotel
1933	Cavalcade
1934	It Happened One Night*
1935	Mutiny on the Bounty
1936	The Great Ziegfeld
1937	The Life of Emile Zola
1938	You Can't Take It with You
1939	Gone with the Wind

* Winner of Oscars for "Best Director", "Best Actor", "Best Actress", and "Best Screenplay"

The first Academy Awards, now popularly known as the Oscars, were presented at a ceremony at the Hollywood Roosevelt Hotel on 16 May 1929, and were for films released in the period 1927–28. A second ceremony held at the Ambassador Hotel on 31 October of the same year was for films released in the period 1928–29, and was won by Broadway Melody (MGM), the first talkie and the first musical to win an Oscar.

THE 10

"BEST PICTURE" OSCAR WINNERS OF THE 1940s

1940	Rebecca
1941	How Green Was My Valley
1942	Mrs. Miniver
1943	Casablanca
1944	Going My Way
1945	The Lost Weekend
1946	The Best Years of Our Lives
1947	Gentleman's Agreement
1948	Hamlet
1949	All the King's Men

Several of the "Best Picture" winners are now regarded as film classics, many critics numbering Casablanca among the greatest films of all time. Mrs. Miniver (which won a total of six Oscars) and The Best Years of Our Lives (seven Oscars) were both directed by William Wyler and reflected the concerns of wartime and post-war life respectively. How Green Was My Valley and Going My Way each won five Oscars. Rebecca and Hamlet both starred Laurence Olivier, who also directed the latter, winning not only the "Best Picture" award but also that for "Best Actor".

THE 10

"BEST PICTURE" OSCAR WINNERS OF THE '950s

1950	All about Eve
1951	An American in Paris
1952	The Greatest Show on Earth
1953	From Here to Eternity
1954	On the Waterfront
1955	Marty
1956	Around the World in 80 Days
1957	The Bridge on the River Kwai
1958	Gigi
1959	Ben-Hur

The first film of the 1950s, All about Eve, received the most nominations (14), while the last, Ben-Hur, won the most (11).

THE 10

"BEST PICTURE" OSCAR WINNERS OF THE 1980s

1980	Ordinary People
1981	Chariots of Fire
1982	Gandhi
1983	Terms of Endearment
1984	Amadeus
1985	Out of Africa
1986	Platoon
1987	The Last Emperor
1988	Rain Man
1989	Driving Miss Daisy

The winners of "Best Picture" Oscars during the 1990s are: 1990, Dances with Wolves; 1991, The Silence of the Lambs – which also won Oscars for "Best Director", "Best Actor", "Best Actress", and "Best Screenplay"; 1992, Unforgiven; 1993, Schindler's List – which also won Oscars for "Best Director", "Best Adapted Screenplay", "Best Film Editing", "Best Art Direction", "Best Cinematography", and "Best Original Score"; 1994, Forrest Gump; which also won Oscars in a total of five other categories; 1995, Braveheart; and 1996, The English Patient.

THE 10

"BEST PICTURE" OSCAR WINNERS OF THE 1960s

1960	The Apartment
1961	West Side Story
1962	Lawrence of Arabia
1963	Tom Jones
1964	My Fair Lady
1965	The Sound of Music
1966	A Man for All Seasons
1967	In the Heat of the Night
1968	Oliver!
1969	Midnight Cowboy

The Apartment (1960) was the last black-and-white film to receive a "Best Picture" Oscar until Steven Spielberg's Schindler's List in 1993, which won seven Oscars.

THE 10

"BEST PICTURE" OSCAR WINNERS OF THE 1970s

1970	Patton
1971	The French Connection
1972	The Godfather
1973	The Sting
1974	The Godfather, Part II
1975	One Flew over the Cuckoo's Nest*
1976	Rocky
1977	Annie Hall
1978	The Deer Hunter
1979	Kramer vs. Kramer

* Winner of Oscars for "Best Director", "Best Actor", "Best Actress", and "Best Screenplay"

OSCAR WINNERS – STARS

"BEST ACTOR IN A SUPPORTING ROLE" OSCAR WINNERS OF THE 1980s

Year	Actor	Film
1980	Timothy Hutton	*Ordinary People*
1981	John Gielgud	*Arthur*
1982	Louis Gossett, Jr.	*An Officer and a Gentleman*
1983	Jack Nicholson	*Terms of Endearment*
1984	Haing S. Ngor	*The Killing Fields*
1985	Don Ameche	*Cocoon*
1986	Michael Caine	*Hannah and Her Sisters*
1987	Sean Connery	*The Untouchables*
1988	Kevin Kline	*A Fish Called Wanda*
1989	Denzel Washington	*Glory*

There have only ever been three occasions when the same film has received three nominations for "Best Supporting Actor": *On the Waterfront*, *The Godfather*, and *The Godfather, Part II*.

OLDEST OSCAR-WINNING ACTORS

	Actor/actress	Award/film	Year	Age*
1	Jessica Tandy	"Best Actress" (*Driving Miss Daisy*)	1989	80
2	George Burns	"Best Supporting Actor" (*The Sunshine Boys*)	1975	80
3	Melvyn Douglas	"Best Supporting Actor" (*Being There*)	1979	79
4	John Gielgud	"Best Supporting Actor" (*Arthur*)	1981	77
5	Don Ameche	"Best Supporting Actor" (*Cocoon*)	1985	77
6	Peggy Ashcroft	"Best Supporting Actress" (*A Passage to India*)	1984	77
7	Henry Fonda	"Best Actor" (*On Golden Pond*)	1981	76
8	Katharine Hepburn	"Best Actress" (*On Golden Pond*)	1981	74
9	Edmund Gwenn	"Best Supporting Actor" (*Miracle on 34th Street*)	1947	72
10	Ruth Gordon	"Best Supporting Actress" (*Rosemary's Baby*)	1968	72

* *At time of Award ceremony; those of apparently identical age have been ranked according to their precise age in days at the time of the ceremony*

Among those senior citizens who received nominations but did not win Oscars is Ralph Richardson, who was nominated as "Best Supporting Actor" for his role in *Greystoke: The Legend of Tarzan* (1984) at the age of 82. Eva Le Gallienne was the same age when she was nominated as "Best Supporting Actress" for her part in *Resurrection* (1980). Outside the four acting categories, the oldest director to be nominated for a "Best Director" Oscar was John Huston, aged 79 at the time of his nomination for *Prizzi's Honor* (1985), and the oldest winner was George Cukor for *My Fair Lady* (1964), when he was aged 65.

"BEST ACTRESS IN A SUPPORTING ROLE" OSCAR WINNERS OF THE 1980s

Year	Actress	Film
1980	Mary Steenburgen	*Melvin and Howard*
1981	Maureen Stapleton	*Reds*
1982	Jessica Lange	*Tootsie*
1983	Linda Hunt	*The Year of Living Dangerously*
1984	Peggy Ashcroft	*A Passage to India*
1985	Anjelica Huston	*Prizzi's Honor*
1986	Diane Wiest	*Hannah and Her Sisters*
1987	Olympia Dukakis	*Moonstruck*
1988	Geena Davis	*The Accidental Tourist*
1989	Brenda Fricker	*My Left Foot*

Only one film has received three nominations for "Best Supporting Actress" – Diane Cilento, Dame Edith Evans, and Joyce Redman for *Tom Jones*. The winners during the 1990s are: 1990 Whoopi Goldberg for *Ghost*; 1991 Mercedes Ruehl for *The Fisher King*; 1992 Marisa Tomei for *My Cousin Vinny*; 1993 Anna Paquin for *The Piano*; 1994 Dianne Wiest for *Bullets Over Broadway*; 1995 Mira Sorvino for the film *Mighty Aphrodite*; and 1996 Juliette Binoche for *The English Patient*.

DENZEL WASHINGTON
Denzel Washington's Oscar-winning career spans films from Glory, *to* Cry Freedom, *to* Much Ado About Nothing.

YOUNGEST OSCAR-WINNING ACTORS

	Actor/actress	Award/film (where specified)	Year	Age
1	Shirley Temple	Special Award – outstanding contribution during 1934	1934	6
2	Margaret O'Brien	Special Award (*Meet Me in St. Louis*)	1944	8
3	Vincent Winter	Special Award (*The Little Kidnappers*)	1954	8
4	Jon Whitely	Special Award (*The Little Kidnappers*)	1954	9
5	Ivan Jandl	Special Award (*The Search*)	1948	9
6	Tatum O'Neal	Best Supporting Actress (*Paper Moon*)	1973	10
7	Anna Paquin	Best Supporting Actress (*The Piano*)	1993	11
8	Claude Jarman, Jr.	Special Award (*The Yearling*)	1946	12
9	Bobby Driscoll	Special Award (*The Window*)	1949	13
10	Hayley Mills	Special Award (*Pollyanna*)	1960	13

CHILD STAR
After winning an Oscar at the age of six, Shirley Temple's film career faded during the 1940s. In 1968 she found a new role as a diplomat, first with the UN and later as a US ambassador.

"BEST ACTOR" OSCAR WINNERS OF THE 1980s

Year	Actor	Film
1980	Robert De Niro	*Raging Bull*
1981	Henry Fonda	*On Golden Pond* *
1982	Ben Kingsley	*Gandhi* #
1983	Robert Duvall	*Tender Mercies*
1984	F. Murray Abraham	*Amadeus* #
1985	William Hurt	*Kiss of the Spider Woman*
1986	Paul Newman	*The Color of Money*
1987	Michael Douglas	*Wall Street*
1988	Dustin Hoffman	*Rain Man* #
1989	Daniel Day-Lewis	*My Left Foot*

* Winner of "Best Actress" Oscar   #Winner of "Best Picture" Oscar

The "Best Actor" Oscar winners of the 1990s to date are: 1990 Jeremy Irons for *Reversal of Fortune*; 1991 Anthony Hopkins for *The Silence of the Lambs* (which also won "Best Picture" and "Best Actress"); 1992 Al Pacino for *Scent of a Woman*; 1993 Tom Hanks for *Philadelphia* – who also won the award in 1994 for *Forrest Gump* (also the winner of "Best Picture" Oscar); 1995 Nicolas Cage for *Leaving Las Vegas*; and 1996 Geoffrey Rush for *Shine*. Hanks's achievement in winning the award in two consecutive years is unique in Oscar history. Only four other actors have ever won twice: Marlon Brando (1954 and 1972), Gary Cooper (1941 and 1952), Dustin Hoffman (1977 and 1988), and Spencer Tracy (1937 and 1938).

"BEST ACTRESS" OSCAR WINNERS OF THE 1980s

Year	Actress	Film
1980	Sissy Spacek	*The Coal Miner's Daughter*
1981	Katharine Hepburn	*On Golden Pond* *
1982	Meryl Streep	*Sophie's Choice*
1983	Shirley MacLaine	*Terms of Endearment* #
1984	Sally Field	*Places in the Heart*
1985	Geraldine Page	*The Trip to Bountiful*
1986	Marlée Matlin	*Children of a Lesser God*
1987	Cher	*Moonstruck*
1988	Jodie Foster	*The Accused*
1989	Jessica Tandy	*Driving Miss Daisy* #

* Winner of "Best Actor" Oscar   #Winner of "Best Picture" Oscar

As with the "Best Actor" award, only one actress has ever won in consecutive years – Katharine Hepburn in 1967 and 1968. A further 10 have won twice: Ingrid Bergman, Bette Davis, Olivia De Havilland, Sally Field, Jane Fonda, Jodie Foster, Glenda Jackson, Vivien Leigh, Luise Rainer, and Elizabeth Taylor. The winners of "Best Actress" Oscars during the 1990s are as follows: 1990 Kathy Bates for *Misery*; 1991 Jodie Foster for *The Silence of the Lambs* (also the winner of "Best Picture" and "Best Actor" Oscars); 1992 Emma Thompson for *Howard's End*; 1993 Holly Hunter for *The Piano*; 1994 Jessica Lange for *Blue Sky*; 1995 Susan Sarandon for *Dead Man Walking*; and 1996 Frances McDormand for *Fargo*.

AND THE WINNER IS . . .

T H E 1 0

FIRST WINNERS OF THE BAFTA BEST FILM AWARD

Year	Film	Country of origin
1947	*The Best Years of Our Lives*	USA
1948	*Hamlet*	UK
1949	*Bicycle Thieves*	Italy
1950	*All about Eve*	USA
1951	*La Ronde*	France
1952	*The Sound Barrier*	UK
1953	*Jeux Interdits*	France
1954	*Le Salaire de la Peur*	France
1955	*Richard III*	UK
1956	*Gervaise*	France

T H E 1 0

LAST WINNERS OF THE BAFTA BEST FILM AWARD

Year	Film	Country of origin
1996	*The English Patient*	UK
1995	*Sense and Sensibility*	UK
1994	*Four Weddings and a Funeral*	UK
1993	*Schindler's List*	USA
1992	*Howards End*	UK
1991	*The Commitments*	USA/UK
1990	*Goodfellas*	USA
1989	*Dead Poets Society*	USA
1988	*The Last Emperor*	Italy/UK/China
1987	*Jean de Florette*	France

T H E 1 0

FIRST WINNERS OF THE CANNES BEST FILM AWARD

Year	Film	Country of origin
1949	*The Third Man*	UK
1951	*Miracle in Milan* and *Miss Julie*	Italy* Sweden
1952	*Othello* and *Two Cents Worth of Hope*	Morocco* Italy
1953	*Wages of Fear*	France
1954	*Gates of Hell*	Japan
1955	*Marty*	USA
1956	*World of Silence*	France
1957	*Friendly Persuasion*	USA
1958	*The Cranes Are Flying*	USSR

* *Prize shared*

Although the Cannes Film Festival was established in 1939, World War II delayed its inaugural ceremony until 1946. In that year and 1947 there was no single "Best Film" prize, several films being honoured jointly, including such unlikely bedfellows as David Lean's *Brief Encounter* and Walt Disney's *Dumbo*. The first production to win the coveted Palme d'Or (Golden Palm) was the British film *The Third Man* (1949). There was no Festival in 1948 or 1950.

T H E 1 0

LAST WINNERS OF THE CANNES *PALME D'OR* FOR BEST FILM

Year	Film	Country of origin
1997	*The Eel* *The Taste of Cherries*	Japan Iran
1996	*Secrets and Lies*	UK
1995	*Underground*	Yugoslavia
1994	*Pulp Fiction*	USA
1993	*Farewell My Concubine/* *The Piano*	China Australia

Year	Film	Country of origin
1992	*Best Intentions*	Sweden
1991	*Barton Fink*	USA
1990	*Wild at Heart*	USA
1989	*sex, lies, and videotape*	USA
1988	*Pelle the Conqueror*	Denmark

T H E 1 0

FIRST WINNERS OF THE BAFTA BEST DIRECTOR AWARD

Year	Director	Film	Country of origin
1968	Mike Nichols	*The Graduate*	USA
1969	John Schlesinger	*Midnight Cowboy*	USA
1970	George Roy Hill	*Butch Cassidy and the Sundance Kid*	USA
1971	John Schlesinger	*Sunday, Bloody Sunday*	UK
1972	Bob Fosse	*Cabaret*	USA
1973	François Truffaut	*Day for Night*	France
1974	Roman Polanski	*Chinatown*	USA
1975	Stanley Kubrick	*Barry Lyndon*	UK
1976	Milos Forman	*One Flew over the Cuckoo's Nest*	USA
1977	Woody Allen	*Annie Hall*	USA

T H E 1 0

LAST WINNERS OF THE BAFTA BEST DIRECTOR AWARD

Year	Director	Film	Country of origin
1996	Joel Cohen	*Fargo*	USA
1995	Michael Radford	*Il Postino*	Italy
1994	Mike Newell	*Four Weddings and a Funeral*	UK
1993	Steven Spielberg	*Schindler's List*	USA
1992	Robert Altman	*The Player*	USA
1991	Alan Parker	*The Commitments*	USA/UK
1990	Martin Scorsese	*Goodfellas*	USA
1989	Kenneth Branagh	*Henry V*	UK
1988	Louis Malle	*Au Revoir les Enfants*	France
1987	Oliver Stone	*Platoon*	USA

THE 10

FIRST WINNERS OF THE BAFTA BEST ACTOR AWARD

Year	Actor	Film	Country of film's origin
1968	Spencer Tracy	*Guess Who's Coming to Dinner*	USA
1969	Dustin Hoffman	*Midnight Cowboy/*	USA
		John and Mary	USA
1970	Robert Redford	*Tell Them Willie Boy Is Here/*	USA
		Butch Cassidy and the Sundance Kid/	USA
		Downhill Racer	USA
1971	Peter Finch	*Sunday, Bloody Sunday*	UK
1972	Gene Hackman	*The French Connection/*	USA
		The Poseidon Adventure	USA
1973	Walter Matthau	*Pete 'n Tillie/*	USA
		Charley Varrick	USA
1974	Jack Nicholson	*The Last Detail/*	USA
		Chinatown	USA
1975	Al Pacino	*The Godfather Part II/*	USA
		Dog Day Afternoon	USA
1976	Jack Nicholson	*One Flew Over the Cuckoo's Nest*	USA
1977	Peter Finch	*Network*	USA

Other than Peter Finch's double, British actors made a poor showing in the early years of the BAFTA "Best Actor" award. However, the balance was redressed in the early 1980s with wins for John Hurt in *The Elephant Man* (1980), Ben Kingsley in *Gandhi* (1982), and Michael Caine in *Educating Rita* (1983).

THE 10

FIRST WINNERS OF THE BAFTA BEST ACTRESS AWARD

Year	Actress	Film	Country of film's origin
1968	Katharine Hepburn	*Guess Who's Coming to Dinner/*	USA
		The Lion in Winter	UK
1969	Maggie Smith	*The Prime of Miss Jean Brodie*	UK
1970	Katharine Ross	*Tell Them Willie Boy Is Here/*	USA
		Butch Cassidy and the Sundance Kid	USA
1971	Glenda Jackson	*Sunday, Bloody Sunday*	UK
1972	Liza Minnelli	*Cabaret*	USA
1973	Stephane Audrane	*The Discreet Charm of the Bourgeoisie/*	France/Spain/Italy
		Just Before Nightfall	France
1974	Joanne Woodward	*Summer Wishes, Winter Dreams*	USA
1975	Ellen Burstyn	*Alice Doesn't Live Here Anymore*	USA
1976	Louise Fletcher	*One Flew over the Cuckoo's Nest*	USA
1977	Diane Keaton	*Annie Hall*	USA

Just as US-made films dominated the early years of the BAFTA Awards, so American actresses scooped a disproportionate number of the prizes for "Best Actress", a situation that has been reversed as British actresses and British-made films have flourished in recent years. Maggie Smith has won four awards, and Katherine Hepburn, Jane Fonda, and Emma Thompson have each won on two occasions.

THE 10

LAST WINNERS OF THE BAFTA BEST ACTOR AWARD

Year	Actor	Film	Country of film's origin
1996	Geoffrey Rush	*Shine*	Australia
1995	Nigel Hawthorne	*The Madness of King George*	UK
1994	Hugh Grant	*Four Weddings and a Funeral*	UK
1993	Anthony Hopkins	*The Remains of the Day*	US
1992	Robert Downey, Jr.	*Chaplin*	UK
1991	Anthony Hopkins	*The Silence of the Lambs*	USA
1990	Philippe Noiret	*Cinema Paradiso*	Italy/France
1989	Daniel Day Lewis	*My Left Foot*	UK
1988	John Cleese	*A Fish Called Wanda*	USA
1987	Sean Connery	*The Name of the Rose*	USA

THE 10

LAST WINNERS OF THE BAFTA BEST ACTRESS AWARD

Year	Actress	Film	Country of film's origin
1996	Brenda Blethyn	*Secrets and Lies*	UK
1995	Emma Thompson	*Sense and Sensibility*	UK
1994	Susan Sarandon	*The Client*	USA
1993	Holly Hunter	*The Piano*	Australia
1992	Emma Thompson	*Howards End*	UK
1991	Jodie Foster	*The Silence of the Lambs*	USA
1990	Jessica Tandy	*Driving Miss Daisy*	USA
1989	Pauline Collins	*Shirley Valentine*	USA/UK
1988	Maggie Smith	*The Lonely Passion of Judith Hearne*	UK
1987	Anne Bancroft	*84 Charing Cross Road*	UK

FILM STARS – ACTORS

TOP 10

HARRISON FORD FILMS

1	Star Wars	1977
2	Indiana Jones and the Last Crusade	1989
3	Return of the Jedi	1983
4	Raiders of the Lost Ark	1981
5	The Empire Strikes Back	1980
6	The Fugitive	1993
7	Presumed Innocent	1990
8	Clear and Present Danger	1994
9	Indiana Jones and the Temple of Doom	1984
10	Patriot Games	1992

Harrison Ford is in the fortunate position of having appeared in so many successful films that if any film were deleted from this Top 10, several similarly profitable films in which he starred could easily replace it, among them *Apocalypse Now* (1979) – although his role in it amounted to little more than a cameo, *Working Girl* (1988), *Witness* (1985), *Regarding Henry* (1991), and *Blade Runner* (1982). One film organization has recently voted Ford "Box Office Star of the Century".

TOP 10

SEAN CONNERY FILMS

1	Indiana Jones and the Last Crusade	1989
2	The Rock	1996
3	The Hunt for Red October	1990
4	Thunderball	1965
5	Never Say Never Again	1983
6	Goldfinger	1964
7	First Knight	1995
8	Diamonds Are Forever	1971
9	You Only Live Twice	1967
10	From Russia with Love	1964

If Sean Connery's fleeting cameo entry in the final two minutes of *Robin Hood: Prince of Thieves* (1991) is taken into account, it would be placed 2nd in this list.

TOP 10

CLINT EASTWOOD FILMS

1	In the Line of Fire	1993
2	Any Which Way You Can	1980
3	The Bridges of Madison County	1995
4	A Perfect World	1993
5	Every Which Way But Loose	1978
6	Unforgiven	1992
7	Sudden Impact	1983
8	Heartbreak Ridge	1986
9	Firefox	1982
10	The Enforcer	1976

TOP 10

MICHAEL DOUGLAS FILMS

1	Basic Instinct	1992
2	Disclosure	1994
3	Fatal Attraction	1987
4	Romancing the Stone	1984
5	The War of the Roses	1989
6	The Jewel of the Nile	1985
7	The American President	1995
8	Black Rain	1989
9	Wall Street*	1987
10	Falling Down	1993

* *Academy Award for "Best Actor"*

TOP 10

ROBERT DE NIRO FILMS

1	Heat	1995
2	Sleepers	1996
3	Mary Shelley's Frankenstein	1994
4	Cape Fear	1991
5	Backdraft	1991
6	The Untouchables	1987
7	The Godfather, Part II*	1974
8	Awakenings	1990
9	Goodfellas	1990
10	Casino	1995

* *Academy Award for "Best Supporting Actor"*

TOP 10

SYLVESTER STALLONE FILMS

1	Rambo: First Blood Part Two	1985
2	Cliffhanger	1993
3	The Specialist	1994
4	Rocky IV	1985
5	Rocky III	1982
6	Rocky	1976
7	Judge Dredd	1995
8	Daylight	1996
9	Rocky II	1979
10	Assassins	1995

TOP 10

ARNOLD SCHWARZENEGGER FILMS

1	Terminator 2: Judgment Day	1991
2	True Lies	1994
3	Total Recall	1990
4	Eraser	1996
5	Last Action Hero	1993
6	Jingle All the Way	1996
7	Twins	1988
8	Kindergarten Cop	1990
9	Junior	1984
10	Predator	1987

TOP 10

SIR ANTHONY HOPKINS FILMS

1	Bram Stoker's Dracula	1992
2	The Silence of the Lambs*	1991
3	Legends of the Fall	1995
4	A Bridge Too Far	1977
5	Magic	1978
6	Howard's End	1992
7	The Elephant Man	1980
8	Shadowlands	1993
9	The Remains of the Day	1993
10	The Lion in Winter	1968

* *Academy Award for "Best Actor"*

TOP 10

JOHN TRAVOLTA FILMS

1	Grease	1978
2	Saturday Night Fever	1977
3	Look Who's Talking	1989
4	Phenomenon	1996
5	Pulp Fiction	1994
6	Broken Arrow	1996
7	Staying Alive	1983
8	Get Shorty	1995
9	Michael	1996
10	Look Who's Talking Too	1990

TOP 10

KEVIN COSTNER FILMS

1	Dances with Wolves	1990
2	The Bodyguard	1992
3	Waterworld	1995
4	JFK	1991
5	Robin Hood: Prince of Thieves	1991
6	A Perfect World	1993
7	Tin Cup	1996
8	The Untouchables	1987
9	Field of Dreams	1989
10	The Big Chill	1983

TOP 10

TOM HANKS FILMS

1	Forrest Gump*	1994
2	Apollo 13	1995
3	Sleepless in Seattle	1993
4	Philadelphia*	1993
5	Big	1988
6	A League of Their Own	1992
7	Turner & Hooch	1989
8	Splash!	1984
9	Dragnet	1987
10	Joe Versus the Volcano	1990

* Academy Award for "Best Actor"

TOP 10

TOM CRUISE FILMS

1	Mission: Impossible	1996
2	Rain Man	1988
3	Top Gun	1986
4	The Firm	1993
5	A Few Good Men	1992
6	Interview with the Vampire	1994
7	Days of Thunder	1990
8	Jerry Maguire	1996
9	Cocktail	1988
10	Born on the Fourth of July	1989

TOP 10

MEL GIBSON FILMS

1	Lethal Weapon 2	1989
2	Lethal Weapon 3	1992
3	Braveheart	1995
4	Ransom	1996
5	Forever Young	1992
6	Maverick	1994
7	Bird on a Wire	1990
8	Lethal Weapon	1987
9	Tequila Sunrise	1988
10	Mad Max Beyond Thunderdome	1985

TOP 10

JACK NICHOLSON FILMS

1	Batman	1989
2	A Few Good Men	1992
3	One Flew Over the Cuckoo's Nest*	1975
4	Terms of Endearment#	1983
5	Wolf	1994
6	The Witches of Eastwick	1987
7	The Shining	1980
8	Broadcast News	1987
9	Reds	1981
10	Mars Attacks!	1996

* Academy Award for "Best Actor"
\# Academy Award for "Best Supporting Actor"

T. HANKS SAYS "THANKS"
Tom Hanks won an Oscar for "Best Actor" in 1994 for his role in Philadelphia, and the following year he was awarded an Oscar in the same category for his role in Forrest Gump. Hanks was the first actor to win an Oscar in two consecutive years since Spencer Tracy, who won "Best Actor" awards in 1937 and 1938.

FILM STARS – ACTRESSES

TOP 10

SALLY FIELD FILMS

1	Forrest Gump	1994
2	Mrs. Doubtfire	1993
3	Smokey and the Bandit	1977
4	Steel Magnolias	1989
5	Smokey and the Bandit II	1980
6	Hooper	1978
7	Eye for an Eye	1995
8	The End	1978
9	Absence of Malice	1981
10	Soapdish	1991

Sally Field provided the voice of Sassy in the animal adventure films *Homeward Bound: The Incredible Journey* (1993) and its sequel *Homeward Bound II: Lost in San Francisco* (1996). If taken into account, they would appear in 10th and 8th places respectively, either side of *The End*, thereby evicting *Absence of Malice* and *Soapdish* from her Top 10.

TOP 10

SIGOURNEY WEAVER FILMS

1	Ghostbusters	1984
2	Ghostbusters II	1989
3	Aliens	1986
4	Alien	1979
5	Working Girl	1988
6	Dave	1993
7	Alien³	1992
8	Copycat	1995
9	Gorillas in the Mist	1988
10	1492: Conquest of Paradise	1992

TOP 10

MICHELLE PFEIFFER FILMS

1	Batman Returns	1992
2	Dangerous Minds	1995
3	Wolf	1994
4	The Witches of Eastwick	1987
5	Up Close and Personal	1996
6	Tequila Sunrise	1988
7	Scarface	1983
8	Dangerous Liaisons	1988
9	One Fine Day	1996
10	The Age of Innocence	1993

TOP 10

SHARON STONE FILMS

1	Basic Instinct	1992
2	Total Recall	1990
3	The Specialist	1995
4	Last Action Hero	1993
5	Sliver	1993
6	Casino	1995
7	Police Academy 4: Citizens on Patrol	1987
8	Intersection	1994
9	Action Jackson	1988
10	Above the Law	1988

SUPERSTAR SHARON STONE
Sharon Stone's film career began in 1980 with her non-speaking and brief appearance in Woody Allen's Stardust Memories as "Pretty Girl on a Train".

TOP 10

MEG RYAN FILMS

1	Top Gun	1986
2	Sleepless in Seattle	1993
3	French Kiss	1995
4	When Harry Met Sally	1989
5	Courage Under Fire	1996
6	When a Man Loves a Woman	1994
7	Joe Versus the Volcano	1990
8	The Doors	1991
9	I.Q.	1994
10	Innerspace	1987

TOP 10

SUSAN SARANDON FILMS

1	The Rocky Horror Picture Show	1975
2	The Client	1994
3	The Witches of Eastwick	1987
4	Bull Durham	1988
5	Little Women	1994
6	Thelma & Louise	1991
7	Dead Man Walking*	1995
8	The Player	1992
9	White Palace	1991
10	The Great Waldo Pepper	1975

* Academy Award for "Best Actress"

Susan Sarandon also provided the voice of the spider in the animated film of Roald Dahl's children's story *James and the Giant Peach* (1996). If included in the ranking, it would be in 8th place.

TOP 10

JODIE FOSTER FILMS

1	Sommersby	1993
2	The Silence of the Lambs*	1990
3	Nell	1994
4	Maverick	1994
5	The Accused*	1988
6	Taxi Driver	1976
7	Freaky Friday	1976
8	Little Man Tate	1991
9	Home for the Holidays	1995
10	Alice Doesn't Live Here Any More	1975

* Academy Award for "Best Actress"

TOP 10

DEMI MOORE FILMS

1	Ghost	1990
2	Indecent Proposal	1993
3	A Few Good Men	1992
4	Disclosure	1995
5	Striptease	1996
6	The Juror	1996
7	About Last Night	1986
8	St. Elmo's Fire	1985
9	Young Doctors in Love	1982
10	Now and Then	1995

Demi Moore provided the voice of Esmeralda in the animated film *The Hunchback of Notre Dame* (1996). If included in her Top 10, it would be in 2nd place.

JULIA ROBERTS
Julia Roberts is best known for her role in Pretty Woman, *which made her one of the most highly paid actresses in Hollywood.*

TOP 10

JULIA ROBERTS FILMS

1	Pretty Woman	1990
2	The Pelican Brief	1993
3	Sleeping with the Enemy	1991
4	Hook	1991
5	Steel Magnolias	1989
6	Flatliners	1990
7	Something to Talk About	1995
8	Dying Young	1991
9	I Love Trouble	1994
10	Michael Collins	1996

TOP 10

EMMA THOMPSON FILMS

1	Junior	1994
2	Sense and Sensibility	1995
3	Dead Again	1991
4	Howard's End*	1992
5	In the Name of the Father	1993
6	The Remains of the Day	1993
7	Much Ado about Nothing	1993
8	Henry V	1989
9	Impromptu	1991
10	Carrington	1995

* Academy Award for "Best Actress"

TOP 10

MERYL STREEP FILMS

1	The Bridges of Madison County	1995
2	Kramer vs. Kramer*	1979
3	Out of Africa	1985
4	Death Becomes Her	1992
5	The Deer Hunter	1978
6	Manhattan	1979
7	Postcards from the Edge	1990
8	Silkwood	1983
9	Sophie's Choice#	1982
10	Julia	1982

* Academy Award for "Best Supporting Actress"
# Academy Award for "Best Actress"

It is perhaps surprising that *Sophie's Choice*, the film for which Meryl Streep won an Oscar, scores so far down this list, while one of her most celebrated films, *The French Lieutenant's Woman* (1981), does not make her personal Top 10 at all.

TOP 10

NICOLE KIDMAN FILMS

1	Batman Forever	1995	6	To Die For	1995
2	Days of Thunder	1990	7	Billy Bathgate	1991
3	Far and Away	1992	8	Dead Calm	1989
4	Malice	1993	9	Portrait of a Lady	1996
5	My Life	1993	10	Flirting	1991

COMEDY STARS

TOP 10
WHOOPI GOLDBERG FILMS

1	Ghost	1990
2	Sister Act	1992
3	Made in America	1993
4	The Color Purple	1985
5	Sister Act 2: Back in the Habit	1993
6	The Little Rascals	1994
7	Soapdish	1991
8	Star Trek: Generations	1994
9	Eddie	1996
10	National Lampoon's Loaded Weapon 1	1993

Whoopi Goldberg's appearance in *National Lampoon's Loaded Weapon 1* was an uncredited cameo; if excluded, her new No. 10 would be *Jumpin' Jack Flash* (1986). She provided the voice of Shenzi in *The Lion King* (1994). If that were taken into the reckoning, it would appear in No. 1 position in her Top 10.

TOP 10
EDDIE MURPHY FILMS

1	Beverly Hills Cop	1984
2	Beverly Hills Cop II	1987
3	Coming to America	1988
4	Boomerang	1992
5	Harlem Nights*	1989
6	Trading Places	1983
7	Another 48 Hours	1990
8	The Golden Child	1986
9	48 Hours	1982
10	Eddie Murphy Raw	1987

* Also director

Eddie Murphy Raw is an unusual entrant, in that it is not a feature film but is a documentary featuring Murphy live on stage. It is one of an elite handful of "non-fiction" films that rank alongside major feature films in terms of their earnings, from screenings, video sales, and rental.

TOP 10
GOLDIE HAWN FILMS

1	The First Wives Club	1996
2	Bird on a Wire	1990
3	Private Benjamin	1980
4	Housesitter	1992
5	Death Becomes Her	1992
6	Foul Play	1978
7	Shampoo	1975
8	Seems Like Old Times	1980
9	Best Friends	1982
10	Deceived	1991

GOLDEN GIRL
Goldie Hawn (born Goldie Jean Studlendgehawn) made her first appearance in 1968 in the long-running TV series Rowan and Martin's Laugh-In. *She has effectively reprised her role as a zany, eternally youthful blonde in comedy films ever since, with* Private Benjamin *earning her a Best Actress Oscar nomination.*

TOP 10
WOODY ALLEN FILMS

1	Manhattan*#✚	1979
2	Hannah and Her Sisters*#✚	1986
3	Annie Hall*#✚	1977
4	Casino Royale*	1967
5	Everything You Always Wanted to Know about Sex (But Were Afraid to Ask)*#✚	1972
6	What's New, Pussycat?*#	1965
7	Sleeper*#✚	1973
8	Crimes and Misdemeanors*#✚	1989
9	Radio Days*#✚	1987
10	Bullets over Broadway#✚	1994

* Appeared in
\# Scriptwriter
✚ Directed

This list includes films that Woody Allen has either written, starred in, or directed. If it were restricted only to films he has directed, *Casino Royale* and *What's New, Pussycat?* would be dropped from the list, and the new 9th and 10th entries would be *Zelig* (1983) and *Love and Death* (1975), both of which he starred in, wrote, and directed. *Annie Hall* prompted the first occasion since 1941 on which one individual was nominated for "Best Picture", "Best Actor", "Best Director", and "Best Screenplay".

TOP 10
PETER SELLERS FILMS

1	The Revenge of the Pink Panther	1978
2	The Return of the Pink Panther	1974
3	The Pink Panther Strikes Again	1976
4	Murder by Death	1976
5	Being There	1979
6	Casino Royale	1967
7	What's New, Pussycat?	1965
8	A Shot in the Dark	1964
9	The Pink Panther	1963
10=	Dr. Strangelove	1963
10=	The Fiendish Plot of Dr. Fu Manchu	1980

TOP 10

BETTE MIDLER FILMS

1	The First Wives Club	1996
2	Get Shorty	1995
3	Ruthless People	1986
4	Down and Out in Beverly Hills	1986
5	Beaches*	1988
6	Outrageous Fortune	1987
7	The Rose	1979
8	Big Business	1988
9	Hocus Pocus	1993
10	Hawaii	1966

* Also producer

Bette Midler's role in *Get Shorty* is no more than a cameo, and that in *Hawaii*, her first film part, is as an extra. If excluded, *Stella* (1990) and *For the Boys* (1991) would join the list. Her voice appears as that of the character Georgette in the animated film *Oliver and Company* (1988).

TOP 10

DANNY DEVITO FILMS

1	Batman Returns	1992
2	Romancing the Stone	1984
3	One Flew Over the Cuckoo's Nest	1975
4	Twins	1988
5	Terms of Endearment	1983
6	Junior	1994
7	The War of the Roses*	1989
8	Get Shorty	1995
9	Ruthless People	1986
10	The Jewel of the Nile	1985

* Also director

Danny DeVito had a relatively minor role in *One Flew Over the Cuckoo's Nest*. If this is discounted from the reckoning, his 10th most successful film is *Throw Momma from the Train* (1987). He directed, appeared in, and narrated *Matilda* (1996), which just fails to make his Top 10.

TOP 10

DAN AYKROYD FILMS

1	Ghostbusters	1984
2	Casper	1995
3	Indiana Jones and the Temple of Doom	1984
4	Ghostbusters II	1989
5	Driving Miss Daisy	1989
6	Trading Places	1983
7	Spies Like Us	1985
8	My Girl	1991
9	Dragnet	1987
10	The Blues Brothers	1980

If his 20-second cameo appearance as Weber in *Indiana Jones and the Temple of Doom* is excluded, Aykroyd's next most successful film is *Sneakers* (1992). If his unbilled part (as Doctor Raymond Stantz) in *Casper* is eliminated, the Spielberg-directed *1941* joins the list – although it is technically regarded as a "flop" because it cost more to make than it earned at the box office. His directorial debut with *Nothing But Trouble* (1991), in which he also played the starring role, was his least commercially successful film.

TOP 10

BILL MURRAY FILMS

1	Ghostbusters	1984	6	What About Bob?	1991
2	Tootsie	1982	7	Scrooged	1988
3	Ghostbusters II	1989	8	Meatballs	1979
4	Stripes	1981	9	Caddyshack	1980
5	Groundhog Day	1993	10	Little Shop of Horrors	1986

TOP 10

ROBIN WILLIAMS FILMS

1	Mrs. Doubtfire	1993
2	Jumanji	1995
3	Dead Poets Society	1989
4	The Birdcage	1996
5	Nine Months	1995
6	Good Morning, Vietnam	1987
7	Hook	1991
8	Jack	1996
9	Awakenings	1990
10	Popeye	1980

TOP 10

JIM CARREY FILMS

1	Batman Forever	1995
2	The Mask	1994
3	Dumb & Dumber	1994
4	Ace Ventura: When Nature Calls	1995
5	Ace Ventura: Pet Detective	1994
6	Peggy Sue Got Married	1986
7	The Dead Pool	1988
8	Pink Cadillac	1989
9	Once Bitten	1985
10	Earth Girls Are Easy	1989

TOP 10

STEVE MARTIN FILMS

1	Parenthood	1989
2	The Jerk*	1979
3	Father of the Bride	1991
4	Father of the Bride Part II	1995
5	Housesitter	1992
6	Planes, Trains, and Automobiles	1987
7	Dirty Rotten Scoundrels	1988
8	Roxanne	1987
9	Three Amigos!*	1986
10	Little Shop of Horrors	1986

* Also co-writer

Steve Martin was also one of the many "guest stars" in *The Muppet Movie* (1979). If included, it would appear in 4th place.

DIRECTOR'S CUT

238

MASTER OF SUSPENSE
British-born Alfred Hitchcock directed almost 60 films in his 50-year career, including some of the most popular thrillers of all time.

TOP 10

FILMS DIRECTED BY ALFRED HITCHCOCK

1	*Psycho*	1960
2	*Rear Window*	1954
3	*North by Northwest*	1959
4	*Family Plot*	1976
5	*Torn Curtain*	1966
6	*Frenzy*	1972
7	*Vertigo*	1958
8	*The Man Who Knew Too Much*	1956
9	*The Birds*	1963
10	*Spellbound*	1945

TOP 10

FILMS DIRECTED BY BLAKE EDWARDS

1	*10*	1979
2	*Revenge of the Pink Panther*	1978
3	*The Return of the Pink Panther*	1975
4	*The Pink Panther Strikes Again*	1976
5	*Blind Date*	1987
6	*Mickie & Maude*	1984
7	*The Great Race*	1965
8	*Victor/Victoria*	1982
9	*Operation Petticoat*	1959
10	*Skin Deep*	1989

TOP 10

MOST PROLIFIC DIRECTORS

	Director	Active period	No. films directed
1	D.W. Griffith	1908–36	545
2	Dave Fleischer	1918–48	392
3	Friz Freleng	1934–83	262
4	Chuck Jones	1938–	240
5	Theo Frenkel	1908–28	216
6	Allan Dwan	1911–61	189
7	Robert McKimson	1946–69	175
8	Sam Newfield	1933–58	165
9	William Beaudine	1917–66	156
10	Gilberto Martinez Solares	1936–94	150

Several of the most prolific directors, including D.W. Griffith, Theo Frenkel, Allan Dwan, and William Beaudine, spent at least the early years of their careers directing silent films. In some instances, not all the films for which they were responsible have been identified, so the totals include certain "probable" but unconfirmed titles. Some directors worked in fairly narrowly defined genres, such as Sam Newfield who was responsible for a large number of cowboy films, while four included here were responsible chiefly for animated films: Dave Fleischer (*Popeye*), Friz Freleng (*Bugs Bunny*), Chuck Jones (*Tom & Jerry* and *Bugs Bunny*), and Robert McKimson (*Daffy Duck*, etc.).

TOP 10

FILMS DIRECTED BY FRANCIS FORD COPPOLA

1	*Bram Stoker's Dracula*	1992
2	*The Godfather*	1972
3	*Jack*	1006
4	*The Godfather, Part III*	1990
5	*Apocalypse Now*	1979
6	*The Godfather, Part II*	1974
7	*Peggy Sue Got Married*	1986
8	*The Cotton Club*	1984
9	*The Outsiders*	1983
10	*Tucker: The Man and His Dream*	1988

TOP 10

FILMS DIRECTED BY SIDNEY LUMET

1	*The Verdict*	1982
2	*Dog Day Afternoon*	1975
3	*Murder on the Orient Express*	1974
4	*Serpico*	1974
5	*Network*	1976
6	*The Wiz*	1978
7	*The Morning After*	1986
8	*Guilty As Sin*	1993
9	*Deathtrap*	1982
10	*A Stranger Among Us*	1992

THE GREAT DIRECTOR

David Lewelyn Wark (known as "D.W.") Griffith, who died 50 years ago on 23 July 1948, was one of the most influential figures in the history of the cinema. Kentucky-born Griffith started his career as an actor in the early years of the cinema, and then turned to writing and directing, pioneering techniques such as fades and flashbacks.
The most prolific director of all time, at one stage in his film-making career he was making an average of 21 films a week. His *The Birth of a Nation* (1915) was the highest-earning film made until 1937 (when *Snow White and the Seven Dwarfs* overtook it), while his controversial epic *Intolerance* was one of the first films to have "a cast of thousands" – and the first major film flop.

YEARS AGO • YEARS AGO • YEARS AGO
50

TOP 10

FILMS DIRECTED BY JOHN HUSTON

1	*Annie*	1982
2	*The Bible*	1966
3	*Prizzi's Honor**	1985
4	*The Man Who Would Be King*#	1975
5	*Casino Royale*	1967
6	*The Life and Times of Judge Roy Bean*	1972
7	*Moby Dick*	1956
8	*Night of the Iguana*	1964
9	*Moulin Rouge**	1952
10=	*Heaven Knows, Mr. Allison*#	1957
10=	*Victory (or Escape to Victory)*	1981

* *Academy Award nomination for "Best Picture"*
\# *Academy Award nomination for "Best Screenplay"*

John Huston (1906–87) was a man of prodigious and diverse talents who wrote the scripts of some 30 films, acted in 40, and directed more than 40. He is perhaps best remembered for films that were greater critical than commercial successes, among them *The Maltese Falcon*, *The Treasure of Sierra Madre*, and *The African Queen*.

TOP 10

FILMS DIRECTED BY HOWARD HAWKS

1	*Hatari*	1962
2	*Sergeant York*	1941
3	*El Dorado*	1967
4	*Rio Bravo*	1959
5	*Gentlemen Prefer Blondes*	1953
6	*The Outlaw**	1943
7	*Red River*	1948
8	*Rio Lobo*	1970
9	*I Was a Male War Bride*	1949
10	*To Have and Have Not*	1945

* *Co-directed with Howard Hughes*

TOP 10

FILMS DIRECTED OR PRODUCED BY GEORGE LUCAS

1	*Star Wars**	1977
2	*The Empire Strikes Back*#	1980
3	*Indiana Jones and the Last Crusade*#	1989
4	*Return of the Jedi*#	1983
5	*Raiders of the Lost Ark*#	1981
6	*Indiana Jones and the Temple of Doom*#	1984
7	*American Graffiti**	1973
8	*Willow*#	1988
9	*The Land Before Time*#	1988
10	*Tucker: The Man and His Dream*#	1988

* *Director*
\# *Producer*

George Lucas made the move from directing to producing after the phenomenal success of *Star Wars*, but he clearly has a Midas touch in both fields. The first five films on this list rank among the 25 highest-earning of all time, and his Top 10 earned more than $2.5 billion at the box office. Lucas was also responsible for writing the stories for the first eight films in this catalogue of triumphs.

TOP 10

FILMS DIRECTED BY MARTIN SCORSESE

1	*Cape Fear*	1991
2	*The Color of Money*	1986
3	*Goodfellas*	1990
4	*Casino*	1995
5	*The Age of Innocence*	1993
6	*Taxi Driver*	1976
7	*Raging Bull*	1980
8	*Alice Doesn't Live Here Anymore*	1975
9	*New York, New York*	1977
10	*New York Stories**	1989

* *Part only; other segments directed by Francis Ford Coppola and Woody Allen*

TOP 10

FILMS DIRECTED BY STEVEN SPIELBERG

1	*Jurassic Park*	1993
2	*E.T.: The Extra-terrestrial*	1982
3	*Indiana Jones and the Last Crusade*	1989
4	*Jaws*	1975
5	*Raiders of the Lost Ark*	1981
6	*Schindler's List*	1993
7	*Close Encounters of the Third Kind*	1977/80*
8	*Indiana Jones and the Temple of Doom*	1984
9	*Hook*	1991
10	*The Color Purple*	1985

* *Re-edited and re-released as a "Special Edition"*

Steven Spielberg has directed some of the most successful films of all time: the top four in this list appear among the top 13 films of all time. If his credits as producer are included, further blockbusters such as *The Flintstones*, *Casper*, *Twister*, *Gremlins*, and *Poltergeist* would also score highly.

OUT-TAKES

TOP 10

FILM-PRODUCING COUNTRIES

	Country	Films produced p.a.
1	India	754
2	USA	686
3	Japan	278
4	Hong Kong	154
5	France	134
6	UK	111
7	China	110
8	Italy	99
9	Spain	91
10	Pakistan	88

The list is of full-length (generally at least 1,600 m/5,250 ft) feature films, and for most countries is for numbers of films produced in 1996. India has maintained its pre-eminence for several years, while the resurgence of the British film industry has elevated it from its former position at the bottom of the Top 10.

CINEMA GIANT
India's insatiable demand for films has resulted in its film industry outstripping even that of Hollywood.

TOP 10

FILM-GOING COUNTRIES

	Country	Annual cinema visits per inhabitant
1	Singapore	7.16
2	Hong Kong	6.01
3	India	5.83
4	China	5.14
5	Monaco	5.06
6	USA	4.82
7	Iceland	4.74
8	Malaysia	3.56
9	Russia	3.15
10	Australia	3.00
	UK	*1.99*

The popularity of films on a country-by-country basis can be roughly measured by analysing the average number of visits to the cinema per head of the population. This analysis produces one of the very few world lists in which Iceland appears in close proximity to the United States.

TOP 10

FILMS WITH THE MOST EXTRAS

	Film/country/year	Extras
1	*Gandhi* (UK, 1982)	300,000
2	*Kolberg* (Germany, 1945)	187,000
3	*Monster Wang-magwi* (South Korea, 1967)	157,000
4	*War and Peace* (USSR, 1967)	120,000
5	*Ilya Muromets* (USSR, 1956)	106,000
6	*Tonko* (Japan, 1988)	100,000
7	*The War of Independence* (Romania, 1912)	80,000
8	*Around the World in 80 Days* (USA, 1956)	68,894
9=	*Intolerance* (USA, 1916)	60,000
9=	*Dny Zrady* (Czechoslovakia, 1972)	60,000

TOP 10

COUNTRIES WITH MOST CINEMAS

	Country	Cinema screens
1	USA	25,737
2	India*	13,002
3	France	4,397
4	Italy	3,800
5	Germany	3,709
6	Indonesia	2,517
7	China	2,000
8	UK	1,890
9	Spain	1,791
10	Japan	1,734

* Including approximately 4,000 mobile cinemas

For many years UNESCO and other international agencies produced statistics for indoor cinemas equipped to show 35 mm films and, in some instances, 16 mm films. The total for the former USSR, once said to be as high as 176,172, always seemed incredible, and was concluded to be a reflection of the value placed on film in the Soviet Union as a medium not only of entertainment but also political ideology. More believable figures are now emerging for the former Soviet republics.

TOP 10

COUNTRIES WITH THE MOST CINEMA SCREENS PER MILLION

	Country	Cinema screens per million
1	Czech Republic	168
2	Sweden	133
3	USA	102
4	Latvia	95
5	Norway	91
6	Iceland	90
7	France	76
8	Switzerland	69
9	New Zealand	67
10	Italy	66

TOP 10

LONGEST FILMS EVER SCREENED

	Title/country/year	Duration hr	min
1	*The Longest and Most Meaningless Movie in the World*, UK, 1970	48	0
2	*The Burning of the Red Lotus Temple*, China, 1928–31	27	0
3	****, USA, 1967	25	0
4	*Heimat*, West Germany, 1984	15	40
5	*Berlin Alexanderplatz*, West Germany/Italy, 1980	15	21
6	*The Journey*, Sweden, 1987	14	33
7	*The Old Testament*, Italy, 1922	13	0
8	*Comment Yukong déplace les montagnes*, France, 1976	12	43
9	*Out 1: Noli me Tangere*, France, 1971	12	40
10	*Ningen No Joken (The Human Condition)*, Japan, 1958–60	9	29

The list includes commercially screened films, but not "stunt" films created solely to break endurance records (particularly those of their audiences), among which are the 85-hour *The Cure for Insomnia* and the 50-hour *Mondo Teeth*. Those in the list are no more watchable: *The Longest and Most Meaningless Movie in the World* was later cut to a more manageable 1 hr 30 min, and remained just as meaningless. Outside this Top 10, Abel Gance's *Napoleon* has not been shown at its full length of nine hours since it was first released, but as new segments of it have been discovered, it has been meticulously reassembled to a length approaching that of the original version. Among more conventional yet extremely long films of recent times are *Wagner* (UK/Hungary/Austria, 1983; 9 hr 0 min), *Little Dorrit* (UK, 1987; 5 hr 57 min), the colossally expensive and commercially disastrous *Cleopatra* (USA, 1963; 4 hr 3 min) and the *Greatest Story Ever Told* (USA, 1965), which was progressively cut from 4 hr 20 min to 2 hr 7 min, but in the end was no less tedious as a result.

PRECIOUS RUBIES
The magical ruby slippers worn by Judy Garland in the 1939 film The Wizard of Oz were sold in 1988 for $165,000, making them the most expensive items of film costume ever sold at auction. As they were one of four pairs made for her role, history could yet repeat itself.

TOP 10

MOST EXPENSIVE ITEMS OF FILM MEMORABILIA EVER SOLD AT AUCTION

	Item/sale	Price (£)*
1	Vivien Leigh's Oscar for *Gone with the Wind*, Sotheby's, New York, 15 December 1993 ($562,500)	380,743
2	Clark Gable's Oscar for *It Happened One Night*, Christie's, Los Angeles, 15 December 1996 ($607,500)	361,500
3	Poster for *The Mummy*, 1932, Sotheby's, New York, 1 March 1997 ($453,500)	252,109
4	James Bond's Aston Martin DB5 from *Goldfinger*, Sotheby's, New York, 28 June 1986 ($275,000)	179,793
5	Clark Gable's personal script for *Gone With The Wind*, Christie's, Los Angeles, 15 December 1996 ($244,500)	146,700
6	"Rosebud" sled from *Citizen Kane*, Christie's, Los Angeles, 15 December 1996 ($233,500)	140,000
7	Herman J. Mankiewicz's scripts for *Citizen Kane* and *The American*, Christie's, New York, 21 June 1989 ($231,000)	139,157
8	Judy Garland's ruby slippers from *The Wizard of Oz*, Christie's, New York, 21 June 1988 ($165,000)	104,430
9	Piano from the Paris scene in *Casablanca*, Sotheby's, New York, 16 December 1988 ($154,000)	97,469
10	Charlie Chaplin's hat and cane, Christie's, London, 11 December 1987, (resold at Christie's, London, 17 December 1993, for £55,000)	82,500

* *$/£ conversion at rate then prevailing*

This list excludes animated film celluloids or "cels" – the individually painted scenes that are shot in sequence to make up cartoon films – which are now attaining colossal prices: just one of the 150,000 colour cels from *Snow White* (1937) was sold in 1991 for $209,000/£115,000, and in 1989 $286,000/£171,250 was reached for a black-and-white cel depicting Donald Duck in *Orphan's Benefit* (1934). If memorabilia relating to film stars rather than films was to be included, Orson Welles' annotated script from the radio production of *The War of the Worlds* ($143,000/£90,500 in 1988) would qualify for this Top 10. Among near-misses are: posters for two 1933 films, *Flying Down to Rio* ($81,000/£49,020) and *King Kong* ($79,500/£47,700), both of which were sold in 1996; such costume items as the witch's hat from *The Wizard of Oz* ($33,000/£20,886 in 1988) and Marilyn Monroe's "shimmy" dress from *Some Like It Hot* (£19,800 in 1988); and the stand-in model of Boris Karloff as Frankenstein's monster from the 1935 film *The Bride of Frankenstein* (£16,500 in 1988).

TV FIRSTS

T H E 1 0

FIRST GUESTS ON
THE TONIGHT SHOW –
STARRING JOHNNY CARSON

1	Groucho Marx	Comic actor
2	Joan Crawford	Actress
3	Rudy Vallee	Singer/actor
4	Tony Bennett	Singer
5	Mel Brooks	Comic
6	Tom Pedi	Actor
7	The Phoenix Singers	Vocal trio
8	Tallulah Bankhead	Actress
9	Shelley Berman	Comedian
10	Artie Shaw	Band leader

Source: Carson Productions

Originally a two-hour week nightly show taped in New York, Carson took over *The Tonight Show* on 1 October 1962, with his final show airing on 22 May 1992.

T H E 1 0

FIRST MUSIC VIDEOS
BROADCAST BY MTV EUROPE

	Video	Artist
1	*Money for Nothing*	Dire Straits
2	*Fake*	Alexander O'Neal
3	*You Got the Look*	Prince with Sheena Easton
4	*It's a Sin*	Pet Shop Boys
5	*I Wanna Dance with Somebody*	Whitney Houston
6	*I Want Your Sex*	George Michael
7	*Who's That Girl*	Madonna
8	*I Really Didn't Mean It*	Luther Vandross
9	*Misfit*	Curiosity Killed The Cat
10	*Higher and Higher*	Jackie Wilson

MTV Europe began its pan-European broadcasting on 1 August 1987.

10 US TV FIRSTS

1 The first President to appear on TV

Franklin D. Roosevelt was seen opening the World's Fair, New York, on 30 April 1939.

2 The first king and queen televised in the US

King George VI and Queen Elizabeth were shown visiting the World's Fair on 10 June 1939.

3 The first televised NFL baseball game

The game between the Cincinnati Reds and the Brooklyn Dodgers at Ebbets Field, Brooklyn, New York, was broadcast on 26 August 1939.

4 The first televised professional football game

The Brooklyn Dodgers vs. Philadelphia Eagles match at Ebbets Field was shown on 22 October 1939.

5 The first TV commercial

A 20-second commercial for a Bulova clock was broadcast by WNBT New York on 1 July 1941.

6 The first soap opera on TV

The first regular daytime serial, DuMont TV network's A Woman to Remember, *began its run on 21 February 1947.*

7 The first broadcast of a current TV show

NBC's Meet the Press *was first broadcast on 6 November 1947.*

8 The first televised atomic bomb explosion

An "Operation Ranger" detonation at Frenchman Flats, Nevada, on 1 February 1951, was televised by KTLA, Los Angeles.

9 The first networked coast-to-coast colour TV show

The Tournament of Roses parade at Pasadena, California, hosted by Don Ameche, was seen in colour in 21 cities nationwide on 1 January 1954.

10 The first presidential news conference televised live

President John F. Kennedy was shown in a live broadcast from the auditorium of the State Department Building, Washington, DC, on 25 January 1961. (A filmed conference with President Eisenhower had been shown on 19 January 1955.)

T H E 1 0

FIRST MUSIC VIDEOS BROADCAST BY MTV (USA)

	Video	Artist		Video	Artist
1	*Video Killed the Radio Star*	Buggles	6	*We Don't Talk Anymore*	Cliff Richard
2	*You Better Run*	Pat Benatar	7	*Brass in Pocket*	Pretenders
3	*She Won't Dance with Me*	Rod Stewart	8	*Time Heals*	Todd Rundgren
4	*You Better You Bet*	Who	9	*Take It on the Run*	REO Speedwagon
5	*Little Susie's on the Up*	PhD	10	*Rockin' the Paradise*	Styx

50 YEARS OF TV

Television started on both sides of the Atlantic in the 1930s, but dates its inexorable rise as the world's foremost broadcast medium from the 1940s. The year 1948 was significant for a number of developments – not least the use of the abbreviation "TV", which first appeared in print in that year in the American magazines *Fortune* and *Time*. The first regular television news service broadcast in Britain was inaugurated on 5 January 1948 – although the first news presenters were heard, but not seen. In the US, *The Ed Sullivan Show* began its 23-year run on 20 June 1948. The first TV cartoon series, first animated TV commercial, and the first TV cowboy series (*Hopalong Cassidy*) shown in the US also all date from 1948.

THE COMING OF TV

The arrival and spread of television is one of the most significant developments of the 20th century. Scottish electrical engineer John Logie Baird (1888–1946) is generally recognized as the pioneer of television. He first demonstrated low-definition broadcasts in 1926, and, although flawed, it was introduced in the UK by the BBC in 1929. Subsequent improvements led to the introduction of high-definition television in the UK on 2 November 1936 and in the US on 30 April 1939. World War II hampered developments until the 1940s. Since then, television has become established globally, to the extent that there are now scarcely any countries that do not have television.

PIONEER OF TELEVISION
Scottish inventor John Logie Baird is seen here demonstrating his original television system.

THE 10

FIRST COUNTRIES TO HAVE TELEVISION*

	Country	Year
1	UK	1936
2	USA	1939
3	Former USSR	1939
4	France	1948
5	Brazil	1950
6	Cuba	1950
7	Mexico	1950
8	Argentina	1951
9	Denmark	1951
10	Netherlands	1951

* *High-definition regular public broadcasting service*

TV COMES OF AGE
By the 1950s, television was commonplace in many countries.

FAMILY VIEWING
Baird's system was used for the first low-definition broadcasts in the UK in 1929.

FIRST TVs
The earliest Baird television sets were cumbersome, unreliable, and expensive, but paved the way for all later developments.

TOP TELEVISION

WHO SHOT J.R.?
*Viewers worldwide tuned in to the episode of
Dallas that revealed it was Kristin Shepard –
shown here – who shot J.R. Ewing.*

T O P 1 0

TV-OWNING COUNTRIES IN THE WORLD

	Country	Homes with TV		Country	Homes with TV
1	China	227,500,000	6	Germany	36,295,000
2	USA	94,200,000	7	India	35,000,000
3	Russia	48,269,000	8	UK	22,446,000
4	Japan	41,328,000	9	France	21,667,000
5	Brazil	38,880,000	10	Italy	20,812,000

The estimated world total for TV households is 854,225,000, with the Top 10
countries accounting for almost 69 per cent – a five-fold increase during the past
30 years and a rise of nearly 60 per cent since 1984.

T O P 1 0

NIELSEN'S TV AUDIENCES OF ALL TIME IN THE US

	TV programme	Date	Households viewing total	per cent
1	*M*A*S*H* Special	28 Feb 1983	50,150,000	60.2
2	*Dallas*	21 Nov 1980	41,470,000	53.3
3	*Roots* Part 8	30 Jan 1977	36,380,000	51.1
4	*Super Bowl XVI*	24 Jan 1982	40,020,000	49.1
5	*Super Bowl XVII*	30 Jan 1983	40,500,000	48.6
6	*XVII Winter Olympics*	23 Feb 1994	45,690,000	48.5
7	*Super Bowl XX*	26 Jan 1986	41,490,000	48.3
8	*Gone with the Wind* Part 1	7 Nov 1976	33,960,000	47.7
9	*Gone with the Wind* Part 2	8 Nov 1976	33,750,000	47.4
10	*Super Bowl XII*	15 Jan 1978	34,410,000	47.2

© Copyright 1997 Nielsen Media Research

As more and more households acquire television sets (there are currently 94,000,000 "TV
households" in the US), the most recently screened programmes naturally tend to be watched
by larger audiences, which distorts the historical picture. By listing this Top 10 according to
percentage of households viewing, we get a clearer picture of who watches what.

T O P 1 0

CABLE TV COUNTRIES IN THE WORLD

	Country	Cable TV subscribers
1	USA	60,495,090
2	Germany	14,600,000
3	Netherlands	5,700,000
4	Belgium	3,610,000
5	Switzerland	2,235,900
6	Sweden	1,850,000
7	France	1,620,000
8	Austria	1,000,000
9	UK	908,018
10	Finland	830,000

T O P 1 0

PAY CABLE CHANNELS IN THE US

	Channel	Subscribers*		Channel	Subscribers*
1	Home Box Office	19,200,000	6	The Disney Channel	6,130,000
2	Encore Plex	8,969,000	7	Starz	3,279,000
3	Cinemax	8,900,000	8	The Movie Channel	3,100,000
4	Showtime	8,100,000	9	Encore/Westerns	1,517,000
5	Encore	6,868,000	10	Encore/Mystery	1,515,000

* As at March 1997

T O P 1 0

TV AUDIENCES OF ALL TIME IN THE UK

	TV programme	Date	Audience
1	Royal Wedding of Prince Charles to Lady Diana Spencer	29 Jul 1981	39,000,000
2	Brazil *vs.* England 1970 World Cup	10 Jun 1970	32,500,000
3=	England *vs.* West Germany 1966 World Cup Final	30 Jul 1966	32,000,000
3=	Chelsea *vs.* Leeds Cup Final Replay	28 Apr 1970	32,000,000
5	*EastEnders* Christmas episode	26 Dec 1987	30,000,000
6	*Morecambe and Wise Christmas Show*	25 Dec 1977	28,000,000
7=	World Heavyweight Boxing Championship: Joe Frazier *vs.* Cassius Clay	8 Mar 1971	27,000,000
7=	*Dallas* (episode revealing who shot J.R. Ewing)	22 Nov 1980	27,000,000
9	*To the Manor Born* (last episode)	11 Nov 1979	24,000,000
10	*Torvill and Dean Olympic Dance*	21 Feb 1994	23,950,000

The 22 November 1980 screening of *Dallas* was the most-watched because it was the episode that revealed who shot J. R. Ewing. *To The Manor Born* gained its greatest ever number of viewers for its last ever episode. The most-watched film of all time on British television is *Live And Let Die*. Although already seven years old when it was first broadcast on 20 January 1980, it attracted an audience of 23,500,000.

T O P 1 0

LONGEST-RUNNING PROGRAMMES ON BRITISH TELEVISION

	TV programme	First shown
1	*Panorama*	11 Nov 1953
2	*What the Papers Say*	5 Nov 1956
3	*The Sky at Night*	24 Apr 1957
4	*Grandstand*	11 Oct 1958
5	*Blue Peter*	16 Oct 1958
6	*Coronation Street*	9 Dec 1960
7	*Songs of Praise*	1 Oct 1961
8	*Top of the Pops*	1 Jan 1964
9	*Horizon*	2 May 1964
10	*Match of the Day*	22 Aug 1964

Only programmes appearing every year since their first screenings are listed; all are BBC programmes except *Coronation Street*.

T O P 1 0

NETWORK CABLE CHANNELS IN THE US

	Channel	Subscribers*
1	ESPN	71,100,000
2	CNN	71,000,000
3	TNT	70,549,000
4	TBS	69,920,000
5	C-SPAN	69,700,000
6	USA Network	69,677,000
7	The Discovery Channel	69,499,000
8	TNN	68,875,000
9	Lifetime	67,000,000
10	Family	66,900,000

* *Covering period January–February 1997 Source: NCTA*

Numbers 1, 4, and 8 are all owned by Turner Broadcasting System based in Atlanta, Georgia, from where in 1993 he also successfully launched the Cartoon Network – which already has more than 11,000,000 subscribers.

T O P 1 0

BESTSELLING BBC TV PROGRAMMES*

	TV programme	First UK transmission
1	*EastEnders*	1985
2	*The Living Planet*	1984
3	*The Trials of Life*	1990
4	*Miss Marple*	1984
5	*Police Rescue*	1991
6	*Tender Is the Night*	1985
7	*Elizabeth R*	1971
8	*Realms of the Russian Bear*	1992
9	*The Human Animal*	1994
10	*Pole to Pole*	1992

* *Ranked by total revenue earned*

BBC Worldwide Television is responsible for selling BBC TV programmes to TV stations around the world. Drama, comedy, documentary and educational programmes all feature strongly among their bestsellers – *Elizabeth R* (a documentary about Queen Elizabeth II) and *Miss Marple* have been sold in more than 50 countries.

T O P 1 0

TV AUDIENCES IN THE UK, 1996

	Programme/ channel/date	Audience
1	*Only Fools and Horses*, BBC1, 29 Dec	24,400,000
2	*Eastenders**, BBC1, 17/20 Oct	22,700,000
3	*Coronation Street**, ITV, 28 Feb	19,800,000
4	*Casualty*, BBC1, 24 Feb	18,000,000
5	*A Touch of Frost*, ITV, 4 Feb	17,600,000
6=	*Euro 96, England* vs. *Germany*, BBC1, 26 Jun	17,500,000
6=	*Heartbeat*, ITV, 8 Dec	17,500,000
8	*You've Been Framed*, ITV, 27 Oct	17,300,000
9=	*The National Lottery Live*, BBC1, 6 Jan	16,600,000
9=	*London's Burning*, ITV, 13 Oct	16,600,000

* *Aggregate audience*

TOP VIDEO

T O P   1 0

COUNTRIES WITH MOST VCRs

	Country	Percentage of homes	No. video households
1	USA	81.4	78,125,000
2	Japan	78.0	32,224,000
3	Germany	58.5	21,221,000
4	Brazil	42.8	20,458,000
5	UK	77.0	16,771,000
6	France	65.3	14,142,000
7	Italy	44.0	9,879,000
8	Canada	70.3	7,810,000
9	Spain	55.1	6,543,000
10	Russia	13.5	6,515,000

The 1980s have rightly been described as the "Video Decade". According to estimates published by *Screen Digest*, the period from 1980 to 1990 saw an increase in the number of video recorders in use worldwide of more than 27 times, from 7,687,000 to 210,159,000. The estimated total for the UK alone is more than double the entire world total for 1980. Since 1992 more than one-third of all homes throughout the world with TV have also had video.

T O P   1 0

VIDEO RENTAL CATEGORIES IN THE US, 1996

	Genre	Annual revenue ($)
1	Action	630,950,000
2	Comedy	611,450,000
3	Drama	219,830,000
4	Suspense	197,510,000
5	Family	194,270,000
6	Thriller	185,410,000
7	Romance	110,600,000
8	Science-fiction	103,700,000
9	Humour	74,180,000
10	Animated	57,510,000

Source: Video Store Magazine

T O P   1 0

VIDEO CONSUMERS IN EUROPE*

	Country	Spending per video household ($)		
		rental	purchase	total
1	Norway	118.49	34.83	153.32
2	Ireland	92.10	33.26	125.36
3	UK	52.93	64.46	117.39
4	Denmark	45.31	58.26	103.57
5	France	25.19	75.42	100.61
6	Italy	28.73	67.03	95.76
7	Switzerland	26.75	49.75	76.50
8	Belgium	25.84	48.74	74.58
9	Luxembourg	25.38	41.13	66.51
10	Netherlands	33.72	31.31	65.03

* *Based on figures prepared by* Screen Digest

On a world basis, total spending per head of population, rather than per household with video, produces a different picture. The field is led by Japan ($43.66), the US ($42.64), Canada ($40.63), and Australia ($39.55). Collating these figures on a worldwide basis is not undertaken annually, but when they are next published they may indicate the emergence of new trends and national habits in the ratio of spending on video rentals and purchases.

T O P   1 0

MOVIE RENTALS ON VIDEO, 1996

	Film	Label	Release	Revenue ($)*
1	*Twister*	Warner	1 Oct	41,840,000
2	*Independence Day*	Fox Video	22 Nov	41,040,000
3	*Broken Arrow*	Fox Video	2 July	39,830,000
4	*Ace Ventura: When Nature Calls*	Warner	12 Mar	36,100,000
5	*Toy Story*	Buena Vista/Disney	29 Oct	34,480,000
6	*Eraser*	Warner	29 Oct	34,140,000
7	*Babe*	Universal	18 Mar	32,660,000
8	*Braveheart*	Paramount	12 Mar	32,640,000
9	*Dangerous Minds*	Buena Vista/Hollywood	12 Feb	31,970,000
10	*A Time To Kill*	Warner	31 Dec	30,390,000

* *Spent by US consumers renting the title during its first four months of release*
Source: Video Store Magazine

The success of movies on video closely mirrors the popularity of their cinema release, the exception here being *Broken Arrow*, which would be in 9th place if ranked by US box office income, but accelerates to third as a result of its popularity on video. Release date is also significant: *Independence Day* earned almost twice as much as *Twister* at the box office, but was released after it on video, so was apparently less successful – a position that a longer-term analysis will almost certainly reverse.

T O P 1 0

BESTSELLING MUSIC VIDEOS OF ALL TIME IN THE US*

1 *Hangin' Tough Live*, New Kids on the Block

2 *Hangin' Tough*, New Kids on the Block

3 *Step by Step*, New Kids on the Block

4 *Live Shit: Binge And Purge*, Metallica

5 *Moonwalker*, Michael Jackson

6 *In Concert*, Jose Carreras, Placido Domingo, Luciano Pavarotti

7 *Live At The Acropolis*, Yanni

8 *Garth Brooks*, Garth Brooks

9 *Justify My Love*, Madonna

10 *Video Anthology 1978–1988*, Bruce Springsteen

* Excluding children's videos
Source: The Popular Music Database

In a diverse list ranging through opera, R&B, rock and country, the three New Kids' titles are now joined by Metallica as the only music video releases to sell over 1,000,000 units each in the US.

T O P 1 0

MOST RENTED VIDEOS OF ALL TIME IN THE UK*

1 *Four Weddings and a Funeral*

2 *Dirty Dancing*

3 *Basic Instinct*

4 *Crocodile Dundee*

5 *Sister Act*

6 *Home Alone*

7 *Forrest Gump*

8 *Ghost*

9 *Speed*

10 *Braveheart*

* To 31 December 1996

Following its international box office success, the British comedy *Four Weddings and a Funeral* was a consistently huge UK renter on video at the tail-end of 1994 and through much of the following year. It wrests the all-time champion slot from the long-resident *Dirty Dancing*. Recent major renters *Speed* and *Braveheart* attain all-time Top 10 status for the first time.

T O P 1 0

MOST RENTED VIDEOS OF 1996 IN THE UK

	Film	Approx. rentals
1	*Braveheart*	4,170,000
2	*Se7en*	3,860,000
3	*Die Hard With a Vengeance*	3,475,000
4	*Bad Boys*	2,800,000
5	*Waterworld*	2,670,000
6	*The Usual Suspects*	2,600,000
7	*Apollo 13*	2,585,000
8	*Trainspotting*	2,570,000
9	*Heat*	2,375,000
10	*Babe*	2,315,000

The UK public's video rental watching during 1996 was largely concentrated on big-budget action and thrillers, usually involving major Hollywood names (Mel Gibson, Brad Pitt, Bruce Willis, *et al*), but perhaps the biggest news in this list is the strong showing of a minuscule-budget British movie, in the shape of *Trainspotting*.

T O P 1 0

VIDEO-RENTING REGIONS IN THE UK

	Region	Per cent of total UK rentals
1	London	19.0
2	The Midlands	15.0
3	Scotland	13.0
4	Wales & West/ Southwest England	10.5
5	Northwest England	10.0
6	Southern England	9.0
7	Yorkshire	8.5
8	East Anglia	6.5
9	Northeast England	5.0
10	Northern Ireland	3.5

Broadly estimated by dividing the UK up by its commercial TV regions this Top 10 shows where the most tapes are rented.

T O P 1 0

MOST-PURCHASED VIDEO CATEGORIES IN THE UK

	Category	Per cent of total sales
1	Feature films	40.5
2	Children's entertainment	26.5
3	TV shows	12.0
4	Music	8.5
5	Live comedy	6.5
6	Sport (excluding football)	1.8
7	Fitness	1.5
8=	Football	1.2
8=	Miscellaneous	1.2
10	Reality video	0.3

Based on an analysis of 1995's UK high street video sales, it is clear that the biggest proportion of people who buy tapes do so in order to own copies of feature films and, to a lesser extent, favourite TV programmes.

T O P 1 0

BESTSELLING VIDEOS OF 1996 IN THE UK

1 *Toy Story*

2 *101 Dalmations*

3 *Lord of the Dance*

4 *Babe*

5 *Pocahontas*

6 *Sleeping Beauty*

7 *Braveheart*

8 *The X-Files – The Unopened File*

9 *Wallis & Gromit – A Close Shave*

10 *Trainspotting*

It is usual on both sides of the Atlantic for Walt Disney, whose titles have universal appeal, to dominate the annual video best sellers; 1996 was no exception, with four Disney titles in this Top 10, and a pair of those in the top two positions.

ON THE RADIO

GOING FOR A SPIN

The universal appeal of popular music of all types means that radio stations that play it dominate the world's airwaves.

TOP 10
RADIO FORMATS IN THE US

	Format	Share (percent)*
1	News/talk	16.8
2	Adult Contemporary	14.5
3	Country	10.5
4	Top 40	8.6
5=	Album Rock	7.2
5=	Urban	7.2
7	Spanish	6.2
8	Oldies	5.6
9	Modern Rock	4.1
10	Classic Rock	3.9

* *Of all radio listening during an average week, 6 am to midnight, Fall 1996, for listeners aged 12+*

Source: Copyright 1996 The Arbitron Company. May not be quoted or reproduced without the prior written permission of Arbitron

News/talk, only recently elevated to the top of this survey, has continued to maintain its premier position.

TOP 10
RADIO-OWNING COUNTRIES

	Country	Radio sets per 1,000 population
1	USA	2,118
2	Guam	1,403
3	Australia	1,273
4	Bermuda	1,260
5	Gibraltar	1,173
6	Netherlands Antilles	1,165
7	UK	1,146
8	Monaco	1,126
9	Denmark	1,033
10	Canada	1,030

TOP 10
MOST LISTENED-TO RADIO STATIONS IN THE US

	Station	City	Format	AQH*
1	WKTU-FM	New York	Dance Contemporary Hit Radio	186,100
2	WQHT-FM	New York	Urban/Contemporary Hit Radio	160,400
3	KLVE-FM	Los Angeles	Hispanic Adult Contemporary	123,200
4	WLTW-FM	New York	Soft Adult Contemporary	136,200
5	WCBS-FM	New York	Oldies	135,500
6	WRKS	New York	Urban Adult Contemporary	126,300
7	WOR	New York	Talk	108,800
8	KFI	Los Angeles	Talk	107,300
9	KKBT-FM	Los Angeles	Urban Contemporary	105,700
10	KPWR-FM	Los Angeles	Urban/Contemporary Hit Radio	104,700

* *Average Quarter Hour statistic based on number of listeners aged 12+ listening between Monday and Sunday 6.00 am to midnight*

Source: Duncan's American Radio from Spring 1996 Arbitron data

TOP 10
RADIO STATIONS IN THE US BY AUDIENCE SHARE

	Station	City	Format	Share (percent)
1	WTHI-FM	Terre Haute, IN	Country	32.5
2	WXBQ-FM	Bristol, TN	Country	29.0
3	WFGY-FM	Altoona, PA	Country	25.8
4	WDRM-FM	Huntsville, AL	Country	25.6
5	WQBE-FM	Charleston, WV	Country	24.9
6	WKSF-FM	Asheville, NC	Country	24.8
7	WIVK-FM	Knoxville, TN	Country	27.0
8	WOVK-FM	Wheeling, WV	Country	23.8
9	WIKY-FM	Evansville, IN	Adult Contemporary	22.0
10	WXHT-FM	Montgomery, AL	Urban Contemporary	20.8

Source: Duncan's American Radio from Spring 1996 Arbitron data

THE 10

FIRST SONY RADIO AWARDS

Gold Award	Year	Personality/ Broadcaster of the Year
Frank Muir, Denis Norden	1983	Brian Johnston, Sue MacGregor
David Jacobs	1984	Brian Matthew, Margaret Howard
British Forces Broadcasting Service	1985	Jimmy Young
John Timpson	1986	Douglas Cameron
The Archers	1987	Derek Jameson
Gerald Mansell	1988	Alan Freeman
Tony Blackburn	1989	Sue Lawley
Roy Hudd	1990	Chris Tarrant
Charlie Gillett	1991	James Naughtie
Sir James Savile	1992	Danny Baker

TOP 10

LONGEST-RUNNING PROGRAMMES ON BBC RADIO

	Programme	First broadcast
1	The Week's Good Cause	24 Jan 1926
2	Choral Evensong	7 Oct 1926
3	Daily Service	2 Jan 1928*
4	The Week in Westminster	6 Nov 1929
5	Sunday Half Hour	14 Jul 1940
6	Desert Island Discs	29 Jan 1942
7	Saturday Night Theatre	3 Apr 1943
8	Composer of the Week (originally This Week's Composer)	2 Aug 1943
9	Letter From America (originally American Letter)	24 Mar 1946
10	From Our Own Correspondent	4 Oct 1946

Experimental broadcast; national transmission began December 1929

TOP 10

RADIO STATIONS IN THE UK IN 1995

	Station	Listener hours*
1	BBC Radio 2	102,655,000
2	BBC Radio 1	99,949,000
3	BBC Radio 4	89,141,000
4	Capital Radio#	46,991,000
5	Virgin#	33,172,000
6	Atlantic 252	30,494,000
7	BBC Radio 5 Live	24,843,000
8	Classic FM	24,573,000
9	Southern Radio#	18,523,000
10	Metro Yorkshire	16,961,000

* Total number of hours spent by all adults
   listening to the station in an average week
Split frequency stations

TOP 10

LUXURIES CHOSEN BY CASTAWAYS ON *DESERT ISLAND DISCS*

1	Piano
2	Writing materials
3	Bed
4	Guitar
5	Typewriter
6	Radio receiver
7	Golf club and balls
8	Painting materials
9	Wine
10	Perfume

TOP 10

BBC RADIO COLLECTION TITLES

1	Round The Horne Vol. 1
2	Goon Show Vol. 1
3	Alan Bennett, Talking Heads
4	The Queen and I
5	Alan Bennett Diaries 1980–1990
6	Victoria Wood
7	The Navy Lark Vol. 1
8	Wind in the Willows
9	Goon Show Vol. 2
10	Joyce Grenfell Requests

The BBC Collection presents a diverse range of audio cassettes of popular radio programmes culled from its extensive archive of recordings. The principal thread in this Top 10, and among the runners-up, is that of comedy, with Alan Bennett and Victoria Wood representing the contemporary era, and *Round the Horne* and *Goon Show* evoking a bygone era. *The Navy Lark*, a new entrant in the Top 10, was first broadcast on 29 March 1959, and the last show, a special programme for the Queen's Jubilee, on 26 June 1977, making it the longest-running comedy series in British radio history.

ACKNOWLEDGMENTS

I would like to thank Caroline Ash for her unfailing assistance in compiling *The Top 10 of Everything*, along with Luke Crampton, Barry Lazell, Ian Morrison, Dafydd Rees, and the following individuals, organizations, and publications who kindly supplied the information to enable me to prepare many of the lists:

John Amos, Richard Braddish, Steve Butler, Shelly Cagner, Dr. Stephen Durham, Christopher Forbes, Darryl Francis, Max Hanna, Peter Harland, William Hartston, Duncan Hislop, Tony Hutson, Robert Lamb, Bernard Lavery, Allen Meredith, Giles Moon, Tim O'Brien, Adrian Room, Rocky Stockman MBE, James Taylor, Arthur H. Waltz

Academy of Motion Picture Arts and Sciences, AEA Technology, Airport Operators Council International, American Association of Botanical Gardens and Arboreta, American Automobile Manufacturers Association, American Forestry Association, American Kennel Club, American Library Association, American Society of Association Executives, *Amusement Business*, Angels & Bermans Fancy Dress Hire, *Animal World*, *Annual Abstract of Statistics*, Arbitron, Art Sales Index, Associated Press, Association of American Railroads, Association of British Investigators, Association of Comics Enthusiasts, Audit Bureau of Circulations, Automobile Association, BAFTA, Bank of England, BBC Publicity, BBC Radio, BBC Worldwide Television, BBC Written Archives, Ben & Jerry's, Beverage Marketing Corporation, *Billboard*, BMI, Bonhams, Bookwatch Ltd., *BP Statistical Review of World Energy*, British Astronomical Society, British Broadcasting Corporation, British Library, British Museum, British Rate & Data, British Video Association, Bureau of Engraving and Printing, Bureau of Federal Prisons, Bureau of Justice Statistics, Cablevision, Cadbury Schweppes Group, Cameron Mackintosh Ltd., Carbon Dioxide Information Analysis Center/Greg Marland/Tom Boden, Carson Productions, Cat Fanciers' Association of the USA, Central Intelligence Agency, Championship Auto Racing Teams (CART), Channel Four Television, Charities Aid Foundation, Chartwell Information, Christie's East, Christie's London, Christie's South Kensington, Civil Aviation Authority, *Classical Music*, Coca-Cola, Coca-Cola Great Britain and Ireland, Corporate Intelligence Ltd., Corporate Resources Group, Council for the Care of Churches, Countryside Commission, *Crime in the United States*, Criminal Justice Reference Service, *Criminal Statistics England & Wales*, Dateline, Death Penalty Information Center, Department of the Army, Corps of Engineers, Department of Health, Department of Trade and Industry, Department of Transport, Diamond Information Centre, Duncan's American Radio, Electoral Reform Society, Environmental Protection Agency, ESPNET Sports Zone, Euromonitor, Federal Bureau of Investigation, Feste Catalogue Index Database/Alan Somerset, Food and Agriculture Organization of the United Nations, Food Marketing Institute, *Forbes Magazine*, Ford Motor Company Ltd., Foundation Center, Generation AB, Geological Museum, London, George Foster Peabody Awards, Giga Information Group, Gideons International, Global Network Navigator, Inc., Gold Fields Mineral Services Ltd., Governing Council of the Cat Fancy, Hamleys of Regent Street Ltd., Harley Medical Group, Harrods Ltd., Health and Safety Executive, H.J. Heinz Co. Ltd., Higher Education Statistics Agency, Hollywood Foreign Press Association, Home Office, Indianapolis 500, Infoplan, Information Resources, Inc., Institute of Sports Medicine, International Civil Aviation Organization, International Cocoa Organization, International Coffee Organization, International Council of Shopping Centers, International Dairy Foods Association, International Ice Cream Association, International Monetary Fund, International Tea Committee, International Union for the Conservation of Nature, International Union of Geological Sciences Commission on Comparative Planetology, *International Water Power and Dam Construction Handbook*, ITV Network Centre, Kellogg Company of Great Britain, Kennel Club, John Lewis Partnership,

Library Association, Lloyds Register of Shipping, London Heathrow Airport, London Regional Transport, London Theatre Record, London Transport Lost Property, Magazine Publishers of America, Major League Baseball, Mansell Color Company, Inc., MARC Europe, *Market Focus*, Mars, Inc., Mars UK Ltd., Meteorological Office, Metropolitan Opera House, New York, *Modern Bride*, Modern Language Association of America, MORI, MRIB, MTV, NASA, National Association for Stock Car Auto Racing (NASCAR), National Basketball Association (NBA), National Canine Defence League, National Center for Education Statistics, National Center for Health Statistics, National Climatic Data Center, National Criminal Justice Reference Service, National Dairy Council, National Football League (NFL), National Gallery, London, National Gallery of Art, Washington, DC, National Grid Company plc, National Hockey League (NHL), National Oceanic and Atmospheric Association, National Piers Society, National Public Radio, National Railway Museum, National Retail Federation, National Safety Council, National Solid Waste Management Association, National Sporting Goods Association, NCAA, NCTA, Nestlé UK Ltd., New York Drama Desk, *New York Post*, New York Transit Authority, Niagara Falls Museum, A.C. Nielsen Co. Ltd., Nielsen Media Research, Nobel Foundation, *NonProfit Times*, Office of National Statistics, Ordnance Survey, Pasta Information Centre, PBS, *People*, Perrier UK Ltd., *Petfood Industry Magazine*, Pet Industry Joint Advisory Council, PGA Tour, Inc., Phillips West Two, Phobics Society, Popular Music Database, Produktschap voor Gedistilleerde Dranken, Professional Golf Association (PGA), Public Library Association, *Publishers Weekly*, *Railway Gazette International*, RAJAR, Really Useful Group, Recording Industry Association of America (RIAA), Registrar General, Relate National Marriage Guidance, Royal Aeronautical Society, Royal Mint, Royal Opera House, Royal Society for the Prevention of Cruelty to Animals, Royal Society for the Protection of Birds, RSA Examinations Board, Science Museum, London, Scotch Whisky Association, Scout Association, *Screen Digest*, Shakespeare Birthplace Trust, Siemens AG, Society of Actuaries, Sotheby's London, Sotheby's New York, *Spaceflight*, Spink & Son Ltd., Sports Council, *Statistical Abstract of the United States*, Sugar Bureau, Taylors of Loughborough, Telecom Security, Theatre Museum, Theatre Record, *Time*, *The Times*, Trebor Bassett Ltd., Tree Register of the British Isles, UNESCO, *Uniform Crime Statistics*, Union Bank of Switzerland, United Nations, Universal Postal Union, University of Westminster, University Statistical Record, US Board on Geographic Names, US Bureau of Labor Statistics, US Bureau of the Census, USCOLD, US Department of Agriculture, US Department of Agriculture Forest Service, US Department of Justice, US Department of Labor, US Department of the Interior, National Park Service/National Register of Historic Places, US Department of Transportation, Federal Aviation Administration, US Department of Transportation, Federal Highway Administration, US Department of Transportation, National Traffic Safety Administration, US Fish and Wildlife Service, US Geological Survey, US Immigration and Naturalization Service, US Mint, US Postal Services, US Social Security Administration, *USA Today*, *Variety*, *Video Store Magazine*, *Waste Age*, *Wines & Vines*, World Association of Girl Guides, World Bank, World Health Organization, World Tourism Organization, Zenith International,

PICTURE CREDITS

t=top left, c=centre, a=above, b=below, l=left, r=right:
© Academy & Motion Picture Arts & Sciences ® 226 cla;
Allsport 118bc /Simon Bruty 129br /Dave Cannon 129crb, 137tr /J.D. Cuban 117ca;
BFI/United International Pictures 209bc;
Bridgeman Art Library/National Gallery, London 193br /Victoria & Albert 183tl;
British Museum front jacket cl;
Camera Press 1cr /Impress/N. Diaye 25crb;
Christie's Images 195br, 241tr;
Corbis/Bettmann 156tl /UPI 222tr, 243cla /Everett 223br, front jacket cra /Nasa, back jacket cra;
Ecoscene 1bc, 99br;
Mary Evans Picture Library 52bc, 157br, 190cb, 243clb;
FLPA 175tl;
Ford Motor Company 59br;
Getty Images 113cra, 129cra, 171br;
Glasgow Museum 209tr;
Robert Harding Picture Library /G & P Corrigan 96br, 160tl;
Image Bank 175br /Peter Hendrie 92bl /Bill Hickey 8cra /Laurence Hughes 153br /Bernard Roussel 191tr /Joe Szodzinski 21clb;
David King Collection 184tl;
London Transport Museum 60bl;
Los Angeles Police Department 144br;
Mary Evans 59acr;
Military Picture Library /Julie Collins 155tr /John Peart 154bl;
Nasa 70bl, 76bl /Finley-Holiday Films 71acr;
National Gallery, London 194tc;
National Maritime Museum 100tr;
National Motor Museum, Beaulieu 2clb, 59tr, 59 tr, 167cla, tr;
Peter Newark's Historical Pictures 108tl;
NHPA /Daryl Balfour 85bc;
Robert Opie 46tc;
Paramount /Courtesy of Kobal 209cra;
Range /Reuter /Bettmann 159tr;
Redferns /David Redfern 248tl;
© 1996 Les Editions Albert René Goscinny-Uderzo 185cra;
Rex Features 17bl, 55br, 111br, 187bc, 197tl, 202tr, 225br, 228bl, 229tr, 235tc, 236bl /Peter Brooker 1br, 233br /Frank Doran 209cla /Jim Graham 199tr /Charles Knight 132tc /Dave Lewis 234bl /Jim Selby 244cla /Sipa 102cra, 238tl, front jacket ca/ Peter Heimsath;
© Royal Geographical Society, London 113cr, 113br, 113bl;
Science Photo Library /J. Baum & N. Henbest 65crb /David A. Hardy 69tr /Nasa 2cra, 66tl, 67br;
Sotheby's 213tc;
South American Pictures /Tony Morrison 97cr;
Frank Spooner Pictures /Bassignac 2cl, 23tl /Alain Benainous 214tl /Clasos Press 173clb /Liaison 3bl, 68bc /Singh Spooner 240bl /Stills 219br;
Sporting Pictures (UK) Ltd 125tr, 129tr, 129bl, 136br;
Tony Stone Images /Doug Armand 21cl /Ben Edwards 9tr, 167clb /Tony Garcia 150cla /Bill Heinsohn 38–39tc /Arnulf Husmo 35tl /Chuck Keeler 167cra /Hideo Kurihara 18tr /Ben Osborne 169tl /Peter Pearson 3tc, 21bc / Jon Riley 31ca / Dave Saunders 37tl /Jack Vearey 37br /Terry Vine 179tr /Baron Wolman 29tr /Herbert Zetti 217br;
Syndication International 196br;
Text 100 /Microsoft 41br;
Topham Picturepoint 152ca, 164br, 165br, 201tr, 209br, 221cl;
Universal /Courtesy Kobal 209clb;
Zefa Pictures 1cl, 12bc, 21crb, 56tr, 57br, 73tr, 75tr, 80cb, 142cb, 143tr, 174bl, 177tc, 178cb.

Every effort has been made to trace the copyright holders and we apologize in advance for any unintentional omissions. We would be pleased to insert the appropriate acknowledgement in any subsequent edition of this publication.

ILLUSTRATIONS
Richard Benson, Richard Ward, Mick Loates, Eric Thomas.

PUBLISHER'S ACKNOWLEDGMENTS
Dorling Kindersley would like to thank the following people for administrative, design, editorial, and DTP assistance: Zirinna Austin, Sasha Kennedy, Jason Little, Simon Murrell, Anna Youle.

!NDEX
Susan Cawthorne